Wired for Learning

An Educator's Guide to Web 2.0

Wired for Learning

An Educator's Guide to Web 2.0

edited by

Terry T. Kidd
Texas A&M University

Irene L. Chen
University of Houston–Downtown

INFORMATION AGE PUBLISHING, INC.
Charlotte, NC • www.infoagepub.com

Library of Congress Cataloging-in-Publication Data

Wired for learning : an educator's guide to web 2.0 / edited by Terry T. Kidd, Irene L. Chen.
   p. cm.
 Includes bibliographical references.
 ISBN 978-1-60752-096-2 (pbk.) – ISBN 978-1-60752-097-9 (hardcover)
1. Web-based instruction. 2. Instructional systems–Design. 3. Web 2.0.
I. Kidd, Terry T. II. Chen, Irene L.
 LB1044.87.W57 2009
 371.33'44678–dc22

                                           2009006756

Printed in the United States of America

CONTENTS

v

PART III

WEB 2.0 ENVIRONMENT AND USER CENTER DESIGN

PART IV

LEARNING MANAGEMENT WITH WEB 2.0

PART V

WEB 2.0: CASE STUDIES AND IDEAS FOR EDUCATORS

ACKNOWLEDGEMENTS

Completing a project of this magnitude is a great challenge and an opportunity many choose never to undertake. It was with the help of many individuals who have inspired and motivated me to complete the journey that lie ahead.

I would first like to take this opportunity to acknowledge the considerable time and effort the authors have invested in their respective publications in this book. The authors presented within this book are well seasoned in their practice and respective areas. Without the hard work, dedication, and in some cases sacrifice, this book would not be made into reality without the assistance of the authors. Thank you for being so gracious and patient under fire and accepting to my comments and ideas on your chapters. I would like to send a special acknowledge and thanks to my good friend and co-collaborator, Dr. Irene Chen.

Gratitude and acknowledgements go out to the reviewers who spent countless hours reading, proofing, and articulating their comments from the proposal stage to the final chapter revisions.

Special thanks must also go to the Information Age Publishing team for their administrative support and help to bring this vision into reality.

I would also like to acknowledge and thank my good friend Ms. Peggy Powell at the University of Texas School of Public Health as well as, Dr. Irene Cech, Dr. Gene Schroder, Dr. Sharon Cooper, and Dr. George Delclos for their encouragement, advice, and mentorship in my career.

Further, I would like to pay a special tribute my to my nephew, who shows me it's a good thing to be a kid sometimes.

Wired for Learning: An Educator's Guide to Web 2.0, pages ix–x
Copyright © 2009 by Information Age Publishing
All rights of reproduction in any form reserved.

And lastly, to my ancestors who were silenced and never saw freedom, this book is dedicated to them.

—Terry T. Kidd, PhD (Candidate)

I would like to express our appreciation to the number of people that have contributed in some way to this publication. These include the chapter authors as well as the editors and designers from Information Age Publishing, without them this publication would not have been possible.

—Irene L. Chen, EdD

PREFACE

Time magazine picked the public as "Person of the Year" for 2006, because the editors were convinced that the public was "seizing the reins of the global media," creating "an explosion of productivity and innovation," and helping to frame a new digital democracy. The editors who made the choice wrote,

> Web 2.0 is a story about community and collaboration on a scale never seen before. Web 2.0 is about the cosmic compendium of knowledge Wikipedia and the million channel people's network YouTube and online metropolis MySpace. Web 2.0 is about the many wresting power from the few and helping one another for nothing and how that will not only change the world, but also change the way the world changes. (Grossman, 2006)

The fascinating story described by the editors at *Time* magazine was made possible by the brand new Web 2.0 tools.

As of February 2009, the term "Web 2.0" coined by O'Reilly Media in 2003 has more than 363 million citations in Google. Web 2.0 refers to the recent expansion of the Web which can be thought of as a new layer on top of the Web and refers to the ways the platform, the Web, is used. Previously, WWW sites were relatively static sites and provided the user information. This second generation of Web tools includes communication tools, interaction with media and humans, and collaboration and sharing. Many readers of this book probably have learned the differences of Web 1.0 and Web 2.0 by watching Jeff Utecht's Web 2.0 video and Mike Wesch's "The Machine is Us/ing Us" on YouTube.

Wired for Learning: An Educator's Guide to Web 2.0, pages xi–xx
Copyright © 2009 by Information Age Publishing
xi

For education to not step up and maximize the Web 2.0 resources for teaching and learning is to risk becoming marginalized as a viable influence in helping to shape the 21st century (McLester, 2007). But there is still a huge amount of disagreement about what Web 2.0 means to education. This book is an attempt to clarify the potential applications of Web 2.0 for teaching and learning in K–12 and higher education through the lens of the three dimensions discussed by Tutty and Martin.

Tutty and Martin in the chapter "User Generated Design: Teaching and Learning with Web 2.0" explain three dimensions of learner and technological characteristics to designing learning for the Web 2.0 environment—the collaborative/social dimension, the user generated design dimension, and the knowledge management. In the collaborative/social dimension, the learners collaborate and personalize their learning. Web 2.0 environment provides the framework for learners to design, interact, receive feedback, and construct their own learning at various levels of self-determination while contributing to a social community. In the user generated design dimension, users have the opportunity to use Web 2.0 tools, to creatively accumulate knowledge based on their interest, and build on meaningful information aligned with the intended outcomes. In the knowledge management dimension, the learners evaluate the learning that has occurred with the help of Web 2.0 tools.

While these three dimensions are unique, they are by no means independent. In fact, they are quite interdependent. Web 2.0 as social learning tools, user as designer, and Web 2.0 as knowledge management tools combine into a larger conceptual strand of Web 2.0, one that sees users as playing more of a foundational role in information architecture.

Research shows that teachers who use technology in traditional ways, such as direct instruction and drill-and-practice programs, are still in the majority (Howard & Taylor, 2005). To date, few active teaching methods with the assistance of Web 2.0 tools in education have been reported. It is even more unusual to read reports detailing ways in which Web 2.0 applications can function as intellectual partners with the learner, in order to engage and facilitate critical thinking and higher-order learning.

The current concepts, projects, and practices of Web 2.0 are fluid and emergent. And, these Web 2.0 practices will continue to evolve. At the same time, educational institutions must make a concerted effort to investigate, design, and implement uses for this new technology.

Users' experience with Web 2.0-class tools is setting the bar of what tools can and should be. Web 2.0's inevitable arrival within the education system is likely to follow the pattern set by the first generation of the Web, only to become more pervasive and essential. These issues are in need of further research.

ORGANIZATION

Despite the difficulty to catalog current and upcoming Web 2.0 tools into discrete dimensions, the editors divide the text into five major sections with a total of twenty-two chapters. These chapters serve as a brief introduction to Web 2.0, its framework and its tools for the collaborative/social dimension, user generated designs, and learning management. Each section chapter includes numerous references to help interested readers readily locate comprehensive resources on Web 2.0. A brief description of the sections and chapters follows.

Part I: Introducing Web 2.0—Trends, Signs, and User Designs

What made us identify one application or approach as Web 1.0 and another as Web 2.0 in education? O'Reilly (2005) outlines a set of seven main characteristics that he thinks are crucial for Web 2.0: the Web as platform; harnessing collective intelligence; data is the next Intel Inside; end of the software release cycle; lightweight programming models; software above the level of a single device; and rich user experiences. When applied to the education arena, these seven characteristics need further investigation and elaboration.

Kang, Chen, and Kidd study the patterns of Web 1.0, the seven characteristics of Web 2.0, and the future trends of Web 3.0. With their chapter Trend of Web 1.0, Web 2.0, Web 3.0, and Beyond, these authors introduce key technologies and concepts of Web 1.0, Web 2.0, and Web 3.0.

Gannon Cook addresses how the inclusion of interdisciplinary knowledge and semiotics initiated by Web 2.0 could reintroduce aspects of cultural and social competencies and resonate with learners to nurture deeper, self-authorized and transformative, ways of knowing. In "Web 2.0: How Signs, Symbols and Pod casts Affect Learning" Gannon Cook suggests that new technologies, such as pod casts, Second Life, and You Tube are shaping how teachers provide content knowledge and communicate with students in higher education. However, the rush to create e-learning could cause many universities to overlook important aspects of instructional design that provide learning on deeper levels. This chapter uses the qualitative case study methodology to examine whether semiotic tools could mediate learners' existing knowledge and Web 2.0 technologies to facilitate deeper e-learning. This chapter also addresses how the inclusion of interdisciplinary knowledge and semiotics could reintroduce aspects of cultural and social competencies and resonate with learners to nurture deeper, self-authorized and transformative, ways of knowing.

Tutty and Martin proposes analyzing the relevance of Web 2.0 to teaching and learning through three signature application dimensions: social learning; user as designer; and knowledge management. In "User Generated Design: Teaching and Learning with Web 2.0," Tutty and Martin proposes a Web 2.0 Instructional Design Model (ID) that has been designed to guide users to utilize Web 2.0 tools to improve learning and performance. This model is built upon the socio-constructivist philosophies of learning and emphasizes on three dimensions to designing learning for the Web 2.0 environment—social/collaborative, user as the designer and knowledge management. The chapter explains the three phases of the model in detail 1) the analysis phase where the learner as the designer interacts with a facilitator to analyze the learning that has to happen, 2) the design phase where the learners collaborate and personalize their learning, 3) and finally the evaluation phase where the learners interact with the facilitator who helps them evaluate the learning that has occurred. Several Web 2.0 tools that help in this collaboration/personalization phase are described. Two case studies where the Web 2.0 model has been applied in a classroom setting have also been described.

Part II: Social Learning, Networking, and the Web 2.0 Movement

With Web 2.0, social learning/social networking/collaboration tools and software allow users to come together around an idea or topic of interest (Lehmann, 2007). Lehmann suggests that educators use social-networking technology for academic benefit and call it academic networking. With the openness of Web 2.0, such as the collaborative referencing features of wikis, come the uncertainty of meaning and the uncertainty about the accuracy of the information that is posted and the difficulty of sifting through to find what is relevant. For some, it becomes challenging to maintain focus, direction and deliberation, but others like the value added by users.

In "Designing Collaborative Communities of Inquiry through the Application of Web 2.0 Tools," Vaughan and Garrison describe how Web 2.0 instructional strategies and tools can be used to design collaborative communities of inquiry. The chapter presents overview of the community of inquiry framework and its three inter-related elements of social, cognitive and teaching presence. In addition, eight categories of Web 2.0 tools are presented along with corresponding software application examples and associated collaborative learning activities. Instructional strategies for using these tools to support a collaborative community of inquiry, in a blended learning environment, are then illustrated and discussed.

The chapter "Instructional Design and Pedagogical Issues with Web 2.0 Tools" argues that as educators move into online environments for teaching and learning, production, socialization and collaboration technologies, using 3D virtual immersive worlds and other Web 2.0 technologies, reveal significant challenges for us for how best to use them. Each provides a new opportunity to foster deeper online student engagement, to support new forms of learning communities and to develop new teaching and learning environments when compared with more traditional tools. The authors profile a 3D environment called AET Zone. From this work, a pedagogical framework known as Presence Pedagogy (P2) has emerged that provides a model for utilizing these tools to promote active teaching and learning.

"Incorporating Web 2.0 into Education: Instructional Design and Pedagogical Issues" provide a discussion of instructional strategies and techniques used to successfully integrate Web 2.0 tools in classroom teaching and learning. It highlights pedagogical issues that arise with the implementation of Web 2.0 into the educational setting. Case studies describing how various Web 2.0 applications can be incorporated in variety of courses in the areas of nursing, education, and computer information systems are presented. Finally, recommendations for teachers and students on how to effectively use Web 2.0 tools to improve teaching and learning process are outlined.

After a brief discussion of the historical and technological background of Web 2.0, in the chapter "Web 2.0 in Academia: Blogs and Wikis as Instruments for Learning and Teaching," the author Panke outlines scenarios that illustrate opportunities and challenges of applying social software (more specifically weblogs and wikis) in learning contexts. The article summarizes findings reported in literature as well as data collected from empirical investigations on the use of Web blogs and wikis for formal and informal learning setting. A content analysis of blogs in three different university classes explores usage patterns and student participation. The findings are contrasted with interview data on two self-organized wiki communities in the German speaking area (namely Pflegewiki and Wikiversity).

Part III: User Design in the Web 2.0 Environment

The "user as designer" dimension remains a hallmark of the Web 2.0 emergent movement, both in ideology and in technology. With open source, lightweight programming, lightweight technologies, and public interface (or API), Web 2.0 applications lead to creativity and better educational applications. Course applications are now designed above the level of a single device, and are intended to integrate services across handheld devices, PCs, and Internet servers.

In "Wiki Environments for Learning," Larusson and Alterman provide a brief overview of some of the more interesting wiki-uses in education and examples of learning activities that wikis have been used to support. A wiki is an asynchronous collaboration platform that encourages and facilitates collective knowledge construction through collaborative writing of wiki pages. Thus wiki-use in the classroom closely adheres to the Web 2.0 technology ideology by turning students into producers of knowledge. It enables students to learn by observing and experiencing ideas alternate to their own through participation in a collective enterprise. Wikis have many other properties that make it a suitable technology to support various kinds of learning activities. Recent and ongoing research emphasizes the added benefit of using wiki-based technology to supplement and enhance traditional modes of learning and permanently places wikis as a key-technology in the future educational arena.

The authors of "Reflective learning for the Net Generation" argue that reflective learning is essential for lifelong learning and a component of many undergraduate curricula but many Net Generation students do not engage in the process within formal educational settings since it does not align with their preferred learning style. The combination of familiar Web 2.0 technologies, such as blogs and media sharing sites, with multimedia motivates students to creatively produce digital stories that stimulate reflective learning. Digital stories present a personal and reflective narrative using a range of media, especially photographs and video. In addition, students can feel empowered and develop multiple literacies that are essential for lifelong learning.

Calandra and Harmon in "SimSpaces: Custom Virtual Worlds for Learning by Design" describe the SimSpaces project, which is based on the development and implementation of a situated learning generator. The SimSpaces application generates situated, participatory and ultimately transformative learning experiences for teachers and students using virtual world technology. Calandra and Harmon argue that their implementation of the SimSpaces project entails two distinct, yet integrally linked phases: 1) the collaborative design and development of simulated, situated learning spaces; and 2) the purposeful use of these simulated environments as practice spaces for teaching professionals.

Jones and Gelb, in "Course Co-Creation vs. Course Management: Wikis as a Potential Alternative to Traditional Learning Management Systems," note that the information architecture of traditional Learning management systems (LMS) embody a power dynamic that leaves administrators and instructors firmly in control over the online educational environment. These hardwired inequalities pose significant challenges in creating truly collaborative learning experiences. This chapter suggests that the power differentials inherent in traditional LMSs can be radically redefined by adopting wiki technology as a complement to or even replacement of the traditional LMS.

Part IV: Learning Management with Web 2.0

The extensive growth of Web 2.0 projects has recently given rise to learning management with Web 2.0. Learning management with Web 2.0 allows one to save and share searches over a specific period of time. As live content changes, tools such as topic stream, trend visualizations, or word generator let a student analyze how news, an issue, or a discussion changes over time. When Web 2.0 is used as a learning management tool, web sites let users form RSS feeds from their many incoming streams. Users can then view their results or the searches of others by tags or keywords.

The chapter "Meaningful Learning with Wikis: Making a Connection" explores the pedagogical framework of wikis and how the design principles of meaningful learning can guide the design of wikis for instructional purposes. Major types of wikis use in education are also discussed with examples.

Carpenter and Taylor explored ways in which Type II computer technology applications offer learners and educators ways to interpret works of art and visual culture that expand traditional linear conventions and encourage multi-linear possibilities. In "You've Got to See This: Looking Back on/ Forward from On-line Hypermediated Art Criticism and Collaborative Digital Technology," they argue that Web 2.0 based applications such as Voice-Thread allow users to upload presentations that combine images, video, text, and voice. Readers may add their own text and voice comments as well as visual elements that embrace and extend the hypermediated criticism approaches we used with Type II applications. In the chapter, the authors consider how to take our previous engagements with hypermediated criticism and apply them to the interpretation of visual culture, using Web 2.0 technologies of VoiceThread, blogs, image galleries, and Second Life. Their focus on visual culture emphasizes a shift from traditional interpretive practices in visual studies from the perspectives of producers to those of the consumers who become participants in the process of meaning making. From their analysis of these Web 2.0 hypermediated criticism experiences their provide suggestions for pedagogical and curricular implications of engaging Web 2.0 in K–12 and other educational settings.

The chapter "Web 2.0 Affordances for Literacies: Using Technology as Pedagogically Strong Scaffolds for Learning" by McLeod and Vasinda illustrates an approach to using technology in the classroom in which research based literacy strategies are carefully and purposefully matched with Web 2.0 affordances. Using an established literacy strategy that is well known to the teacher and making a new application of that strategy with a new technology provides a bridge for educational practice that combines the known with the new. By maintaining the integrity of the strategy and identifying and harnessing the affordances of the Web 2.0 tool, the combination can move practice forward to the technology-rich teaching and learning of the future. The process is described and illuminated with three classroom examples.

Schroeder in "Semester Without End: Keeping the Class Connection Open via RSS" argues that whether we called it semester, quarter, intersession, session, term, or module—instructional units have been just that, quantifiable measures in terms of time, content, and location. Classes have a beginning, duration, and end. When the term of that instructional unit was met, there is a cessation of teaching and learning. With RSS, there is the potential to keep the class connection open beyond the end of the term.

Part V: Web 2.0: Case Studies and Ideas for Educators

Collaborative learning and situations for active exploration and/or social collaborations are pedagogical methods associated with constructivism. Immediately wikis, blogs, social bookmarking, and RSS feeds come to mind as useful tools to help foster the collaboration and learning. Web 2.0 will fit well into a constructivist classroom. At the same time, educational institutions such as K–12 schools have to make a concerted effort to investigate, design, and implement uses for this new technology. A key goal of education is student engagement and these new tools give educators a fantastic opportunity to engage learners. In Part V, Utecht shares tips of creating a Web-based school portal, Jost and Chen documents a dialogue between a district Educational Technologist and a higher education faculty, Grant and Mims link the use of Web 2.0 technologies to contemporary constructivist and cognitivist learning environments, Polly and Mims examine the issue of designing professional development to support web 2.0 technology integration and Samuel, Sanson, and Hinson guide readers to looking behind the curtain on support issues to understand what must be in place in order to take advantage of Web 2.0 tools, and Parton and Hancock brought up the accessibility issues of Web 2.0.

Utecht, in the chapter "Planning for 21st Century Technologies" argues that, with the onset of Web 2.0 tools in the 21st century, schools have had to rethink the use of technology within the learning environment. School stakeholders from teachers to parents to students are asking schools to allow them seamless access to information via the Internet. This chapter focuses on creating a Web-based school portal that puts student learning at the center of a comprehensive technology plan. From communication between school wide systems to supporting and implementing a technology plan within a school, this chapter looks to connect the power of Web 2.0 tools in creating a comprehensive information system for users within a school community.

The chapter "Is There a Place in Second Life® for K–12 Education?" by Jost and Chen documents a dialogue between an Educational Technologist for a large urban school district and a faculty member of teacher education. The Educational Technologist has taught for 19 years, 18 of them in Pre-Kindergarten through 6th grade computer labs. She is interested in exploring new virtual reality technologies and how they can be useful for increasing student achievement.

In "Web 2.0 in Teacher Education: Characteristics, Implications and Limitations," Grant and Mims concentrates on the use of Web 2.0 technologies in contemporary constructivist and cognitivist learning environments. Grant and Mims present the characteristics of Web 2.0 tools to support teaching and learning, including low threshold applications, a variety of tools and models, as well as access to tools and knowledge. The authors then identify the limitations and challenges that exist with using these tools, such as immature applications, longevity of applications, number of applications, unconsolidated services and security and ethics.

The authors of "Designing professional development to support the integration of Web 2.0 technologies" argue that the emergence of Web 2.0 technologies has transformed the way that people collect, organize and generate knowledge. Still, like most digital technologies, Web 2.0 technologies are not being used to their full potential in schools. Using the framework of technological pedagogical content knowledge (TPCK), the author describes an empirically-based model of learner-centered professional development that shows promise to impact student learning by supporting the effective integration of Web 2.0 technologies in PK–12 classrooms.

In "Technically Speaking: Supporting 1.0 Teachers in a 2.0 World," Samuel, Sanson, and Hinson intend to help educators assemble their Web 2.0 toolkit that enables the creation of Web 2.0 learning objects. Its primary objective is to discuss infrastructure, interfaces, hardware, and software to fill in information gaps. Too often, teachers return from Web 2.0 seminars to discover during classroom implementation that they do not have enough information or technical expertise to make the applications work. They may also need help supporting students as they retrieve content at school via high bandwidth or remotely from home via dial-up access, or creating feeds that render correctly in different feed readers and media players. This chapter, in essence, is "looking behind the curtain" to understand what must be in place in order to take advantage of Web 2.0 tools.

The chapter, "Accessibility Issues for Web 2.0," written by Parton and Hancock informs readers to the issues of web usability and accessibility. Given Web 2.0's heavy reliance on collaborative applications and the tendency to have content built by teachers and students, Web accessibility training is paramount. This chapter provides rationale for addressing accessibility compliance, review historical failures of the Web design community to address these standards, and provide solutions for what we can do as a community to improve Web 2.0 accessibility.

REFERENCE

Grossman, L. (2006, December 13). *Time's Person of the Year: You.* Time.

Lehmann, C. (2007). How to: Use social-networking technology for learning. *Edutopia.* Retrieved February 6, 2009, from http://www.edutopia.org/how-use-socialnetworking-Technology.

McLester, S. (2007). Web 2.0 for educators. *Technology & Learning, 27*(9), 9–19.

O'Reilly, T. (2005). What is web 2.0. *O'Reilly Network.* Retrieved on July, 6, 2008, from http://www.oreillynet.com/pub/a/oreilly/tim/news/2005/09/30/what-is-web-20.html

PART I

INTRODUCING WEB 2.0:
TRENDS, SIGNS, AND USER DESIGN

CHAPTER 1

THE TREND OF WEB 1.0, WEB 2.0, WEB 3.0, AND BEYOND

Te-Ping Kang
National Cheng Kung University

Jengchung V. Chen
National Cheng Kung University

Terry T. Kidd
Texas A&M University

ABSTRACT

This chapter introduces the current use and future trend of Web 2.0. Because of the plethora of processes in developing Web 2.0, it's impossible to introduce them in a short article, so we'll focus on the most important technologies and concepts. Understanding Web 2.0 will introduce us to the future trend of Web 3.0, which appeared in the middle of 2007.

INTRODUCTION

In this chapter, the main theme is split into two phases. The first phase introduces the present situation of using Web 2.0 concepts in the World Wide Web. The second phase explains how Web 2.0 concepts lead to Web 3.0. In the first section, the definition and terminology of Web 2.0 is explained clearly, and the technology of presenting Web 2.0, for example, AJAX (Asynchronous JavaScript and XML), RSS (Really Simple Syndication)/ Atom, Semantic Web, and Web-based applications, will also be specified. Existing Internet enterprise models and business applications will be introduced in the final part of this section, for example, Google, Wikipedia, Yahoo!, and Flickr.

The second phase is the trend of Web 2.0 and Web 3.0. In this section, clear definitions are also required. However, Web 3.0 is not as explicit as Web 2.0 in concepts and technology, so only existing technology will be introduced. For example, transforming the Web into an available database, lead Internet into artificial intelligence, and the realization of SOA (Service-oriented architecture) and semantic Web. At the end of this section, some semantic Web or Web 3.0 pioneer's ideas will be taken as future trends, and this chapter will end with a thorough survey of all the above.

BACKGROUND

After the middle of 2007, most information technology (IT) industrial leaders began using the innovative term "Web 3.0." Although most of them emphasized that "Web 3.0," just like the previous term "Web 2.0," did not refer to an update to any technical specifications or actual alteration. And most of the abstract changes could not be expressed easily; they merely explained these concepts by using easy examples to present the difference between Web 2.0 and Web 3.0. But actually, we can find similar key points in their discussions—for example, the urgency of developing semantic Web and Internet artificial intelligence. These technology terms will have important roles in this chapter which can help us take a closer look at Web 2.0 and Web 3.0. Before we recount the rapid growth of the World Wide Web in the past ten years, you may need to know some basic Internet history and terms. So we'll start at the very beginning before the emergence of Web 2.0.

FROM WEB 1.0 TO WEB 2.0

In Internet development history, "Web 1.0" is a retronym that represents most websites between 1994 and 2004. This term is used to differentiate from "Web 2.0"—to provide a boundary between them. So before the Web 2.0 term appeared, there was no hard definition of what a "next generation Web" was. According to the definition, we can find some specifications of Web 1.0, so-called "old style pages," including single static pure HTML pages, online guest books, non-realtime data, and the like. The most obvious similarity is that a company, or a webmaster, had to own a single host, which possessed all the data which browsers needed. It meant providing all the information to a single peer or user.

However, information and Web technology on the Internet were growing rapidly. Providing pure information has become only one aspect of the Internet. People want to shop or sell goods on the Internet, communicate with friends, and publish their point of view on their own site. Nevertheless, not everyone is able to establish a website. On the other hand, it is impractical to own all the information of every single user. For example, if you owned an online shop with thousands of items, it is unrealistic to appraise all the goods on the shopping list. Furthermore, peers might want to see others' comments but not always the same one. Under such concepts, more and more community or social web sites have emerged, and some of them are extremely successful—for example, eBay and Flickr. Those sites did not simply appear after the emergence of "Web 2.0," rather they evolved among other competitors with new ideas and technologies. And what technologies or changes made them so special? We'll first present some key features of Web 2.0.

FIRST STEP OF WEB 2.0

The term "Web 2.0" was initially noticed on the first O'Reilly Media Web 2.0 conference in 2004. According to Tim O'Reilly's speech (O'Reilly, 2005), although Web 2.0 suggests a new version of the World Wide Web, it does not refer to an update to any technical specifications. At first the concept was only brainstorming and sought to clarify the differences between Web 1.0 and Web 2.0 (Table 1.1). For example, personal websites are Web 1.0, blogging is Web 2.0, which means the Web 2.0 is not only a new marketing buzzword, but in fact exists on the Internet. It also doesn't have a hard boundary, but rather, a gravitational core, like the "meme map" of Web 2.0. Furthermore, Web 2.0 means an Internet that is even more interactive, customized, social, and media-intensive (Shannon, 2006). Based on these concepts, O'Reilly (O'Reilly, 2005) suggested seven main characteristics that could describe this term:

1.   The Web as Platform

O'Reilly suggested three groups of websites and then compared them by showing the advantage of Web applications. He showed the drawback of a desktop application which requires the user to pay... and the risk of competition which lowers the market share of specific application—for example, a Web browser. He also pointed out the power of "Long Tail," which emphasizes the collective power of the small sites that make up the bulk of the Web's content. Finally he exemplified BitTorrent, which illustrates the concept: "the service gets better automatically the more people use it."

2.   Harnessing Collective Intelligence

Web 2.0 emphasizes the power of collective intelligence. He gave the example of successful websites which provide the collective information from users, but not websites themselves. It also points out the organic growth of the Web 2.0 nature, and concludes that network effects from user contributions are the key to market dominance in the Web 2.0 era. Finally, he pointed out the hottest feature of Web 2.0 blogging (which aggregated the wisdom of crowd) would also be an essential part of harnessing collective intelligence.

3.   Data is the Next "Intel Inside"

This concentrates on the competitiveness of owning data. He gave the example of online Map service providers. Although they publish the map service in a different way, they need the original map data to implement all these applications. Thus his conception: the owner of the data may have a chance to own the market.

4.   End of the Software Release Cycle

This paragraph shows that current modern Web 2.0 sites were trying to shorten their release cycle in order to follow up the newest requirement or resist any kind of accident. It also mentioned the open source dictum, "release early and release often" would be a trend of Web 2.0 sites.

5.   Lightweight Programming Models

This paragraph pointed out the advantage of using light weight programming models. For example, using lightweight service by Amazon and the simplicity of organic Web services introduced by Google. O'Reilly also addressed three significant facts. First, support lightweight programming models that allow for loosely coupled systems, which lower the complexity of Web service. Second, think syndication, not coordination. This means webs should try to syndicate data outwards, but not control what happens when it gets to the other end of the connection. Third, design for "hackability" and remixability, which emphasized that only if one service's barriers to re-use were low, it could enjoy the success of redistribution and popularity.

6. *Software above the Level of a Single Device*

It gave an example of iTunes, which was a desktop application, but combines the massive Web back-end to provide more information. It didn't install every data but seamlessly reaches the same idea of owning the whole Web database in your local system. Although it wasn't a Web application, it leveraged the power of the Web platform which using the core principle of Web 2.0.

7. *Rich User Experiences*

By using some of the newest technology or the combination of old ones, it provided a lot of new user experiences which never existed before. And those improvements were one of the most attractive characteristics of Web 2.0.

All of the above briefly explain the development of the current Web 2.0 trend. Most of the technologies have already existed before the appearance of this terminology. So they attempt to clarify the concept of the developing situation. At least, Tim O'Reilly (O'Reilly, 2006) presented a more compact definition of Web 2.0: "Web 2.0 is the business revolution in the computer industry caused by the move to the Internet as platform, and an attempt to understand the rules for success on that new platform." It was the most es-

TABLE 1.1   Difference between Web 1.0 and Web 2.0

Web 1.0		Web 2.0
DoubleClick	→	Google AdSense
Ofoto	→	Flickr
Akamai	→	BitTorrent
mp3.com	→	Napster
Britannica Online	→	Wikipedia
personal websites	→	Blogging
evite	→	Upcoming.org and EVDB
domain name speculation	→	Search engine optimization
page views	→	Cost per click
screen scraping	→	web services
publishing	→	participation
content management systems	→	wikis
directories (taxonomy)	→	tagging ("folksonomy")
stickiness	→	syndication

sential part of the topics he mentioned above. Web 2.0 also includes a social element where users generate and distribute content, often with freedom to share and re-use. This can result in a rise in the economic value of the Web to businesses, as users can perform more activities online (Barnwal, 2007). However, those implementations are based on some technologies that we can't ignore. So we'll discuss more specific details in the next section.

KEY TERMS

Although Web 2.0 itself didn't infer any specific technology, the realization of such features was built under many important progresses of Internet technologies (Laningham, 2006). Technologies which increase the developing speed of Web 2.0 kept developing not only after the term came out, but most of them were used for awhile on the Internet. However, they may not catch too much attention before being widely used. Some critical technology are shown as follows:

- **AJAX**:   AJAX stands for Asynchronous JavaScript and XML. It isn't a single technology, but several technologies, each flourishing in its own right, and then coming together in powerful new ways. The most important characteristic is the increased responsiveness and interactivity of Web pages achieved by exchanging partial data with the server asynchronously behind the Web actions. AJAX incorporates standards-based presentation using XHTML and CSS; dynamic display and interaction using the Document Object Model; data interchange and manipulation using XML and XSLT; asynchronous data retrieval using XMLHttpRequest; and JavaScript binding everything together (O'Reilly, 2005). The incorporation makes it possible to generate Web pages immediately and allows all applications in the same platform to work independently. For example, if you are uploading a photo to a Flickr photo album, you might find that you can change a photo's description directly. After you click the save button, you may not experience a full page refresh like old style websites. The page will only refresh partially and you can do other work while waiting for the response of the server side. This asynchronous mechanic provides a more friendly and intuitive user experience. Another widely discussed feature was initially a suggestion by Google. When you are typing key words in the textbox of a Google search, similar suggestions will appear below the words you are typing. It helps a user who is unsure whether the input is right or wrong. A user could also find the exact word he wants, which elminates typing and prevents typing error.

- **Web feeds (RSS/Atom):**   RSS and Atom are the two most common Web feeds. The definitions of RSS vary. RSS 0.91 stands for Rich Site Summary, RSS 0.90 and RSS 1.0 stand for RDF Site Summary, and RSS 2.0 stands for Really Simple Syndication. Although they have different meanings for the same acronym, most of their technology specifics are similar, and just like Atom, are a standard for Web feeds. The benefit of using Web feeds is the aggregation of content from multiple Web sources into one place, so the data could be reused in a different form or format. And this kind of Web feed syndication is also designed to be human-readable as well as machine-readable. This means that Web feeds can also be used to automatically transfer information between many websites without any human intervention. Initially, however, most sites didn't introduce the use of Web feeds. But the ease of using Web feeds is allowing visitors to use feed readers to get newest data without visiting the site again. So, after the weblogs gained popularity, visitors only wanted to check new items or read the contents in their familiar format. Web feeds provide a simple and quick way to view the information. This simplicity and accessibility was most successful, so most of the weblog space providers support RSS or ATOM in order to attract more users. The biggest advantage of using Web feeds for readers is ignoring content format, so they can always choose an easier way to read those articles, via pure text or clearer paragraph arrangement. By using a Web feed reader application, readers could also focus on the content they need.
- **Semantic Web:** It is used to semantic the information and services on the World Wide Web, and then make it possible for the Web to understand and satisfy the requests of people and machines to use the Web content (Berners-Lee, Hendler, Lassila, 2001). The reason for semantic Web is that most information on Web pages is designed to be read by people, not machines. In the end, the computers cannot parse the raw data into information directly. So by formatting the data in a formal specification in a semantic way, the information could be reused and exchanged by other application. The original 2001 *Scientific American* article by Berners-Lee described an expected evolution of the existing Web to a Semantic Web (Berners-Lee, 2001). Such an evolution has yet to occur. Indeed, a more recent article from Berners-Lee and colleagues stated: "This simple idea, however, remains largely unrealized" (Shadbolt, Hall, Berners-Lee, 2006). Although the concept of semantic Web is not widely used at present due to the issues of practical feasibility, privacy, need of information, and so on. Some projects have

already been working for special propose (Feigenbaum, Herman, Hongsermeier, Stephens, 2007).

- **Folksonomy:** This is the practice and method of collaboratively creating and managing tags to annotate and categorize content. Usually it freely choses keywords instead of from a controlled vocabulary (Voss, 2007). The advantage of using folksonomy lowers the barrier of participation and tagging data is used in new ways to find information. For example, tag clouds are frequently used to visualize the most used tags of a folksonomy. They are the collection of metadata. More related information or content will increase the weight to a specific folksonomy. After the collections grow bigger, users can discover who created a given folksonomy tag, and see the other tags that this person created. In this way, folksonomy users often discover the tag sets of another user who tends to interpret and tag content in a way that makes sense to them. The result is often an immediate and rewarding gain in the user's capacity to find related content. Under this interaction between users by the tags, more and more information would be provided because of the cross linking of similar tags. This will help the accessibility of the information created by a single user. Flickr and del.icio.us were widely cited examples of websites using folksonomic tagging. We'll discuss Flickr in the next section.

- **Rich Internet Application (RIA):** Rich Internet applications are Web applications that have the features and functions of traditional desktop applications. Traditional Web applications center all activity around a client–server architecture with a thin client. Under this system all processing is done on the server, and the client is only used to display static content. The biggest drawback with this system is that all interaction with the application must pass through the server, which requires data to be sent to the server, the server to respond, and the page to be reloaded on the client with the response. By using a client-side technology which can execute instructions on the client's computer, RIAs can circumvent this slow and synchronous loop for many user interactions. There are many benefits of using RIA. First, most of the RIA need only small installation, because the using of existing Web techniques—for example, Adobe Flash, pure Javascript, or AJAX—significantly reduces the overhead compared to a desktop application. Also updates to new versions can be automatic or transparent to the end user, and reduce the complexity of reliability. Under the nature of Web application, users can use the application from any computer with an Internet connection. And most RIA technologies allow the user experience to be the same, regardless of the operating system. We'll talk about the RIA example of Google gears in the next section.

Those are the most important technologies we could find on Web 2.0 sites. There are also quantities of new features derived from the technologies above, but they use similar concepts. Webs keep advancing, so after we have a basic review of the theory, we could talk about some actual websites which use these ideas.

EXEMPLARY WEB 2.0 APPLICATIONS

Previous technologies we discussed were only the key features of Web 2.0. But when we talk about classic examples of Web 2.0, we cannot just deem those technical features as the most important part of it. Besides, analyzing some prosperous commercial or non-commercial sites using the concept of Web 2.0 on the Internet will be a good guideline to research the next step of Web development. Some of them enjoy great success and, more or less, effect the development of Web 2.0. Some industry leaders and pioneers are shown below.

Google

When it began in January 1996, Google was only research which focused on search engines. The two researchers, Larry Page and Sergey Brin, hypothesized that a search engine that analyzed the relationships between websites would produce better ranking of results than existing techniques. The main searching algorithm uses a system called "PageRank" to help rank Web pages that match a given search string. "PageRank" is a link analysis algorithm that assigns a numerical weighting to each element of a hyperlinked set of documents, such as the World Wide Web, with the purpose of measuring its relative importance within the set. So by using this algorithm, Google search could find a more precise and objective result of websites. It helped users find more useful and related sites using keywords. The powerful research quickly became one of the best in the search engine market.

After the success of Google search, Google provided more and more features under the AJAX-based Web applications—for example, Google Mail, and Google Docs. Google Mail provides an online platform to send or receive email. It emphasizes that storage is almost unlimited, and allows user searching, filtering, and tagging mail content which other Web mail providers cannot offer. It also introduced the instant message system just inside the application, so there is no need to open another messenger program at the same time. Google Docs provides an online document editing application which works soundly without any installation on the computer. It takes the concept of "the Web as platform" which changes the usual practice of running every program on your personal computer. It means maybe there will be more and more programs you can run on the Web platform; it decreases the inconvenience of installing programs; and lowers the gaps between different platforms—for example, Macintosh and Microsoft Windows. So since you can work on the Web, you can work anywhere despite the platform you are using. Google Docs also provides the mechanics to share your document with many editors. Thus, everyone who owns the authority of this document could edit it anytime. Such applications are called Rich Internet applications (RIA) which replace the traditional desktop applications, and are one of the important features in Web 2.0.

"iGoogle" is a desktop-like Web start page. Users could add any feature (called gadgets on Google) provided by Google. Google also creates its own Web framework called Google Web Toolkit (GWT). By using GWT, third-party developers are able to create Web applications which can be published on iGoogle and used by everyone. Most of them won't create a gigantic application which contains every single feature, but provides only one specific application at once, and this would be the best example of the "lightweight programming model." This platform, like desktop startpage, accomplishes the concept of "the Web as platform" and shares the techniques of all developers who use the GWT around the world, not only the employees of Google.

Finally, we can find most of the critical Web 2.0 concept was used on these applications, including Web platform, communicating, unifying, knowledge collecting, and the like. If you talk about successful Web 2.0 models presently, you can never ignore Google. It may be the best reason why Google is leading the industry.

Wikipedia

Wikipedia is a free and open content encyclopedia project operated by the non-profit Wikimedia Foundation. Articles have been written collaboratively by volunteers around the world, and nearly all of its articles can be edited by anyone, and all text is covered by GNU Free Documentation License (GFDL). It isn't just people working together. It's not a committee, it's a community as well as an encyclopedia (Sidener, 2006). By collecting the intelligence of all the editors in the world, Wikipedia not only obtains the information from a specific user, but communicates with all the editors. That information was discussed again and again, and finally presented by multi-editors who came from different jobs and masters throughout the world. Finally, almost all of the contents will be revised by people from similar domains which greatly enhanced the reliability of the information.

It's much different than the traditional encyclopedia edited by a group of specific people. The source of this resource is worldwide. Different countries may also deliver different points of view, which could give some special reference materials that the original editors couldn't provide. Another special feature is the existing of "Wikipedia bot." Some data mining and spelling corrections were automatically done by these Internet robots and more complex robots were created to complete the mission of integrating or formatting information. Wikipedia may be the best example of the collection of intelligence on Web 2.0.

Flickr

Flickr was one of the earliest Web 2.0 personal photograph album applications widely used by bloggers as a photo repository. It also provides video hosting, Web service suite, and remains one of the biggest online communities. The most important feature of Flickr is using tags to organize images so users can search images concerning a certain topic to find related images. It enhanced the relation between different topics and provides a more precise way to categorize information. Moreover, Flickr allows users to organize their photos into multiple different sets rather than a single physical hierarchy, so users could find specific group of photos by using multiple set metadata. An early website to implement tag clouds, it provides access to images tagged with the most popular keywords. More popular or recent keywords would be presented in a larger font to attract the visitor. Because of the support for tags, Flickr has been cited as an important example of using folksonomy.

WEB 3.0

Like Web 2.0, Web 3.0 is a term that describes the recent evolution of the World Wide Web, and hypothesizes about a future wave of Internet innovation. Until now, the trends are varying greatly because of the different views and directions of Internet development.

Some critics debated that the existing of Web 3.0 is another market buzzword after the slowdown of current World Wide Web environment. Most of the definitions of Web 3.0 are blurry and still controversial, because until now, the main theme remains divergent and incomplete. Different industry leaders discussed their own concept of Web 3.0, although there may be some, but little, similarity. Another question is the lack of actual example. Some currently existing debates were only preceptorial guidelines. Few of them worked in practice; most of them were only in research. It was much different from Web 2.0, because when the term exists, most changes were not present on the surface, but Web 2.0 was based on the existing technique or websites. However, there are some existing industry leaders processing the future of Web 3.0. For example, development of semantic Web, implement of artificial intelligence, the service-oriented architecture (SOA), and a lot of innovative thinking.

Consequently, we foresee a great change to the World Wide Web—not only an outward of Web application, but an evolution inside the Internet's core. For example, currently the main Web 3.0 technologies, such as intelligent software that utilize semantic data, have been implemented and used on a small scale by multiple companies for the purpose of more efficient data manipulation (Copeland, 2007). Those implementations are invisible for a normal Web user, but are changing or improving the experience of visiting a website. For example, Amazon, one of the biggest online shops collects every click and browsing history to predict your sex, age, and interest—without your profile. They use a more precise algorithm to evaluate which group of people assimilate your shopping habit or preference. Then they provide some related items which might interest you. In recent years, there has been an increased focus on bringing semantic Web technologies to the general public. We'll discuss those technologies in the next section.

EXISTING TECHNOLOGY USING WEB 3.0 CONCEPT

Web 3.0 is not only a slogan of World Wide Web evolution, but is currently being practiced. The following are some critical technologies which build the backbone of Web 3.0.

Web Data Mining

Most Web 3.0 concepts are derived from the large scale of Web data collection, so many industry leaders emphasize the importance of the data Web as structured data records should be published in reusable and queryable formats—such as XML, RDF or other microformats. The wide use and development of query and re-formatting technology like SPARQL and XSLT also provide a great opportunity to help the data integration and application interoperability (see the example of Amazon we mentioned in the previous section). In old-style data collection methods, a website would ask you to register and give some basic information, including your age, work, interest, and income. The online shop realized they can't collect all the necessary information with just a few questions. Necessary data may not be obtained because questionnaires annoy people. Besides collecting the information of unregistered users, results may be further unreliable because some users may give false information. So they collect the information from user behavior. For example, what a visitor previously bought, what they're interested in, what was the average price, and when they bought these goods. This data is much more meaningful than asking the visitor what they want. They accumulate this information to further classify and analyze. Another good example: People who buy a classical music CD also find a suitable headphone on the website. So when another visitor seeks the same classical music, Amazon may recommend this headphone, and perhaps a discount. These features are generated by a special framework. All they have to do is give a specific product. Other data mining works were finished by the machine. It also greatly decreases the manpower of maintaining such a great database. The semantic Web may have the chance to develop only when the construction of Data Web as a whole database which is built by structured or semi-structured content was available in RDF or other kind of format. It is similar to other data mining we run in practice. But, the data is spread over the whole Internet with more complication and chaos. So data mining will keep progressing as a top priority.

Internet Artificial Intelligence

Another important evolutionary path for the Web leads to artificial intelligence that can simulate the Web into a quasi-human fashion. IBM and Google are now implementing technologies that simulate the trend of Web development by complex algorithm and immense data collection. Although some research brought this into practice, the realization of Web intelligence system is still controversial. The Internet artificial intelligence is trying to find a method to predict the trend of a real human trend. They use some simple event to simulate the whole Web behavior—or by using the intelligent system such as via collaborative filtering services like del.icio.us and Flickr that extract meaning and order from the existing Web and how people interact with it. That kind of organic system will develop and keep simulating the quasi-human environment (Markoff, 2006). And by adjusting the trend with real statistics, the system may present a more precise result for reference.

Realization of the Semantic Web and SOA

SOA (Service-oriented architecture) is an architecture that relies on service-orientation as its fundamental design principle. In an SOA environment, independent services can be accessed without knowledge of their underlying platform implementation and also separate functions into distinct units, or services (Bell, 2008). Web 2.0 is sometimes characterized by building on the existing Web server architecture and using services. So Web 2.0 itself can therefore be regarded as displaying some SOA characteristics (Schroth, Janner, 2007; Hinchcliffe, 2005). Under this characteristic, some researches pointed out that Web 3.0 may be linked to a possible convergence of SOA and semantic Web (Provoost, 2006; Bornier, 2006). So the semantic Web could provide the data which SOA needed, and the SOA could implement higher level of services. Those SOA structures provide a chance to morph the Internet into the "Internet of Service." Specific services provided by one machine may be communicable with other machines with a standard format of data. This kind of cooperation could expand the range of information reusability, and also reorganize the knowledge base between different databases. Useful information could finally extract from those databases, which is ready to be used for constructing the Semantic Web.

Those abstracts are theoretically available, but debates come from the scale of these ideas. Different from the evolution of Web 2.0, most of the concepts or techniques could be practiced in Web 2.0 era because of the low barrier and lightweight design pattern. Small websites could advance jointly because of those easy concepts. Also some of the successful small websites were using only a special design of Web 2.0. But after they win a great number of the market share, they might sell their site and find other new ideas for the next step. However, the current main theme of Web 3.0 is built of huge data quantity and higher barrier of entry. Some critics deem the term Web 3.0 as the overuse of "next generation Web." Nevertheless, those subjects are worthy to discuss, and the definition will keep expanding in the future.

INNOVATIVE CONCEPTS FOR WEB 3.0

Until now, the definition of Web 3.0 is still controversial and unclear. But some of the characteristics and technology are used quietly by some innovative companies. Although we cannot reach a conclusion currently, the opinion of pioneers who develop applications by using the concept of Web 3.0 would be a best telescope to see the process in a short future. Nova Spivack (Spivack, 2006) stated the cycle of third-generation Web will continue for five to ten years since 2007, and will result in making the Web more connected, more open, and more intelligent. As he compared the difference between Web 1.0, 2.0, and the third-generation Web, the use of semantic Web, microformats, natural language search, and so on, which emphasize machine-facilitated understanding of information in order to provide a more productive and intuitive user experience deserve the name of Web 3.0. He also expanded the definition of Web 3.0 in order to provide more actual major technology trends that are about to reach a new level of maturity at the same time, including:

- ubiquitous connectivity
- network computing
- open technologies
- open identity
- the intelligent Web

Some of these technologies are not new in Web 3.0; however, they may not have been respected. So Web 3.0 not only develops vertically in technology, but also contains the horizontal expansion in existing technology and other application.

FUTURE TRENDS

The development of Web 3.0 will keep changing the World Wide Web in almost every aspect—not only technological changes, but also the transformation of the entire Web environment. Different from the gap between Web 1.0 and Web 2.0, Web 3.0 contains many unprecedented concepts for the current World Wide Web, including the reconstruction of Web contents into standard RDF format or other microformats, interactions through Web not only human-to-machine but machine-to-machine, and moreover, the development of artificial intelligence. These innovations are going to change not only applications on the Internet, but the way we provide and receive the information. Consequently, Web 3.0 won't take change only on specific Web application or a single site. We can foresee a challenging result of the overall progress once the Web 3.0 finds the technical breakthrough.

Future research can aim on two aspects of Web 3.0. The first one is the technical aspect. We can choose a specific article—for example, semantic Web, then try to determine the easier way to approach. Because most of the Web 3.0 technologies are difficult to implement, it is much different than Web 2.0. Another one is the combination of different Web 3.0 technologies or the coalescence with current technologies. For example, the combination of RIA and Semantic Web. By collecting the information of RIA user behavior, maybe we could concrete the GFDL documents or contents with special format to implement the Semantic Web.

There's an obvious goal of future Web development, information integration. It would be the most important lesson for the Web developers. Since the improvement of hardware and broadband Internet access, many achievements seemingly impossible before, are now available. Many experts on Web development keep introducing new design patterns for the new framework of the next revolution. These will be the biggest propeller of the next generation Webs.

CONCLUSION

From the research, debates, and the industry state of play, we can conclude:

1. Web 3.0 is a technology derived from Web 2.0, however, there is no hard boundary but a huge technical gap between them.
2. Most of the core concepts of Web 3.0 are difficult to implement at this moment.
3. Web 3.0 pays more attention to machine-to-machine communication, in order to decrease the unnecessary waste of time. It also attempts to find a way to construct a quasi-human network to simulate the complex decision of a human on the Internet.
4. Data mining and information gathering needs a more exact format (for example, RDF) to create the complete data web.

These conclusions can't cover all the aspects of Web 3.0, but they present some concrete problems and advantages. Although the feasibility of Web 3.0 is controversial, we can see that Web 3.0 will be the most important issue in the near future for the World Wide Web. This importance will increase after Web 2.0 matures.

REFERENCES

Barnwal, R. (2007). Web 2.0 is all about understanding the economic value of social interaction. *AlooTechie* (para. 7–8). Retrieved February 23, 2008, from http://www.alootechie.com/news/1977.asp

Bell, M. (2008). *Service-oriented modeling: Service analysis, design, and architecture.* Hoboken, NJ: Wiley.

Berners-Lee, T. (2001). The semantic web. *Scientific American.* Retrieved March 13, 2008, from http://www.sciam.com/article.cfm?id=the-semantic-web

Berners-Lee, T., Hendler, J., & Lassila, O. (2001, May 17). The semantic web. *Scientific American* (para. 9–11, 15–16, 26–32). Retrieved March 26, 2008, from http://www.sciam.com/article.cfm?id=the-semantic-web&print=true

Copeland, M. (2007). Web 3.0: No humans required. *Business2.com* (para. 9–11, 21–25, 50–52). Retrieved October 8, 2007, from http://money.cnn.com/magazines/business2/business2_archive/2007/07/01/100117068/index.htm?postversion=2007070305

Feigenbaum, L., Herman, I., Hongsermeier, T., Neumann, E., & Stephens, S. (2007). The semantic web in action. *Scientific American, 297,* 90–97.

Google + e-mail = gmail. (2004, August 1). *CNN* (para. 18–20). Retrieved February 23, 2007, from http://money.cnn.com/2004/04/01/technology/google_email/index.htm.

Hinchcliffe, D. (2005). Is web 2.0 the global SOA? *SOA Web Services Journal, 28.*

Laningham, S. (2006). *developerWorks interviews: Tim Berners-Lee, July, 28, 2006.* Retrieved February 7, 2007, from http://www.ibm.com/developerworks/podcast/dwi/cm-int082206txt.html

Markoff, J. (2006). Entrepreneurs see a web guided by common sense. *New York Times* (para. 3, 13). Retrieved November 12, 2006, from http://www.nytimes.com/2006/11/12/business/12web.html?pagewanted=1&ei=5088&en=254d697964cedc62&ex=1320987600

O'Reilly, T. (2005). What is web 2.0. *O'Reilly Network.* Retrieved August 6, 2006, from http://www.oreillynet.com/pub/a/oreilly/tim/news/2005/09/30/what-is-web-20.html

O'Reilly, T. (2006). Web 2.0 compact definition: Trying again (para. 3-4). Retrieved January 20, 2007, from http://radar.oreilly.com/archives/2006/12/web_20_compact.html

Provoost, L., & Bornier, E. (2006). Service-oriented architecture and the semantic web: A killer combination? (para. 19–20). University of Utrecht. Retrieved February 5, 2009, from http://lee.webcoder.be/papers/sesa.pdf.

Schroth, C., & Janner, T. (2007). Web 2.0 and SOA: Converging concepts enabling the internet of services. *IT Professional, 9*(3), 36–41.

Shadbolt, N., Hall, W., & Berners-Lee, T. (2006). The semantic web revisited. *IEEE Intelligent Systems, 21*(3), 96–101.

Shannon, V. (2006). A "more revolutionary" web. *International Herald Tribune.* Retrieved May 24, 2006, from http://www.iht.com/articles/2006/05/23/business/web.php.

Sidener, J. (2006). Everyone's encyclopedia. *San Diego Union Tribune.* Retrieved October 15, 2006, from http://www.signonsandiego.com/uniontrib/20041206/news_mz1b6encyclo.html.

Spivack, N. (2006). The third-generation web is coming (para. 9, 10). *KurzweilAI.net.* Retrieved December 17, 2006, from http://www.kurzweilai.net/meme/frame.html?main=/articles/art0689.html?m%3D3.

Voss, J. (2007). Tagging, folksonomy, and co–renaissance of manual indexing? *Proceedings of the International Symposium of Information Science.* 234–254. Retrieved January 26, 2007, from http://arxiv.org/abs/cs/0701072

Web 3.0 technology. (2007). *Java Jazzup Magazine,* 59–64.

CHAPTER 2

WEB 2.0

How Signs, Symbols, and Podcasts Affect Elearning

Ruth Gannon Cook
DePaul University School for New Learning

ABSTRACT

New technologies, such as podcasts, *Second Life*, and *YouTube* are shaping how teachers provide content knowledge and communicate with students in higher education. However, the rush to create elearning could cause many universities to overlook important aspects of instructional design that provide learning on deeper levels. Without thoughtful integration of meditation tools in online degree programs, a student in these programs could end up acquiring new knowledge and still lack a well-rounded education. This chapter uses the qualitative methodologies of case study and action research to examine whether semiotic tools could mediate with learners' existing knowledge and Web 2.0 technologies, such as podcasts, to facilitate deeper elearning. It addresses how the inclusion of interdisciplinary knowledge and semiotics could reintroduce aspects of cultural and social competencies and resonate with learners to nurture deeper, self-authorized and transformative, ways of knowing.

Wired for Learning: An Educator's Guide to Web 2.0, pages 21–41

21

INTRODUCTION

Often in the creation of a new medium of communication, old forms of communication, such as text and graphics, are carried forward into that new technology (a good example would be the Internet and the newest generation, Web 2.0) (Innis, 1951; McLuhan, 1976). But knowledge also includes the forms of representation that convey historical, artistic, and inherently recognizable meanings on multiple levels of cognition. Knowledge also includes understanding of ethics, morality, and human elements, such as kindness and understanding. Not all of these knowledge components may be conveyed in online learning. However, without thoughtful integration of these values, students in online programs could end up learning knowledge kernels, but lacking a well-rounded education.

The Concerns of This Chapter

While, ostensibly, one of the key roles of technology is "the same as the teacher's, that is, to facilitate online learning" (Huang, 2002, p. 31), the separation of communication technologies from interdisciplinary research, educational theories and instructional design principles has become a growing concern. Distance educators often fail to understand that distance it is really about "creating a different kind of structure for learning and teaching, not the use of technology" (Kearsley, 1998 in Huang, 2002, p. 31). Technology and social context are equally important considerations in online learning, or social isolation and minimal learning can result (Spitzer, 1998).

The media of communication (in the instance of the research study utilized in this chapter, including the technologies of the Internet and Web 2.0, "restructure time and space and thereby help shape intersubjective social relations (p. 127). While technical media do not determine cultural meanings, as McLuhan implies (McLuhan,1964, 1976; McLuhan & Fiore, 1967), they do play some role in helping to form the life-world relations" (Stevenson, 1995, p. 127). One concern warns that, because of the use of computers, cell phones and hand-held devices, humans now tend to view social and technical relations as fragmented and "radically separable from the production of meaning" (p. 127). Their communication experiences have been restructured by the media of everyday life (Stevenson, 1995). So the real question is how to help learners transform their online learning of course materials to include their own inner knowing and social construction of meaning so that they become transformative and well-rounded learners.

The Objective of This Study

The objective of this study is to study the use of semiotics in Web 2.0 technologies, primarily podcasts, online learning communities, and Voice-Over-Internet Protocols (VOIP), to see if tool mediation can enhance learner comprehension and provide a bridge from basic assimilation of content data to transformative and well-rounded knowledge.

REVIEW OF LITERATURE

This review of literature will address research on the types of post-secondary education students who take courses online that include new technologies, such as those utilized in Web 2.0. The research will then conduct interdisciplinary research on mass communications and technology, semiotics, and instructional design. (The body of this research also has been utilized for the interdisciplinary research portion of this study).

Research on Online Students

Distance education taught in blended (traditional classroom and via distance delivery methods) and online (also called elearning) environments, has become increasingly popular because of the convenience and availability it offers to students. This study looked exclusively at courses and programs delivered entirely online that use *Blackboard* management software and Web 2.0 technologies.

Traditional and Nontraditional Student Demographics in Traditional Post-Secondary Education

The National Center for Education Statistics' (1997) defines a traditional student as a student who enrolls full-time in college immediately after high school graduation. The definition of a nontraditional student is a student who has any of the following characteristics:

- Delays enrollment (does not enter postsecondary education in the same calendar year that he or she finished high school);
- Attends part time for at least part of the academic year;
- Works full time (35 hours or more per week) while enrolled
- Is considered financially independent for purposes of determining eligibility for financial aid;

- Has dependents other than a spouse (usually children, but sometimes others);
- Is a single parent (either not married or married but separated and has dependents); or
- May have completed high school with a General Education Diploma (GED) or other high school completion certificate).
  (National Center for Education Statistics, 2002, Definition of a nontraditional student, ¶1)

In 1999–2000, 27 percent of all undergraduate students were traditional, and 28 percent were highly nontraditional (National Center for Education Statistics, 2002). (See Appendix A). Another 28 percent were moderately nontraditional and 17 percent were minimally nontraditional (2002). While there was still a large percentage of traditional age (18–24) students who entered higher education between 1990 and 2004, and the enrollment of students under age 25 increased by 31 percent during that period, enrollment of persons 25 years of age and over rose by 17 percent during the same period (National Center for Education Statistics, 2002). From 2004 to 2014, NCES projected a rise of 11 percent in enrollments of persons under 25 and an increase of 15 percent in the number of students 25 years of age and over (National Center for Education Statistics, 2006).

The character of the undergraduate population varied markedly by type of institution. Public two-year and private for-profit institutions had much larger proportions of moderately and highly nontraditional students than four-year institutions, and much smaller proportions of traditional students (National Center for Education Statistics, 2006). At both public two-year and private for-profit institutions, 89 percent of the students were at least mini-

TABLE 2.1 Fall Enrollment in Degree-Granting Institutions[a]

Age	1990	1995	2000	2002	2005[1]	2010[1]	2014[1]
Total	13,819	14,262	15,312	16,612	17,350	18,816	19,470
14 to 17 years old	177	148	145	202	201	216	215
18 and 19 years old	2,950	2,894	3,531	3,571	3,705	4,067	3,951
20 and 21 years old	2,761	2,705	3,045	3,366	3,456	3,848	3,845
22 to 24 years old	2,144	2,411	2,617	2,932	3,143	3,384	3,686
25 to 29 years old	1,982	2,120	1,960	2,102	2,374	2,724	2,913
30 to 34 years old	1,322	1,236	1,265	1,300	1,290	1,399	1,573
35 years old and over	2,484	2,747	2,749	3,139	3,181	3,178	

[a] Total fall enrollment in degree-granting institutions, by age: Selected years, 1990 through 2014 (in thousands)
Source: Courtesy of the National Center for Educational Statistics (2006).

mally nontraditional, compared with 58 percent at public four-year institutions and 50 percent at private not-for-profit four-year institutions (2006).

The research for this study was conducted at a four year private university with a program dedicated to adult learners. The target population at the university in this research study consisted of nontraditional students (considered adult learners from 24 years of age or older) (DePaul University School for New Learning, 2008).In this case, the definitions of a), nontraditional student also included

- The requirement that the students be a minimum of 24 years of age
- The students must have successfully completed a GED high school completion certificate (DePaul University, 2008)

Traditional and Nontraditional Students in Online Courses and Degree Programs

There has been a growing pressure on corporate, public and private educational institutions to deliver more formal training and education via Internet-transmitted technology. The number of adult education participants jumped from 76 million in 1995 to 90 million in 1999 (National Center for Education

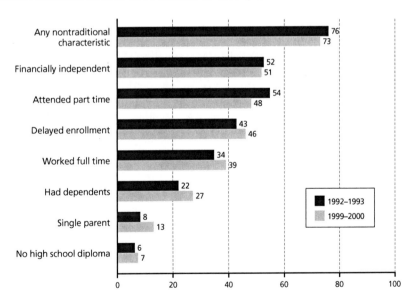

Figure 2.1 Percentage of undergraduates with nontraditional characteristics: 1992–1993 and 1999–2000.
Source: U.S. Department of Education, NCES. National Postsecondary Student Aid Study (NPSAS:2000).

Statistics, 1999). There lies the driving force upon higher education to focus upon distance learning as a viable educational delivery medium.

The demand for distance education (DE) prompts new websites to spring up daily from universities and training facilities offering college credit courses, on-line preparation and certification courses (Gannon-Cook, 2003).

RESEARCH ON ONLINE LEARNERS

The growing demand for online education has been evidenced by the increasing numbers of traditional and non-traditional students taking online courses. What may generally define online learners is accessibility. Online learners may have, in the past, been unable or unwilling to take courses because of the lack of access to higher education that required traditional classroom attendance or long commutes (National Center for Education Testing, 2000; United States Distance Learning Association, 2000; United States Distance Learning Association, 2001; Web-based Education Commission to the President and the Congress of the United States, 2000). Online learning and other forms of distance education now make postsecondary education possible for these students not only because they provide easy access to learning via the Internet and interactive technologies, but because they encourage the students to feel more in control of their learning. But online learning could also present challenges that students may not be prepared for, such as the need to focus on the content materials and to self-regulate their learning. Online learning often needs to include more than content materials; it may need recommendations on how to help the learner gain confidence in an online course, recommendations on how to self-regulate the student's learning, and how to stay disciplined while taking an online course.

Complex Learning

"The propriety of setting goals for learners that they might not set for themselves is at the heart of the educative process" (Taylor, 2006, p. 214). The kind of learning that can lead to a "more complex epistemology" (p. 212) occurs in several ways:

> By elaborating existing frames of reference, by learning new frames of reference, by transforming points of view, or by transforming habits of mind ... We transform frames of reference—our own and those of others—by becoming critically aware of their assumptions and aware of their context—the source, nature, and consequences of taken-for Granted beliefs. (Taylor, 2006, p. 19)

The educator's goal may be to foster "a qualitative evolution of mind" (Taylor, 2006, p. 275) that actually creates a distinction between the instrumental mind (which characteristics include identification with self interests, a lack of empathy; and the need for very specific directions and the socialized mind (which includes values derived from environment and others) to scaffold authentic knowledge and encourage self-authorizing and, optimally, transformative consciousness. The tools of communication used to convey these values are crucial to facilitate the mediation and socialization processes of effective learning.

Research on Mass Communications

The term mass communications, for the purposes of this study, is limited to Technologies that Deliver Online Learning, such as online synchronous and asynchronous chats in online learning communities, Web 2.0 technologies (web logs [blogs]), podcasts, and Voice Over Internet Protocol (VOIP) communications). The term 'mass' comes from the extensive dissemination of communications media and denotes great distribution, range or extent (of people or production) (Wikipedia, 2008d, available online). Mass communication transmission relates to newspaper, magazine publishing, radio, television, film, and electronic media, such as the Internet and has increasingly focused on the convergence of publishing, broadcasting and digital communication (2008d).

Marshall McLuhan, an author of seminal research on mass communication, held that mass communication is a form of social action that can be studied as a process of creating and managing social reality rather than as a technique for describing it (McLuhan, 1976). The new medium reprocesses the old one, yet while the communications tool may evolve, humans still "continue to think in the old, fragmented space and time patterns of the pre-electric age" (McLuhan, 1964, p. ix, p. 20). While new environment has been created, the 'content' is still conveyed in the medium of the old mechanized environment. So, in the end, the content of any medium "is always another medium" (p. 23). McLuhan also coined the phrase, "the medium is the message" to point out that the tool through which the message is conveyed also conveys a message (1976). All media communications also proxemics, "extensions of some human faculty—psychic or physical" (McLuhan & Fiore, 1967, p. 26).

The study of mass communications has included the study of how media has impacted society on a national and global level. For a communicative culture "that seeks... to enlarge thought... through a plurality of voices, particularly of those that are not immediately present in day-to-day encounters, is especially necessary in a globalized and fragmented culture" (Stevenson, 1998, pp. 68–69). Important contributors to the field of mass communications include Jurgen Habermas (1981a, 1981b) and Walter Benjamin (1973), both members of the Frankfort School. Habermas warned that since the eighteenth century there has been a splitting off of knowledge, justice and taste (appreciation for the arts) that has contributed to a "loss of meaning in the context of everyday life" (p. 52). Post-structuralist writers, such as Baudrillard (1975, 1981, 1990), Derrida (1966, 1978), Foucault (1980), and Chomsky (1992), have written about the effects of media on society.

Technology and Mass Communications

> Ours is a brand-new world of allatonceness. "Time" has ceased, "space" has vanished. We now live in a global village . . . a simultaneous happening. We are back in acoustic space. We have begun again to structure the primordial feeling, tribal emotions from which a few centuries of literacy divorced us . . . electric circuitry profoundly involves men with one another . . . our electrically-configured world has forced us to move from the habit of data classification to the mode of pattern recognition. We can no longer build serially, block-by-block, step-by-step, because instant communication insures that all factors of the environment and of experience co-exist in a state of active interplay. (McLuhan & Fiore, 1967, p. 63)

New forms of technology emerge daily so the research on the effects of media upon individuals and society will continue to provide rich data from the academic discipline of mass communications that can contribute to other disciplines, such as Computer Technology, Education, Instructional Design, Political Science and Languages.

Research on Semiotics

The study of semiotics has been largely relegated to the academic studies of discourse, languages and Mathematics. But, research has demonstrated that semiotics has had a profound effect on human communications and interactions throughout history. Plato and Aristotle looked at language and signs as far back as 340 BCE (Cobley & Jansz, 2004). However, semiotics has only been studied as a discipline over the last hundred years. Experts, such as Saussure (1974), Peirce (Hoopes, 1991), Jakobson (1962–87), Derrida (1978), Baudrillard (1975, 1981, 1990), Lacan (1977), and Eco (1976) have been the key contributors to the field of semiotics.

Semiotics is the study of patterned human communication behavior, including auditory/vocabulary, facial expressions, body talk, touch (proxemics), signs, and symbols (Clarke, 1987; Cobley, 1996; Cobley & Jansz, 2003; Eco, 1976; Gannon-Cook, 1998; Hervey, 1982; Hoopes, 1991; Leader, 1995). A semiotician might describe social meaning as a product of the relationships constructed among people and the signs they use to convey their messages. Research on Semiotics can include:

- Text/inscriptions, including markup languages, SML, HTML, XTML, XML, etc.
- Pictures/icons/signs/symbols/metaphors
- Audio/oral narratives/storytelling/folktales
- Rites/rituals/narratives/journals
- Proxemic technologies/computers

As sociocultural tools, such as signs and symbols, included in semiotics, take on enriched meaning, affecting the functions of human consciousness as well as their environment. Ultimately, everyday language and discourse come under the scrutiny of this discipline since it becomes a metalinguistic descriptor of ordinary communication (Dant, 1991). Ordinary language identifies and uses written material and verbiage to communicate and express meaning. It is also uses these "tools" to construct meaning and, in some psychological schools of thought, i.e., the structuralist school of thought, analysis of these tools is applied in order to study the social context of language in a meaningful way (Gannon-Cook, 2000). Literacy includes the forms of representation that convey anthropological, historical, artistic, and inherently recognizable meaning on multiple levels of cognition.

Text

Since the study of semiotics often focuses on the "essence of text," the study of the underlying knowledge of signs and symbols has been somewhat overlooked. Text (which includes the alphabet) has been the primary means of communication since the invention of the alphabet(BCE) and the mass availability of books that came with Gutenberg printing press in 1468 (Schlain, 1999). "Printing was the Reformation: Gutenberg made Luther possible" (Durant, 1957). But other forms of language, such as Cyrillic, and most Asian languages, do not use text; they use signs and symbolic representations that represent alphabets and, consequently, have evolved different cultures and communication styles.

Without an awareness of how signs work as tools in mediation with consciousness, a comprehensible knowledge of words and other signs in text is obscured. The social construction of observable knowledge needs to be qualified on a continuous basis so that more than "text" is emphasized (Dant, 1991).

Signs

"A picture is worth a thousand words" (a paraphrased Chinese Proverb, author unknown). Signs can include symbols that represent communications, pictures, icons, inscriptions, and metaphors. Vygotsky defined the sign as "the basic unit of communication" (Turner, 1993, p. 87). He deemed "signs" to be important "psychological tools" that mediated with consciousness. He elaborated examples of signs as being language, counting systems, algebraic symbols, writing, diagrams, maps, and conventional signs and stressed signs' importance as origins of meaning. He noted that the analysis of sign meaning was, to him, "the only adequate method for analyzing human consciousness" (Wertsch, 1985, p. 106).

Claude Levi Strauss (1970) posited that symbolic forms and metaphoric language were recognized in the same manner by both ancient and modern minds, and the unconscious structure underlying customs and institutions should be studied to obtain a principle of valid interpretation across cultures (Dant, 1991). In truth, the word design comes from de (Latin root meaning from) and sign. If that is the case, then perhaps it might account in part for why novices seem to adopt software using metaphors more readily (Gannon Cook, 1999, 1998). Computer companies have included icons that have universal recognition in their software designs, including symbols like trash cans, pencils, pictures and paint buckets. "These symbols have helped users all over the world find something that already had meaning to them and made them more comfortable using the technology" (Gannon-Cook, 1999).

Metaphors

Metaphors are figures of speech that attribute a similar quality or name to something which is not literally applicable to it (Webster 1989). By reasoning through metaphors, anchoring of information can occur that facilitates understanding of new ideas (Gallini, Seaman, Terry, 1995). Studies conducted on metaphors, a type of semiotic tool, indicate that metaphors seem to inspire iconic thinking, fill conceptual gaps, and become absorbed into society, taking on a literal quality as symbolic descriptors of culture (Innis, 1951; McLuhan, 1968; Turbayne, 1962). They also suggested that metaphors were not just alternatives to literal language, but were embedded in thought, frozen in memory, and some metaphors even triggered bodily response, such as a metaphor of a sumptuous banquet might trigger hunger, or a metaphor of jumping off a diving board may raise adrenaline (Danesi, 1993; Dant, 1991,Verene, 1993). These studies postulated that metaphors seemed to inspire iconic thinking, filled conceptual gaps, and became absorbed into society, taking on literal qualities as symbolic descriptors of culture (Gordon, 1998; McLuhan, 1968; Turbayne, 1962).

The adoption of metaphors to define and describe courseware and content in technology maintains the tradition of subconscious pattern recognition set long ago by the use of these descriptors ((Danesi, 1993; Levi-Strauss, 1970, Turbayne, 1962). Metaphoric terms like *Netscape, Webspinner, Dreamweaver*, surfing the net, chatting in cybercafes, webs, *Second Life*, podcasts, are but a few of these descriptors used to describe electronic software packages and activities. Without metaphoric descriptors, electronic courses might not have the allure and subconscious pattern recognition needed to prompt interest and acceptance of the new technological vehicle of information delivery (Lieber, 1997). Current iconic representations and metaphors used in technology are rapidly taking on grass-roots recognition among peoples of many cultures and languages. So, to assure this new evolving "techno culture" is thoroughly integrated into on-line courseware design, the "old" knowledge must converge with the new. This can be "food for thought" for today's instructional designer who must design courses that can not only convey information, but also knowledge.

Audio/Oral Narratives/Storytelling/Folktales

Metaphors are usually verbal, so stories, folktales and narratives are verbal accounts of fiction or refashioned true events often told as metaphors. The actual shared transmissions, along with speech patterns and method of delivery, all play a part in the successful understanding of both the metaphor and the topic being narrated by the storyteller. One of the more famous metaphors is that of Plato's cave and one of his explanations of how one learns. Prisoners see only shadows on the cave walls, but when released they see the light of the real world. Other metaphors used as analogies include that of the mind to a computer, maps of the world and of the mind, climbing mountains, sailing ships, and too many more to mention here.

Rites/Rituals/Narratives/Journals

"Make a wish, it's your birthday, and don't tell anyone that wish so it will come true." (unknown origin). Each family in every country has its own rites and rituals. Rites and rituals were established in temples and churches over the last ten thousand years, ranging from Hindu rites to today's Catholic church rituals. Another form of semiotic is poetry.

> *There I beheld the emblem of a mind*
> *that feeds upon infinity . . . intent to hear*
> *its voices issuing forth to silent light*
> *In one continuous stream*
> (Rothstein, 1996, p. 239)

Written narratives and journals also usually are centered on a metaphoric theme, such as that of the journey along life's highway, climbing the mountain to the summit, walking the tightrope of business, and so forth, and all are designed to resonate with the reader or decoder.

Tool Mediation and Proxemic

Vygotsky (Wertsch, 1985) offered an innovative, explanation for mental functions. He suggested that the primary tools of activities, represented in signs and symbols, acted as agents for, and subsequently provided definition for, culture, and served as intervening links to consciousness. Mediation of these tools, which Vygotsky called tool mediation, was the structural and genetic central feature of mental functioning which, in turn, became a necessary liaison to consciousness. Another term coined by Vygotsky, the "unit of analysis", served as the primary unit of organization, and provided a building block in the foundation of explanatory theoretical principles of psychology. His seminal research transformed existing methodologies with his introduction of this intermediate link of action/object (of study). He believed the "historical study of behavior is not an auxiliary aspect of theoretical study, but rather forms its very base" (Lee, 1985, p. 55). What emerged for Vygotstky was an organic system of assessment of activity (tools and symbols) that provided a key to the psychological paradigm of external projection and internal control. The body of research initiated by Vygotsky offered the basis for a culturally grounded theory of cognition, with the concept of "mediated tools" linking culture to the functions of consciousness (Gannon-Cook, 2000).

The traditional dictionary meaning assigned to the word "tool" is "anything, which, held in the hand, assists a person to do manual or nonmanual work. (Webster's Dictionary, 2007)." Vygotsky used the word "tool" in a similar context, assigning it meaning in relation to work. Vygotsky's "tools" included not only physical tools like hammers, but mental tools like metaphors, symbols, and semiotic representations of communication, like auditory/vocal and visual expressions; body talk (kinesthetics); touch (proxemics); and prostheses (extensions of limbs). Vygotsky's definition of tools would also include technological instruments, robotics, computer hand devices, optical scanners, even cell phones. His interpretation of tool mediation Wertsch, 1985) would agree with McLuhan's (McLuhan & Fiore, 1967), that the equipment (tools) become extensions of the user's body. As McLuhan stated "All media are extensions of some human faculty, psychic or physical" (p. 26). By changing the environment, media "evoke(s) in us unique ratios of sense perceptions. The extension of any one sense alters the way we think and act—the way we perceive the world" (p. 41).

Research on Instructional Design

Instructional design is described as "the process of solving instructional problems by systematic analysis of the conditions for learning" (Seels & Glasgow, 1998, p. 1). Instructional design can be utilized in both traditional and on-line environments and is usually based on theory, research, best practices, and practical experience (Gagne, 1987; Merrill, 1983; Merrill, Tennyson, & Power, 1992; Moore & Kearsley, 1996).

Instructional design is a systematic way of designing, carrying out, and evaluating the whole process of learning and teaching in terms of specific objectives, based on research and human learning and communication, and employing a combination of human and nonhuman resources to bring about more effective instruction" (Seels & Glasgow, 1998, p. 8).

Analysis, design, development, implementation and evaluation are integral stages of the instructional design process (Seels & Glasgow, 1998), but how these phases are integrated is generally up to both the organization using instructional design and the instructional designer. In the university where this study was conducted, on-line courses were implemented with standardized processes for both content and style. There are also interactivities in electronic courses that are designed to enlist and engage the student to participate in her or his learning. But in these stages and activities, there is seldom attention paid to the inclusion of the communications aspects of semiotics. Despite all the research conducted in the fields of communications and language that acknowledges the massive amount of embedded knowledge conveyed through semiotic tools, little attention has been paid to the inclusion of semiotics in course design and delivery, hence the reason for this study.

METHODOLOGY

The Research Question

The purpose of the research is to study the use of semiotics in online courses utilizing Web 2.0 technologies, such as podcasts, online learning communities, and Internet phones, to see if semiotic tools can positively influence students to develop deeper, transitional, learning.

The methodology is based on design and development research (Richey & Klein, 2007). Design and development research "not only enhance(s) our knowledge base, but (will) also provide(s) the empirical basis for the construction of a comprehensive theory of design and development" (p. 6). The research in this study consists of a triangulation of qualitative research: action research, case study, and a review of interdisciplinary research.

> This (design and development research) will give the field a fourth theory base, supplementing the understandings we have already acquired from psychological and learning theory, instructional and teaching-learning theory, and communication and message-design theory. (p. 6)

Action Research

Action research is "a comparative research on the conditions and effects of various forms of social action and research leading to social action" that uses "a spiral of steps, each of which is composed of a circle of planning, action, and fact-finding about the result of the action" (Wikipedia, 2008, available online).

In this study the action research was conducted by the researcher who monitored technologies used in an online course at a large private university in the Midwest. The Web 2.0 technologies used in the study were online learning communities, voice over Internet protocols (VOIP) and teleconferences; and podcasts. (In addition to conducting the investigation, the class was also taught by the researcher).

Case Study

A case study is a study of some social unit or organization that attempts to determine what factors led to its success or failure; it is also a detailed analysis of a person or group from a social, psychological or medical point of view (Wordnet 2.1, 2008). Case studies have been used in varied investigations, particularly in sociological studies, but increasingly, in instruction (Tellis, 1997). By design, in case studies the data are usually triangulated to maximize the reliability of the results (Tellis, 1997). Yin (1994) has developed robust procedures that have been developed and tested to bring out the details from the participants by using multiple sources of data. Yin (1994) presented the protocol as a major tool to be used in case studies to assert the reliability of the case study research. A typical protocol should have the following sections:

- An overview of the case study project (objectives, issues, topics being investigated)
- Field procedures (credentials and access to sites, sources of information)
- Case study questions (specific questions that the investigator must keep in mind during data collection)
- A guide for case study report (outline, format for the narrative) (Yin, 1994, p. 64, in Tellis, 1997).

This case study was conducted as a tool development case study with the students in an online course during the summer of 2007. (The researcher was also the primary investigator that conducted the case study).

Participants

The participants in the study were 20 adult learners enrolled in an online Technology, Training, and Human Performance course at a large private Midwestern university. There were 8 men and 12 women who participated in the study.

Data Collection Procedures

For the action research portion of the study, the researcher kept a journal of the online discussions and events that took place over the summer quarter that the online class was taught.

For the case study, the researcher combined interviews with podcast experts, conducted field observations of student behaviors, assessed the Web 2.0 technologies used in the course, and utilized explanatory research to aggregate a comprehensive analysis of the contents, delivery and interactivities of the course used in the study.

ANALYSIS

The researcher analyzed the findings of the qualitative research, that of the action research, the case study, and interdisciplinary review of research, to see which techniques may have worked more effectively and what lessons have been learned from this study.

The researcher had set up the course with several Web 2.0 interactivities, primarily establishing an online learning community, conducting voice-Internet conferences (VOIP) (both in a group and individually), and posting podcasts with course aids to help students get better visual and subliminal connections to and understanding of the new course materials and the assignment requirements. Throughout the eleven week course, the teacher acted as facilitator, posting responses and conversations with students in the online community. There were at least one individual VOIP conference and two class VOIP conferences, the first held two weeks into the course, and the second held two weeks prior to the end of the course. Podcast course aids were posted four times during the quarter, both within the proprietary web management course with links to the podcast site, and were actually published on the university proprietary iPod site.

Findings

The findings of the action research and case study indicated that online learners often felt isolated and disconnected from their classmates initially, even with the newest technologies, but with ongoing interaction through emails, online communities, Internet phone conferences, and podcast study aids, the students quickly moved passed the intimidation and frustration phases of learning to the assimilation and integration of the course contents. The course design, that included not only Web 2.0 technologies, but semiotic tools that were incorporated to help students recognize inherently familiar signs and mentally dialog with them, was effective in keeping students interested enough, initially, to remain in the course and complete it. The researcher could not attribute the semiotic design of the course to the retention, but felt future research could shed more light on how the students' sociocultural experiences may have been mediated by the semiotic course tools.

There will also be an ongoing need to guide the development of online coursework, and take into consideration the historic references of semiotics to assure some initial degree of conscious mental recognition and positive predisposition towards new content and technologies in online courses. There will need to be quality control to assure consistency of design and semiotic tool integration throughout the design and implementation process. Accommodation to new technologies, such as those of Web 2.0, and research, will require systematic design standards like the ones used in course studied in this research.

Constructive approaches, like those used in the course used in this study, emphasize the "forging of connections between individuals' experiences and various elements from their system of influences . . . Meaning or learning is generated from within the individual in relation to his or her experience of the world" (Patton, 2005, pp. 23–24). When adult learners are expected to be self-directed, they may not have any idea of how to carry out that mandate. If they can be encouraged to enter the new electronic passages with familiar signs and inscriptions that resonate with what they already know, they are more likely to try to persist and navigate the new learning environment. What is less obvious to the learners in this process, is that they are also being presented with new opportunities to scaffold onto their prior learning new ways of seeing themselves and the world (Kegan, 1994).

"Social constructivists admirably remind us of the value, power, and virtue of social participation and community" (Kegan, 1994, p. 289), but educating adult learners in on-line environments requires much work to create a "discourse community" (p. 288). To bring on-line learners through the transformation to self-authorship involves facilitating the learner's acceptance of that responsibility. It takes more than technological interactivity tools to make that happen; it takes ongoing mentoring, communicating and diligently working to bring each student into a safety zone that is not only virtual, but virtually encouraging to engage in discourse.

CONCLUSION

The findings of this study will serve to inform the body of research in several disciplines, those of mass communications, linguistics, and instructional design. The primary intention of this study has been to review semiotics and how the inclusion of semiotics in on-line course design can facilitate better assimilation of new knowledge and use of new technologies, such as those of Web 2.0.

The qualitative research conducted in this study revealed that on-line courseware designed using familiar symbols and stories, and other forms of semiotics, helped to pave the way for learning and transformation, more so than did courseware without those representations, even when the courseware included new interactive technologies.

Semiotic tools can provide rich legacies of multi-culturalism to instructional design and to research. New technologies, such as Web 2.0 are creating a new global language, one that is still translated and integrated, however, using the same old languages and symbolic representations of past generations. But it is necessary for course designers and teachers to better understand how tool mediation can work more effectively with semiotics since students mediate their new knowledge with their existing knowledge via the proxemics of technology.

Representational language and semiotics have seldom been prioritized in the overall design of courseware. Yet the benefits of technology have been widely acknowledged. Somehow, the accumulations of human communication forms through history should have a place in online course design, along with new technologies, such as Web 2.0. So a better understanding by course designers and teachers of semiotics and technology tool mediation can help to bring learners to a new level of acceptance and comprehension.

New learning technologies, along with the social factors of twenty-first century living, will continue to impact learners in on-line courses and programs. These findings could be important for future research on because, without thoughtful integration of meditation tools into online degree programs, students in these programs could end up acquiring new knowledge and still lack a well-rounded education. Renewed use of semiotics in the creation of course design could evolve and, ultimately, expedite a new strand of global semiotics.

The main focus of this research has been to review semiotic elements, in addition to Web 2.0 technology, to see how instructional designers can best enlist and involve students in online learning. The study addressed how the inclusion of semiotics into course design could reintroduce aspects of cultural and social competencies that resonate and nurture deeper, self-authorized and transformative, ways of knowing for online learners. Future trends seem to indicate that the past communication forms, such as text, graphics, and metaphors, will continue to be incorporated into the newer technologies (Gannon-Cook, 1998, 1999; Innis, 1951; McLuhan, 1964; Schlain, 1998), as evidenced by the new software names that carry forth the text meanings, such as Wikipedias (web encyclopedias), web logs (blogs), pod-casting (a mixed metaphor containing the concept of clusters or pods, and casting a fishing line), and so forth. Since the prospects of Web 2.0 will invariably contain semiotic elements, future research on which aspects of semiotics could best resonate with students could provide invaluable insights into how to enlist and retain students in Web 2.0 courses.

REFERENCES

Baudrillard, J. (1975). *Mythologies*, translated by Annette Lavers. St. Albans, Paladin.

Baudrillard, J. (1981). *Requi(e)m for the media, in for a critique of the political economy of the sign*. St. Louis, MO: Telos.

Baudrillard, J. (1990). *Mass media culture, in revenge of the crystal: Selected writings on the modern object and its destiny, 1968–1983* (ed. and trans. P. Foss & J. Pefanis). London: Pluto Press.

Benjamin, W. (1973). The work of art in an age of mechanical reproduction. In *Illuminations*. London: Fontana.

Chomsky, N. (1992). Media and the war: What war? In H. Mowlana, G. Gerbner, & H. I. Schiller, (Eds.), *The media's war in the Persian Gulf—A global perspective* (pp. 216–233). Boulder, CO: Westview Press.

Clarke, D. S. (1987). *Principles of semiotic*. London: Routledge.

Cobley, P., (Ed.). (1996). *The communication theory reader*. London: Routledge.

Cobley, P., & Jansz, L. (2004). *Introducing semiotics*. London: Icon Books.

The Continuing Education Group of the University of Wisconsin-Extension website. (2001). Retrieved February 11, 2008, from http://www.uwex.edu/disted.

Danesi, M. (1993). *Vico, metaphor, and the origin of language*. Bloomington: Indiana University Press.

Dant, T. (1991). *Knowledge, ideology, and discourse: A sociological perspective*. London: Routledge.

DePaul University. (2008). *School for New Learning website*. Retrieved February 15, 2008, from http://snl.depaul.edu.

Derrida, J. (1966). *Structure, sign, and play in the discourse of the Human Sciences*. Lecture delivered at Johns Hopkins University. Baltimore, MD: John Hopkins University.

Derrida, J. (1978). *Writing and difference* (trans. Alan Bass). London: Routledge.

Durant, W. (1957). *The story of civilization. Vol. 6, The reformation*. New York: Simon & Schuster.

Eco, U. (1976). *A theory of semiotics*. Bloomington: Indiana University Press.

Foucault, M. (1980). *Power/knowledge: Selected interviews and other writings, 1972–1977*. New York: Pantheon.

Franklin & Marshall College. (2008). *Definition of a well-rounded person*. Retrieved February 15, 2008, from http://en.wikipedia.org/wiki/Franklin_&_Marshall _College.

Gallini, J., Seaman, M., & Terry, S. (1995). *Universal teaching strategies* (2nd ed.). New York: Allyn & Bacon.

Gannon-Cook, R. (1998). Semiotics in technology, learning and culture. *Bulletin of Science, Technology & Society, 18*(3), 174–179.

Gannon-Cook, R. (1999 June). *Exhuming McLuhan; Lessons distance education can learn from communications*. Paper presented at the Annual Professional Teacher Training Conference (PTTC), Arlington, Texas.

Gannon-Cook, R. (2000 November). *TechnoCulture and semiotics: Getting the picture for online course design*. Paper presented at the meeting of the Association for the Advancement of Computing in Education's (AACE) WebNet 2000: World Conference on the World Wide Web and Internet in Orlando Florida.

Gannon-Cook, R. (1999 June). *Exhuming McLuhan; Lessons distance education can learn from communications*. Paper presented at the Annual Professional Teacher Training Conference (PTTC), Arlington, Texas.

Gannon-Cook, R. (2003 May). *Factors influencing faculty participation in distance education in postsecondary education in the United States: A study conducted at a major public university in the southwestern United States*. Unpublished doctoral dissertation, University of Houston, Houston, Texas.

Goodyear, P. (2006 July). Technology and the articulation of vocational and academic interests: Reflections on time, space, and e-learning. *Studies in Continuing Education, 28*(2), 83–98.

Gordon, W. T. (1998). *Marshall McLuhan: Escape into understanding*. New York: Basic Books.

Habermas, J. (1981a). *The theory of communicative action, Vol.1: Reason and rationalization*. Boston: Beacon Press.

Habermas, J. (1981b Winter). *Modernity versus postmodernity*. Germany: New German Critique.

Hervey, S. (1982). *Semiotic perspectives*. London: Allen and Unwin.

Hoopes, J., (Ed.). (1991). *Peirce on signs: Writings on semiotic*. Chapel Hill: University of North Carolina Press.

Huang, H. M. (2002). Toward constructivism for adult learners in online learning environments. *British Journal of Educational Technology, 33*(1), 27–37.

Jakobson, R. (1962–1987). *The selected writings of Roman Jakobson*. The Hague: Mouton Publishing.

Lacan, J. (1977). *Ecrits: A selection* (trans. A. Sheridan). London: Tavistock.

Leader, D. (1995). *Lacan for beginners*. Cambridge: Icon.

Levi-Strauss, C. (1970). *The elementary structures of kinship*. London: Tavistock.

Levi-Strauss, C. (1977). *Structural anthropology* (trans. C. Jacobson & B. Grundfest Schoepf). Harmondsworth: Penguin.

Lieber, R. (1997). Storytelling: A new way to get close to your customers. *Fortune, 2*(1), 102–110.

McLuhan, M. (1964). *Understanding media: The extensions of man*. New York: Signet Books.

McLuhan, M. (1976). *The medium is the messenger*. New York: Simon & Schuster.

McLuhan, M., & Fiore, Q. (1967). *The medium is the massage.* New York: Touchstone Books.

Mezirow, J. (2000). *Learning as transformation.* San Francisco: Jossey-Bass.

National Center for Education Statistics. (1997, October). *Distance education in higher education institutions.* Washington, DC: United States Department of Education, Office of Educational Research and Improvement.

National Center for Education Statistics. (1999a). *Lifelong learning national household education survey, adult education interview.* Washington, DC: Author.

National Center for Education Statistics. (2002). *National postsecondary student aid study: Nontraditional undergraduates.* Retrieved February 15, 2008, from http:// nces.ed.gov/programs/coe/2002/analyses/nontraditional/sa01.asp

National Center for Educational Statistics (2006). *Digest of education statistics, 2005 (NCES 2006-030).* Table 170. Retrieved February 15, 2008, from http://nces. ed.gov/fastfacts/display.asp?id=98

O'Reilly, T. (2005 September 30). What is Web 2.0? *O'Reilly Network.* Retrieved August 6, 2008, from from http://www.oreillynet.com/pub/a/oreilly/tim/ news/2005/09/30/what-is-web-20.html.

Palermo, J. (1992). *Dewey on the pedagogy of occupations: The social construction of the hyper-real.* Retrieved February 15, 2008, from http://www.ed.uiuc.edu/eps/ PES-Yearbook/92_docs/Palermo.HTM

Richey, R., & Klein, J. (2007). *Design and development research.* Mahwah, NJ: Erlbaum.

Rothstein, E. (1996). *Emblems of mind: The inner life of music and mathematics.* New York: Avon Books.

Saussure, F. (1974). *Course in general linguistics.* London: Fontana.

Shlain, L. (1999). *The alphabet versus the goddess: The conflict between word and image.* New York: Penguin Press.

Sherry, L. (1996). Issues in distance education. *International Journal of Distance Education 11*(4), 337–365. Retrieved August 28, 2001, from http://www.cudenver. edu/public/education/edschool/issues.html#abstract.

Spitzer, D. R. (1998, March/April). Rediscovering the social context of distance learning. *Educational Technology,* 52–56.

Stake, R. (1995). *The art of case research.* Newbury Park, CA: Sage.

Stevenson, N. (1995). *Understanding media cultures: Social theory and mass communication.* London: Routledge.

Taylor, K. (2006). Autonomy and self-directed learning: A developmental journey. In C. Hoare (Ed.), *Handbook of adult development and learning* (pp. 196–218). New York: Oxford University Press.

Tellis, W. (1997, July). Introduction to case study [68 paragraphs]. *The Qualitative Report* [On-line serial], *3*(2). Retrieved February 15, 2008, from: http://www. nova.edu/ssss/QR/QR3-2/tellis1.html

Turbayne, C. (1962). *The myth of metaphor.* New Haven, CT: Yale University Press.

Turner, G. (1993). Film languages: Culture and language. In D. Graddol & O. Boyd-Barrett (Eds.), *Media tests: Authors and readers* (pp. 119–135). London: Multilingual Matters.

United States Department of Education, National Center for Education Statistics (2000). *National Postsecondary Student Aid Study (NPSAS:2000).* Washington, DC: Author.

United States Distance Learning Association. (1996). *Report on Distance Learning.* Retrieved May 7, 2002, from http://usdla.org.

Webster's New Lexicon Dictionary. (2007). New York: Lexicon Publications, Inc.

Verene, D. (1993). Metaphysical narration, science, and symbolic form. *Review of Metaphysics, 47,* 115–132.

Wikipedia (2008a). *Intersubjective social relations.* Retrieved February 15, 2008, from http://en.wikipedia.org/wiki/Social_relations

Wikipedia (2008b). *A definition of action research.* Retrieved February 15, 2008, from http://en.wikipedia.org/wiki/Action_research

Wikipedia. (2008c). *Definition of Web 2.0.* Retrieved February 15, 2008, from http://en.wikipedia.org/wiki/Web_2.0

Wikipedia. (2008d). *Definition of mass media.* Retrieved February 15, 2008, from http://en.wikipedia.org/wiki/Mass_communication

Wikipedia. (2008e). *Definition of social constructivism.* Retrieved February 15, 2008, from http://en.wikipedia.org/wiki/Social_constructionism

Wordnet 2.1 (2008). *A definition of case study.* Retrieved February 15, 2008, from http://uk.ask.com/reference/dictionary/wordnetuk/36993/case%20study.

Yin, R. (1994). *Case study research: Design and methods* (2nd ed.). Thousand Oaks, CA: Sage.

CHAPTER 3

USER GENERATED DESIGN

Teaching and Learning with Web 2.0

Jeremy I. Tutty
Boise State University

Florence Martin
University of North Carolina Wilmington

ABSTRACT

The Web 2.0 Instructional Design Model (Web 2.0 ID) has been designed to guide users to utilize Web 2.0 tools to improve learning and performance. Web 2.0 ID is built upon the socio-constructivist philosophies of learning and emphasizes three dimensions to designing learning for the Web 2.0 environment—social/collaborative, user generated design and knowledge management. The chapter explains the three phases of the model in detail 1) the analysis phase where the learner as the designer interacts with a facilitator to analyze the learning that has to happen, 2) the design phase where the learners collaborate and personalize their learning, 3) and finally the evaluation phase where the learners interact with the facilitator who helps them evaluate the learning that has occurred. Several Web 2.0 tools that help in this collaboration/personalization phase are described. Two case studies where the Web 2.0 model has been applied in a classroom setting are also described.

Wired for Learning: An Educator's Guide to Web 2.0, pages 43–58
Copyright © 2009 by Information Age Publishing

INTRODUCTION

Advancements in technology have revolutionized the opportunities for educators to teach and the means for students to learn. In the last decade, educational opportunities have evolved within the movement towards Web-based instruction, online learning, and even more dramatically with the combination of social learning, inquiry-based interactive learning, and knowledge construction. The contention exists that the nature of knowledge and learning themselves has changed (Siemens, 2004). The pedagogical methods used for years are instructionally sound and defendable, but they can quickly become outdated as students adapt their learning to the networked world.

The recent emergence of approaches to learning that are based on self-determination and networked contexts such as heutagogy (Phelps, Hase, & Ellis, 2005) and connectivism (Siemens, 2005) help us understand learning as making connections with ideas, facts, people and communities. Learning has grown beyond mere consumption of knowledge and become a knowledge creation process. In the current world of proliferated mass social media, it is Web 2.0 tools that provide an excellent vehicle for making such connections. The question becomes what can we do to promote effective learning using Web 2.0 tools.

The authors of this chapter have designed an instructional model that can be used to guide users to utilize Web 2.0 tools to improve learning and performance. Web 2.0 Instructional Design (Web 2.0 ID) provides both a new model for teaching that builds upon the inherent capacity of networked communication to support improvement in learning and performance, and a new model of learning where learners engage in the process of design that supports individual and collective learning with Web 2.0 tools. Learning with the Web 2.0 platform is learner driven rather than instructor driven. These tools are ready when needed by the learner. Learning in this new paradigm stems from innovation rather than instruction.

The Conceptual Framework of the Web 2.0 Instructional Design Model

Web 2.0 ID is built upon the notion that learning is no longer an internal, individualistic activity, and that learner-designed contexts have the capacity to connect the formal learning agenda of educational institutions with the personal learning goals of students. Drawing from socio-constructivist philosophies of learning such as: social learning theory (Vygotsky, 1978) and Social Construction of Technology (SCOT) (Bijker, Pinch, & Hughes, 1987; Collins, 1985; & Woolgar, 1991); Web 2.0 ID approaches learning as grounded in the theories of distributed cognition (Salomon, 1993), and social construction of knowledge (Glasersfeld, 1995). Web 2.0 places all participants in learning at the intersection of these two theories, in that, the social context and distributed environment are now one in the same.

Web 2.0 ID was developed to allow for flexibility along and within the continuum of teacher-directed pedagogy to learner-directed heutagogy. Garrison, Anderson, and Archer (2003) identify social presence, cognitive presence, and teaching presence as the conditions for developing an online learning community. Web 2.0 ID reflects our assertion that teaching presence may be established anywhere along the pedagogy-heutagogy continuum. This assertion dictates that the design model must provide for co-configuration, co-creation, or co-design of learning (Bakardjieva, 2005). McLoughlin (2002) provides a framework for designing learner support for an online environment, which includes task support, social support, and peer support. Tait and Mills (2003) indicate support systems must relate to different cultures, learners, economic systems, and programs of study.

Web 2.0 tools make it possible for social connections to be made easily. Participants are able to collaborate based on a learning/performance outcome and look for peers and experts to guide them through the process.

DIMENSIONS OF WEB 2.0 ID

Web 2.0 ID applies three dimensions of learner and technological characteristics to designing learning for the Web 2.0 environment. Theses include the collaborative/social, user generated design, and the knowledge management characteristic.

Collaborative/Social

Web 2.0 ID is collaborative. Collaborative learning environments offer a new perspective on the importance of creating a supportive context within which learners can navigate the process of learning, self-regulate, collaborate, and contribute (Gunawardena & McIsaac, 2004; Strijbos, Martens, & Jochems, 2004). Unlike early models of independent study that stressed individual learning, Web 2.0 ID provides the framework for learners to design, interact, receive feedback, and construct their own learning at various levels of self-determination while contributing to a social community.

We believe that to successfully achieve such a self-regulating community requires an investment by the instructor. The teacher serves as the facilitator allowing students to inquire, research, discover, analyze, and evaluate according to their needs and what is being studied. The emphasis shifts from giver of knowledge to one who supports, encourages, challenges, questions, and promotes intellectual curiosity with the learner being held responsible for what is accomplished (Cooper, 2003).

User Generated Design

As designers, learners have the opportunity to use Web 2.0 tools, to creatively accumulate knowledge based on their interest, and build on meaningful information aligned with the intended outcomes (See Figure 3.1).

In the learner as designer phase, learners become intellectual partners with the technology and engage in constructive learning processes (Salomon, Perkins & Globerson, 1989; Bhattacharya & Bhattacharya, 2006). The model involves the learners in the intellectual process of building their knowledge rather than isolating them from the process.

Knowledge Management

Knowledge Management is an approach to achieving learning and performance objectives by efficient use of knowledge. In Web 2.0 ID, we rely on intelligence-based knowledge management, which is a composite construct of data, information, rules, procedures, best practices and traits such as attention, motivation, creativity, commitment and innovation (Malhotra, 2003).

In the learner as designer phase, social Web users collaborate towards their learning and performance outcome. This paradigm represents a change from the days when users preferred to keep the knowledge locked

Figure 3.1 Dimensions of Web 2.0 ID.

Figure 3.2 Intelligence-based knowledge management.

and users were concerned about copyright, privacy and secrecy. Web 2.0 ID is build about users that are willing to share their knowledge across boundaries as long as it is valued and beneficial. Users personalize the knowledge gained by reflecting and actualizing it towards their outcome. Finally, they also receive feedback on their understanding and provide feedback to the other users within the Web 2.0 environment. This cycle results in a continuous collaboration towards the learning/performance outcome, and the reinforcement of intrinsically and extrinsically motivated Web 2.0 learners (Figure 3.2).

The technological capabilities of the Web 2.0 platform support the computational aspects of knowledge management, and the social collaborative aspect provides an opportunity for the re-use of knowledge in an efficient manner. Web 2.0 ID utilizes the co-identity of the social context, the paradigm of intelligence-based knowledge management, and the distributed environments; to not only center the final outcome about the learner, but the design process as well. Web 2.0 ID is built around a leaner design cycle based on continuous collaboration and performance improvement (Stokes & Richey, 2000), which capitalizes on the duality of Web 2.0 as both the social context and distributed environment.

PHASES OF WEB 2.0 ID

The model has been designed such that it can be adapted into a face-to-face, blended or an online classroom. Instructors may direct students to the Web 2.0 world to achieve learning objectives, or learners may use it to achieve their own learning objective.

Analysis

In an attempt to improve pedagogy, the analysis phase is designed such that the learners work with a facilitator who sets the stage for learning. This facilitator could be a peer, an instructor, or learners can self-facilitate. With guidance from the facilitator, the participants are able to analyze the tools available, identify the strengths and weaknesses of these tools and identify the learning outcomes that can be achieved using these tools. In this critical step, the learner navigates a process whereby multiple perspectives are challenged, accommodated, and negotiated with peer learners and experts. The intent of which is to solve a problem, discover something, or to work together to achieve a common learning goal.

Identify Learning/Performance Outcomes (Outcome Analysis)
The purpose of the analysis phase is to guide the learners towards the design phase with an accomplishable learning outcome that promotes collaboration and ongoing formative assessment. This is driven by the identification of a learning outcome. The phases of a formal linear analysis are transferred to the learner in the design phase.

For the instructor, purposive design in this step must include the understanding that the extent to which the performance outcome is individually or collaboratively designed exerts an impact on the remaining process. This outcome then dictates the parameters for the design and instruction. On one end of the continuum, the task analysis approach an instructional designer will use depends on the context that surrounds the instruction to be developed. Instructional designers are to have a clear understanding of what learners are to be able to accomplish by participating in instruction. At the other end, the unintentional experiences of the learners are as important if not more so than the planned outcome.

Identifying the learning/performance outcome encompasses the following tasks:

- Devising an authentic task—The source of the outcome may be derived from a number of sources, be that a curricular requirement, instructor preference, learner negotiated content, or a desired outcome a learner brings to the formal classroom. Obviously, when learners assume the designer role, they lack the expertise to clearly understand what the outcome will look like, and for novices, what designing will look like. So, an indirect consequence of the process is the learner learning to learn. Identifying an open-ended, authentic performance outcome (problem-based or project-based) will allow learners to optimize the collaborative experience.

- Identify strengths, weaknesses, opportunities, and threats (SWOT) posed by various Web 2.0 tools (Tool Analysis)—Using the correct tools and technology is important in attaining the learning or performance outcome. Understanding the technology is the focus of the tool analysis. SWOT Analysis is a powerful technique for understanding the strengths and weaknesses, and for looking the opportunities and threats you face on using the tools. SWOT analysis is an industrial technique to uncover opportunities, understand weaknesses, and eliminate threats that would otherwise catch you unaware. In this task, the capabilities of the available technologies must be evaluated in light of the capability to support the learning/performance task in an open-ended learning environment.

- Identify users' technical competencies (Actual Competency Analysis)—Assuring the performance task is appropriate to the learners' current technical capacity may require a pre-assessment of learner skills. The technology may provide the necessary capabilities to support acquisition of the identified outcomes, but the learners must have the competency to participate.

- Identify cultural and ethical values aligned with the use of the tools (Value Analysis)—Web 2.0 platforms rely on user-generated content to aggregate attention and community. Having the freedom to access content and collaborate should not bring unethical behaviors. Learners moving to design must proceed toward an outcome that does not compromise values. The level of ethical identity and individuals' perception of member empowerment created here is critical to the design and learning process. Instructors must foster: a safe environment for exchange of diverse views and multiple perspectives as the instruction moves to virtual spaces for social interaction. Instructors should address expectations that promote social equality and commitment to the learning outcome. Providing protocols for respectful communication facilitate learners moving into design with confidence.

Collaboration and Personalization

The collaboration and personalization phases comprise an iterative cycle, in which learners collaborate as their reliance on the scaffolding of the performance objective is replaced by social interaction and the achievement of a common performance goal. In this phase, learners become intellectual partners with the technology and engage in constructive learning process (Salomon, et al., 1989; Bhattacharya & Bhattacharya, 2006). The model involves the learners in the intellectual process of building their knowledge rather than isolating them from the process. Thus promoting a mindset of constantly seeking ways to improve performance. Implicit in this focus is the sense of identifying benchmarks and constantly implementing improvements.

Continuous improvement focuses on improving learning and performance to match the learning/performance outcome.

In this phase learners:

- Collaborate towards their learning/performance outcome
- Contribute expertise to help other participants achieve their learning outcomes
- Derive knowledge from each other
- Personalize the information gained
- Receive and provide feedback
- Continuously collaborate to improve learning/performance

Each formative cycle is punctuated by a formal formative evaluation, and concludes with a summative evaluation. Each cycle represents a formative loop that produces an assessable output to the evaluation phase. Each assessable output designates the completion of a cycle. During early cycles, learners begin to generate initial ideas to address the identified outcomes and begin to utilize the tools for establishing beneficial social interaction. During intermediate cycles, learners access relevant resources from both external sources and from peers. The role of peer feedback expands as advanced learners introduce information not considered in the initial cycles.

Self-assessment and peer-assessment lead to revision and the sharing of new perspectives. It is at this point, that commitment to the learning outcome is most challenged. Finally, learners engage in a process of reflection and reorganization that personalizes the learning process. The learners then work together to produce shared artifacts to document attainment of the learning/performance outcome of the collaborative learning experience.

Some of the Web 2.0 tools that help in this collaboration/personalization phase are described below.

Social Networking

Most of the social networking sites are Web-based and provide various techniques for interaction, such as chat, messaging, email, video, voice chat, file sharing, etc.

Though most of the social connections are established for non-education purposes, a small percentage of social connections are also established for educational purposes. Social networking can be beneficial, valuable and effective when used by students in higher education settings to collaborate on various activities towards their learning goal. Keyword searches help them connect to the other social Web users who are interested in the same learning goal as them and they are able to derive knowledge from each other. Several of the networking sites have different language capability and there are sites developed for users from specific nations.

Blog

A Weblog, more commonly referred to as a blog, is a Web-based publication consisting primarily of periodic. The blog provides an opportunity for the blogger (one who writes the blog) to share his knowledge with the blog readers who interact with the blog poster by using the comments or email feature on the blog post. A typical blog combines text, images, and links to other blogs, Web pages, and other media related to its topic. Though most of the blogs are online journals are used for a variety purposes, there is a category of blogs called edublogs that are written by those with an educational purpose. Edublogs include blogs written by or for teachers, blogs maintained for the purpose of classroom instruction, or blogs written about educational policy.

Since 2002, blogs have gained increased attention for their role in knowledge dissemination. Unlike the previous collaborative activities that were restricted within the walls of the classroom and discussion forums on learning management systems, with these Web 2.0 collaborative tools, students find themselves discussing a wide range of topics with peers worldwide. Blogs are widely available to all social Web users to read. Though many blogs include only one blog poster, there are group blogs where a group of participants blog and communicate with each other. Classroom blogs have become common where teachers are creating blogs for their students in class. Activities are conducted where students collaborate with peers from all over the world. There are a number of blog services providers.

Wikis

Wikis are a Website or a collection of Web pages that allow users to add and edit content collectively. The wiki enables documents to be written collaboratively, in a simple markup language using a Web browser. Wiki pages can be created and updated in no time. Most of the Wiki's are available to the general public to read and edit, however there are private wiki's that require secure access to alter the pages and even at times to read content.

Using wiki's, enable a group of learners to collaborate towards a common learning/performance outcome. All the learners are able to add, and

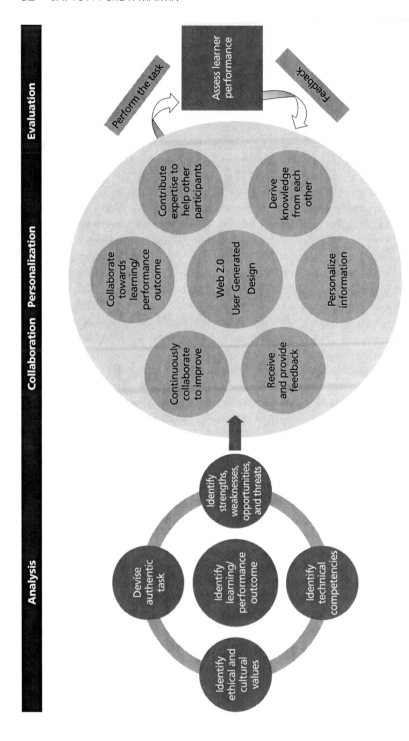

Figure 3.3 Web 2.0 instructional design model.

edit information at the same time making it possible for users to derive information from each other, providing expertise on the areas they are familiar with, and drawing from other collaborators in novice areas.

Aggregators/RSS Feeds

RSS (Really Simple Syndication) is a method of describing news or other Web content that is available for "feeding" from an online publisher to Web users. RSS feed subscribers are able to receive updates on news, research or any other information in which they are interested. This information is brought to the user by an aggregator. An aggregator is client software that uses a Web feed to retrieve syndicated Web content such as Weblogs, podcasts, vlogs, and mainstream mass media Websites. Users do not have to go in search of all the updated information; instead the updated information is brought to them. This is an aspect of intelligence-based knowledge management where content created by other social Web users are available for the users to read using aggregators.

Using an aggregator, a user can read all types of information including news, books, project reports, blogs, research updates. Even research databases have integrated Web feeds, so users can receive the updated articles through their aggregators.

Social Bookmarking

Social bookmarking is a method for the social Web users to store, organize, search, manage and share bookmarks of Web pages on the Internet with the help of metadata. The social Web users book mark sites so that they can remember the sites at a later date and to share it with the other users. The sites bookmarked are organized in such a way that the knowledge is managed efficiently and effectively. When a user returns at a later date the site can be pulled out by using the appropriate tag. Bookmarking Websites can be accessed from anywhere in the world, which provides a definite advantage to the older bookmarking technique using favorites. Some social bookmarking services provide Web feeds for their lists of bookmarks and this allows subscribers to become aware of new bookmarks as they are saved, shared, and tagged by other users. Social bookmarking helps the collaborators access the tagged content that helps them achieve their learning/performance goal.

Podcasts/Vodcasts

A podcast is a digital media file that is made available on the Internet using syndication feeds, for playback on mobile devices and personal computers. Podcasts are used in a wide variety of ways, including distribution of school lessons, tutorials, music shows, commentaries etc. Podcasting is becoming increasingly popular in education. Podcasts, vodcasts and presentations that can be shared to collaborators with the purpose of helping them achieve their learning/performance goal. Rather than trying to reinvent the wheel, the users search for existing knowledge and learn from the experiences on specific learning and performance tasks of other social Web users.

Evaluation

Evaluation is most effective when it reflects an understanding of learning as multidimensional and integrated and when it effects change in specific student performance outcomes. In general, evaluation should focus on outcomes of student learning, should be aligned with the identified outcomes.

The role of the evaluation phase is similar to that of the facilitator in the analysis phase. The intent is to ensure that the required enabling contexts, resources, features, and scaffolding are present throughout the learning process. If the instruction was instructor-facilitated in the analysis phase, learning could be instructor-evaluated in this phase. Peer or self-evaluation is possible. However, it is important that the evaluator be an expert to provide meaningful contributions to improving learner performance. Novice peers may not be much help in evaluating the learning that has occurred.

In Web 2.0 ID, the evaluation phase is also incremental. It is likely that several collaboration cycles will occur at the formative level before attainment of the learning/performance outcome is achieved. At the conclusion of each formative cycle the evaluator provides feedback both on the product and the design process. As learners advance though each formative cycle, their performance is scaffolded and the learners extend their understanding.

- Design tasks for the evaluator include:
- Establishing a feedback cycle
- Ensuring the accessibility of necessary resources
- Encouraging collaborative interaction
- Clarifying and addressing misconceptions
- Making a determination of outcome attainment

These tasks serve several purposes. They ensure the health of the user designed community. They model the appropriate peer feedback methodology that occurs during each formative cycle. And maintain a supportive context within which learners can navigate the process of learning. Eventually, the traditional formative cycles coalesce in the collaborative Web 2.0 environment and the evaluation reaches the summative stage.

The iterative nature of the process of user-generated learning with Web 2.0 provides for continual gains in the capacity to achieve more complex outcomes. As learners gain increasing design skills, the cycle of collaboration, contribution, and performance grows. Even summative outcomes may serve as a springboard for further learning.

FUTURE TRENDS—CASE STUDIES

To further illustrate the flexibility of Web 2.0 ID, we present two case study applications, one in which the instructor assigned a learning outcome, and one in which the learning outcome was student negotiated with the instructor. Both applications utilized learner-generated design.

A Multimedia Model Design Activity in a Computer-Based Instruction Course

The model was used in a graduate "Computer-Based Instruction" course taught at a university in the southeastern United States. The instructor of the course assigned the learning outcome to the students, which was to design a multimedia design and development model. The students were given the option to select one or more Web 2.0 tools to achieve this learning outcome (Blogs, Wiki, Forums, Virtual worlds, Podcasts, Mashups).

The instructor acted as the facilitator for this task and helped the learners analyze the tool (tool analysis) by a detailed Web 2.0 presentation. The users were able to analyze their technical competency and the cultural and ethical values aligned with the use of each of the Web 2.0 tools. This helped the learners reach the optimal competency level for using the tool before they collaborated to achieve the learning outcome.

The learners then collaborated with peers on the Web 2.0 platform to achieve their learning outcome. Once completed the task of the multimedia model design they submitted the results to the instructor for evaluation. The model in this situation was adapted such that the instructor was the facilitator who assigned the learning outcome; the learners collaborated with peers and constructed their learning and personalized it and finally submitted it to the instructor to be evaluated. The instructor, serving in the evaluator role provided feedback.

Defining Emerging Trends in an Introductory Instructional Technology Course

In this case, the model was used in an online graduate Introduction to Instructional Technology course at a university in the northwestern United States. Students were given the general learning outcome category of emerging trends in the field of instructional technology. Students were then encouraged to research emerging trends and technologies available for the assignment. The students negotiated their trend selection and the parameters of the product of learning outcome with the instructor. The only instructor-imposed limitations on the products were that they should be instructional in nature and no two groups/individuals may cover the same trend.

In contrast to the previous case, the activity was entirely peer facilitated with the instructor serving in the evaluator role. Given the task, each step of the analysis was peer assisted. Students self-selected into groups based on preliminary interest areas and identified strengths, weaknesses, technical competencies, and values associated with potential tools and formats for the final instructional product. The results of these analyses were presented to the instructor in the form of parameters for negotiation. Once parameters such as: group membership, topic, tool, and product format were determined, the learners then collaborated with peers using the determined tool to develop their instruction product and achieve their learning outcome. The majority of students remained in their interest group and collaborated to develop a wiki on their selected trend. Other products included instructional blogs, a podcast, and a collaborative video. The activity was completed with one evaluation cycle, in which the instructor provided feedback on the product. The activity culminated with presentations of the instructional products to the class.

This case is an example of how Web 2.0 ID can be used to introduce new concepts while allowing students to collaborate, socially construct new knowledge, and control their learning environment. Web 2.0 tools, such as the wiki, facilitate the iterative design process because the process essentially is the product. The application of Web 2.0 ID as used in this case is excellent for authentic tasks that require consensus building.

CONCLUSION

The emergence of approaches to learning that are based on self-determination and networked contexts such as heutagogy (Phelps, et al., 2005) and connectivism (Siemens, 2005) help us understand learning as making connections with ideas, facts, people and communities. Learning has grown beyond mere consumption of knowledge and become a knowledge creation process. New strategies for teaching require the examination of how the emergence of Web 2.0 redefines the competencies that are needed by instructors, peers and learners.

This chapter contributes to many fields by presenting an instructional design model designed to improve learning and performance using Web 2.0 tools. The three phases of the model (analysis, collaboration and personalization, and evaluation) each contribute uniquely to facilitate user-centered design across disciplines. During analysis, users are able to analyze available tools, identify the strengths and weaknesses of each tool and identify potential outcomes. Collaboration and personalization engages users in a constructive learning process and cycle of continuous improvement. In evaluation, the feedback cycle is established to ensure attainment of any identified outcomes.

The model draws upon the theoretical principles of social learning theory and Social Construction of Technology and combines distributed cognition and social construction of knowledge to enhance the learning process. The model reflects the authors' assertion that social collaborative learning may occur anywhere along the pedagogy-heutagogy continuum. The model also reflects the merger of collaborative/social, learner designed, and intelligence-based knowledge managed learning dimensions that follow from the dictates of providing for co-configuration, co-creation, and/or the co-design of learning.

REFERENCES

Bakardjieva, M. (2005). *Internet society. The internet in everyday life.* London: Sage.

Bhattacharya, Y. & Bhattacharya, M. (2006). *Learner as a designer of digital learning tools.* Proceedings of the Advanced Learning Technologies, 2006. Sixth International Conference, July 2006, pp. 133–134

Bijker, W., Pinch, T., & Hughes, T. (1987). *The social construction of technological systems: New directions in the sociology and history of technology.* Cambridge: MIT Press.

Collins, H. M. (1985). *Changing order: Replication and induction in scientific practice.* Beverly Hills, CA: Sage.

Cooper, S. (2003). *Interactive online courses: Fact or fiction, AECT,* Retrieved October 14, 2007, from http://www.aect.org/Divisions/jones.asp

Garrison, D. R., Anderson, T. & Archer, W. (2003). A theory of critical inquiry in on-line distance education. In M. G. Moore, & W. G. Anderson (Eds.), *Handbook of distance education* (pp. 113–127). Mahwah, NJ: Erlbaum.

Glasersfeld, E. V (1995). A constructivist approach to teaching. In L. Steffe & J. Gale (Eds.), *Constructivism in education* (pp. 3–16). Mahwah, NJ: Erlbaum.

Gunawardena, C. N., & McIsaac, M. S. (2004). Distance education. In D. Jonassen (Ed.), *Handbook of research on educational communications and technology* (2nd ed., pp. 355–395). Mahwah, NJ: Erlbaum.

Malhotra, Y. (2003). Why knowledge management systems fail: Enablers and constraints of knowledge management in human enterprises. In C. W. Holsapple (Ed.), *Handbook of knowledge management* (pp. 577–600). Berlin: Springer-Verlag.

McLoughlin, C. (2002) Learner support in distance and networked learning environments: Ten dimensions for successful design. *Distance Education, 23*(2), 149–162.

Phelps, R., Hase, S., & Ellis, A. (2005) Competency, capability, complexity and computers: exploring a new model for conceptualizing end-user computer education.*British Journal of Educational Technology, 36*(1), 67–84.

Salomon, G. (1993) No distribution without individual's cognition: A dynamic interactional view. In G. Salomon (Ed.), *Distributed cognitions: Psychological and educational considerations* (pp. 111–138). Cambridge: Cambridge University Press.

Salomon, G., Perkins, D. N., & Globerson, T. (1991). Partners in Cognition. Extending human intelligence with intelligent technologies. *Educational Researcher, 20*(3), 2–9

Siemens, G. (2004). Connectivism: A learning theory for the digital age. *ELearnspace.* Retrieved October 5, 2007, from http://www.elearnspace.org/Articles/connectivism.htm

Siemens, G (2005). Connectivism: Learning as network-creation. *ELearnspace.* Retrieved November 15, 2007, from http://www.elearnspace.org/Articles/networks.htm

Stokes, J.T., & Richey, R.C. (2000) Rapid prototyping methodology in action: A developmental study. *Educational Technology Research and Development, 48*(2), 63–80.

Strijbos, J. W., Martens, R. L., & Jochems, W. M. (2004). Designing for interaction: six steps to designing computer-supported group-based learning. *Computers & Education, 42,* 403–424.

Tait, A. & Mills, R. (2003) *Rethinking learner support in distance education: Change and continuity in an international context.* New York: Routledge Falmer.

Vygotsky, L.S. (1978). *Mind in society.* Cambridge, MA: Harvard University Press.

Woolgar, S. (1991). The turn to technology in social studies of science. *Science, Technology & Human Values, 16,* 20–50.

PART II

SOCIAL LEARNING, NETWORKING,
AND THE WEB 2.0

CHAPTER 4

DESIGNING COLLABORATIVE COMMUNITIES OF INQUIRY THROUGH THE APPLICATION OF WEB 2.0 TOOLS

Norm D. Vaughan
D. Randy Garrison

ABSTRACT

The purpose of this chapter is to describe how Web 2.0 instructional strategies and tools can be used to design collaborative communities of inquiry. The chapter begins with an overview of the Community of Inquiry framework and the three inter-related elements of social, cognitive and teaching presence. Eight categories of Web 2.0 tools are presented along with corresponding software application examples and associated collaborative learning activities. Instructional strategies for using these tools to support a collaborative community of inquiry, in a blended learning environment, are then illustrated and discussed.

Wired for Learning: An Educator's Guide to Web 2.0, pages 61–83
Copyright © 2009 by Information Age Publishing

61

INTRODUCTION

Sustained collaboration in the construction and confirmation of knowledge represents a new era in educational practice. The New Media Consortium and the EDUCAUSE Learning Initiative's 2008 Horizon Report identifies collaborative learning as a challenge that "is pushing the educational community to develop new forms of interaction..." (p. 5). They identify collaboration and communication as a significant trend in expanding the possibilities for learning and creativity. A significant driver of this transformation in learning has been the emergence of Web 2.0 tools.

While the tools present exciting opportunities, the challenge is in understanding instructional design and pedagogical issues associated with the best use of Web 2.0 tools such as blogs, wikis, online communities and voice over internet protocol (VOIP) technologies (e.g., Elluminate, Horizon Wimba). The tools only become useful in the context of understanding worthwhile educational goals and higher order learning activities. The true potential of these tools is in the creation of synchronous and asynchronous communities of inquiry that are sustainable over time and space. What is not well understood is the educational significance of this shift to collaborative learning and the issues in adopting powerful Web 2.0 tools for the greatest educational advantage. After exploring the why of Web 2.0 tools, we will describe how, when and where to use these tools in the context of creating and sustaining collaborative communities of inquiry.

CONCEPTUAL CORE

The premise of this chapter is that online learning is experiencing a transformative shift from issues of accessing and sharing information to designing communities of inquiry where participants are actively engaged in deep and meaningful learning. Web 2.0 is about using the web in a way that capitalizes on its greatest asset—bringing people together in learning communities; communities where participants (students and teachers in the case of education) with a common interest can collaborate on purposeful activities for the benefit of all. Brown and Adler (2008) argue that Web 2.0 capabilities have "shifted attention from access to information toward access to people" (p. 18). Web 2.0 tools are allowing people to come together in collaborative learning communities.

Online communities of inquiry are places where all voices can be heard while testing and rejecting unproductive contributions. Historically, this has been the ideal of learning environments in higher education. Only in the last half-century, with the enrolment growth in higher education, has the practice been diminished as a result of larger classes and passive lectures. As

Web 2.0 tools emerge, educators are presented with the opportunity to realize the historical ideal of higher education to learn in collaborative communities of inquiry.

Collaboration

The key to unlocking the potential of Web 2.0 tools is to recognize and capitalize on their potential to support collaborative learning activities. To do this we must step back and rethink what we are doing. We need to clarify the core values of an educational experience and better align our activities and goals with the need for creative and innovative graduates that can work productively in collaborative environments. In this regard, educators are increasingly realizing that we must provide more interactive and engaged learning experiences (Kuh, Kinzie, Scuh, Whitt and Associates, 2005). Collaborative learning is the key to engaging learners in deep and meaningful learning. It the antithesis of the passive lecture approach to learning that dominates higher education today. Engagement in collaborative discourse and reflection has historically been the hallmark of higher education. The key is to understand that the new and emerging technologies that are the focus of this chapter and book represent the opportunity to redesign more active and collaborative learning experiences. The first lesson is to avoid simply layering Web 2.0 tools onto a deficient educational design.

Collaborative learning is characterized by a sharing of personal meaning and the validation of understanding through discourse. Philosophically, collaborative learning is founded in the tradition of constructivist learning theory. Individuals are expected to assume the responsibility to make sense of new content but with the support and feedback of a collaborative community of learners. At the core of collaborative learning is inquiry. Understanding the nature of collaborative inquiry is crucial in guiding the use of powerful Web 2.0 social networking tools.

Community of Inquiry

The Community of Inquiry (CoI) framework (Garrison & Anderson, 2003) has been instrumental in helping researchers and practitioners appreciate the core elements of collaborative learning and what it takes to create and sustain collaborative communities. The CoI is a generic framework that directs attention to the process of constructing and confirming deep understanding. The three main elements of the CoI framework are social presence, cognitive presence, and teaching presence. Each of these elements and their overlap must be considered in the design and delivery of collaborative learning activities and outcomes. Social presence is defined as the ability of participants to identify with the interests of the community (e.g., the course of study), communicate purposefully in a trusting environment, and develop inter-personal relationships by way of participants projecting their individual personalities. The CoI framework is about deep and meaningful learning experiences operationalized through cognitive presence. Cognitive presence is defined in terms of the practical inquiry model. Practical inquiry represents phases (problem, exploration, integration, and resolution) of a collaborative-constructive educational experience. The final element, teaching presence, provides the leadership that focuses and sustains a productive collaborative community. Teaching presence is responsible for the design, facilitation and direction of the educational experience (Figure 4.1).

Each presence is multi-dimensional with categories that dynamically reflect progressive and developmental aspects of each of the elements and the educational experience broadly. Our understanding of online social presence has evolved the most over the last decade. While much work remains to understand the role of social presence in various contexts, it is safe to speculate that social presence is much more than socio-emotional support. Social presence must be directed to support the purpose and interests of the participants. A CoI is not simply a social support group. There are aspects of social presence that may well have greater priority in establishing

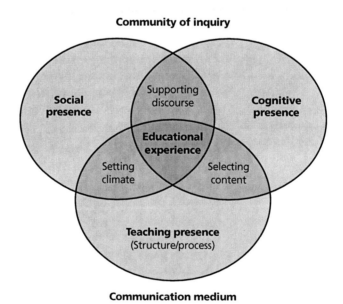

Figure 4.1 Community of inquiry framework.

a purposeful community of inquiry. Rogers and Lea (2005) suggest that to build social presence and community in an educational context, it is important to begin with group identity.

> If the intended result of social presence is to confer on the group greater capacity to communicate and collaborate, then the group will work more productively to the extent that group members identify with the group, thus making the group more cohesive. (p. 153)

For this reason, we hypothesize that it would be more productive to focus first on open communication in the task of creating a risk-free climate as well as group cohesion to build on group identity and provide the foundation for collaboration. The emphasis over time will naturally shift from open communication, to cohesion and then interpersonal relationships. Purposeful communities will most likely develop naturally in that sequence.

Cognitive presence, as operationalized through the Practical Inquiry model, exhibits an inherent developmental progression. This process has its genesis in the scientific method and John Dewey's (1933) work to apply this to the educational context. The categories of teaching presence are perhaps also discernable in terms of their developmental progression as responsibilities shift from design to facilitation and then direction. With all of the presences, the developmental phases may telescope into each other depending on circumstances (Table 4.1). Similarly, the identification of each of the presences, as evidenced in recent validation research, will depend on the particular context (Garrison & Arbaugh, 2007; Swan, Shea, Richardson, Ice, Garrison, Cleveland-Innes, & Arbaugh, 2008).

TABLE 4.1   Community of Inquiry Elements, Categories, and Indicators

Elements	Categories	Indicators (examples only)
Social presence	Open communication	Learning climate/risk-free expression
	Group cohesion	Group identity/collaboration
	Interpersonal/affective	Self projection/expressing emotions
Cognitive presence	Triggering event	Sense of puzzlement
	Exploration	Information exchange
	Integration	Connecting ideas
	Resolution	Applying new ideas
Teaching presence	Design and organization	Setting curriculum & methods
	Facilitating discourse	Shaping constructive exchange
	Direct instruction	Focusing and resolving issues

Tools and Applications

Web 2.0 tools can be used to support collaborative learning in a variety of formats (Leslie & Landon, 2008). For example, social bookmarking applications can be used to share personal collections of Web-based resources to complete group projects. Blogs can facilitate student self-reflection and peer review of course assignments. Students can use wikis to collaboratively summarize course discussions, refine research papers or even co-create online books. Social networking applications such as Facebook and MySpace can be used to extend the boundaries of the classroom to create online communities and discussions/debates that include past students, potential employers and subject matter experts. Audio, graphic and video files can now be created and shared through social media applications such as Podomatic, Flickr and YouTube. These files and other data sources can then be recombined to create new meaning and interpretations by using mashup applications such as Intel's Mash Maker and MIT's Piggy Bank.

VOIP technologies such as Skype and Elluminate Live! allow students to communicate and collaborate outside of the classroom. Moreover, virtual world applications such as Second Life provide opportunities for rich synchronous interaction in 3-D immersive worlds to support collaborative and creative project-based work.

An overview to each of these categories of Web 2.0 tools, including examples of software applications and ideas for collaborative learning activities, is provided in Table 4.2.

The next section of this chapter describes instructional strategies for using these Web 2.0 tools to design collaborative communities of inquiry in a blended learning context.

INSTRUCTIONAL STRATEGIES

We define blended learning as "the organic integration of thoughtfully selected and complementary face-to-face and online approaches and technologies" (Garrison & Vaughan, 2008, p. 148). Designers of blended learning courses have shown leadership in using Web 2.0 collaborative learning tools. The primary reason for blended learning taking the lead in this area is the necessity to understand the relative strengths of synchronous and asynchronous environments in terms of creating and sustaining collaborative communities of inquiry.

As noted previously, the CoI framework is based on an inquiry approach to learning. Inquiry learning is problem or question-driven learning involving critical discourse, self-direction, research methods, and reflection

TABLE 4.2 Categories of Web 2.0 Tools

Category	Description	Software application examples	Collaborative learning activities
Social bookmarking	• Sharing personal collections of URLs on a Web-based server • Ability to re-use and re-purpose existing collections of links • Tagging of resources helps develop relationships between concepts and people	Del.icio.us http://del.icio.us/ Connotea http://www.connotea.org/ Edtags http://edtags.org/ Furl http://www.furl.net/	• Course reading list • Article critique assignments • Group project resources
Blogs	• A Web-based public diary with dated entries, usually by a single author, often accompanied by links to other blogs that the author of the site visits on a regular basis (Downes, 2004). • Reflective writing and reading activity • Opportunity for students to receive external feedback and to make contributions to the dialogue in their field of study • RSS subscription to other blogs to receive automated content updates	Google's Blogger http://blogger.com/ Edublogs http://edublogs.org/ Bloglines http://www.bloglines.com/	• Article critiques • Peer review • Assignment self-reflections • Field journal • Practicum/clinical journal • Citizen journalism
Wikis	• A wiki is a collection of Web pages that can be edited by anyone, at any time, from anywhere. The possibilities for using wikis as a platform for collaborative projects are limited only by one's imagination and time. (Leuf & Cunningham, 2001) • Support collaborative and creative project-based work	Wikispaces http://www.wikispaces.com/ Pbwiki http://pbwiki.com/ Seedwiki http://seedwiki.com/ Google Docs http://documents.google.com/	• Class books • Online discussion summaries • Group essays

(continued)

TABLE 4.2 Categories of Web 2.0 Tools (continued)

Category	Description	Software application examples	Collaborative learning activities
Social networking	• Focuses on building and verifying of online social networks for communities of people who share interests and activities • Additional "communication channel" to reach students (i.e., RSS feeds from institutional learning management systems)	Facebook http://www.facebook.com MySpace http://www.myspace.com/ Friendster http://www.friendster.com/ Bebo http://www.bebo.com/ Ning http://www.ning.com/	• Online discussion board • Study groups • Course communication
Social media sharing	• Simplify the process of posting and sharing content on the Web (i.e., text, audio, images and video) • Provide a wealth of re-usable media resources for learners and educators	Podomatic http://www.podomatic.com/ Flickr http://flickr.com/ YouTube http://youtube.com/ Slideshare http://www.slideshare.net/	• Interviews with external experts • Case studies • Storytelling • Project work
Mashups	• Allow non-technical individuals to mix-up data, find new meaning and present it in interesting ways	IBMs Many Eyes http://services.alphaworks.ibm .com/manyeyes/home	• Mapping activities • Data visualization • Presenting student project and research work

Type	Features	Tools	Uses
	• Allow users to put together different types of data • Mapping mashups—maps are overlaid with different types of information • Music mashups—mixing tracks from two or more different source songs	Intel's Mash Maker http://mashmaker.intel.com/web/ MIT's Piggy Bank http://simile.mit.edu/wiki/Piggy_Bank Wordle http://www.wordle.net/ Visuwords http://www.visuwords.com/	
VOIP (voice over internet protocol)	• Synchronous communication opportunities (i.e., text messaging, audio, video) • Support 'real-time' collaborative and creative project-based work	Skype http://skype.com/ WiZiQ http://www.wiziq.com/ Dimdim http://www.dimdim.com/ Elluminate Live! http://www.elluminate.com/ Horizon Wimba http://www.wimba.com/	• External guest presentations • Group project work
Virtual worlds	• Synchronous interaction in 3-D immersive worlds • Support collaborative and creative project-based work that goes beyond text-based and audio communication	Second Life http://secondlife.com/ Croquet http://www.opencroquet.org The Palace http://www.thepalace.com/ Moove http://www.moove.com	• Experimentation • Simulations • Group project work

TABLE 4.3 Practical Inquiry Phases

Description	Category/Phase	Indicators
The extent to which learners are able to construct and confirm meaning through sustained reflection, discourse, and application within a critical community of inquiry.	1. Triggering event	1. Inciting curiosity and defining key questions or issues for investigation
	2. Exploration	2. Exchanging and exploring perspectives and information resources with other learners
	3. Integration	3. Connecting ideas through reflection
	4. Resolution/application	4. Applying new ideas and/or defending solutions

throughout the learning experience. This process is outlined in the four phases of the Practical Inquiry model (see Table 4.3).

We suggest that an inquiry through blended learning approach can be utilized to intentionally integrate Web 2.0 tools to support the progression of inquiry through to resolution and/or application. This approach consists of four inter-connected phases:

1. Before a synchronous session
2. Synchronous session
3. After a synchronous session
4. Preparation for the next synchronous session

Before a Synchronous Session

The first phase involves the use of Web 2.0 tools in advance of a synchronous session to 'plant the seeds' for triggering events that will then be more thoroughly defined within the actual synchronous session. Ausubel (1968) refers to these as "advance organizers" or anchoring events that provide entry points for connecting new information with the recall of prior related learning experiences. There are a variety of learning activities and related Web 2.0 applications that can be used to support this phase. They include the use of Web-based readings with an accompanying online survey, quiz or discussion forum. This activity and several other examples are provided in Table 4.4.

The first priority is to establish communication with the learners so that they are clear about the rationale and expectations for the pre-class assignments. This communication can be facilitated through a weekly course an-

TABLE 4.4   Design Considerations before a Synchronous Session

Nature of Inquiry	Learning Activities	Web 2.0 Tools

Learner
• Create a *triggering event*
• Advanced organizer
• Stimulate connections
Teacher
• Determine learner's prior knowledge or experience with the topic or issue
	a) Reading/Writing
	  • Pre-reading assignment or activity on a specified topic or issue
	  • Followed by a self assessment quiz, survey or discussion forum
	b) Listening/Writing
	  • Auditory/visual presentation of information
	  • Followed by a self assessment quiz, survey or discussion forum activity
		i) Communication
		  • Announcement sent to students via an RSS feed through a Social Networking Tool (i.e., Facebook) or News Aggregator Application (i.e., Bloglines)
		ii) Posting or linking to pre-reading assignments
		  • Social Bookmarking Tools (i.e., Del.icio.us, Edtags)
		iii) Digital learning objects
		  • Podcasts (i.e., Podomatic)
		  • PowerPoints (i.e., Slideshare)
		  • Videos (i.e., YouTube)
		iv) Self assessment quizzes
		  • Assessment tools (i.e., Moodle)
		v) Anonymous surveys
		  • Survey Tools (i.e., getfast .ca)
		vi) Discussion Forum
		  • Pre-class online discussion regarding questions and issue related to the required reading (i.e., Facebook, Ning)

nouncement, which can be transmitted via an RSS feed to a social network such as Facebook or a news aggregator application like Bloglines.

Teachers often require students to participate in a reading activity before a class session. Traditionally, this activity involved a reading from the course textbook. Social bookmarking systems such as Del.icio.us and Edtags can now be used to provide students with access to relevant and engaging Web-based articles and resources. Some instructors also require students to find their own course related articles and then post these resources to a social bookmarking network so that all members of the class can access and comment on these Web sites.

Social media sharing tools can also be used by both teachers and students to create, post and share digital learning objects before a class session. For example, teachers can use podcasts (e.g., Podomatic), narrated PowerPoint

Figure 4.2   Narrated PowerPoint presentation.

presentations (e.g., Slideshare, Adobe Presenter) or video (e.g., YouTube) to communicate course concepts, scenarios and case studies with students before class time. The advantages of using these types of learning objects are that they allow students to listen and view course-related material outside of class time, at their own pace, and as often as required to gain understanding (see Figure 4.2).

Despite the ability to access learning material in a variety of formats there still exists the common challenge of getting students to meaningfully engage in these pre-class activities. Novak, Patterson, Gavrin and Christian (1999) have used a survey or quiz tool to create triggering events for students in advance of a synchronous session. They have coined the term Just-in-Time Teaching (JiTT) to describe the process of getting students to read a textbook chapter or Web-based article and then respond to an online survey or quiz, shortly before a class. The instructor then reviews the student submissions 'just in time' to adjust the subsequent class session in order to address the students' needs, identified by the survey or quiz results. A typical survey or quiz consists of four concept-based questions with the final question asking students: "What did you not understand about the required reading and what would you like me [the instructor] to focus on within the next synchronous session?" An alternative to this activity would be to construct an online discussion forum in a social networking application like Facebook to allow students to post questions or issues related to the pre-class reading. This can be a powerful learning forum as students are able to read and respond to each other's questions in advance of the synchronous session.

During a Synchronous Session

The second phase of the blended inquiry cycle involves a synchronous session where Web 2.0 tools can be used to define the triggering event(s), provide opportunities for exploration and create a first step towards the integration phase. These sessions can take place either face-to-face or online through the use of VOIP applications such as Elluminate Live or Horizon Wimba. The focus of these sessions should not be on information transmission such as lecturing, but instead, be used to diagnose student misconceptions, foster critical dialogue, and support peer instruction. Table 4.5 outlines several synchronous learning activities that can be supported with

TABLE 4.5 Design Considerations during a Synchronous Session

Nature of Inquiry	Learning Activities	Web 2.0 Tools
• Defining the *triggering events* (key questions) • Beginning to *explore* the questions	a) Talking/Listening • Dialogue with teacher and fellow learners about the specified issue or topic • Mini-lecture and/or tutorial to address the results of the pre-class quiz or survey • Large or small group discussion or activity • Case study • Initiation of an individual or group project	i) Displaying quiz or survey results • Online—display in the VOIP application (i.e., Horizon Live) • Classroom—computer projection or overhead ii) Conducting in-class quizzes and surveys to promote dialogue and small group work • Online—survey tool and break-out room features in a VOIP application (i.e., Elluminate Live) • Classroom—Personal response systems (clickers) and think, pair, share activities iii) Displaying digital learning objects and resources • Online/classroom—using social media sharing sites (i.e., Flickr, Slideshare, YouTube) and repositories such as merlot.org iv) Displaying assignments • Online/classroom—course blogs or wikis can be used to post assignment handouts, tutorials, resources and links to examples of previous student work

Web 2.0 applications. These activities are further described in the subsequent paragraphs.

If a survey, quiz or online discussion forum has been used to support the pre-class reading, then the synchronous session will often begin with a debriefing of this activity. Anonymous survey or quiz results can be uploaded to a VOIP application such as Elluminate Live or projected in a classroom (either by computer or with an overhead acetate print out) and reviewed by all students. The ensuing debate helps to clearly define the triggering event and allows members of the class to begin sharing and comparing their perspectives and experiences related to the question or issue (see Figure 4.3).

Web-based learning objects, such as interactive demand and supply curves for economic principles, can also be accessed and discussed during class time to help students visualize and understand the relationships between key course concepts. These digital learning objects can be retrieved from social media sharing applications (i.e., Flickr, Slideshare and YouTube) or from repositories such as MERLOT (Multimedia Educational Repository for Learning Online Teaching–http://www.merlot.org/). Links to these objects can be made from the course blog or wiki allowing students to manipulate and review these learning resources after the synchronous session.

Discussion and debate can be facilitated online through the use of the quiz and break-out room features in a VOIP application (i.e., Horizon Live) and with personal response systems, commonly referred to as clickers, in a classroom. Crouch and Mazur (2001) describe how synchronous quizzes can

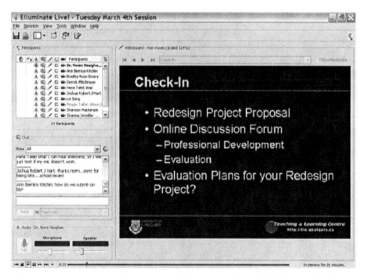

Figure 4.3 Synchronous session in the Elluminate Live VOIP application.

be used to support a form of peer instruction. The process begins with the instructor posing a question or problem. The students initially work individually toward a solution and 'vote' on what they believe is the correct answer by selecting the desired response in a VOIP application or by clicking a numbered or lettered response on their clicker in a classroom. The results are then projected for the entire class to view. For a good question, there is usually a broad range of responses. Students are then required to compare and discuss their solutions online in a break out room or with the person next to them in a classroom in order to come to a consensus. Another 'vote' is taken but this time only one response or clicker per group can be utilized. In most circumstances, the range of responses decreases and usually centers around the correct answer. An alternative to this process is to have groups of students generate the quiz questions in advance of the synchronous session.

Synchronous sessions also provide a good opportunity to initiate or clarify individual or group projects. To help students understand the expectations for these assignments, previous student work can be displayed and critiqued. Students can then either develop or use a pre-existing assessment rubric to review the examples of past coursework. Similar to digital learning objects, these previous assignments can be linked to the course blog or wiki so that students have access to this material after class time.

As class time is usually reduced in a blended learning course, we recommend that each of these synchronous sessions conclude with a discussion to establish student responsibilities and action items. This discussion can also be combined with a Web-based anonymous exit survey, which asks the students to state what they learned during the session and what they are still unclear about. This closing discussion and survey helps the students begin to integrate the new information received during the session with their prior learning experience. The survey data collected also provides valuable feedback for the teacher in terms of planning future synchronous sessions and activities.

As indicated previously, transforming the focus of these synchronous sessions from information dissemination (lecturing) to active and collaborative learning opportunities for students can be challenging. There are several additional resources that we recommend to help facilitate this process. For example, Kuh et al. (2005) in their book *Student Success in College: Creating Conditions that Matter* provide examples of effective practice for increasing levels of active and collaborative learning and student-faculty interaction within courses, programs and institutions. Bean's (2001) book on *Engaging Ideas: The Professor's Guide to Integrating Writing, Critical Thinking, and Active Learning in the Classroom* has an excellent section on designing tasks for active thinking and learning. Similarly, Barkley, Cross and Major's (2005) handbook on *Collaborative Learning Techniques* outlines specific techniques that can be used to facilitate group work in synchronous sessions.

Between Synchronous Sessions

The use of Web 2.0 tools between the synchronous sessions provides opportunities for the students to further explore and reflect on course-related activities. This phase begins with the use of a course blog or wiki, to post a summary and a list of follow-up items from the synchronous session. An RSS feed can be used to "push" this announcement out to students through a social networking system but it is also recommended that this summary be composed in a word processing document so that it can be copied and pasted as a group email message to the students. Sreebny (2007) states "Email is still the most widely used collaboration tool in the world" (p. 3). An overview of how Web 2.0 technologies can be used to support a series of reflective learning activities is provided within Table 4.6. Each of these activities is then discussed in the accompanying paragraphs.

TABLE 4.6   Design Considerations after a Synchronous Session

Nature of Inquiry	Learning Activities	Web 2.0 Tools

• Further *exploration* towards *tentative integration* with the ability to connect theory to practice application	a) Reading/Writing
	  • Anonymous class exit survey
	    – What did you learn from the class session?
	    – What are you still unclear about?
	  • Online discussion with student moderation
	b) Talking/Listening + Reading/Writing
	  • Individual or group project work, case studies
	
	Preparation for next class
	a) Reading/Writing
	  • Pre-class reading assignment or activity on a specified topic or issue
	  • Followed by a self assessment quiz, survey or discussion forum
		i) Anonymous surveys
		  • Survey tools (i.e., getfast.ca)
		ii) Communication
		  • Announcement section of a course blog or wiki for student "to do" list
		  • Group email for the student "to do" list
		  • Email for individual student questions or clarification (try to put common questions into a Frequently Asked Questions discussion forum)
		  • Online discussion forums in social networking systems (i.e., Facebook) to facilitate student moderated discussions
		  • VOIP and Virtual Worlds (i.e., Elluminate Live, Second Life) for synchronous working sessions among student groups
		iii) Individual and Group Project Work
		  • Study groups within social networking systems (i.e., MySpace, Ning)
		  • Blogs for reflective journaling (i.e., Blogger)
		  • Wikis for collaborative writing projects (i.e., Seedwiki)
		  • Mashup tools for data analysis and representation of collaborative projects (i.e., Intel's Mash Maker)

Figure 4.4   Online discussion forum in Facebook.

In terms of communication, students can email the instructor for individual questions or clarification of assignments but it is recommended that a "Frequently Asked Questions" online discussion forum be created within a social networking system (i.e., Facebook). Students can then share in the responsibility of answering questions and problem solving course-related issues. Online discussion forums can be used to promote individual reflection and critical dialogue between the synchronous sessions. For example, a series of online discussion forums can be created by the instructor in Facebook related to the key modules/topics for the course (Figure 4.4).

Groups of students (three to five) then select a module based on course readings, previous experience and/or interest in the topic. Each group is responsible for moderating and summarizing their selected online discussion for a set period of time (often one or two weeks). Brookfield and Preskill's (2005) book, *Discussion as a way of teaching: Tools and techniques for democratic classrooms,* provides examples of the types of questions that can be used by students to create reflective discussion summaries or "discussion audits" (p. 72). These questions can be modified for online discussions. For example:

- What are the one or two most important ideas that emerged from this week's online discussion?
- What remains unresolved or contentious about this topic?
- What do you understand better as a result of this week's online discussion?

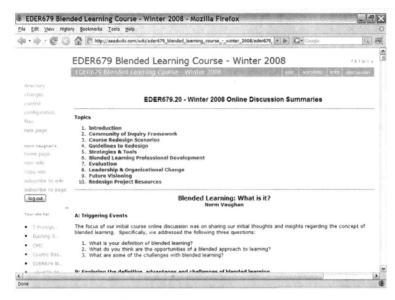

Figure 4.5 Wiki online discussion summary.

- What key word or concept best captures our discussion this week?
- What are some resources (e.g., Web sites, articles, books) that could be used to find further information/ideas about this topic?

A wiki can then be used to make draft notes and a final summary (synthesis and analysis) of the online discussion based on these questions or additional guidelines that are co-created by the students and the course instructor (see Figure 4.5).

Blogs can be used to support self-reflection and peer review of course assignments allowing students to take a deeper approach to their learning by going "public" with their work (Vaughan, 2008). At the beginning of the semester, the teacher can require each student to create their own blog. Once an assignment has been completed and the student has received assessment feedback they then post responses to questions such as the following on their blogs:

1. What did you learn in the process of completing this assignment?
2. How will you apply what you learned from this assignment to the next class assignment, other courses and/or your career?

A peer review process can also be supported through the use of blogs. Students can post drafts of course assignments to their blogs and then their peers can review these documents and post comments to the author's blog (Figure 4.6). Guiding questions for this peer review process could include:

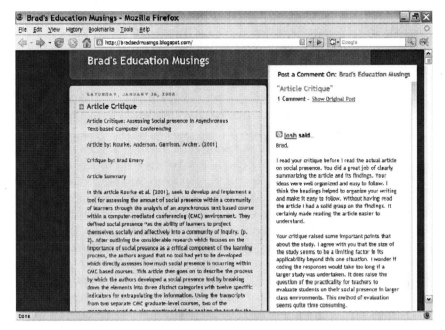

Figure 4.6 Peer review of a blog posting of an article critique.

1. What did you learn from reviewing this document?
2. What were the strengths (e.g. content, writing style, format and structure) of the document?
3. What constructive advice and/or recommendations could you provide for improving the quality of this document?

A common complaint from students about group work is the lack of time and the difficulty in arranging meetings between the class sessions. Web 2.0 tools such as VOIP systems and Virtual Worlds can be utilized to overcome this challenge. These applications allow students to participate in 'real-time' online group meetings over the Internet. For example, VOIP tools like Elluminate allow students to use a whiteboard to brainstorm ideas; a common Web browser to explore and review Web sites; and shared desktop applications such as word processors, spreadsheets, graphics software to create and revise documents together. Students can also use these applications to synchronously access Mashup tools such as Intel's Mash Maker and MIT's Piggy Bank in order to analyze and visually represent project data. In addition, Virtual Worlds such as Second Life allow learners to collaborate on project work in rich 3-D immersive environments.

Toward the end of this phase, another related inquiry through blended learning cycle is introduced with a new learning activity such as the posting of another Web-based reading and survey/quiz. This activity should be designed to help students synthesize their learning from the current cycle and prepare for the subsequent synchronous session.

Next Synchronous Session

In the next synchronous session, Web 2.0 tools continue to play a key role in helping to complete an inquiry through blended learning cycle or module by 'closing the loop' between the asynchronous and synchronous components of a blended learning course. Table 4.7 describes the type of learning activities that can be used to help students achieve a sense of resolution and/or application to the course related inquiry.

This process can be facilitated with a class discussion at the beginning of the synchronous session. The inquiry phases of integration and tentative resolution are addressed by first reviewing the results of the anonymous exit survey from the last synchronous session (see Figure 4.7) and then discussing any student questions or concerns raised from this survey. If there was an online discussion between the synchronous sessions, the student moderators or the teacher can provide an oral summary or some reflections about the discussion. Students can also be invited to demonstrate assignments 'in-progress'. These types of activities help to clarify assignment expectations and consolidate student learning within the course.

An inquiry through blended learning cycle concludes with a brief 'wrap-up' discussion, including final thoughts or comments, and then moves onto the next related question or topic that in turn triggers the next related inquiry cycle.

TABLE 4.7   Design Considerations for the Next Synchronous Session

Nature of Inquiry	Learning Activities	Web 2.0 Tools

• Resolution/ Application	a) Talking/Listening/ Writing
	  • Review of online discussion activities
	  • Individual or group presentations
	  • Final group thoughts on the topic or issue
	  • Initiation of dialogue on the next topic or issue
		i) Display quiz or survey results
		  • Online—display in the VOIP application (i.e., Horizon Live)
		  • Classroom—computer projection or overhead
		ii) Display of online discussion forum
		  • Online discussion forums within social networking systems (i.e., Facebook)
		iii) Display assignments and student work
		  • Links to student blogs and wikis

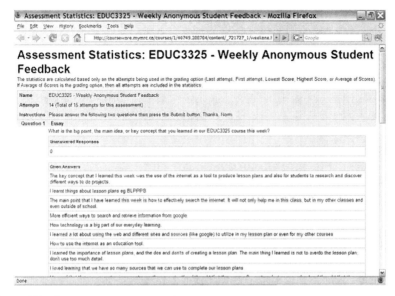

Figure 4.7   Anonymous survey results.

FUTURE TRENDS

Predicting the future is a mug's game in any context but even more un-productive in terms of technology and its possible applications. For this reason we shall focus on identifiable trends that will most likely continue to significantly shape educational practice in the near future. We suggest that the future of Web 2.0 tools in an educational context can best be un-derstood through the analysis of three trends. The first and perhaps most significant is the recognition that through the adoption of Web 2.0 tech-nologies communities can be created and sustained over time and place. This makes possible what Brown and Adler (2008) refer to as "learning 2.0." They state, "…communities are harbingers of the emergence of a new form of technology-enhanced learning—learning 2.0—which goes be-yond providing free access to traditional course materials and educational tools and creates a participatory architecture for supporting communities of learners" (p. 28).

The second trend is the adoption of collaborative approaches to teach-ing and learning. This goes beyond simple interaction and sharing of infor-mation. It represents a purposeful partnering to solve relevant problems. It provides an environment to test conceptions and validate personally constructed knowledge. The third trend of Web 2.0 tools and learning is that of a diversity of educational purposes, approaches and audience. While we can identify trends and even principles of practice, the decentralization of the teaching and learning process will inevitably lead to greater diversity and opportunities to learn. This choice of what and how to learn can only be a positive for educators and students.

As opportunities for interaction and collaboration increases through the proliferation of Web 2.0 tools, more pressure will be placed on educational institutions to adopt collaborative-constructivist approaches that engage learners in communities of inquiry. Collaborative learning goes beyond passively sharing information. For this reason, Web 2.0 tools and learning will have a transformative influence in both formal and informal learning environments.

CONCLUSION

The historical ideal of higher education has been to learn in collaborative communities of inquiry. This chapter has demonstrated the potential of using Web 2.0 instructional strategies and tools to recapture this vision, even in large, introductory undergraduate courses. The key is to redesign our courses for active and collaborative learning experiences that enable students to take responsibility for their learning and validate their understanding through discourse and debate with their peers.

REFERENCES

Ausubel, D. P. (1968). *Educational psychology: A cognitive view.* New York: Holt, Rinehart and Winston.

Barkley, E. F., Cross, K. P., & Major, C. H. (2005). *Collaborative learning techniques: A handbook for college faculty.* San Francisco: Jossey-Bass.

Bean, J. C. (2001). *Engaging ideas: The professor's guide to integrating writing, critical thinking, and active learning in the classroom.* San Francisco: Jossey-Bass.

Brookfield, S. D., & Preskill, S. (2005). *Discussion as a way of teaching: Tools and techniques for democratic classrooms* (2nd ed.). San Francisco: Jossey-Bass.

Brown, J. S., & Adler, R. P. (2008). Minds on fire: Open education, the long tail, and learning 2.0. *EDUCAUSE Review, 43*(1), 16–32.

Crouch, C. H., & Mazur, E. (2001). Peer instruction: Ten years of experience and results. *American Journal of Physics, 69,* 970–977.

Dewey, J. (1933). *How we think* (rev. ed.). Boston: D.C. Heath.

Downes, S. (2004). Educational blogging. *EDUCAUSE Review, 39*(5), 14–26.

Garrison, D. R., & Anderson, T. (2003). *E-learning in the 21st century: A framework for research and practice.* London: Routledge/Falmer.

Garrison, D. R., & Arbaugh, J. B. (2007). Researching the community of inquiry framework: Review, issues, and future directions. *Internet and Higher Education, 10*(3), 157–172.

Garrison, D. R., & Vaughan, N. (2008). *Blended learning in higher education.* San Francisco: Jossey-Bass.

Kuh, G. D., Kinzie, J., Scuh, J. H., Whitt, E. J. and Associates (2005). *Student success in college.* San Francisco: Jossey-Bass.

Leslie, S., & Landon, B. (2008). Social software for learning: What is it, why use it? *Report for The Observatory on Borderless Higher Education.* London: OBHE.

Leuf, B., & Cunningham, W. (2001). *The wiki way: Quick collaboration on the web.* New York: Addison-Wesley.

Novak, G. M., Patterson, E. T., Gavrin, A. D., & Christian, W. (1999). *Just-in-time teaching: Blending active learning with web technology.* Upper Saddle River, NJ: Prentice Hall.

Rogers, P., & Lea, M. (2005). Social presence in distributed group environments: The role of social identity. *Behavior & Information Technology, 24*(2), 151–158.

Sreebny, O. (2007). Digital rendezvous: Social software in higher education. *Educause Center for Applied Research (ECAR) Research Bulletin, 2,* 1–12

Swan, K., Shea, P., Richardson, J., Ice, P., Garrison, D. R., Cleveland-Innes, M., & Arbaugh, J. B. (2008). Validating a measurement tool of presence in online communities of inquiry. *E-Mentor, 2*(24), 1–12. Retrieved February 5, 2009, from http://www.e-mentor.edu.pl/e_index.php?numer=24&all=1

The Horizon Report. (2008). The New Media Consortium. Retrieved February 11, 2008, from http://www.nmc.org/pdf/2008-Horizon-Report.pdf

Vaughan, N. D. (2008). The use of wikis and weblogs to support deep approaches to learning. *The University College of Fraser Valley Research Review,* 1(3), 47–60. Available online at: http://journals.ucfv.ca/rr/RR13/article-PDFs/6-vaughan.pdf

CHAPTER 5

INSTRUCTIONAL DESIGN AND PEDAGOGICAL ISSUES WITH WEB 2.0 TOOLS

Amelia W. Cheney
Robert L. Sanders
Nita J. Matzen
John H. Tashner
Appalachian State University

ABSTRACT

As educators move into online environments for teaching and learning, production, socialization and collaboration technologies, such as 3D virtual immersive worlds and other Web 2.0 technologies, reveal significant challenges for us for how best to use them. Each provides a new opportunity to foster deeper online student engagement, to support new forms of learning communities and to develop new teaching and learning environments when compared with more traditional tools. For eight years, faculty at Appalachian State University has employed these types of technologies in a 3D environment called AET Zone. From this work, a pedagogical framework known as Presence Pedagogy (P2) has emerged, which provides a model for utilizing these tools to promote active, engaged teaching and learning.

Wired for Learning: An Educator's Guide to Web 2.0, pages 85–99
Copyright © 2009 by Information Age Publishing
All rights of reproduction in any form reserved.

INTRODUCTION

Students in a cohort in the Instructional Technology Master's program are challenged: how can each discover instructional resources that are personally relevant and meaningful, and how might they best share their findings with colleagues and others? They find that calling out URLs during their rare face-to-face meetings or sharing findings through a group listserv is cumbersome, and posting on the class discussion board is no guarantee that all who may benefit from the resource will find it easily. The instructor offers a suggestion: What about Del.icio.us? Within minutes, keyboards are clicking as the class participants search for the suggested site and learn more. One student begins the process, and as others begin to contribute, they work together to develop commonalities in the way they tag the sites they find to optimize their value. In this scenario, students find that traditional ways of sharing knowledge are inadequate, and adapt their own community tool to accomplish their goal and further their own learning opportunities.

As educators move into online environments for teaching and learning, production, socialization and collaboration technologies, such as Del.icio.us and others, reveal significant challenges for us for how best to use them. Each provides a new opportunity to foster deeper online student engagement, to support new forms of learning communities and to develop

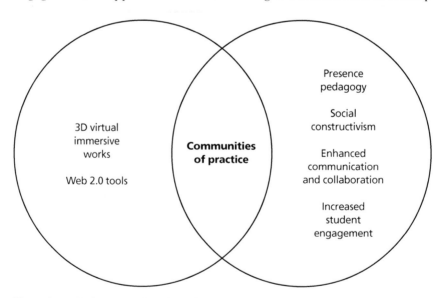

Figure 5.1 Pedagogy and tools enable communities of practice.

new teaching and learning environments when compared with more traditional tools. In many web-based instructional systems, it is difficult—and sometimes impossible—to offer kinds of rich engagement of small peer group research, discussions and communication that serve as the very essence of constructivist learning environments. Web 2.0 tools, embedded within three-dimensional (3D) immersive virtual worlds, enhance online student engagement in new and profound ways. In this chapter, we will discuss lessons learned from eight years of use of these tools in an instructional environment, with particular focus on the ways in which Web 2.0 tools enhance instruction within the framework of *Presence Pedagogy (P2)*.

BACKGROUND

AET Zone at Appalachian State University

The faculty within Appalachian State University's Reich College of Education have developed a Conceptual Framework (Reich College of Education–Appalachian State University, 2005), based upon social constructivism (Vygotsky, 1978), that guides teaching and learning. The following concepts serve as the foundation for this framework:

- Learning occurs through participation in a Community of Practice;
- Knowledge is socially constructed and learning is social in nature in a Community of Practice;
- Learners proceed through stages of development from Novice to Expert under the guidance of more experienced and knowledgeable mentors and among like-minded peers in the Community of Practice;
- An identifiable knowledge base that is both general in nature and also specific to specialties emerges from focused activity within the Community of Practice;
- All professional educators develop a set of Dispositions reflecting attitudes, beliefs, and values common to the Community of Practice.

These social constructivist principles guided faculty in the Instructional Technology program as we began investigating web-based alternatives for our program. A number of systems which had widespread acceptance in higher education, including WebCT and Blackboard, were considered but rejected, primarily because such platforms did not provide for the types of communication and interaction thought to be necessary for meaningful learning environments. These learning systems seemed to take the traditional lecture-oriented, one-way movement of information and move it into a web environment. In order to provide a different experience for participants, it was decided to develop a 3D immersive virtual world system with ActiveWorlds, (www.activeworlds.com), one of the leading 3D platforms available at the time. To this kernel many additional tools were added and continue to be added to enhance the environment for education, including Web 2.0 tools such as VoIP, threaded discussions, wikis, blogs, podcasting, and other recent technologies. The result has been the development of a patent-pending 3D world named the AET Zone, a teaching and learning environment with embedded Web 2.0 tools that enhance online learning in deep and profound ways. This platform provides a means to build virtual worlds for students, instructors, and other invited guests to meet and work together in ways not found in other learning environments that are currently available. Teaching and learning in AET Zone is a unique experience. Concepts of space, movement, physical presence and co-presence combine with conversational, collaborative, production and presentation tools in ways that create effective small and large group shared workspaces.

Participants within AET Zone are represented by avatars: human-like graphical representations of themselves. Each avatar moves through the 3D world interacting with each other and objects or with embedded artifacts. These artifacts may be linked to different resources, web pages or tools necessary to provide content and support for various kinds of synchronous and asynchronous interactions. Small and large group shared workspace tools enable interactive conversations in text chats, threaded discussion boards, audio chats and group production and sharing of documents, web pages, and other types of application software, as well as other resources.

Our online learning environment is designed to meet the needs of learners engaged in meaningful self-directed and instructor-led activities within

Figure 5.2 Students interacting in a course in AET Zone.

a community of practice of novices as well as experts. During the time in which graduate level programs at Appalachian State University have been working in the AET Zone, the environment has been uniquely developed to include students and faculty from multiple discipline areas and currently includes programs in instructional technology, library science, school administration, and educational leadership working together forming to form a rich and complex educational community of practice. Detailed descriptions of this 3D virtual immersive learning environment have been noted in other research (Bronack, Riedl, Tashner, 2006; Riedl, R., Bronack, S., & Tashner, J., 2006; and Tashner, J., Bronack, S., & Riedl, R.; 2005).

Our work with AET Zone has left us acutely aware of the important design issues surrounding the effective instructional use of virtual immersive worlds and other Web 2.0 tools has emerged. Likewise, our commitment to social constructivism suggests that simply upgrading to the latest technologies is not enough. Instead, pedagogical changes and adaptations must occur for Web 2.0 tools to enhance learning, provide access to resources, and enable communication, production, sharing and collaboration in small and large groups across distance and time. It is not just the tools per se, but how the tools are used within the structured pedagogy and the learning environment created that develops a deep learning experience.

SOCIAL CONSTRUCTIVISM, PEDAGOGY AND DESIGN

Development of a Community of Practice

Brown and Adler (2008) discuss the notion of 'social learning', which is based on the premise that understanding is socially constructed through conversations about content and grounded in interactions around problems or actions—that the focus is not on *what* is being learned but *how* it is being learned. They note that Web 2.0 tools in particular:

> . . . are examples of a new user-centric infrastructure that emphasizes participation (e.g., creating, re-mixing) over presentation, that encourages focused conversation and short briefs (often written in a less technical, public vernacular) rather than traditional publication, and that facilitates innovative explorations, experimentations, and purposeful tinkerings that often form the basis of a situated understanding emerging from action, not passivity. (p. 30)

Our experience and understanding of this point, based on feedback, observation, interview and survey results, suggests that 3D virtual worlds developed for education support deep learning in these ways. As AET Zone has grown to a community of over 2400 citizens, including faculty, current students, alumni, guests, and content experts, we have seen the development of the types of community fundamental to the social constructivist ideal. Interactions and activities that are both formal and informal, and both planned and serendipitous, have allowed students and faculty to interact in a continuous, collaborative fashion in this 3D immersive environment.

Our efforts have been guided by some key questions. For example, what elements are necessary to support social learning in a community of practice in a virtual world setting? How do Web 2.0 tools facilitate this process? As might be expected, each difficult question leads not only to important lessons, but also other, equally important questions. Of all lessons learned during the implementation of a 3D virtual immersive learning environment, perhaps the most important is this: while the tools provide devices for communication and collaboration, the truly important considerations are the changes in pedagogy and facilitation of student engagement enabled by these new opportunities for interaction. As we grow in our understanding of Web 2.0 tools and our ongoing design and development of the AET Zone, we continue to explore the goal of supporting a community of learners as a fundamental tenet to the pedagogical strategies we develop for teaching in this environment. What do we do to help facilitate and encourage this type of community? What do we model? How do activities, both planned and unplanned, contribute to the development of a social constructivist 3D virtual world?

Presence Pedagogy

Traditional face-to-face classrooms characteristically have a sense of presence in working with and among students, experts and other guests during scheduled class meetings. This includes a sense of physical presence; that is, the feeling of being someplace. This sense is heightened when combined with the sense of being someplace with others, whether it be with large or small groups or other individuals. The classroom is a learning space in which people interact with one another in meaningful and significant ways.

Typical web-based learning management systems support anywhere, anytime learning, but do not foster the feeling of being someplace else with someone else in a realistic way. Synchronous and asynchronous Web 2.0 tools can be used within appropriate pedagogical frameworks to regain this sense of presence and co-presence lost in these more traditional online learning environments. As the tools and the pedagogies continue to mature, powerful and new learning communities are forming to provide anywhere, any time online learning opportunities through which novices and experts are working together to understand complex issues and to share new knowledge. Thoughtfully combining Web 2.0 tools with 3D immersive environments offers students and instructors a real sense of space, context and the active presence of others. When participants are able to immerse themselves in on online environment in such a way, often each experiences a psychological shift from "Click Here" to "You ARE Here." Effectively combining the contextual richness of 3D with the social basis of Web 2.0 tools creates a dynamic rarely seen in online learning; that is, one in which members of the learning community rarely feel alone and are both encouraged and required to capitalize on the presence of others in meeting their personal and course learning objectives.

Presence Pedagogy (P2), as it has evolved within the AET Zone, is described in detail in the literature (Bronack et al., 2008). While presence is a necessary element of the P2 model, neither presence and its corollary co-presence, nor the tools used to create this attribute, are sufficient to explain the uniqueness of P2. Rather it is the use and applications of the tools along with the presence phenomena that makes a substantive difference. Social constructivism (Vygotsky, 1978) and Situated Learning (Lave and Wenger, 1991) guide this new pedagogical model. The P2 model offers educators a substantial shift in how we can best approach teaching and deep learning using Web 2.0 tools embedded in 3D immersive virtual worlds.

The P2 model is similar to teaching in a face-to-face (F2F) environment in terms of the presence of faculty and students in the same space and at the same time. However, this F2F sense of presence is fundamentally different when discussed in P2 terms. Unlike F2F presence, P2 can provide continuous access to instructors, colleagues and other students. No longer do students attend class for a set number of hours on a set day of the week. Rather, students and faculty may be present in a virtual space at most times of the day, week, and semester. Interactions that occur when students are present may be planned and pre-arranged. However, they may also happen serendipitously. Members of the virtual community engaged in P2 interact with those who are present together at the same time, regardless of "assigned" course, program, department, or role. P2 expects and anticipates these unplanned interactions and subsequently integrates these chance meetings into the very fabric of what is being learned and the activity that takes place as part of the living curriculum it creates.

P2 emerges as a unique pedagogical approach out of the praxis of the philosophical frameworks of social constructivism and situated learning. It is not simply a model of best practice in teaching or for the most effective use of a particular set of tools. Rather, P2 is a model for best practice in teaching *when using* these new tools. It suggests ways of thinking about engaging students and taking advantage of the opportunities these emerging tools offer. In practice, it is a fundamental shift in how we approach teaching and learning in environments that support online education.

The changing nature of the ways in which individuals access and use knowledge is central to a consideration of P2. Presence Pedagogy (P2), characterized by a substantive change in what constitutes teaching and learning, focuses on the ways in which educators and learners interact in online environments:

- ask questions and correct misperceptions;
- stimulate background knowledge and expertise;
- share tools and resources;
- facilitate interactions and encourage community;
- provide and delineate context and goals to act upon;
- encourage exploration and discovery;
- facilitate distributed cognition;
- encourage reflective practice;
- capitalize on the sense of presence and co-presence;
- utilize technologies to achieve and disseminate results. (Bronack, et al, 2008)

We see all of these factors as essential to an effective approach to teaching in a Web 2.0 environment, and will describe how our implementation of what we consider *Presence Pedagogy* informs our decisions regarding each of these factors. This P2 model serves as the catalyst for social constructivist learning in an immersive virtual world. The P2 pedagogy causes a "churn" that encourages purposeful interactions, goal oriented projects, increased productivity and collaborative processes which result from an intentional learning environment.

Constructivist Attributes of Web 2.0

Hargadon (2008) suggests a paradigm shift attributable to Web 2.0 tools that is of particular importance to education. The author identifies eleven key factors of this shift:

From:	To:
Consuming	Producing
Authority	Transparency
Expert	Facilitator
Lecture	Hallway
Access to information	Access to people
Learning about	Learning to be
Passive learning	Passionate learning
Presentation	Participation
Publication	Conversation
Formal schooling	Lifelong learning
Supply-push	Demand-pull.

Brown (2005) asserts that this move from supply-push to demand-pull causes a revisiting of constructivist practice, in which learning occurs in (virtual) communities of practice, and is characterized by tinkering, designing, creating, remixing, and re-searching. This reconsideration of constructivist principles leads to a discussion of the ways in which Web 2.0 enables the shift described above.

A framework for Web 2.0 tools from TechSoup (n.d.) provides a valuable organizational tool when considering the ways in which P2 is enabled and supported. The site categorizes these tools into: 1) tools to collaborate with others, 2) tools to network and build community, 3) tools to publish and disseminate information, 4) tools to share stories, and 5) tools for creating new tools. Table 5.1 outlines the P2 Principles, Web 2.0 Categories, examples of applicable Web 2.0 tools, and examples of ways in which these tools are used within AET Zone. The table is followed by a more in-depth discussion.

Collaboration with Others

One important element of the P2 model involves the collaboration among all members of the community of practice. These collaborations serve as a means of addressing two particular principles of P2, both "Asking Questions and Correcting Misconceptions" and "Supporting Distributed Cognition."

In the P2 approach, Web 2.0 tools are embedded in a 3D immersive environment to provide a variety of ways to interact and collaborate, both synchronously and asynchronously. Students and faculty use tools such as discussion boards and blogs to generate ongoing conversations about topics and themes related to course content. Synchronous tools such as text chat and instant messaging are built into the environment to allow users to approach one another in the environment and engage in live conversation. Likewise, web-conferencing tools such as Talking Communities and Elluminate provide private forums for real-time interactions, document sharing and production, as well as opportunities for questions to be asked and answered, and for ideas to be challenged and clarified. Through this process of questioning and clarifying, both student peers and faculty "experts" serve as catalysts to promote explicit learning. It is important to note that class activities are designed to promote the use of all these tools to enhance various kinds of interactions for different purposes between and among participants.

These multiple manifestations of presence made possible through the students' use of all the Web 2.0 tools available to them in the virtual world help to create an open space in which students and faculty of various backgrounds, levels, and disciplines can interact and share in their thinking

TABLE 5.1 Tenets of Presence Pedagogy and Web 2.0

P2 Principle	Web 2.0 Categories	Applicable Web 2.0 Tools	Examples of Web 2.0 Uses in P2 Environment (AET Zone)
Ask questions and correct misconceptions Support distributed cognition	Collaborate with Others	• Discussion Boards • Small and Large Group Audio Chats/Conferencing • Wikis • Blogs • Social Bookmarking • Document Sharing/Production	• Course Discussion Boards • Expert Guest Speakers Interacting in Audio Chats • Creation of Course Texts Using Wikis • Shared Social Bookmarking/Tagging of Resources • Products Produced Together (i.e., Wikis, Blogs, Websites, Virtual Spaces)
Stimulate background knowledge and expertise Capitalize on the presence of others Facilitate interactions and encourage community Encourage exploration and discovery Delineate context and goals	Social Network and Build Community	• Wikis • Social Bookmarking • Interactive Databases • Document Sharing • 3D Immersive Learning Environments (AET Zone) • Discussion Boards • Small and Large Group Audio Chats/Conferencing • Blogs • Social Networking • Free Access to Web 2.0 Tools • Integration of Tools into 3D Environments • RSS • Environment as Mashup	• Course Spaces in 3D Immersive World • Collaborative Writing and Sharing of Case Studies via the Web • Assignments Where 'Newbies' Find 'Veterans' to Learn Tips for Using Available Tools • Virtual Presence of ASU Library Services in World • Interactive Databases for Sharing of Resources • Cross-Cohort and Cross-Program Projects Using Web 2.0 Tools
Foster reflective practice Utilize technology to achieve and disseminate results Share tools and resources	Publish and Disseminate Information Share Stories Create New Tools	• Blogs • Social Networking • Wikis • Photo and Video Sharing • Podcasting • Social Networking • Digital Storytelling • Interactive Databases • Tagging • Document Sharing/Production	• Blogs for Reflection During Courses and Internships • Creation of Group Websites Utilizing Hypermedia Tools • Shared Social Bookmarking and Tagging • Building of Resources in AET Zone

about educational problems and issues, and their collective actions directed toward solutions to these problems. Expertise in, understanding of, and responsibility for these solutions are shared by students and faculty through the embedded use of wikis, blogs, RSS feeds, social bookmarking, and other tools that support interaction and collaboration.

Social Networking and Building Community

Several of the P2 Principles are closely aligned with the use of Web 2.0 tools to social network and build community through the stimulation of students' background knowledge and expertise. The P2 model encourages activities that require the sharing of personal and professional experiences among engaged members of the learning community of practice that forms in the 3D immersive environment. This community is perpetuated through cross-course, cross-cohort, cross-program, and cross department interactions, and collectively recognizes the background and expertise that each member brings to the community.

Web 2.0 tools support the sharing and storing of the knowledge and expertise important to the P2 model. While wikis and social bookmarking sites like Del.icio.us are natural choices for addressing the above principle, there are a variety of other tools and interactive databases embedded in the virtual environment that enable all members of the community to make contributions concerning what they know and learn.

The P2 model is fundamentally about creating a learning community of practice. The P2 model capitalizes on this sense of presence and co-presence by recognizing the ways in which students and faculty can serendipitously interact with one another as a direct result of this greater awareness of another. The use of naming conventions to identify student, cohort, program, and even nationality help students feel safe and to provide a context for questions and conversation to occur in the context of the broader educational community rather than limited by the course or program in which they are enrolled. Faculty members move through the space, interacting with students and other faculty, as a means of supporting students across programs, not just those enrolled in "their" courses.

A variety of Web 2.0 tools such as discussions, chats, web-conferencing, blogs, wikis, social networking sites, and the 3D immersive environment itself all serve to facilitate these interactions between and among members of this growing community as a means of delineating context and goals of learning. Students choose the tools most appropriate to the way in which they want to communicate and interact. Those wanting to share information or reflect may choose blogs or any number of social networking tools. Others who want to engage in real-time dialogue may choose a chat or web-conferencing tool. And, those who want to engage in ongoing collaboration may choose a wiki or discussion board to support that style of interaction. Regardless of the goal or tool used to achieve that goal, active and engaged participation in the community furthers the learning that takes place in the context of these interactions.

Publishing and Disseminating Information/Sharing Stories/Creating Tools

Web 2.0 tools can be utilized to provide new and creative ways to publish and disseminate information, results, stories and resources to others. Throughout any course offered in the AET Zone, students are required to engage in reflective practice in terms of what they are doing and learning, privately through blogs and publicly through discussion boards and group meetings in chats and web-conferencing spaces. As part of the course requirements, students engage in activities that require utilization of in-world tools and resources to think, reflect, and experiment with ideas.

These reflective practices help students work through issues, questions, and challenges as their thinking about education and, in particular, their own instructional practice evolves. Web 2.0 research and productivity tools embedded in the AET Zone provide the means of achieving their project goals. Upon completion of the research and planning phases of a project, students consider the utilization of other Web 2.0 tools such as MySpace, Facebook, YouTube, and Flickr to present and disseminate the results of student learning. These tools, products, and resources are shared and maintained indefinitely in the AET Zone, thus creating a persistent presence of a living curriculum that is adapted, modified, and added to on an ongoing basis from semester to semester.

FUTURE TRENDS

Much has been written concerning the need to move from the static lecture format to more authentic pedagogies. History is replete with examples such as Ralph Waldo Emerson's (1844) statement, "We are shut up in schools, and colleges and recitation-rooms, for 10 or fifteen years and come out at last with a bag of wind, a memory of words and do not know a thing," or Albert Einstein's (1946) lament, "It is, in fact, nothing short of a miracle that the modern methods of instruction have not yet entirely strangled the holy curiosity of inquiry." These men would be happy to know that several significant pedagogical trends are emerging as a result of the collaborative communications tools referred to as Web 2.0. While it is increasingly difficult to predict the future, several trends portend near and intermediate substantive changes in educational pedagogies.

Schneider (2008) cites many concerns with the current lecture oriented classrooms that form the overriding pedagogy of today. The evolution of computer delivered instruction has attempted to take that same pedagogical model we have always used and upload it for online delivery to students. This one way delivery of information was perhaps the best we could do with the tools that we have had with which to work until quite recently. However, the development of newer tools included in the Web 2.0 applications has enabled us to rethink both *what* and *how* we educate students. A basic question that is emerging is "what does a 21st century educated person look like?"

More than one hundred years ago, companies switched from generating their own electric power and joined the developing electric grid. A series of transformations was set into motion that changed our economy and society in profound ways. A similar transformation is occurring today as individual computers are increasingly connected to a vast internet forming a "world wide computer" (Carr, 2008). This suggests a global transition from desktop computers to regional Internet nodes that create a form of computer utilities. Most of the emerging computer power and usefulness is derived from all the software and information that is available out on the Net, including the current Web 2.0 applications. Students are learning and using these tools outside of school for their own purposes, including autonomous collaborations, sharing and productions, as well as communications and networking. Individuals are choosing to engage in "virtual communities" rather than physical ones. Likewise, the control of media is moving to individuals. Elementary, middle, secondary schools as well as higher education are all moving online. Traditional institutions, including our traditional concept of "school" as a brick and mortar place may not be as important.

Perhaps the most salient trend though deals with the economics of our transitioning society. Benkler (2006) argues that this newly networked economy enables individuals and private groups to be more productive than many traditional formally organized groups. The Web 2.0 tools and applications "offer defined improvements in autonomy, democratic discourse, cultural creation, and justice" (p. 168) Weinberger (2007) notes that "For 2,500 years, we've been told that knowing is our species' destiny and its calling. Now we can see for ourselves that knowledge isn't in our heads: It is between us. It emerges from public and social thought and it stays there, because social knowing, like the global conversations that give rise to it, is never finished" (p. 147).

As educators continue to examine the content of the disciplines, they will increasingly find further applications of these Web 2.0 tools. The tools are becoming a part of the content of the subjects. Studying the tool within the context of content will become commonplace and part of the practice of education.

CONCLUSION

The thoughtful and careful integration of Web 2.0 tools to engage students in authentic learning experiences will be necessary for these tools to find their place in today's educational system. As of now, the current system is working against them; teaching is done to students; learning is done alone and competitively; and, sharing and collaboration is generally discouraged. However, in part due to current globalization and the developing needs of the emerging information society, social constructivism may provide a solid foundation for beliefs about social learning, and emerging pedagogical approaches such as Presence Pedagogy. These trends will continue to encourage and support the ongoing integration of these Web 2.0 tools to enhance learning, provide access to resources, and enable communication, production, networking and collaboration in small and large groups across distance and time.

REFERENCES

Benkler, Y. (2006). *The wealth of networks: How social production transforms markets and freedom*. Retrieved May 20, 2008, from http://www.benkler.org/Benkler_Wealth_Of_Networks.pdf.

Bronack, S., Riedl, R., & Tashner, J. (2006) Learning in the zone: A social constructivist framework for distance education in a 3D virtual world. *Interactive Learning Environments 14*(3), 219–232.

Bronack, S., Sanders, R., Cheney, A., Riedl, R., Tashner, J., & Matzen, N. (2008). Presence pedagogy: Teaching and learning in a 3D immersive world. *International Journal of Teaching and Learning in Higher Education, 20*(1), 59–69.

Brown, J. S. (2005). New learning environments for the 21st century. *Aspen Symposium 2005*. Retrieved May 10, 2008, from http://net.educause.edu/ir/library/pdf/ffp0605.pdf.

Brown, J. S., & Adler, R. P. (2008). Minds on fire: Open education, the long tail and learning 2.0. *Educause Review*. Retrieved April 30, 2008, from http://net.educause.edu/ir/library/pdf/ERM0811.pdf.

Carr, N. (2008). *The big switch: Rewiring the world, from Edison to Google*. New York: Norton.

Christiansen, C. M., & Horn, M. B. (2008). *Disrupting class: How disruptive innovation will change the way the world learns*. New York: McGraw-Hill.

Einstein, A. (1946). Retrieved May 23, 2008, from http://www.quoteworld.org/quotes/4061.

Emerson, R. W. (1844). *Quotations: Education/learning.* Retrieved May 23, 2008, from http://www.4degreez.com/quotes/quotes_edu.mv.

Hargadon, S. (2008). *Web 2.0 is the future of education.* Retrieved May 3, 2008, from http://www.stevehargadon.com/2008/03/web-20-is-future-of-education.html.

Lave, J., & Wenger, E. (1991). *Situated learning: Legitimate peripheral participation.* New York: Cambridge University Press.

Reich College of Education–Appalachian State University. (2005). *Conceptual framework.* Retrieved November 6, 2006, from http://ced.appstate.edu/about/conceptualframework.aspx.

Riedl, R., Bronack, S., & Tashner, J. (2006, January). *3D web-based worlds for instruction.* Published in Proceedings of The Society for Information and Teacher Education, Phoenix, AZ.

Schneider, J. (2007). *Chalkbored: What's wrong with school and how to fix it.* Retrieved May 24, 2008, from http://www.chalkbored.com/.

Tashner, J., Bronack, S., & Riedl, R., (2005, March). *Virtual worlds: Further development of web-based teaching.* Published in Proceedings of the Hawaii International Conference on Education, Honolulu, HI.

TechSoup. (n.d.) *Everything you need to know about Web 2.0.* Retrieved May 18, 2008, from http://www.techsoup.org/toolkits/web2/.

Vygotsky, L. S. (1978). *Mind in society: The development of higher psychological processes.* Cambridge, MA: Harvard University Press.

Weinberger, D. (2007). *Everything is miscellaneous.* New York: Times Books/Henry Holt.

CHAPTER 6

INCORPORATING WEB 2.0 INTO EDUCATION

Instructional Design and Pedagogical Issues

Elena Qureshi
Phillip Olla
Madonna University

ABSTRACT

Web 2.0 is opening new capabilities for human interaction. It also broadens the ways we can use technology to help us collaborate more effectively. The book chapter will discuss instructional strategies and techniques used to successfully utilize Web 2.0 tools for classroom collaboration. It will also highlight pedagogical issues that arise with the implementation of Web 2.0 into the educational setting. Case studies describing how various Web 2.0 applications can be incorporated in variety of courses in the areas of nursing, education, and computer information systems will be presented. Finally, recommendations for teachers and students on how to effectively use Web 2.0 tools to improve teaching and learning process will be outlined.

Wired for Learning: An Educator's Guide to Web 2.0, pages 101–117
Copyright © 2009 by Information Age Publishing
All rights of reproduction in any form reserved.

INTRODUCTION

Web 1.0 has had a phenomenal impact in the educational setting creating opportunities in e-learning, information access, publishing and research. Some University presidents were concerned that the Internet would destroy the traditional campus life (Ryan, 2001). This is far from the case and the Internet has presented new opportunities along with some significant challenges to the educational setting. The emergence of Web 2.0 into the education setting is having the same impact as Web 1.0 but is much more pervasive and powerful. The idea that students can collaborate in real-time to create digital contents such as words, programs, images, or theories is a compelling notion. In addition to content creation students can now access a vast amount of information from a variety of excellent and dubious sources. The challenge for educators is to comprehend how to utilize the tools and applications to improve the teaching and learning process.

This chapter will present case studies describing how Web 2.0 applications and tools can be implemented in variety of courses in the areas of nursing, education, and computer information systems. The chapter will discuss Instructional design techniques and pedagogical issues that arise with the implementation of Web 2.0 into the educational setting. Specifically, the chapter will be broken down into the following sections:

- **Section 1: Instructional Design.** This section will focus on the overview of the concept of Instructional Design and general phases of Instructional design.
- **Section 2: Web 2.0 concepts and terminology.** This section will categorize Web 2.0 services and will discuss various types of collaboration software.
- **Section 3: Case Studies.** This section will focus on a few specific examples of using Web 2.0 applications in graduate and undergraduate courses in the areas of nursing, education, and computer information systems. The section will also present applications that can be used to create multimedia applications.
- **Section 4: Recommendations and Future Trends.** This section will outline recommendations for teachers and students to effectively use Web 2.0 tools to improve collaboration. Basic definitions of terms will be provided at the end of the chapter.

The authors hope that this chapter will become a valuable resource for students and teachers at the higher education level and K–12 alike. Web 2.0 is changing the landscape of higher education and the application of learning technologies. The new web will be a platform that joins up all the functions and data with a new network of connections below the application level, enabling a new generation of applications that will make teaching and learning easier, more productive, and more fun.

SECTION 1: INSTRUCTIONAL DESIGN

While it is believed that Web 2.0 is changing the landscape of higher education and the application of learning technologies, the reality is that many instructors are still unfamiliar with emerging social networking tools. Those teachers who are on the cutting edge have concerns about the appropriate use of various Web 2.0 applications in the classroom environment (Selwyn, 2008). As a result, there is a great need to carefully examine various Instructional design models and evaluate their potential for successful inclusion of Web 2.0 resources to improve teaching and learning process.

Definition Overview

Educational research contains a wide variety of definitions for instructional design. Briggs, Gustafson, and Tillman (1991) defined instructional design as a systematic approach to creating effective instruction that had not had the test of time such as scientific principles for example. Merrill, Drake, Lacy, and Pratt (1996) defined instructional design as a technology for the development of learning experiences and environments, which promotes the acquisition of specific knowledge and skill by students. Instructional design is also a technology that incorporates known and verified learning strategies into instructional experiences which make the acquisition of knowledge and skill more efficient, effective, and appealing. Spector (as cited in Morgan, 1997) referred to instructional design as a structuring of the learning environment for the purpose of facilitating learning or improving learning effectiveness. This definition of instructional design is adopted in this chapter as well.

General Instructional Design Phases

Instructional design refers to the process of instructional program development from start to finish (Braxton, Bronico, & Looms, 1995). Many models exist for use by different levels of instructional designers and for different instructional purposes; however, Braxton et al. summarized the process into five general phases (See Figure 6.1).

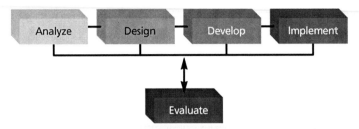

Figure 6.1 Five phases of instructional design process.

The *Analyze* phase is the foundation for all other phases of instructional design. During this phase, one must define the problem, identify the source of the problem and determine possible solutions. The phase may include specific research techniques such as needs analysis, job analysis and task analysis. The outputs of this phase often include the instructional goals, and a list of tasks to be instructed. These outputs will be the inputs for the Design phase.

The *Design* phase involves using the outputs from the Analyze phase to plan a strategy for developing the instruction. During this phase, one must outline how to reach the instructional goals determined during the Analyze phase and expand the instructional foundation. Some of the elements of the Design phase may include writing a target population description, conducting a learning analysis, writing objectives and test items, selecting a delivery system, and sequencing the instruction. The outputs of the Design phase will be the inputs for the Develop phase.

The *Develop* phase builds on both the Analyze and Design phases. The purpose of this phase is to generate the lesson plans and lesson materials. During this phase one will develop the instruction, all media that will be used in the instruction, and any supporting documentation. This may include hardware (e.g., simulation equipment) and software (e.g., computer-based instruction).

The *Implementation* phase refers to the actual delivery of the instruction, whether it is classroom-based, lab-based, or computer-based. The purpose of this phase is the effective and efficient delivery of instruction. This phase must promote the students' understanding of material, support the students' mastery of objectives, and ensure the students' transfer of knowledge from the instructional setting to the job.

The *Evaluation* phase measures the effectiveness and efficiency of the instruction. Evaluation should actually occur throughout the entire instructional design process—within phases, between phases, and after implementation. Evaluation may be formative or summative.

Instructional Design Theories

Instructional theory describes a variety of methods of instruction (different ways of facilitating human learning and development) and the situations in which those methods should be used. The methods can be broken into simpler component methods and the methods are probabilistic (Reigeluth, 1999, p. 7). Researchers agree that instructional design theories are based on learning theories. Although there are many learning theories, three theories—behaviorism, cognitivism, and constructivism- dominate instructional design.

Research shows that instructional design models that are based on constructivist approach that values collaboration and focuses on students rather than an instructor can be easily adapted to a wide variety of instructional situations. Reynard (2007) suggested that to reach a level of instructional success, instructor has to apply effective instructional design strategies and plan ahead. Instructional success also requires an equal access to content for students, and creating a culture of ideas exchange leading to dialog, not simply conversation. Further, the emergency of Web 2.0 has brought with it a variety of new interaction styles and concepts such as blogs, wikis, podcasts, and other. These tools are opening new capabilities for human interaction. Web 2.0 also broadens the ways we can use technology to help us collaborate more effectively. It is important to realize, however, that simply providing tools to students will not achieve a desired instructional outcome.

The next section will examine the concept of Web 2.0 and its application in the educational setting.

SECTION 2: WEB 2.0 CONCEPTS AND TERMINOLOGY

Web 2.0 Concept and Terminology

Web 2.0 is a difficult concept to understand or define. The problem stems from the diverse views on the topic by industry experts. There are two contradictory views on the Web 2.0 phenomenon. The first perspective synonymous with Tim O'Reilly is that *Web 2.0* is a trend in the use and design of Internet based technology that aims to promote concepts such as creativity, knowledge generation, information sharing, and collaboration. These important concepts have facilitated the development and evolution of virtual communities and online services, such as social-networking sites, social bookmarking, blogs, and wikis. The Web 2.0 term was coined at the first O'Reilly Media Web 2.0 conference (O'Reilly, 2005).

Tim O'Reilly is the founder of O'Reilly Media and defines Web 2.0 as "the business revolution in the computer industry caused by the move to the Internet as a platform, and an attempt to understand the rules for success on that new platform" (O'Reilly, 2006).

The main problem with the Web 2.0 concept is that some people believe that it insinuates new version of the World Wide Web, when in fact it does not introduce any new technical specification updates to the original www. It just transforms the way software developers and end-users use web. The most famous adversary to the Web 2.0 concept is Sir Tim Berners-Lee, the inventor of the Web. Tim Berners-Lee once described the term "Web 2.0" as a "piece of jargon" in a podcast. His argument was that Web 2.0 is all about blogs and wikis, which are people to people. The notion of people to people is the original premise of the Internet (Anderson, 2006). Another criticism of Web 2.0 is the lack of sustainable business models from the companies operating in this arena.

Categorization of Educational Web 2.0 Services by Functionality

Due to the constantly evolving technology and the lack of a clear consensus on what Web 2.0 really is or whether Web 2.0 actually exists, it is difficult to categorize applications and services that are deemed Web 2.0 compliant. To resolve this issue, this article uses the concept of service functionality to categorize the applications.

Most of the applications mentioned in the following subsections are already being incorporated into education to various degrees. These following applications are not real technologies, but a collection of interconnected services or user processes that utilize the Internet open standards and building blocks (Anderson, 2007). Although the whole range of applications listed in Figure 6.2 can be incorporated into education, social networking, social bookmarking and mash-up websites have not made the same impact on education as blogs, wikis, and collaboration software.

Blogs

The term *blog* was created from shortening the term *web log*. A blog is a site maintained by an individual, organization or group or people, which contains recurrent entries of commentary, view points, descriptions of events, or multimedia material, such as images, pictures or videos. The entries are typically displayed in reverse chronological order with the most recent post being the current focus. For the most part, blogs provide views or information on a specific and distinct subject; while other blogs function as

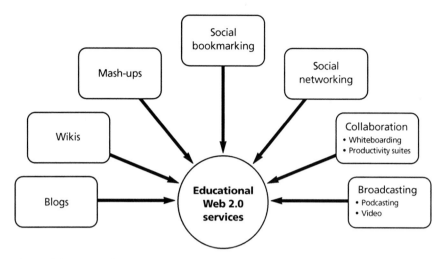

Figure 6.2 Educational Web services.

personal online diaries. Typically a blog combines text, images, videos, and links to other blogs, web pages, and other media related to its topic being discussed. An important functionality of a blog that has immense benefits in the educational context is the ability for readers to leave comments in an interactive format (Benkler, 2006, p. 217). Blogs typically have a textual focus; there is a growing concentration of blogs in the social media arena, such as photographs (photoblog), sketchblog, videos (vlog), music (MP3 blog), and audio (podcasting). It is difficult to get an actual figure of how many blogs exist but as of May 2008, blog search engine Technorati was tracking more than 120 million blogs.

TABLE 6.1   Blogs Used in Education

Website	Purpose	Comments
http://wordpress.org/	Software to create blogs	WordPress is an online publishing platform with a focus on aesthetics, web standards, and usability. Free.
http://www.blogger.com	Software to create blogs	Google website, very easy to use with a variety of templates.
http://blogs.warwick.ac.uk/	Educational blog	This is an example of how a university is using blogging. They have over 5,000 blogs with 106,836 entries.

Examples of Educational Blogs

Podcast Broadcasting. A podcast is a series of digital files distributed over the Internet using RSS for playback on portable media players, such as iPods, PDA, smartphones, or computers. The term *podcast*, like *broadcast*, can refer either to the series of content itself or to the method by which it is syndicated. Although podcasts are typically audio recordings, recently they have become synonymous with video or audio. Video podcast is sometime shortened to vidcast or vodcast and refers to the online delivery of video content. Podcasts can be in MP3 format and can contain talks, reviews, commentaries, interviews, and lectures (Felix & Stolarz, 2006). Podcasting is becoming widespread in education (Brittain et al., 2006; Ractham & Zhang, 2006). Educational Feeds and Podcasts can be located at http://www.educational-feeds.com

Collaboration Software. Prior to the Web 2.0, Collaboration software was known as groupware and was typically desktop based and integrated various aspects of work on a single project by multiple users from separated workstations and various time intervals (Kaplan, 2002). It is critical in the current competitive business environment that students are taught how to plan proficiently, schedule competently, communicate effectively and share resources efficiently. Introducing students to effectively use collaboration applications prepares them to become successful members of the workforce.

Web 2.0 collaboration learning environments come with a variety of innovative features and functionality, such as audio/video conferencing, whiteboarding, shared workspace, content sharing, etc. illustrated in Figure 6.3.

In addition to the functionality, simplicity and user-friendly access are the most important attributes to consider (Kaplan, 2002). Users should spend little time leaning the application or the technology that runs the collaboration site and spend more time performing the tasks and learning about the content. The technology should be transparent to the instructor as well as the learner; no prior technical expertise should be required to customize or manage the environment.

Wikis

A wiki is website that allows users with access to collaboratively create, edit, link, and categorize the content of a website in real time covering a variety of reference material. Wikis have evolved from being purely a reference site into collaborative tools to run community websites, corporate intranets, knowledge management systems and educational sites.

Advocate of Wikis are enthusiastic about the ease of use, flexibility, open access, however, there are considerable problems with using wikis in the educational setting (Ebersbach et al., 2006; Lamb, 2004). Even though there have been some high profile cases involving the use of Wikipedia for

Figure 6.3 Collaboration site functionality.

malicious editing and vandalism (Stvilia et al., 2005), the proponents point out that the moderation process quickly identifies and resolves these issues. Another alternative that is being used for professional work is to restrict editing access to specific registered users (Cych, 2006).

The essence of the Wiki functionality is described as follows (Anderson, 2007):

1. A wiki invites all users to edit any page or to create new pages within the wiki Web site, using a standard web browser with no additional software requirements.
2. A wiki promotes meaningful topic associations between different pages by making page link creation almost intuitively easy and showing whether an intended target page exists or not.
3. A wiki is not a carefully crafted site for casual visitors. Instead it seeks to involve the visitor in an ongoing process of creation and collaboration that constantly changes the Web site landscape.

SECTION 3: CASE STUDIES

Case 1: Group Project and Collaboration Using Basecamp

The Information Systems Seminar course is a capstone course for the Management Information Systems (MIS) major. This course is offered by school of business and is one of the final classes that must be taken by the students to demonstrate a variety of skills learned in the previous courses. The students were tasked with developing a web portal for a local nonprofit community organization. It was the students' responsibility to conduct all the analysis and design, manage the project activities and co-ordinate with the instructor and the client. One of the first tasks was for the students to identify a Web 2.0 application that could be used to co-ordinate their activities. Initially, they chose Google docs and used the spreadsheet feature. This approach did not work too well so they were assigned space on a website called Basecamp. Basecamp is used mainly by project teams in small/medium organizations but the flexibility makes it ideal for use within the educational arena for group work. The applications is completely online and allows a group to easily track and organize all aspects of a project or team effort in a central place accessible from anywhere.

Some of the features used by the students included:

1. Dashboard overview
2. To-do lists
3. Chat Feature
4. Milestones and iCal
5. Messages and comments
6. File sharing
7. File versioning
8. Time tracking
9. Online shared Journal for reflection

In the project reflection session, all the students agreed that it would have been impossible to manage the tasks and workload without the shared workspace. Another important comment from the students was their ability to share recourses and avoid duplication of effort by better coordination and assignment of tasks.

This exercise was an excellent way to teach students project management skills along with collaborative development. From an instructional design perspective, there was minimal deviation from the previous instructional components. The most important change is that students can work together as a group even though each student has a distinct piece of work to complete for a unique client. The benefit of this is that students were able to harness collective knowledge from the group and also negotiate tasks exchanges within the group. By decomposing their work into manageable tasks viewable to the who group, students could trade tasks based on their strengths and weaknesses; an example is the Improve Status logo in Figure 6.4 this was created by one student for another students client in exchange for a Google Map inserted into another clients page.

Another benefit is the fact that people can be invited to join the project by the students and instructor. If this course was managed within the institution's Learning Management System, the external clients would not have been able to participate in this project.

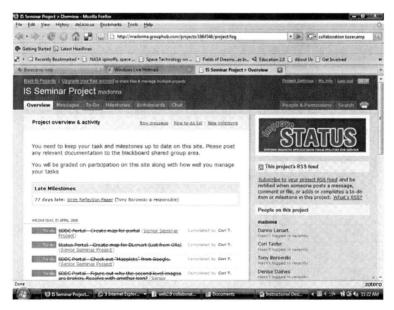

Figure 6.4 Basecamp overview screen.

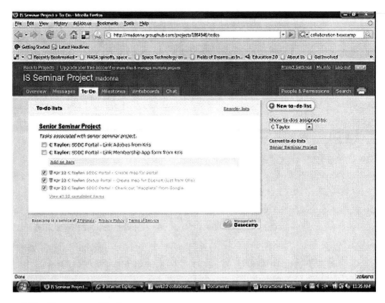

Figure 6.5　Basecamp Tasks screen.

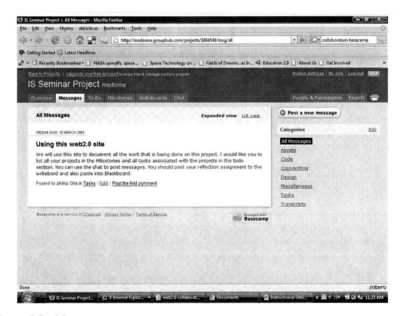

Figure 6.6　Messages screen.

Case Study 2: Collaboration Applications—Simulating a Telemedicine Consultation

The Nursing Informatics (MIS 5230) course was designed to present applications of informatics systems to nursing and healthcare practitioners. The course addressed healthcare informatics issues covering hardware, software, databases, communications applications, computer developments and associated legal and ethical issues. Graduate students typically take this class from the School of Nursing. These students have practical and managerial expertise in the Nursing field and are currently working on the Masters of Business Administration.

The assignment for the class involved separating the students into two groups.

Group A: Rural Hospital. The objective of this group was to present a patient exhibiting a variety of conditions using the telemedicine infrastructure to Group B.

Group B: Urban Hospital. The objective of this group was to diagnose the condition as quickly as possible and suggest a treatment plan.

The students used a web collaboration platform called Vyew. This website (http://www.vyew.com) provides real-time interaction between people

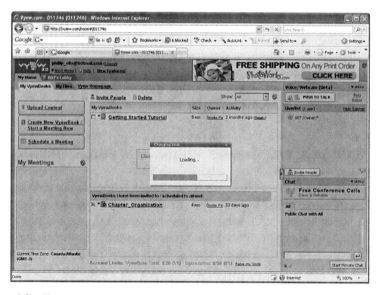

Figure 6.7   Yvew screen.

and content. Vyew is flexible and allows users to import documents in a variety of formats, such as MS Office documents, PDF, Flash, MP3, video, graphics, and screen captures. It also provides support for saving, tracking and logging all meeting activities.

The medical conditions used in the telemedicine scenario were researched by the students who were all qualified nurses. The information was presented in a manner that would make the diagnosis difficult as this was a time challenge. The students made use of the following functionality:

- Document Sharing: The patient notes were uploaded to the workspace for both groups to discuss.
- Video conferencing: The students used the web camera to show images of a rash that the patient had on his arm.
- Chat features: At one point the Group A students disabled the video/audio connection and were only accessible via chat. This was done as a ploy to slow down the process.

Outcome:

1. Both groups were very successful in completing the task relativity quickly (seven minutes and ten minutes).
2. The students were very impressed at how easy they could set-up exercise. They all agreed that this was a valuable task that could be replicated in the real world if security and privacy could be guaranteed.
3. There was no prior warning about this activity and no training on using the application, however, the students completed the activity with minimum supervision.

SECTION 4: RECOMMENDATIONS AND FUTURE TRENDS

Collaborative learning provides an environment to enrich the learning process. Introducing Web 2.0 tools into an educational system creates more realistic social contexts, thereby increasing the effectiveness of the system. Such an environment would help sustain the student's interests and would provide a more natural learning habitat. It is apparent that Web 2.0 collaboration is becoming one of the promising learning paradigms at the higher education level. Despite the complexity involved in the design of effective collaborative learning, more research efforts should be spent to explore this paradigm to provide better learning environments.

Lessons that were learned in the process of utilizing Web 2.0 applications in the classroom environment include the following:

1. Slow Internet connection can disrupt the class; therefore, it is important to test the website in the classroom with more than one computer connected.
2. Software updates: Web-based applications such as Java and Flash must be up-to-date. Valuable class time will be wasted if students have to download and install new versions of Flash or Java to support the Web 2.0 site.
3. Always have a plan B. There is a chance that during an in-class session the Web 2.0 site could be down for maintenance, it is vital that the instructor has an alternative exercise for the class.
4. It is very important that the students and faculty take regular backups of data that is stored on the Web 2.0 site. All the applications discussed in this paper provide the option for downloading the data in a variety of formats.
5. If the Web 2.0 site is critical for the class, the instructor must register for news updates and newsletter from the site, this will prevent surprises like takeovers or the service becoming unavailable.
6. Most of the functionality used in the case studies was free. There are always limitations of the basic or free model, therefore, it is important that the instructor / faculty understands the business model of the website to ensure that the limitations do not interrupt the class exercise.
7. Most of the free sites have adverts. This was an acceptable inconvenience for our classes, but this may not work for everyone. Check to make sure that the adverts being presented to the students are in line with the mission of your institution.
8. Using wireless networks to access Web 2.0 sites can cause network issues. Make sure this is tested properly before the class.
9. Sometimes the free version does not allow more than five users to connect to the same session. This problem was avoided by allowing the students to work in groups. This also helped with the network load.
10. All students must have an active email address to sign up for services. This should not be a problem; however, our experience showed that some students did refuse to register because they did not have an active personal email. Also, they refused to use their work emails for fear of spam.

CONCLUSION

The chapter presented instructional strategies and techniques used to successfully utilize Web 2.0 tools for classroom collaboration. The case studies described in this chapter provided examples of how Web 2.0 could be used in University courses. They demonstrated various pedagogical issues that arise with the implementation of Web 2.0 into the educational setting.

This book chapter was an attempt to consolidate some of the helpful online products and services that can help students, teachers, and administrators utilize valuable Web 2.0 resources into their teaching and learning. It is obvious that the new Web will be a platform that joins up all the functions and data with a new network of connections below the application level, enabling a new generation of applications that will make teaching and learning easier, more productive, and more fun. We live in a society that is heavily dependent on computer technology, and there is strong evidence that students can benefit from using various Web 2.0 tools in their collaborative efforts.

REFERENCES

Anderson, N. (2006). *Tim Berners-Lee on web 2.0: "Nobody even knows what it means."* [Online]. Retrieved May 2, 2008, from http://arstechnica.com/news.ars/post/20060901-7650.html.

Anderson, P. (2007). What is web 2.0? Ideas, technologies and implications for education. *Technology & Standards Watch Report.* [Online] Retrieved May 2, 2008, from http://www.jisc.ac.uk/media/documents/techwatch/tsw0701b.pdf.

Benkler, Y. (2006). *The wealth of networks: How social production transforms markets and freedom.* New Haven, CT: Yale University Press.

Brittain, S., Glowacki, P., van Ittersum, J., & Johnson, L. (2006). Podcasting lectures. *Educause Quarterly 29*(3). [Online]. Retrieved January 15, 2007, from http://www.educause.edu/apps/eq/eqm06/eqm0634.asp.

Braxton, S., Bronico, K., & Looms, T. (1995). *Models for instructional design.* The George Washington University in Washington, DC: Computer Science Department. [Online]. Retrieved September 5, 2001, from http://www.student.seas.gwu.edu/~sbraxton/ISD/learning_theory.html.

Briggs, L., Gustafson, K., & Tillman, M. (1991). *Instructional design: Principles and applications* (2nd ed.). Englewood Cliffs, NJ: Educational Technology Publications.

Cunningham, W. (2006). *What is a wiki?* [Online] Retrieved May 2, 2008, from http://www.wiki.org/wiki.cgi?WhatIsWiki.

Cych, L. (2006). Social networks. In BECTA (Ed.), *Emerging technologies for education* (pp. 32–41). Becta ICT Research: Coventry, UK. [Online] Retrieved May 1, 2008, from http://becta.org.uk/corporate/publications/documents/Emerging_Technologies_Accessibility.pdf.

Ebersbach, A., Glaser, M., & Heigl, R. (2006). *Wiki: Web collaboration.* Berlin: Springer-Verlag.

Felix, L., & Stolarz, D. (2006). *Hands-on guide to video blogging and podcasting: Emerging media tools for business communication.* St. Louis: Focal Press.

Kaplan, S. (2002). *Building communities—Strategies for collaborative learning.* [Online] Retrieved April 27, 2008, from http://www.learningcircuits.org/2002/aug2002/kaplan.html%20.

Lamb, B. (2004). Wide open spaces: Wikis, ready or not. *Educause Review 39*(5), 36–48. [Online]. Retrieved January 15, 2007, from http://www.educause.edu/pub/er/erm04/erm0452.asp.

Merrill, D., Drake, L., Lacy, M., & Pratt, J. (1996). Reclaiming instructional design. *Educational Technology, 36*(5), 5–7. [Online]. Retrieved September 5, 2001, from http://www.coe.usu.edu/it/id2/reclaim.html.

Millen, D., Feinberg, J., & Kerr, B. (2005, Novermber). Social bookmarking in the enterprise. *ACM Queue.* [Online]. Retrieved December 2, 2007, from http://www.acmqueue.com/modules.php?name=Content&pa=showpage&pid=344.

Morgan, S. (1997). *What is instructional design theory?* [Online] Retrieved September 3, 2001, from http://hagar.up.ac.za/catts/learner/smorgan/IDTHEORY.html.

National School Board Association (NSBA). (2007). Creating & Connecting: Research and guidelines on online social and educational networking. *National School Board Association.* [Online]. Retrieved May 2, 2008, from http://www.nsba.org/SecondaryMenu/TLN/CreatingandConnecting.aspx.

O'Reilly, T. (2005). What is web 2.0? *O'Reilly Network.* [Online]. Retrieved May 5, 2008, from http://www.oreillynet.com/pub/a/oreilly/tim/news/2005/09/30/what-is-web-20.html.

O'Reily, T. (2006). *Web 2.0 compact definition: Trying again.* [Online]. Retrieved May 5, 2008, from http://radar.oreilly.com/archives/2006/12/web-20-compact-definition-tryi.html.

Ractham, P., & Zhang, X. (2006). Podcasting in academia: A new knowledge management paradigm within academic settings. In *Proceedings of the 2006 ACM SIGMIS CPR Conference (SIGMIS CPR '06) on Computer Personnel Research, Claremont, California, USA, April 13–15* (pp. 314–317). New York: ACM Press.

Reigeluth, C. (1983). Meaningfulness and instruction: Relating what is being learned to what a student knows. *Instructional Science, 12,* 197–218.

Reigeluth, C. (1999). *Instructional design theories and models: Volume II.* Hillsdale, NJ: Erlbaum.

Reynard, R. (2007). Tips for using chat as an instructional tool. *Campus Technology.* [Online]. Retrieved May 2, 2008, from http://campustechnology.com/articles/52470_1/.

Selwyn, N. (2008). *Web 2.0 applications as alternative environments for informal learning—a critical review.* Paper for OECD-KERIS expert meeting (Session 6—Alternative learning environments in practice: Using ICT to change impact and outcomes).

Stvilia, B., Twidale, M., Gasser, L., & Smith, L. (2005). Information quality discussions in Wikipedia. Technical Report, Florida State University. [Online]. Retrieved January 16, 2007, from http://mailer.fsu.edu/~bstvilia/.

CHAPTER 7

WEB 2.0 IN ACADEMIA

Blogs and Wikis as Instruments for Learning and Teaching

Stefanie Panke
Institut für Wissensmedien, Germany

ABSTRACT

After a brief discussion of the historical and technological background of Web 2.0, the chapter outlines scenarios that illustrate opportunities and challenges of applying social software (more specifically weblogs and wikis) in learning contexts. The article summarizes findings reported in literature as well as data collected from empirical investigations on the use of weblogs and wikis for formal and informal learning setting. A content analysis of weblogs in three different university classes explores usage patterns and student participation. The findings are contrasted with interview data on two self-organized wiki communities in the German speaking area (namely Pflegewiki and Wikiversity).

Wired for Learning: An Educator's Guide to Web 2.0, pages 119–134
Copyright © 2009 by Information Age Publishing
All rights of reproduction in any form reserved.

INTRODUCTION

Web 2.0 is a vision for the further development of the Internet that was called into being in 2004 during a conference of the same name, and became prominent through an article by Tim O'Reilly in 2005. Since then, the term has grown noticeably more meaningful: Web 2.0 became a new source of hope in blogs and online news sites and, in 2006 captured the attention of the business sections and feature pages in printed magazines. Reports hinted at a possible new springtime for the Internet or–depending on the author's point of view -, feared a new "dot-com bubble." In the meantime, according to the service "*Google Trends,*" the term "Web 2.0" has overtaken "e-learning" in popularity as a search category. This is reason enough to take a closer look at the philosophy behind the buzzword and, building on that, to conceptualize its benefits for learning and teaching with digital media.

Is Web 2.0 an alternate fuel for the e-learning or Internet market, or is it a fascinating new phenomenon of self-directed user behavior and collaborative knowledge sharing? In one sense, the Internet is going back to its roots. According to Berners-Lee's (1998) personal retrospective, the basic idea of the Web was to create a place for communication and collaborative writing: *"The dream behind the Web is of a common information space in which we communicate by sharing information."* The early days of the Internet were characterized by the fact that the pioneers were not only the users of what was offered on the web, but, as a rule, also the authors of a web presence. During the 1990s, as the Internet increasingly became part of society's everyday media experience, the use of the technology was simultaneously hampered by new limitations: Since web design had become more and more professionalized, it was very difficult to create a state-of-the-art website without profound knowledge of content-management systems, HTML, CSS and script languages. Individuals needed to spend a lot of time, and considerable technical skills were required to maintain and update a website. Users who were not versed in technology faced great difficulties when they tried to play an active part in authoring, linking and commenting. For that reason, the web was perceived by many users only and exclusively as a medium for retrieving information. Today, however, there exist many different providers and programs that allow individuals to utilize the web to suit their own intentions without any prior technical knowledge. The lifecycle of software has become more dynamic (*"perpetual beta"*) and more closely aligned with the needs and requirements of users. Marketing principles like "*the long tail*" (Anderson, 2006) emphasize the importance of niches: whereas the mass media are mainly interested in large numbers of readers or audience viewing rates, Web 2.0 focuses on the best possible fit between supply and demand. This is facilitated by open application programming interfaces (APIs), which allow "mash-ups" from various data sources so that the users' needs are considered across the boundaries of different services and websites.

Through simple tools and web services, the presentation of one's own topics to a large audience has been made available to many more people than ever before. Services such as *Blogger, Twoday* or *Wikihost* allow the creation of one's own weblog or wiki with just a few clicks. A personal profile page can be created easily by users on network platforms such as *MySpace* or *XING*. As these examples illustrate, the web has become simpler, and therefore more open to users. The interconnection between early concepts of hypertext and the current trends labeled as "Web 2.0" is explained in some detail by Millard & Ross (2007).

Users are turning to these new and simple technologies that function as open systems without any rigid role and workflow concepts, since they support creative interaction, further development and change. In this way there is a co-evolution of innovative online services and innovative forms of usage: *"The Web is evolving to become more like an area for social and idea networking"* (D'Souza, 2006). This new orientation has evident implications for the educational system, which are referred to as e-learning 2.0–a term introduced by Stephen Downes (2005). How can Web 2.0 tools for individual and co-operative knowledge management be implemented in the context of education? Franklin & Harmelen (2007) warn not to hold unrealistic expectations: *"Web 2.0 is just one part of the higher education ecosystem."* Thus, there will never be an all-inclusive answer to the question of its pedagogical potential. Whether or not a certain application is suitable, will depend on the target group of the respective activity, on people's personal learning styles, and other contextual factors. For this reason there is no didactic recipe for a Web 2.0 ready-to-serve meal.

In order to give a nuanced picture of the potential of e-learning 2.0, this article explores formal and informal learning settings. As to the technology, the focus is on weblogs and wikis, since these tools so far call the tune in the concert of social software and are well suited for contrasting case studies since their infrastructure is conceptually different. In the Blogosphere, pieces of information and opinions are contributed in a co-operative process, and a discourse takes places in the form of links and commentaries. A wiki is more a form of collaborative writing where individual authors—and their individual responsibility for what they have written—stay in the background: *"Wikipedia is a work made by a community, the blogosphere is a community made by its works"* (Cunningham, 2006).

BLOGS AS TEACHING TOOLS IN HIGHER EDUCATION

By virtue of their specific form of linking entries to individual authors and dates, weblogs are the ideal space for handling, networking and archiving individual views which may (or may not) become the source of the views of a community: "They are perceived as *"unedited personal voices"* (Efimova & Fiedler, 2004). When used for private purposes, weblogs appear as a form of "*micro-publishing*" (Williams & Jacobs, 2004), which may be adapted with great flexibility and integrated into a variety of different contexts, motivations and needs. The focus is on the "*joy of writing*," and the blog is seen as a relatively protected space that encourages exploration and experimenting (Schmidt & Wilbers, 2006).

Responding quickly and being up to date is more important in many cases than accuracy of grammar or typing (Ojala, 2005). Schlobinski & Siever (2005) describe blogs as "*conceptually oral.*" Their emergent structure, which resembles some form of conversation, might also be interpreted as an egalitarian space, a "*communication hub*" with little or no hierarchy (Wijnia, 2004). Reese et al. (2007) summarize the distinctive features of Weblogs as "*ease of use, low barriers to creation and maintenance, dynamic quality, easy interactivity and potential for wide distribution*" (p. 239).

Many authors–like Williams & Jacobs (2004)–have pointed out that weblogs may have great influence in the context of learning arrangements: "*Blogging has the potential to be a transformational technology for teaching and learning*" Oravec (2003) stresses the reflexive qualities of weblogs, as they provide students with a documentation of their learning and writing behavior, which they can have a look at themselves and think about. Weblogs may also be a good form of supporting co-operative work. If a weblog contains and summarizes the learning process, intermediate and final results of the participants, it may be used as an e-portfolio for evaluation. Armstrong & Retterer (2004) report improvements of the learners' writing competence in foreign language instruction. The strategic integration of blogs into teaching at the Harvard Law School is documented by Williams & Jacobs (2004): these belong to the digital portfolio of all students and staff in the same way as an individual e-mail address.

Case Studies

The media technology department of the Knowledge Media Research Center (Tübingen, Germany) is responsible for the design and development of the open source blogging system Bebop. The system has been implemented and tested in various settings (Panke & Oestermeier, 2006). Through a content analysis of three course Weblogs, used in different teaching scenarios throughout the winter semester of 2005/06, the respective communicative and documentary functions ob the weblog use were explored in detail, e.g. the periods of posting, the distribution of activity among students and teachers, and the overall acceptance of the technology (Panke, Gaiser & Draheim, 2007). Table 7.1 shows the different contexts and underlying conditions of the three case studies.

The "*Medialog*" was part of an icebreaker exercise in the very first face-to-face session. The participants introduced themselves through postings, named their private and topic-related interested and expectations in the seminar, adding photographs. During the entire seminar, the weblog functioned as something like a homepage for the course, making available current information (hyperlinks, news) and material (scripts, slides) provided by the lecturer. Students used this platform to post mindmaps, presentations, summaries or other results of their work.

They also used it for their preparation of the final exam. After each session, typical questions which might have been asked during the test were provided through the weblog. During the mass lecture, the "*Psychblog*" served mainly as a repository for the lecturer's slides. In addition, students were encouraged to use the weblog to ask questions on lecture content and answer other students' questions by adding commentaries. The lecturer was satisfied with the high quality of student contributions, saying that the weblog gave her a good feedback on what participants found difficult to understand, and provided a space for bringing in their background knowledge.

In the virtual seminar for graduates working on doctoral theses, the "*VirtuGrade*" weblog was integrated on the basis of "*learning by teaching.*" Each participant was responsible for one topic and its virtual presentation, with only some supervision by academic staff. One problem that occurred in this context was the use the students made of the opportunity to create hierarchies in the category system. Some of them used it to create deep structures with up to four levels. Later, the participants themselves found that this interlocking information structure was badly arranged.

Findings

According to Fiedler (2004), blogs are particularly suitable for self-organized teaching scenarios with no fixed content framework. Our case study has confirmed this experience. The most intensive use of blogs was made during the virtual seminar organized by graduates. They contributed an average (median) of 14.5 postings and 29 commentaries, whereas the two faculty members who were in charge only sent occasional postings at the beginning.

TABLE 7.1 Weblog Case Studies

Blog title, teaching scenario	Institution, course type, topic, extent	Characteristics of target group	Extent of online teaching/ other media used	Using blog required?
"Medialog," enrichment of seminar/class	University of Applied Sciences of Neu-Ulm, 2 hrs/week during semester, "Introduction to media psychology"	21 participants (advanced studies), affinity to computer studies (high technical competence for using media)	on-campus (face-to-face) sessions every 2 weeks, tuition by electronic mail	Recommended but voluntary
"Psychblog," enrichment of mass lecture	University of Tübingen, 2 hrs/week during semester, lecture on "Psychology of motivation"	99 participants (basic studies), little technical competence, no prior experience with e-learning	weekly lecture on campus	compulsory, minimum 2 postings, 4 commentaries
"VirtuGrade," conducting a virtual seminar	"Virtual Graduates' College," seminar on "Knowledge communication in groups"	18 graduates working on doctoral theses from research institutions in different states of Germany	virtual teaching but face-to-face meetings at beginning and end, two synchronous audio conferences	Voluntary

In the blog that accompanied the mass lecture, student participation was close to what was demanded: an average (median) of 2 postings and 5 commentaries, little more above the minimum. 44 per cent of the postings and 39 per cent of the commentaries were sent within the last two weeks before the written test—which would suggest that the students did it just to fulfill this requirement in time.

In the seminar-style course, participants used the Medialog mainly for their preparation of the oral test, to help each other and clarify points. Those who benefited most from these additional communication facilities were some of the advanced and highly motivated students, and this expressed itself clearly in the uneven level of participation: 51 per cent of all commentaries came from the three most active students.

The voluntary use of blogs by students in the context of lectures requires a high level of moderation by the lecturer in order to encourage permanent and regular participation. Hence it is of vital importance to introduce efficient rules for feedback, say, in the form of peer reviewing by students. By quoting valuable contributions during the face-to-face sessions, supervisors can underline the significance of these postings and commentaries. Especially in lectures with large audiences, blogging can be made more attractive by making it compulsory. The content organization and archiving of knowledge can pose further difficulties: Our experience has been that many students did not understand or accept the lecturer's pre-set blog categories, but in their own self-organized settings, the participants' complex ramifications turned out to be unworkable.

WIKIS AS INFORMAL LEARNING ENVIRONMENTS

Using weblogs as instruments in formal teaching scenarios is one thing, but we should also take a closer look at the use of social software "in the wild." Here the design of non-institutional open educational resources deserves special attention. In addition, the collective activity of blogging should be contrasted with the collaborative nature of wikis. In a collective effort, many people provide their individual viewpoint on a given object on the web. This happens, for example, in weblogs, when users add their personal comments to a specific resource, (i.e., a hyperlink) and in this way create a pool of information around this object. In a collaborative system, many contributors with different backgrounds create one object, say, a *Wikipedia* entry, which is crafted by and the product of constant negotiation within the community.

Godwin-Jones (2003) suggests that wikis can serve as focal points for virtual communities by creating a shared repository of expertise in a subject area, which is refined in the course of time by contributions from interested individuals. Just like weblogs, wikis are not perceived as merely a piece of software, but as a distinctive web genre, with a procedural mimicry to open source code: "The wiki takes the ethos of the open-source software movement with its realization of the benefits of collaborative software development, and applies it to information resource management and development" (Tredinnick, 2006, p. 230).

Wikis are permeable systems, because they are not only adaptable, but changes made by individuals have a direct impact on the content itself. Instead of pre-structuring the publishing process through a complex and precise editorial workflow, the editor, reviewer and publisher functions are combined into one role within the wiki. As the wiki syntax can "foresee" that hyperlinks to "nowhere" lead to the creation of a new page, we can observe in a wiki a co-evolution of structures as opposed to editorial planning. Thus, wikis form an incremental, non-hierarchical "meme environment." Another central feature is the transparency of discourse in connection with to the creation of shared artifacts, as a result of the fact that all versions of a document are stored, and that a discussion pages complements each article. Administrators have a specific status within the wiki community. In contrast to standard users, they are able to delete pages, to (temporarily) block out editorial activity and to suspend users from the community. Their function could be described as one of organizers and moderators. They will not impose an editorial "line of approach," but are able to anticipate vandalism and prevent "editorial wars" around controversial topics. It should be underlined, however, that administrators are not exclusively concerned with editorial quality. Any user may add wiki-pages to a personal watch list, and the user will then be notified of changes that were made on these pages. Combined with the version-keeping feature, which allows an immediate restoration of any previous version of a page, this explains why wikis are very robust systems—despite the fact that anyone may access and edit them at any time.

It is not surprising that a number of educational institutions (specifically in higher education) have experimented with wiki environments for collaborative knowledge building. A summary of the potential of wikis in teaching may be found in Ferris & Wilder (2006): Educators may use wikis to provide customized electronic portfolios, to facilitate collaborative activities such as web-writing or problem-solving, for information sources or case libraries, for the submission of student assignments, and for project spaces (for the latter cf. Xu, 2007). But collective authoring is not something that students will do naturally. Initiating a wiki is a real challenge that calls for some pedagogical efforts (Lund & Smordal, 2006; Curbric, 2007). Cubric's (2007) report on wikis in academic teaching comes to the conclusion that students will need to be motivated through regular tutor feedback, clear learning goals and by counting wiki activities in the formal assessment of their performance. Augar, Raitman & Zhou (2004) describe a detailed scenario for an icebreaking exercise while introducing a course wiki.

As Guth (2007) observed, the use of wikis in educational environments is on the increase, but they are often installed within existing institutional learning management systems. Many teaching wikis are set up to last for just one term or semester, and efforts are made to maintain a manageable size of the user group (say, a student class or project team). Openly accessibly wiki projects are usually meant to survive considerable changes of the stock of their users and articles over a long and indeterminate period of time. According to Roth (2007), the viability of a wiki is a coin with two sides, which might be described as population dynamics (recruitment, retention, exclusion or leave) and content dynamics (growth, stabilization, quality), and both sides co-evolve.

What is collaboration in open wikis based on? Bryant et al. (2005) carried out one of the first ethnographic inquiries on this subject, describing the encyclopedia Wikipedia as a community of practice and analyzing it in the framework of activity theory. More specifically, they focused on the concept of legitimate peripheral participation (Wenger, 1998). Wenger, McDermott & Snyder (2002, p. 51) propose seven principles for the cultivation of communities, and the principles of "design for evolution" and "focus on value" provide the general guideline. "Open a dialogue between inside and outside perspectives," "Invite different levels of participation," "Develop both public and private community spaces," and "Combine familiarity and excitement" refer to the process of facilitating the work of such a community when it has been started and is running.

How are these principles of community building reflected within existing open wiki projects? To gain a deeper insight into the potential of implicit, emergent learning structures, we conducted several in-depth, qualitative interviews in 2007, dealing with the concept, design and implementation of the two German wiki projects *Wikiversity* and *Pflegewiki* ("Nursingwiki"). The analysis of these interviews describes these projects in general and covers in more detail their initial stages, editorial quality of contributions during the process of building the wiki, the influence of the community on the development of the project, and the individual learning process of those who were actively involved. Both persons who were interviewed belong to the founder members or initiators of the respective project and reflect their own experiences as a student or academic teacher as well.

Interview on Wikiversity

Wikiversity is a "virtual university," in which academic teaching and research are carried out on the basis of the wiki principle *"anyone may partici-*

pate." The wiki is meant as a platform for teaching and learning beyond the limitations that are set by fees, crowded lecture halls and credit points. Navigation is based on the principle of imitating "rooms" and structures of a classical university. The content is listed by "*faculties*" that carry out projects and run courses. A "*cafeteria*" is provided for informal student meetings.

This is one of the projects of the international "Wikimedia-Foundation" that runs the *Wikipedia* (one of the best-known encyclopaedias) and various other projects (*Wikibooks, Wikinews,* etc.). A first, unofficial pilot version of a German-language Wikiversity was launched in 2005, but abandoned shortly after. The current version of the German-language *Wikiversity*—with its present appearance and the status of an official Wikimedia project—has been in existence since 2006.

I interviewed a student who had previously been involved in the German Wikipedia and—coming from there—in the pilot version of Wikiversity. He is now engaged in building and expanding the current platform by providing content, carrying out administrative tasks (with the rather archaic designation of a "Pedell," "bedel," or "beadle") and doing some public relations work. As Wikiversity is a young and, as it should be, a very dynamic project, the project building and decision-making process during the initial stage of a wiki was of particular interest in this case study.

It all started with a proposal that laid down the aims and functioning of the project and was reviewed by a Board that consisted of elected representatives of the Wikimedia community.

> The Board is a group of people who are involved in the Wikimedia Foundation, and as elected representatives they decide about the existence and termination of individual wiki projects. [In order to allow the community to participate in this discussion, there exists a "meta page" for an open exchange of opinions.] Meta means, above all single projects like Wikiversity, Wikipedia, and so on. All people who are interested can voice their opinion on projects and influence this discussion.

A new project is first launched in a "beta" version. After some time, its development so far is evaluated by initiating a new discussion on the meta page. The final decision is taken by the Board:

> The Board will decide in the end. Either they are convinced, everything is solid enough, the people are there, the internal guidelines for the project are clear, the tendency is okay, we now accept it as an official project. Or, as happened with Wikiversity in the past, the project is good in principle, but you will have to overhaul your guidelines. And this is what happened with Wikiversity in the last few years.

So this decision-making process is characterized by a balance between central, hierarchical control on the one hand, and opportunities for decentralized participation on the other. There are no criteria for excluding anyone; any users may state their opinions. But only those ideas will persist in the long run on which agreement is possible, for which sufficient numbers of others can be mobilized, which are plausible and acceptable. The same applies to decisions that concern structures within Wikiversity. The framework provided by the project idea and general objectives leaves room for trying out new structures, as long as they are in line with the general purpose of the project. But the daily test of their practical use will, in the end, decide if these newly-created structures will survive.

> I started setting up new "institutes," and this started a controversy. Many people criticized that our available content was insufficient for introducing such an additional level of structures. This deterred some people. But we found a pragmatic solution in the end. The official description of our Wikiversity no longer contains "institutes," but this feature can be tried out in the Political Science department, for which I am responsible. After some time, we will see to what extent these "institutes" are accepted by our users, and discuss the matter again.

Personal involvement in a wiki is attractive because this activity leaves much room for creative design, and one's own personal activity takes effect immediately. Our interview partner described his personal learning process as "learning by teaching." Content which was meant to be presented to others had to be worked through more thoroughly and better understood than in the course of just dealing with the same subject matter individually.

> I learned how much more intensively I had to know—and get to know—the subject in order to be able to pass this knowledge on to others. And I learned how much more than I would learn myself when making this effort to try and tell someone else about it, much more than if I had just read a book about it and thought, okay, now I understand. This is a much greater challenge, to prepare this stuff for the wiki, so that others can understand it as well.

Interview on Pflegewiki ("Nursingwiki")

The German "nursingwiki" is a reference source for professional nursing. Its first version went online in 2003 and has been available with the domain name *pflegewiki.de* since 2004. It is based on the *Wikiversity* (Mediawiki) software, but is an independent project, not connected to the Wikimedia Foundation. It now offers 4000 pages and has established itself as an accepted source of reference, both among nursing staff and teachers of nursing theory.

I interviewed the person who initiated this portal. He deals with its administration, with editorial tasks and moderation, and acts as its external representative in his capacity as chairman of the charitable society that runs this website. From Wikipedia he knew the wiki principles, he was familiar with server administration and script languages, and this made it easier to set up a new wiki. As a teacher of nursing theory he had the idea of building an independent wiki on nursing-related topics.

> The main point was to make my own lecture handouts freely available to my students while improving them all the time. As I teacher I had never been sure if what I taught was really state of the art. Nursing theory is a discipline in which knowledge becomes outdated very quickly, and the amount of what you need to know is increasing rapidly. Now I thought, if I make all this available in a wiki, there will certainly be people who tell me this or that is out of date, or I know better, or here is a point that should be added.

As the nursingwiki is now a firmly established project, our main interest focused on the motivation of those people whose participation ensures its continuation, on the techniques used for moderation, and on efforts that are made to maintain a high level of quality.

My interview partner estimates that he spends up to two hours per day working on the wiki, most of the time with technical administration (spam control). The motivation lies in the range of people who use this portal.

> If you see that it is an accepted thing, that people like it. To some extent, it is good for my ego. And the others feel the same.

The editorial quality of contributions for his wiki is guaranteed by an active community. Anyone can edit any page, but in the long run only those things will be relevant and only those things will last which are accepted by the great majority of users or supported by literature and research studies. "In 80 percent of all cases this works quite well."

Quality deficits are clearly marked, both by visual signals and text, to encourage experts in the field to improve the page. Active cooperation by individual users and particularly good contributions are highlighted by a specific code.

> We have "thank you" cards which someone can send to a user page, and we even have an award. A user who has taken great pains to make contributions over a long period of time will be awarded the "Golden Wiki Star" (laughs).

Summary

Both interview partners agreed that a hard core of a committed "inner circle" of active participants is needed to launch a wiki. They need a basic framework of content. Only then will the project be visible to outsiders and attract other users (readers and/or contributors).

The operationalization of the "basic framework of content" was different in the two examples. *Wikiversity* started with a large number of navigation structures, *Pflegewiki* with well-edited real contributions and the open admission that many things might still be missing. Existing material was integrated into the wiki, hoping that community activities would sooner or later close the gaps. A higher degree of planning, or the systematic acquisition of contributions for "top" topics, was reserved for the second stage. The main problem of Wikiversity will be to fill the structures that have been created with real content, and live up to its own expectations.

In both projects, it is a community that guarantees the quality of content. What counts in the long run is what the community says, their arguments, about contributions, expansions and modifications, and not so much the formal role of any "author." Administrators are not "guards" to check the correctness of content, but their job is moderation. Instead of applying some rigid editorial policy of quality management, deficits of content and form are not filtered out, but made transparent and documented in order to be resolved by the community.

The interviews mirror different angles of a learning community—the student and the teacher face. Being active in a wiki project allowed the student to seize the amount of work involved in the preparation of learning material, and the extended opportunities for one's own learning by switching roles with the teacher. From the teacher's point of view it is important no longer to regard oneself as the only authority, but accept others as co-authors on equal terms. Collaboration on an open wiki will not only lead to a higher degree of reflection of one's own role in the learning process, but also to a gain of communicative and social competence. Identification with the product, permanent motivation, a broad readership, user feedback, are the key factors for those dedicated users who are actively involved. In this way, many people, with different degrees and in different forms of participation, will contribute to the viability of a community wiki.

CONCLUSION

If we compare different application contexts of social software, it becomes clear that the users' behavior in virtual learning arrangements will depend on the opportunities which the respective context offers—its "affordances." Using blogs in a space with clear-cut hierarchies and little informal communication will mean using social software in a context with little intrinsic motivation. Informal learning, which is—in principle—a self-organized activity, will require, and may be assisted by, a suitable infrastructure. But not any use of social software will automatically lead to a corresponding practice of informal communication and lively discourse.

The "domestication" of techniques that are mainly used for informal learning, for the purpose of pursuing learning objectives that have been pre-determined by the lecturers will obviously lead to some problems: The "joy of writing," which is a very powerful motivation of Wikipedians and residents of the blogosphere, will not automatically occur when a lecturers asks course participants to use one of these platforms. Their fast and direct communicative culture will in many cases lead to a collision with the hierarchical structures of formal instruction. There are still some disputed legal implications including privacy. Use of Web 2.0 in instructional contexts should always keep students aware of the fact that this may be an area of sensitive interaction with personal information and copyright protected sources.

Future research might also take a closer look at specific e-moderation techniques, like the adaptation of existing paradigms (the 5-steps model by Gilly Salmon, 2000, is an example) to the specific requirements of the blogosphere and wikiverse. If it was better understood how self-organized, informal projects establish a "natural" form of authority and guidance, this might result in better techniques for, so to speak, transplanting social software into a classroom situation with its conflict between student liberty and instructional control. Will we just want to deploy an easy-to-use content management system in a teaching setting, or is it our aim to provide students with a different type of learning experience by implementing and embedding Web 2.0 principles, regardless of the existing technological infrastructure? This will be the choice from the teacher's point of view.

REFERENCES

Augar, N., Raitman, R., & Zhou, W. (2004): Teaching and learning online with wikis. In R. Atkinson, C. McBeath, D. Jonas-Dwyer, & R. Phillips, (Eds.), *Beyond the comfort zone: Proceedings of the 21st ASCILITE Conference* (pp. 95–104). Retrieved July 15, 2008, from http://www.ascilite.org.au/conferences/perth04/procs/lancaster.html

Armstrong, K. & Retterer, O. (2004). Mi Blog es Su Blog: Implementing community and personal weblogs to encourage writing in intermediate Spanish. In L. Cantoni & C. McLoughlin (Eds.), *Proceedings of World Conference on Educational Multimedia, Hypermedia and Telecommunications 2004* (pp. 1135–1137). Chesapeake, VA: AACE.

Berners-Lee, T. (1998). *The world wide web: A very short personal history.* Retrieved July 15, 2008, from http://www.w3.org/People/Berners-Lee/ShortHistory.html

Bryant, S. L., Forte, A., & Bruckman, A. (2005). Becoming wikipedian: Transformation of participation in a collaborative online encyclopedia. In K. Schmidt,

M. Pendergast, M. Ackerman, & G. Mark (Eds). *Proceedings of the 2005 international ACM SIGGROUP Conference on Supporting Group Work* (pp. 1–10). ACM, New York.

Cubric, M. (2007). Wiki-based process framework for blended learning. In K. Schmidt, M. Pendergast, M. Ackerman, & G. Mark (Eds.). *Proceedings of the 2005 international ACM SIGGROUP Conference on Supporting Group Work* (pp. 11–24). ACM, New York.

Cunningham, W. (2006). *Design principles of wikis.* Talk at the 2006 International Symposium on Wikis, Odense, Denmark.

Downes, S. (2005, October 17). E-learning 2.0. *eLearnMagazine.* Retrieved July 15, 2008, from http://elearnmag.org/subpage.cfm?section=articles&article=29-1

Efimova, L., & Fiedler, S. (2004): Learning webs: Learning in weblog networks. In P. Kommers, P. Isaias, & M. B. Nunes (Eds.), *Proceedings of the IADIS International Conference Web Based Communities 2004* (490–494). Lisbon, Portugal.

Ferris, S., & Wilder, H. (2006). Uses and potentials of wikis in the classroom. *Innovate 2*(5). Retrieved July 15, 2008, from http://www.innovateonline.info/index.php?view=article&id=258.

Franklin, T., & van Harmelen, M. (2007). *Web 2.0 for content for learning and teaching in higher education.* JISC study, Great Britain. Retrieved July 15, 2008, from http://www.jisc.ac.uk/publications/publications/web2andpolicyreport.aspx

Godwin-Jones, R. (2003). Emerging technologies. Blogs and wikis: Enviroments for online collaboration. *Language Learning & Technology, 7*(2), Retrieved July 15, 2008, from http://llt.msu.edu/vol7num2/emerging/.

Guth, S. (2007). Wikis in education: Is public better?. In A. Désilets & R. Biddle (Eds.). *Proceedings of the 2007 International Symposium on Wikis* (pp. 61–68). ACM, Montreal, Quebec.

Lund, A., & Smørdal, O. (2006). Is there a space for the teacher in a wiki? In D. Riehle (Ed.). *Proceedings of the 2006 International Symposium on Wikis* (pp. 37–46). ACM, New York.

Millard, D. E., & Ross, M. (2006). Web 2.0: hypertext by any other name? In U. K. Wiil, P. J. Nürnberg, & J. Rubart (Eds.). *Proceedings of the Seventeenth Conference on Hypertext and Hypermedia* (pp. 27–30). ACM, New York.

Oravec, J. A. (2003). Weblogs as an emerging genre in higher education. *Journal of Computing in Higher Education, 14*(2), 21–44.

Panke, S., & Oestermeier, U. (2006). Weblogs als Lerninfrastrukturen: Das Beispiel Bebop. In A. Schwill, (Ed.), *Grundfragen multimedialer Lehre: Proceedings GML 2006* (pp. 70–81). Potsdam: DDI-Verlag.

Panke, S., Gaiser, B., & Draheim, S. (2007). Weblogs als Lerninfrastrukturen zwischen Selbstorganisation und Didaktik. In U. Dittler, M. Kindt, & C. Schwarz (Eds.), *Online Communities als soziale Systeme* (pp. 81–95). Münster: Waxmann Verlag.

Reese, S. D., Rutigliano, L., Hyun, K., & Jeong, J. (2007). Mapping the blogosphere: Professional and citizen-based media in the global news arena. *Journalism, 8*(3), 235–261.

Roth, C. (2007). Viable wikis: Struggle for life in the wikisphere. In A. Désilets & R. Biddle (Eds.). *Proceedings of the 2007 international symposium on Wikis* (pp. 119–124). ACM, Montreal, Quebec.

Salmon, G. (2000). *E-moderating: The key to teaching and learning online.* London: Kogan Page.

Schlobinski, P., & Siever, T. (2005). Sprachliche und textuelle Aspekte in deutschen Weblogs. In P. Schlobinski & T. Siever (Hrsg.). *Sprachliche und textuelle Aspekte in Weblogs. Ein internationales Projekt* (pp. 52–85). Hannover: Networx 46.

Schmidt, J., & Wilbers, M. (2006): Wie ich blogge?! Erste Ergebnisse der Weblogbefragung 2005. *Berichte der Forschungsstelle Neue Kommunikationsmedien, 06-1, Universität Bamberg.* Retrieved July 15, 2008, from http://www.fonk-bamberg.de/pdf/fonkbericht0601.pdf

D'Souza, Q. (2006). *Web 2.0 ideas for educators.* Retrieved July 15, 2008, from http://www.TeachingHacks.com

Tredinnick, L. (2006). Web 2.0 and business. *Business Information Review, 23*(4), 228–234.

Wenger, E. (1998). *Communities of practice: Learning, meaning, and identity.* Cambridge, MA: Cambridge University Press.

Wenger, E., McDermott, R., & Snyder, W. M. (2002). *Cultivating communities of practice. A guide to managing knowledge.* Boston: Harvard Business Press.

Williams, J., & Jacobs, J. (2004). Exploring the use of blogs as learning spaces in the higher education sector. *Australian Journal of Educational Technology, 20*(2), 232–247.

Wijnia, E. (2004): Understanding weblogs: A communicative perspective. In T. Burg (Ed.), *BlogTalk 2.0: The European Conference on Weblogs* (pp. 38–82.) Retrieved July 15, 2008, from http://elmine.wijnia.com/weblog/archives/wijnia_understandingweblogs.pdf.

Xu, L. (2007). Project the wiki way: Using wiki for computer science course project management. *Journal of Computing Sciences in Colleges, 22*(6), 109–116.

PART III

WEB 2.0 ENVIRONMENT AND USER CENTER DESIGN

CHAPTER 8

WIKI ENVIRONMENTS FOR LEARNING

Johann Ari Larusson
Richard Alterman
Brandeis University

ABSTRACT

This chapter will provide a brief overview of some of the more interesting wiki-uses in education and examples of learning activities that wikis have been used to support. A wiki is an asynchronous collaboration platform that encourages and facilitates collective knowledge construction through collaborative writing of wiki pages. Thus wiki-use in the classroom closely adheres to the Web 2.0 technology ideology by turning students into producers of knowledge. It enables students to learn by observing and experiencing ideas alternate to their own through participation in a collective enterprise. Wikis have many other properties that make it a suitable technology to support various kinds of learning activities. Recent and ongoing research emphasizes the added benefit of using wiki-based technology to supplement and enhance traditional modes of learning and permanently places wikis as a key-technology in the future educational arena.

Wired for Learning: An Educator's Guide to Web 2.0, pages 137–151
Copyright © 2009 by Information Age Publishing
All rights of reproduction in any form reserved.

INTRODUCTION

Computer-supported collaborative learning is an active area of research in the learning sciences. One significant advantage to moving some of the cooperative learning online is that it enables students to effectively work asynchronously. A significant issue with computer-mediated learning environments concerns making the technology easy enough to use so that the students will buy-in. Arguing to learn and knowledge-building communities are examples of the many kinds of collaborative learning tasks that can be effectively mediated by technology. Students today have familiarity with a wide variety of applications: one can assume that the students are by-and-large proficient users of technology, although not necessarily programmers and/or engineers.

A wiki is a special kind of web site that supports (a)synchronous co-editing and sharing of wikipages enabling students to meet virtually at their convenience and asynchronously (collectively) work on a class project (Byron, 2005). Wiki environments do not provide much control over the co-editing of documents. Any user can edit either the content or the structure of the wiki text. Since wiki environments automatically log every change made to the wikipages, no matter how insignificant it might be, earlier versions of the documents are always retrievable.

Wikis have received quite a lot of attention in the educational community. The recent workshop at CSCL 2007 (Lund, 2007) and symposium at ICLS 2008 (Pierroux et al., 2008) is testimony to the growing general interest in exploiting wiki-based technology to supplement and enhance traditional methods of collaborative learning. Wikis have many properties that make it a suitable technology to support various kinds of learning activities. Many types of wikis exist and most are offered as open-source and without royalty. Wikis are relatively easy to learn how to use: using a wiki is within the skill set of both science and non-science students in high school or college. Students can share and co-edit documents. Documents can be organized into a network, and contain any number and kinds of attachments. Since the wiki is accessible online, students are free to review, retrieve, and edit documents from any number of physical locations. Because the documents are online the students potentially have access to all of the documents generated by the class, whether they were developed individually or collectively. Wiki environments are extendable, modifiable and can be easily preformatted and scaffolded to support a variety of educational activities.

THE "WIKI"

The wiki was originally developed by Ward Cunningham, and it's major contribution is the fast manipulation of a collection of free-form textual documents (Leuf & Cunningham, 2001). No special software is required as users modify pages in an editor accessible through the standard web browser. Users only work with the actual page content, called wikitext, which does not require any knowledge of complex HMTL tags. The content can be augmented using a simplified markup language to indicate various structural and visual conventions. Some wikis include a WYSIWYG editor for this purpose. Wikis collect metadata about every change made

Figure 8.1 Wikipedia's front page.

to a wikipage not matter how insignificant it is. This information can be reviewed on a page commonly referred to as "Recent changes" where modifications can be easily identified and the page reverted to a previous state. Many wikis associate a separate "discussion" page with each wikipage enabling the community to discuss/debate the content being added to or removed from the actual wiki article.

Wikis are very democratic in nature yet anarchistic. Every user has the same amount of power/control and anonymous users often have the same rights as registered users. Everyone can edit both the content and the structure of the wiki. Because of the equality of rights, there is also no division of labor. There is no director that tells subordinates what to do. Individuals select the role that best fits their preferences. This approach, that appears chaotic at first, has been very successful with Wikipedia being the most famous example.

WIKIS FOR EDUCATION

Schwartz et al. (2004) defined a selection criterion for educational wikis and highlighted how distance learning and education in general can benefit from using wikis and claimed that its full potential in the educational arena is yet to be realized. These criteria are:

- Cost: wiki's are open source
- Complexity: technical support is readily available online and the wiki writing is easy to learn
- Control: access can be restricted
- Clarity: easy to navigate and observe evolution of the wiki content
- Portability: can be accessed through any browser
- A common set of editing features: WYSIWYG editing, image insertion, etc.

Wang & Turner (2004) stated that wiki collaboration encourages students to be co-creators of the course content. Wiki components specific to education that meet the special needs of the classroom are needed that, for example, preserve ownership of content and prevent concurrent edits. Raitman, Augar & Zhou (2005) investigated the utility of online discussions mediated by a wiki. Most students enjoyed participating in the online discussion, however the majority of the students continued to prefer face-to-face discussions. The online discussion worked best for the students who were most willing to "buy-in" to using the technology. The limited functionality of HTML, lack of real time communication, and the feeling that it was too easy to delete someone else's contribution from the wiki were examples of issues that emerged.

Wiki technology has been engineered to support more specific sorts of learning activities like "arguing to learn" or "collaborative story telling." The following discussion presents an overview of a few of these studies.

Collaborative Writing

Collaborative Story Telling

The benefits of creative writing using a computer have been studied quite a bit but primarily amongst students at the post-primary level (Désilets et al., 2005). The collaborative, web-based nature of wikis has great potential in mediating this kind of activity and the wikis' simplistic nature makes them a viable option to support collaborative writing amongst students at the primary level. Désilets et al. conducted five case studies where teams of two to five primary level students used a wiki to collaboratively write a story. The wiki chosen was Lizzy, which focuses on usability by non-technical users (e.g. primary school children). The goal of the study was to have students learn about the (collaborative) technology, investigate the applicability of wikis for the younger students, and help the students practice composition skills.

The activity was divided into two phases. The story was supposed to be non-linear—essentially a web version of the genre that exists in paper form ("Choose your own adventure" books). In the "design phase" students developed an idea off-line and created an *abstract map* of the storyline, showing places, activity, actions et cetera. During the "writing phase," the students practiced composition while they played with alternate scenarios of how readers might potentially traverse the "web of the story." During this phase, each team of students collaboratively created the story while they worked independently on separate wikipages. The students were encouraged to talk to each other to coordinate their work and to seek technical help. After each writing session the teacher reviewed the story contents, and posted comments on the title pages ranging from general praise to criticism.

Overall, this work demonstrated that wiki-based collaborative storytelling is quite feasible at the primary grade level. (If primary school students can effectively use wiki technology, that is "proof" the wiki technology is very easy to.) The students collaborated very closely in the writing phase and although left to self-organize there was a great deal of coordination taking place. The vast majority of the teams did not have a central leader; rather the students were collectively responsible for how they divided up the work. In some teams students randomly navigated the hypertext story hierarchy and filled in the "gaps" when they identified a task not completed. Other teams divided up pages based on interest or feeling of competence in terms of completing a particular task. The most popular strategy was the "random walk" as it was most straightforward. Regardless of the strategy chosen they observed a strong sense of collective responsibility and ownership for the story. Students that had been assigned a particular set of tasks or pages did not hesitate to contribute to other pages or tasks if they felt it was necessary. Conversely students were comfortable with teammates occasionally "helping out" with their work. The wiki also efficiently mediated the asynchronous collaboration between the instructor and the students. The teacher's comments were invariably read by the students at the next work session and immediately acted upon.

The abstract map played a key role in coordination. Unfortunately since the abstract map was not editable online the students could not use it to mark their progress on their joint task. Ideally this kind of coordination artifact should be viewable and editable on the wiki as an overview of the team's progress.

Collaborative Essay Writing

An empirical study presented by Wang et al. (2005) focused on examining the educational benefit of using wikis in a freshman-level course that taught *English as a second language*. The course required the teams of students to collaboratively write an essay in English on a specific topic. An off-the-shelf wiki, SushiWiki, was used to mediate the work. Students (and teacher) interacted during the project by exchanging annotations and comments in and around the essay text. At the end of the semester a final exam was given that assessed the students' acquired knowledge.

The wiki event logs were analyzed, specifically editing behaviors and frequency of writing, and examined in relation to the final exam scores. Overall, the average scores on the exam were quite high which might indicate increased learning as a result of this "new kind" of learning activity. Dividing the teams into *high* and *low wiki usage* teams showed a significant, but inverse, relation between wiki usage and exam performance. The *low usage* teams showed a slightly better performance on the final exam than the *high usage* teams challenging the idealistic hypothesis regarding the "natural" educational benefits of wikis. However, Wang et al. stated that these results should be interpreted cautiously and that they do not necessarily suggest a causal link between *low* or *high* wiki usage and (un)successful learning. The study lacks random grouping thus the possibility of pre-existing (perhaps unsuccessful) student relationships can undermine the validity of the analysis. The empirical evidence, however, can be used to advance educational technology research so as to produce wiki environments that provide the *right* support for the educational domain. Other efforts, for example, have identified a close relationship between the success of a collaborative project and *the amount* and *kinds* of work carried out on the wiki (Larusson & Alterman, 2007).

Arguing to Learn

The CoWeb developed at Georgia Institute of Technology is one of the earliest attempts at developing wiki platforms for educational use (Guzdial et al., 2001; Rick & Guzdial, 2006). Multiple versions of the original CoWeb platform have been developed to support different kinds of tasks and classes.

CoWeb has for example been used in a freshman-level English class where students engaged in two main learning activities (Rick et al., 2002). Initially, students participated in an activity called *close-reading* where a prose or a poem was posted for students to informally discuss and debate its meaning. The discussion, posted on individual pages, linked back directly into the relevant locations of the prose or poem. Students commented upon each other's comments and also upon each other's essays. The original *close-reading* chat session was preserved, and comments on the original discussion were directly linked to it (see Figure 8.2).

There were two sections of the class that were taught by the same instructor. The first section consisting of 24 students used CoWeb to complete their various assignments whereas a comparison section used a threaded-discussion environment for the close reading session and worked individually on the essays. No notable differences between the two groups in terms effort were observed: the students in each class devoted an equal amount of time to the class. The students in the class that used CoWeb had significantly better attitudes toward collaboration than the comparison class. The class that used CoWeb performed better and learned more.

Close-reading   Comments are linked to close-reading

Figure 8.2 Additional comments are directly linked to the initial close-reading discussion.

Twelve students were chosen at random and their assignments reviewed by the instructor and an outside colleague. The students' work on both the close-readings and the essay writing was rated according to a predefined schema. Examples of criterion included: *"Engagement with class material," "Reflective/Recursive Writing Practices," "Formation of critical questions,"* and *"Critical/Close Reading Skills."* In each rating category the students in the class that used CoWeb outperformed the comparison class, in most by a large statistically significant amount. The students in the CoWeb section did significantly better on writing essays than the comparison class, particularly in how they organized their essays. CoWeb students also showed significant superiority in their use of critical vocabulary.

Supporting a Knowledge Community

A *knowledge community* (Scardamalia & Bereiter, 1991) is a type of collaborative activity where learning is elevated through shared sociocultural practices that emerge and evolve as students with shared interests and goals interact as they strive to meet those goals.

Building an Encyclopedia to Produce/Attain Knowledge and Technology Literacy

Because of the rapidly growing networked economy, students entering the workforce must attain skillful usage of collaborative, creative, project-based technologies that support work practices and critical thinking (Bruns & Humphreys, 2005). These skills go beyond basic technology literacy and require a more social constructivist learning process that enables students to explore the social, political, and economic context rendering the standard "history lesson" traditionally provided by the teacher not feasible.

In order to develop these abilities an approach more inline with the ideology behind of the *object of study*, Web 2.0 technology, is required (Bruns & Humphreys, 2005). The technology is not merely a "holding tank" or distribution channel of instructor-produced content consumed by students but rather a collaborative workspace that turns students into producers of knowledge. At the Queensland University of Technology wikis were identified as useful for this purpose with two key benefits. It enables students to *become a knowledge community* through interaction and creativity where they are obliged to create, present, promote, and communicate their understanding. The wiki also helps them *understand the knowledge community* since, through its use, they develop skills necessary for participating efficiently, a learning benefit that is equally important and cannot be ignored.

In 2004, students used MediaWiki to develop an encyclopedic collection of information on new media concepts and topics. Initially, students developed a brief annotated bibliography on a topic of their choice and then formed groups that further collaborated on a major wiki entry covering a communally chosen topic. At later stages individual students expanded on the topic by adding sub topics. The students used the discussion pages and "Recent changes" page to facilitate their group work and keep track of others. The instructors also used the revision history to make sure every student was on top of their task. The wiki was also used to facilitate tutorial work and student interaction outside of classes. Tutors organized discussion groups to coordinate students' emerging projects.

For many students writing wiki articles was not straightforward. Encyclopedic summaries require a different structure and style from the more familiar argumentative essays students are frequently asked to write. The students were required to present both (or all) sides of the argument which introduces a new style of communication and the process of students negotiating and agreeing on how to proceed with constructing the article has educational value which cannot be underestimated (Bruns & Humphreys, 2005). In the long run a key benefit of using wiki technology in this capacity is that an "article" can be reused in future semesters, with each successive generation of students building on top of previous efforts, expanding on the topics or adding new topics. This approach to preserving articles provides a new resource for teaching and research in general and can be used as a networked resource for students. Unlike a textbook, the wiki version of a text can accumulate new commentaries that further explore the content of the text and linkages between various related elements between different articles.

Coordinating the work of some 150 students across six classes was not straightforward; for example, it was increasingly difficult to prevent duplication of work and overlapping topics. While the students were relatively quick at becoming familiar at learning how to interact with the technology (adding and editing pages), they did struggle with the content format. Some of the articles resembled the traditional single viewpoint student essay that arrives at the "one" conclusion. A possible explanation is the nature of the classes. A small number of students studying the same topic might have the same or similar homogenous views of the topic and therefore unintentionally produce a one-sided report instead of a neutral encyclopedia summary that presents multiple "sides of the story."

Building the Teacher into the Wiki

The teacher's role, and place, in the online wiki activity has not received a lot of attention (Lund & Smørdal, 2006):

> One major challenge for learning in technology-rich, collaborative environments is to develop design principles that balance learner exploration with a more goal directed effort. We argue that teachers play a key role in such

efforts and that educational wiki designs need to allow such a role in order to support group knowing.

It is reasonable to assume that wiki-mediated learning can benefit greatly by providing support, not only for the students' needs, but also for the instructor, especially when the wiki mediates the work of younger students.

The study reported in Lund & Smørdal (2006) presents findings from two *English as a foreign language* courses at an Upper Secondary School in Norway. A MediaWiki was used to enable students to construct a knowledge repository about The United States (study 1) and a fictional town influenced by the students' readings of topics related to the United Kingdom (study 2). The goal was to combine the "encyclopedic" characteristics of Wikipedia with a more personal "lived" approach highlighting "what we have learned."

Analyzing the wiki history and survey responses revealed that the students felt a gradual sense of collective enterprise and liked the wikis' structure and sense of community that emerged from joint ownership and the editing of documents. The students' responses were distinctly positive towards the technology, indicating that features such as the revision history was extremely useful when comparing and sharing information on what they were learning. Students also reported that it was a win/win situation where they both helped others and received help in return and were provided with multiple viewpoints on a shared topic of interest.

In a first study, the students did not appear to feel completely engaged in a collective knowledge construction project as they sought to create extensions of the content indefinitely rather than reading and revising their fellow students' contributions. The teacher had to intervene twice and instruct them to change focus resulting in more revisions than additions.

The goal of second study was twofold. First, construct the task so as to create a greater sense of community with a shared goal of producing a collective object. Second, the teacher should provide a greater presence on the wiki in order to provide prompts, structure, and direction. Results from the second study indicated that the teacher's presence on the wiki had only materialized occasionally on the wiki and usually in the form of simple questions regarding categories or namespaces rather than content. Furthermore, analyzing the event logs revealed that topic pages on the wiki usually had only one primary author with other users primarily fixing grammatical errors.

The results of these studies emphasize the need to find the teacher a decent workspace on the wiki, where they are provided with carefully developed tools that enable them to guide and foster students' collective cognition online. The need for more detailed logging mechanisms, visualization and various kinds of display mechanisms that highlight work patterns of students on the wiki would be of great use. It would enable teachers to trigger, stimulate, monitor, and guide online activities conducive to learning in the non-fixed activity space which is the wiki.

Awareness and Navigation

In asynchronous computer-mediated environments it is critical that the technology provides users with ways to acquire awareness as it helps them guide future work and coordinate their efforts (Gutwin & Greenberg, 2002; Gutwin & Greenberg, 2004). In terms of the wiki this refers to awareness of the evolution of the workspace itself but also awareness of how others are interacting with the workspace and each other (Gutwin & Greenberg, 1999). "Keeping current" in online collaborations can be improved by providing visualizations of user activity (Janssen et al., 2007).

On the asynchronous wiki users can get lost in textual hyperspace for a number of reasons (Reinhold, 2006). The wikis' web-in-the-web nature with its infinite possible interlinkages between related pages can make navigation confusing. Without a fixed policy, the participants can easily create a wiki site with a hodgepodge of different kinds of links. If different users add links for different sorts of reasons, it becomes very difficult to anticipate the organization of the site as one navigates.

Navigation would be easier if the wiki provided a visualization of the overall structure of the wiki site and then helped users to identify relationships between articles that he/she is currently reading or editing and the overall wiki structure.

Reinhold (2006) and Reinhold and Abawi (2006) discuss prototype components, WikiTrails and ContextBar, which can be layered on top of existing wikis in order to provide an elaborate visualization of the wiki structure. The goal is to simplify understanding the complex relationships between the wiki elements and reduce the complexity of navigating by displaying the trail traversed by the user as in order to reach the currently selected page and the page's outgoing links.

Eyes of a wiki presented in Han and Kim (2005) provides a similar kind of navigational aid by classifying the wiki page link hierarchy onto 3-levels (see Figure 8.3). The top level shows the "upper" pages, which provide an overview of the main topic, that link to the currently visited page. The middle level includes pages at the same level that the current page links to. The third level shows the sub-pages that provide more detailed information on a particular sub topic that the current page links to. Each page link is assigned a relevance score based on the number of links the wikipage contains to pages covering the same or similar topic.

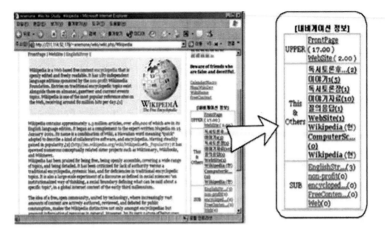

Figure 8.3 Eyes of a wiki classifies related wikipages into a 3-level hierarchy.

In a case study two groups of students collaboratively produce a knowledge repository on Computer Science related topics using a wiki. One group was provided with the navigational map while the other used a standard wiki. The two groups produced similar numbers of wikipages and the number of editing and reading activities was also very similar. The wiki without the navigational map had a much simpler and shallower link structure. Furthermore, the students that used the navigational map also had a significantly higher number of cross-links between articles than the normal wiki. Students using the normal wiki did not as easily position themselves within the chaotic wiki structure. It was harder for them to identify alternate, related, wiki locations of interest, and they felt uncomfortable constructing a more complex information-rich structure.

WikiNavMap presents the user with a map of the overall wiki structure, and it highlights the most recent pages, most active pages, and pages that are important (Ullman & Kay, 2007). Developed as a plugin for TracWiki it has been used and evaluated within the research lab as well as in a course on "learning and technology" where the wiki mediated group work. The students created a very detailed, interlinked collection of a vast number of wikipages (190) whereas the research lab only produced 32 pages documenting their ongoing research work. While the researchers found the component to be very useful making navigation easier the students in the class did not find it quite so helpful. In short, the navigational map quickly became too large to be useful as it was too cluttered to make out, locating information and navigating the wiki.

Ullman & Kay do provide suggestions as to how future work can benefit from this experiment, e.g., by making the fisheye methods more selective

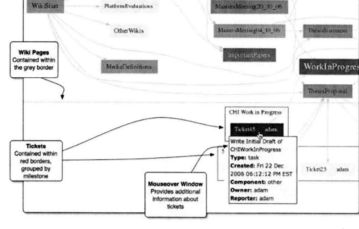

Figure 8.4   WikiNavMap provides a visualization of the entire wiki structure.

about the choice of elements it displays by perhaps presenting more "locally relevant" and interesting content.

FUTURE RESEARCH

Previous research on wikis in education has focused primarily on deploying the technology and evaluating the students' learning "after the fact." Less attention has been paid to studying the collaborative activity itself, and principles for engineering wiki environments to support different kinds of student collaborations. For example, for a team term project mediated by a wiki, how could one engineer a wiki platform so that the students could work in joint problem space? Or another example would concern the on-line discussion of course material. How can a wiki be scaffolded so that substantial discussions of the course material will emerge and be "witnessed" by a large number of students in the class? In both of these cases, the issue is to explore whether wikis can support the "collaborative" part of collaborative learning.

If future research addresses these questions then it becomes possible to produce guidelines and principles that designers/engineers of wiki-based learning environments can apply in order to ensure successful coordination and collaboration and (improve) the learning experience.

CONCLUSIONS

A wiki is an asynchronous collaboration platform that encourages and facilitates collective knowledge construction, in its most basic form through collaborative writing of wiki pages. A wiki is easy to learn how to use. It has an extendable structure, and it is malleable. For these reasons, it is an ideal technology for mediating a wide variety of collaborative learning activities.

Wikis closely adhere to the Web 2.0 technology ideology that turns students into producers of knowledge. It enables students to *learn by observing and experiencing* ideas alternate to their own through participation in a collective enterprise.

Wikis have already received a lot of attention in the learning sciences and educational technology communities. This article provided a brief overview of some of the more interesting wiki-uses in education and examples of learning activities that wikis have been used to support. Recent and ongoing research emphasizes the added benefit of using wiki-based technology to supplement and enhance traditional modes of learning and permanently places wikis as a key-technology in the future educational arena.

REFERENCES

Bruns, A., & Humphreys, S. (2005). Wikis in teaching and assessment: The M/cyclopedia project. In *WikiSym '05: Proceedings of the 2005 international symposium on wikis* (pp. 25–32). New York: ACM Press.

Byron, M. (2005). Teaching with tiki. *Teaching Philosophy, 28*(2), 108–113.

Gutwin, C., & Greenberg, S. (1999). The effects of workspace awareness support on the usability of real-time distributed groupware. *ACM Transactions on Computer–Human Interaction, 6*(3), 243–281.

Gutwin, C., & Greenberg, S. (2002). A descriptive framework of workspace awareness for real-time groupware. *Computer Supported Cooperative Work (CSCW), 11*(3), 411–446.

Gutwin, C., & Greenberg, S. (2004). The importance of awareness for team cognition in distributed collaboration. In E. Salas, S. M., Fiore, & J. A. Cannon-Bowers (Eds.), *Team cognition: Process and performance at the inter- and intra-individual level* (pp. 177–201). Washington, DC: American Psychological Association Press.

Guzdial, M., Rick, J., & Kehoe, C. (2001). Beyond adoption to invention: Teacher-created collaborative activities in higher education. *Journal of the Learning Sciences, 10*(3), 265–279.

Han, H., & Kim, H. (2005). Eyes of a wiki: Automated navigation map. *Lecture Notes in Computer Science, 3815*, 186–193.

Janssen, J., Erkens, G., Kanselaar, G., & Jaspers, J. (2007). Visualization of participation: Does it contribute to successful computer-supported collaborative learning? *Computers & Education, 49*(4), 1037–1065.

Larusson, J. A., & Alterman, R. (2007). Tracking online collaborative work as representational practice: Analysis and tool. In C. Steinfield, B. Pentland, M. Ackerman, & N. Contractor (Eds.), *Communities and Technologies 2007: Proceedings of the Third Communities and Technologies Conference* (pp. 245–264). London: Springer.

Leuf, B., & Cunningham, W. (2001). *The wiki way: Quick collaboration on the web.* Boston: Addison-Wesley.

Lund, A. (2007). *Wiki research: Knowledge advancement and design.* Workshop at CSCL 2007 (Computer Supported Collaborative Learning conference). Rutgers University, New Brunswick, NJ.

Lund, A., & Smørdal, O. (2006). Is there a space for the teacher in a wiki? In *Wiki-Sym '06: Proceedings of the international symposium on Symposium on Wikis* (pp. 37–46). New York: ACM Press.

Pierroux, P., Rasmussen, I., Lund, A., Smørdal, O. Stahl, G., Larusson, J. A., & Alterman, R. (2008). Supporting and tracking collective cognition in wikis. In *Proceedings of ICLS 2008: International Conference for the Learning Sciences: Vol. 3* (pp. 330–337). The International Society of the Learning Sciences.

Raitman, R. A., & Zhou, N. W. (2005). Employing wikis for online collaboration in the e-learning environment: Case study. In *Proceedings of the Third international Conference on information Technology and Applications (Icita '05) Vol. 2* (pp. 142–146). Washington, DC: IEEE Computer Society.

Reinhold, S. (2006). Wikitrails: Augmenting wiki structure for collaborative, interdisciplinary learning. In *WikiSym '06: Proceedings of the international symposium on Symposium on Wikis* (pp. 47–58). New York: ACM Press.

Reinhold, S., & Abawi, D. (2006). Concepts for extending wiki systems to supplement collaborative learning. *Lecture Notes in Computer Science, 3942,* 755–767.

Rick, J., Guzdial, M., Carroll, K., Holloway-Attaway, L., & Walker, B. (2002). Collaborative learning at low cost: CoWeb use in English composition. In G. Stahl (Ed.), *Computer support for collaborative learning: Foundations for a CSCL community. Conference proceedings of the CSCL2002 conference* (pp. 435–442). Mahwah, NJ: Erlbaum.

Rick, J., & Guzdial, M. (2006). Situating CoWeb: A scholarship of application. *International Journal of Computer-Supported Collaborative Learning, 1*(1), 89–115.

Scardamalia, M., & Bereiter, M. (1994). Computer support for knowledge-building communities. *Journal of the Learning Sciences, 3*(3), 265–283.

Schwartz, L., Clark, S., Cossarin, M., & Rudolph, J. (2004). Educational wikis: Features and selection criteria. *International Review of Research in Open and Distance Learning, 5*(1).

Ullman, A. J., & Kay, J. (2007). WikiNavMap: A visualisation to supplement team-based wikis. In *CHI '07: CHI '07 extended abstracts on human factors in computing systems* (pp. 2711–2716). New York: ACM Press.

Wang, C., & Turner, D. (2004). Extending the wiki paradigm for use in the classroom. In *Proceedings of the International Conference on Information Technology* (pp. 255–259). Washington, DC: IEEE Computer Society Press.

Wang, H. C., Lu, C. H., Yang, J. Y., Hu, H. W., Chiou, G. F., Chiang, Y. T., Hsu, W. L., & Sinica, A. (2005). An empirical exploration of using wiki in an English as a second language course. In *Proceedings of the Fifth IEEE International Conference on Advanced Learning Technologies* (pp. 155–157). Washington, DC: IEEE Computer Society Press.

CHAPTER 9

REFLECTIVE LEARNING FOR THE NET GENERATION

John Sandars
Christopher Murray
Maggie McPherson
The University of Leeds

ABSTRACT

Net Generation students enthusiastically use a variety of Web 2.0 technologies for "leisure and pleasure," especially social networking and media sharing sites. Many students skilfully present multimedia personal narratives on these sites but engagement in text based reflective academic work is often low and does not align with their preferred learning style. Our experience is that the innovative use of Web 2.0 technologies can successfully engage these students in reflective learning. In addition, students can feel empowered and develop multiple literacies that are essential for lifelong learning. There are important challenges, and implications for further research, to the use of Web 2.0 technologies for reflective learning. These include tutor and institutional responses to Web 2.0 technologies, the assessment of reflective learning when multimedia is substituted for text, the use of digital stories in e-portfolios, the development of multiple literacies and the use of Web 2.0 in the wider genre of digital storytelling.

Wired for Learning: An Educator's Guide to Web 2.0, pages 153–168
Copyright © 2009 by Information Age Publishing
All rights of reproduction in any form reserved.

INTRODUCTION

Learning by doing is a fundamental process that has allowed the human race to survive. Our cavemen ancestors quickly began to recognise that sabre tooth tigers bite and should be avoided. We can use pedagogic jargon and call this process experiential learning (Jarvis, 1995). Our experiences are incredibly rich and are driven by various motives and beliefs. We try to make sense of why events have occurred and to identify what we can do to alter our future behaviour. This is reflective learning (Jarvis 1995).

Educational theorists have regarded reflective learning as an essential attribute of any learner and a vital component of any educational process (Foley, 2000). Current educational policy, especially in higher and adult education, has now become awash with this concept and reflective learning is widely accepted as an essential competence for professional education and lifelong learning. In the context of medical education, there is hardly any course that does not have reflective learning as one of its stated objectives. However, the enthusiasm of medical educators for reflective learning does not appear to be greeted with the same intensity by their students.

In this chapter, we will explore the possible reasons for low student engagement and discuss how the innovative use of Web 2.0 approaches can help students to become reflective learners. We recognise that some of our initial work has only been within undergraduate medical education but we provide descriptions of the practical use of Web 2.0 technologies to develop reflective learning in both this context and in postgraduate students on an ICT in Education programme. Finally, we highlight the challenges for future development and research in this essential area of education.

BACKGROUND

The educational theorist Dewey (1933) made an enormous impact on progressive education and firmly placed reflective thought at the centre of the process of learning. His ideas were further developed by other educationalists, including Schon (1987) who proposed that reflective learning was the central process by which professionals made sense of their "messy" world, and Mezirow (1991) who emphasised its transformative potential, enabling existing perspectives to be critically challenged. The educational world was quick to adopt reflective learning as the basis for lifelong personal and professional development. Most medical undergraduate degree courses now expect students to keep a regular reflective diary and when assessed it is invariably by a written reflective assignment.

Higher education places great importance on text based media for learning and teaching, with the expectation that students will be able to present their inner thoughts and emotions as written narrative accounts. However, a recent study of undergraduate medical students identified that some students stated that they did not engage in reflective learning since it did not align with their learning preferences (Grant, Kinnersley, Metcalf, Pill & Houston, 2006). Our own unpublished research has also noted this barrier but students also mentioned that they took part in reflection outside their formal educational context and did not need to formalise the process.

Boud and Walker (1998) note that the main challenge for reflective learning is the engagement of students. We responded to this challenge by trying to understand the learner perspective and to develop an approach to reflective learning that was based on these insights.

THE NET GENERATION AND THEIR USE OF WEB 2.0

Our current undergraduate medical students are members of what has been called the Net Generation (Oblinger & Oblinger, 2005). This group of young people has grown up with a variety of new technologies and the Internet as an integral part of daily life and learning. Observers of the evolving nature of the internet have noted that there has been a change from a platform that previously only provided discrete packages of published information, such as web sites, to one in which there is interaction and participation between users. This change in the functionality of the current web has been called Web 2.0 to mark its difference to the previous aspects of the web (O'Reilly, 2005). The new technologies that support this change include blogs, wikis, media sharing sites (such as Flickr and YouTube), social network sites (such as Facebook and MySpace) and social bookmark sites (such as Del.icio.us). In addition, young people are often constantly connected and socially interacting with others, especially by the use of mobile phones and instant messaging.

The Net Generation has not only become more technological savvy but they also appear to learn in fundamentally different ways to previous generations. Prensky (2001) has suggested that this is because the brains of the Net Generation have become wired differently at an early developmental stage, at a time when the neuronal structure has increased plasticity. There are several features that are typical of the way that the Net Generation learns:

- Environments that are rich in multi-media images, especially visual and audio, are preferred to those that are predominantly composed of text.
- There is a preference to be actively engaged in tasks

- Motivation to learn comes from being actively involved in the learning and by their attempts to answer questions that arise during a task.
- There is a preference to work in groups and they regard social interaction as a very important part of their learning.

We surveyed all first year undergraduate medical students in 2007. The average age was 19 years and over 90 per cent used instant messaging, 80 per cent used a media sharing site (such as Flickr or YouTube) and 97 per cent had a profile on a social networking site (such as Facebook or MySpace). Similar results have been found in surveys of first year students in a range of disciplines at the University of Melbourne and the University of Oxford (Kennedy, Krause & Judd, 2006; White, 2007).

We also surveyed all second year undergraduate medical students in 2007 to identify their learning preferences. The most frequent preferences were bodily kinaesthetic (52.8%) and interpersonal (47.8%).

Recent literacy research has highlighted a "digital disconnect" in US school children (Levin & Arafeh, 2002). They do not engage in written work at school but are active informally outside school with the creation and exchange of written text using a range of technologies and media. We suspect that the same dichotomy also occurs in undergraduate medical students.

A study of undergraduate students in a range of disciplines noted that students were highly receptive to the use of new technologies in their courses provided that they could see direct benefit and that it was not being used merely as a gimmick (Conole, de Laat, Dillon & Darby, 2007).

Our conclusion was that our undergraduate medical students were typical of the Net Generation, both regards their high use of new technologies, including Web 2.0, and their learning preferences. We had the expectation that students would be used to working with a range of media, including images, sound and text, in an informal context and with a variety of new technologies. Our challenge was now to offer opportunities for reflective learning that were closely aligned to the student experience.

USING MULTIMEDIA FOR REFLECTIVE LEARNING

Making meaning from experience requires the construction of a narrative. This can be through the use of text but many students find it difficult to describe their thoughts and emotions though words. However, visual and audio media allow these deeply personal experiences to be more easily accessed and portrayed. Gauntlett (2008) has recently highlighted the creative potential of using a range of media to stimulate reflective learning and Hull and Nelson (2005) have emphasised that the use of multiple media (images, words and music) is not simply an additive art but increases the meaning-making potential of any narrative.

There has never been an easier time to combine the use of multimedia with technology to create and present a personal and reflective narrative. Narrative is usually presented as a structured story in which there is an overall coherent theme rather than a random collection of media. This structuring of narrative increases reflective learning through an active and creative process in the author (Ohler 2008). Digital storytelling is process in which digital technology is used to combine a number of media into a coherent narrative.

DIGITAL STORYTELLING FOR REFLECTIVE LEARNING

The genre of digital storytelling is ill defined and includes a variety of approaches and uses. Paul and Fiebich (2005) describe their attempts to develop a taxonomy of digital storytelling but on closer inspection they appear to use the term for documentary style multimedia presentations, either through established media providers (e.g. newspapers) or through community groups. More specific uses of digital storytelling for reflective learning have been described in the literature:

Community Development

Since the early 1990s there have been numerous schemes, with roots in community arts and oral history, to encourage individuals to present their own digital stories, especially using videos. Well known schemes include the Centre for Digital Storytelling in the US (Lambert 2003) and Capture Wales (Meadows 2003). Authors not only originate their own material (video, still photographs and audio) but they are also active in the editing of their own story. Usually the work is facilitated and uses a structured approach to create the story. The benefits for the authors include empowerment and the development of new skills, both technical and for literacy.

K–12 Education

There has been enormous interest in the use of digital storytelling in US schools (Ohler, 2008), with similar benefits to its authors as for its use in community development. The use of a structured storytelling approach (as for community development) is variable and this is dependent on the overall purpose. Identified benefits include the development of self-confidence, literacy skills, computer and multimedia presentation skills, reflection and increased content knowledge.

Digital Faith Stories

Kaare and Lundby (2006) used facilitated and structured digital storytelling (as for community development) with young people to help them to identify their faith beliefs. Participants enjoyed using the new creative media and they stated that the approach helped them to reflect on their belief systems.

Pre-Service Teacher Training

It is not surprising that digital storytelling has also been used for teacher training. The purpose is wide and reflection may be the main focus for some schemes but often it is similar to its use in K–12 education (Lathem, Reyes & Qi, 2006). The use of multimedia production for a reflective portfolio appears to increase reflection (Spurgeon & Bowen 2002).

Teacher Professional Development

Although the term digital storytelling has not been specifically used, the use of photographs to create a visual narrative as a stimulus for reflection for professional development in teachers is well established (Lemon, 2007).

Courses in Higher Education

Video-based storytelling has been used to develop reflection in undergraduate media design courses (McDonnell, Lloyd & Valkenburg, 2004). A recent pilot study has highlighted the high acceptance and effectiveness of this approach for reflective practice in landscape design students (Jenkins & Lonsdale, 2007).

A variety of technological approaches have been used in the above studies. The commonest approaches have been the use of preinstalled storytelling software, such as iLife on Mac computers or PhotoStory 3 and Windows Movie Maker on Windows based computers. These allow the creation of multimedia presentations by combining photographs, videos and audio. Sometimes text is added, usually on as an introductory title page or as subtitles. Occasionally more sophisticated multimedia editing software has been used. PowerPoint offers widely available and familiar presentation software and has mainly been used in K–12 education.

THE GENRE OF MULTIMEDIA BLOGGING FOR REFLECTIVE LEARNING

There appears to be little in the way of the use of Web 2.0 technologies or mobile camera phones in the previous description of reflective digital storytelling but videoblogging, or vlogging, is an emerging genre for reflective learning (Educause, 2005). The basic approach is to use videos, with or without audio, as the primary medium for the blog. These personal often contain reflections on current topics of interest. The videos can be created with the previously described software but they can also be taken by mobile phone and directly uploaded to a blog. This process is called moblogging (Trafford, 2005).

The use of videoblogging, with or without the use of mobile phones, as a specific approach to develop reflective learning is not widely described but it has the potential to be used in an identical way as reflective digital storytelling.

USING WEB 2.0 AND DIGITAL STORYTELLING IN UNDERGRADUATE MEDICAL EDUCATION

Digital storytelling for reflective learning was introduced into a first year undergraduate personal and professional development module. The aim of this module was to encourage students to reflect on their experience of first meeting a patient. All students visited a patient in their home and were expected to identify their thoughts and feelings of what it was like to communicate with a patient who they had not met before but also to consider the perceived thoughts and feelings of the patient.

Students were given an opportunity to choose how to create their digital story but the overall approach used a range of Web 2.0 technologies and mobile phones. Each student had a personal blog that was created by using open source software (http://elgg.org/) on an institutional platform outside the main VLE (Virtual Learning Environment). The blog allowed students to write reflective accounts, to store images from a variety of sources (such as free and publicly accessible media sharing sites and photograph archives), to store images taken from their mobile phones and to create digital stories. This use was analogous to using a reflective diary and a scrap book (Williams & Jacobs, 2004). Students who had a mobile camera phone could collect images as and when they wanted to capture a particular thought or feeling. No patient identifying photographs were taken. The digital story was presented as a PowerPoint show since this presentation software was familiar to all the students, was widely available on the institutional computer system and could be easily uploaded to the blog.

We noted that digital stories were created in three ways. Some students used their mobile camera phones to take images before, during and after the event and these were included in their final presentations. Others took mobile camera phone images but, after considering their story, used a mixture of their own images and others they had sourced through the internet, usually through Flickr or Google Images. The remainder used solely pictures they had sourced from the internet.

THE EVALUATION

Students frequently mentioned the "fun" aspect of the whole process and they enjoyed being creative.

> I don't tend to use pictures in that way but I discovered a new way of expressing my feelings and it was good.

This engagement and enthusiasm contrasted with their thoughts on traditional methods of writing reflective accounts and text-based presentations. Being able to be creative and artistic was a positive for the students, particularly due to the nature of the rest of their course,

> It was good to get away from science and be more artistic!

Students also commented that they liked using technology that they were familiar with, such as mobile phones, media sharing sites and blogs.

The creation of the digital story took place after the visit and the process of choosing the "right" image to convey their emotions was an important aspect. As one student noted,

> When you start to choose the pictures you are thinking about how you felt exactly and comparing it to the picture and thinking that matches that doesn't!

All stages of the digital storytelling process appeared to stimulate reflection, from initial selection of the photographs to the final presentation of the story.

> I find it very useful because while I was trying to choose my pictures I could actually visualise what was going on at that moment and you can think of the

emotions you were feeling. You think that it will only take 5 minutes but you end up putting a lot of effort into it.

You go greater into depth as well to be more honest and show your feelings.

If you were to write a report on your visit I would have been looking for facts. But I found that I was listening more to what she was saying and how she felt and how I felt.

As tutors, we were impressed by the obvious enthusiasm of the students and the depth of reflection in their presentations.

Overall, we appear to have successfully engaged our undergraduate medical students in reflective learning by using a range of Web 2.0 technologies and also by the use of mobile phones. Blogs were used as a personal learning space that combined both media storage with a creative space. Images were obtained from a variety of media sharing sites. The "always to hand" nature of mobile camera phones encourages spontaneous image capture at times of surprise during an experience, the "disorientating dilemma" that Mezirow (1991) regards as being an essential component of transformative reflective learning. The images can also be uploaded immediately to a blog or transferred at a later date.

USING WEB 2.0 AND DIGITAL STORYTELLING IN A POSTGRADUATE ICT IN EDUCATION PROGRAMME

In this case, digital storytelling for reflective learning was introduced to MA ICT in Education (MAICTE) students during a second semester module about the principles and practice of e-learning. The aim of this module was to encourage learners to reflect on their personal experience of e-learning as a student.

At the outset of the module, the students were informed that this reflection would be assessed in their final piece of work:

> In the assignment itself, you are free to structure your reflection of e-Learning in a format which you judge to be appropriate. However, in order to help you to prepare your work, it is suggested that you keep a digital record to tell the story of your personal exploration of the various topics and your own experiences of e-Learning during the module.

The students had free choice over which devices/software to use and were asked to reflect on a range of issues such as:

- Their own learner profile and learning preferences
- Aspects of individual learning engaged in, e.g., reflective, developmental, etc.

- Aspects of group-based activities participated in
- Which activities were most useful, and why
- Which activities were of least use, and why
- Which topics are critical to incorporate e-Learning into professional practice
- What new knowledge is needed to manage the process of e-Learning
- Whether views of e-Learning change during the module
- If personal learning profile/preferences have changed by the end of the module

At the end of the module, the final session entailed students create a presentation that provided advice for future MAICTE students. A number of students opted to create fairly simple PowerPoint presentations, and some used photos to good effect (Figure 9.1).

An equal number were extremely creative in their approach. One individual produced a great cartoon strip (Figure 9.2). His comments that accompanied this were as follows:

> I tried to create something that was purely based on free use software and internet access (i.e., no cameras, video, voice etc in view of our recent chats on the digital divide) and that was a new process for me.

One student also decided that it would be interesting to take an alternative approach and scanned a pictorial guide (Figure 9.3).

In addition, a couple of students decided that their advice was worth sharing more widely and posted lively presentations in YouTube. Since the full videos are well worth watching, and the print medium of this book cannot

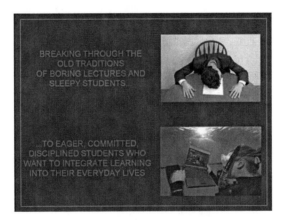

Figure 9.1 Incorporating photos in order to illustrate advice provided to new e-Learners.

Figure 9.2   Comic strip—Luddite Guide for the new e-learner.

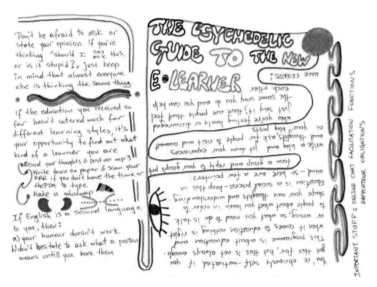

Figure 9.3   Psychedelic Guide to the new e-learner.

do justice to their work, it is suggested that readers try to view the originals at the following URLs: http://www.youtube.com/watch?v=aQNjhNjXvy8, and http://www.youtube.com/watch?v=ixYsLeuELFc.

Finally, these contributions indicate that students had really engaged with the activity and used a wide range of multimedia (video recorders, mobile phones, scanned pictures) and Web 2.0 technologies to carry out the task.

THE EVALUATION

The comments received from many of the MACTE students were extremely positive, highlighting how enjoyable the learning process had been:

> It has been the most enjoyable learning experience I have ever had and overall this course has given me the confidence to do more than I thought I could do. Many thanks to all the tutors and students!

> I am happy that I have chosen this module as I feel full of new knowledge and experiences in a subject that I am very interested in . . .

> I am thankful to e-learning because it provided the opportunity to study something which I am interested in . . .

In particular, one offered the following advice to 'newbies' to the programme:

> Make the most of the experience. It has been the most valuable learning experience I have had to date.

Thus the enthusiasm of the students is patently obvious and they have gone to great lengths to make these contributions despite the fact that these were not to be assessed per se.

FUTURE TRENDS

The use of Web 2.0 technologies for digital storytelling appears to be a valuable pedagogic tool to stimulate reflective learning in the present Net Generation of students and we feel that our experiences have wider application in higher and lifelong learning. Our experience has identified several challenges. The rise in popularity of Web 2.0 technologies for "leisure and pleasure" by young people has resulted in a view by many tutors that these technologies are trivial and not to be used in educational settings. This appears to be compounded by the frequent news stories of misuse by young people. Overcoming this barrier requires strong educational leadership by programme directors. Further research to identify the extent and nature of the views of tutors is recommended.

There is also a tension between the use of Web 2.0 technologies within formal education contexts, especially in higher education, and the more informal public use of the same technologies (Dron, 2007). Students may not be willing to use an institutional VLE but continue to use alternative public approaches that they are already familiar with (White, 2007). The popularity of Web 2.0 approaches by young people is not only the ease of access and usability of the technologies but the important social dimension in which networks of users can be easily developed. An important aspect of reflective learning, especially for young people, is the development of self-identity and this has an essential social dimension (Brown, 1998). Most VLEs have limited ability to provide a similar type of service. The actual constraints, both organisational and technological, of institutional VLEs, and the perceptions of students to institutional systems is important to understand for the further use of digital storytelling and this is an area for further research.

The assessment of reflective learning using multimedia digital stories creates a problem for the current educational system which is heavily biased towards text based assignments (Jackson, 1995). It appears to us that this is divisive for the present generation of learners. One argument that we frequently hear from teachers is that writing is an essential skill for life-long learning but the theory of multiple literacies suggests that this can be achieved through other activities, such as essays on various topics (Hull & Nelson, 2005). There is an argument that the process of writing a story is important to organise thoughts and to stimulate reflection but our experience suggests that many students who create multimedia digital stories go through a similar rigorous process. An area for further research is to compare the student experience and depth of reflection using both approaches. Further research is also required to develop methods of assessment that are more closely aligned with the multimedia aspects of digital storytelling. Collaboration may be required with performance and artistic educators to consider aspects such as how the content is organised and presented to represent a particular experience.

A recent trend in higher education and lifelong learning is the development of e-portfolios in which a variety of artefacts can be collected and presented (Klenowski, Askew, & Carnell, 2006). Digital stories can become one of these artefacts, although most e-portfolios still rely heavily on the collection of text based materials (Barrett, 2006). The use of digital stories in e-portfolios is an area for future research.

Recent literature on multiple literacies has highlighted the need for all lifelong learners to be competent across a range of literacies (Hull & Nelson, 2005). Traditionally, being literate only related to skills in reading and writing in text based media but this notion has now widened to include media and digital literacy. Media literacy refers to the skills required to identify, appreciate and utilise the vast variety of new media, especially visual and audio, that surrounds any learner. There are additional digital literacy skills that are required to ensure that media literacy can be useful to an individual, such as accessing media sharing sites, but there are wider aspects, such as the ability to use the internet and computers. The contribution of digital storytelling to the development of multiple literacies is an area for future research.

There appears to be scant use of Web 2.0 technologies and mobile camera phones in the wide genre of digital storytelling. There are a wide variety of participants, often older than technology savvy Net Generation students, in a wide variety of contexts. The use of new technologies for digital storytelling appears to be an area that is ripe for further development and research.

CONCLUSION

Digital storytelling offers a practical pedagogic application of a variety of Web 2.0 technologies. Our initial work supports the use of this approach to engage Net Generation students in reflective learning but it also appears to stimulate deep reflection. In addition, it empowers students as learners and it has the potential to develop the multiple literacies that are required for lifelong learning. Further development and research is required to see if our experiences can be more widely applied in the various contexts in which the genre of digital storytelling is used for reflective learning. We realise that this new approach can be a significant challenge to higher education institutions and educators, both in control of the learner experience but also assessment procedures.

REFERENCES

Barrett, H. C. (2006). *Researching and evaluating digital storytelling as a deep learning tool.* Paper developed for the Kean University Digital Storytelling Conference June 2005. Retrieved July 15, 2008, from http://www.helenbarrett.com/portfolios/SITEStorytelling2006.pdf.

Boud, D., & Walker, D. (1998). Promoting reflection in professional courses: The challenge of context. *Studies in Higher Education, 23*(2), 191–206.

Brown, J. D. (1998). *The self.* Boston: McGraw-Hill.

Conole, G., de Laat, M., Dillon, T., & Darby, J. (2007). *JISC LXP. Student experiences of technologies. Final report.* Retrieved July 15, 2008, from http://www.jisc.ac.uk/

media/documents/programmes/elearningpedagogy/lxpprojectfinalreport-dec06.pdf.

Dewey, J. (1933). *How we think: A restatement of the relation of reflective thinking to the educative process.* New York: D. C. Heath.

Dron, J. (2007) *Control and constraint in e-learning: Choosing when to choose.* Hershey, PA: Idea Group Publishing.

EDUCAUSE (2005). *7 things you should know about videoblogging.* Boulder, CO: EDU-CAUSE. Retrieved July 15, 2008, from http://www.educause.edu/ir/library/pdf/ELI7005.pdf.

Foley, G. (Ed). (2000). *Understanding adult education and training.* St Leonards, New South Wales: Allen & Unwin.

Gauntlett, D. (2007). *Creative explorations.* Abingdon: Routledge.

Grant, A., Kinnersley, P., Metcalf, E., Pill, R., & Houston, H. (2006). Students' views of reflective learning techniques: An efficacy study at a UK medical school. *Medical Education, 40*(4), 379–388.

Hull, G. A., & Nelson, M. E. (2005). Locating the semiotic power of multimodality. *Written Communication, 22*(2), 224–261.

Jackson, B. (1995). Assessment practices in art and design: A contribution to student learning? In G. Gibbs (Ed.), *Improving student learning through assessment and evaluation* (pp. 154–167). Oxford: The Oxford Centre for Staff Development.

Jarvis, P. (1995). *Adult and continuing education: Theory and practice.* London: Routledge.

Jenkins, M., & Lonsdale, J. (2007). Evaluating the effectiveness of digital storytelling for student reflection. In *Proceedings of the 2007 ASCILITE Conference on ICT: Providing Choices for Learners and Learning*, Singapore.

Kaare, B. H., & Lundby, K. (2006). Constructing digital stories on faith and life: An experiment in religious education. In *Proceedings of the International Conference on Informal Learning and Digital Media*, September 2006, University of Southern Denmark, Odense, Denmark.

Kennedy, G., Krause, K.-L., & Judd, T. (2006). *First year students' experiences with technology: Are they really digital natives?* Report for the Melbourne Centre for Study of Higher Education, University of Melbourne.

Klenowski, V., Askew, S., & Carnell, E. (2006). Portfolios for learning, assessment, and professional development in higher education. *Assessment and Evaluation in Higher Education, 31*(3), 267–286.

Lambert, J. (2003). *Digital storytelling cookbook and travelling companion.* Berkeley CA: Digital Diner Press.

Lathem, S. A., Reyes, C., & Qi, J. (2006). *Literacy autobiographies: Digital storytelling to capture student voice and reflection.* Retrieved July 15, 2008, from http://www.uvm.edu/pt3/?Page=papers.html&SM=researchsub.html.

Lemon, N. (2007). Take a photograph: Teacher reflection through narrative. *Reflective Practice, 8*(2), 177–191.

Levin, D., & Arafeh, S. (2002). *The digital disconnect: The widening gap between internet-savvy students and their schools.* Washington, DC: Pew Internet & American Life Project.

McDonnell, J., Lloyd, P., & Valkenburg, R. C. (2004). Developing design expertise through the construction of video stories. *Design Studies, 25,* 509–525.

Meadows, D. (2003). Digital storytelling: Research-based practice in new media. *Visual Communication, 2*(2), 189–193.

Mezirow, J. (1991). *Transformative dimensions of adult learning.* San Francisco, CA: Jossey-Bass.

Oblinger, D. G., & Oblinger, J. L. (2005). *Educating the net generation.* Washington, DC: EDUCAUSE.

Ohler, J. (2008). *Digital storytelling in the classroom.* Thousand Oaks CA: Corwin Press.

O'Reilly, T. (2005). *What is web 2.0.* Retrieved July 15, 2008, from http://www.oreillynet.com/pub/a/oreilly/tim/news/2005/09/30/what-is-web–20.html.

Paul, N., & Friebich, C. (2005). The elements of digital storytelling. Retrieved July 15, 2008, from http://www.inms.umn.edu/elements/.

Prensky, M. (2001). Digital natives, digital immigrants. *On the Horizon, 9*(5), 1–5.

Schön, D. (1987). *Educating the reflective practitioner.* San Francisco, CA: Jossey-Bass.

Spurgeon, S., & Bowen, J. L. (2002). Digital video/multimedia portfolios as a tool to develop reflective teacher candidates. In *Proceedings of the NECC 2002: National Educational Computing Conference,* San Antonio, TX.

Trafford, P. (2005, July). Mobile blogs, personal reflections and learning environments. *Ariadne, 44.* Retrieved July 15, 2008, from http://www.ariadne.ac.uk/issue44/trafford/intro.html.

White, D. (2007). *Results of the "Online Tool Use Survey" undertaken by the JISC funded SPIRE project.* JISC funded 'SPIRE' Project Report. Retrieved July 15, 2008, from http://www.rolotec.ch/blog/archives/survey-summary.pdf.

Williams, J. B. & Jacobs, J. (2004). Exploring the use of blogs as learning spaces in the higher education sector. *Australasian Journal of Educational Technology, 20*(2), 232–247.

CHAPTER 10

SIMSPACES

Collaboratively Designed
Virtual Learning Environments

Brendan Calandra and Stephen W. Harmon
Georgia State University, Atlanta

ABSTRACT

In this chapter, the authors propose a framework for the collaborative design, development, and implementation of immersive virtual learning environments called SimSpaces, where teams of participants work together to design, develop, and later inhabit a wide range of customized virtual learning spaces. This chapter includes a rationale, a scenario for how the project might be implemented, and suggestions for future directions. Operational definitions and references are also included.

INTRODUCTION

Experience has shown that when children have the chance at physical activities which bring their natural impulses into play, going to school is a joy, management is less of a burden, and learning is easier."
—Dewey, 1916, pp. 194, 195

Wired for Learning: An Educator's Guide to Web 2.0, pages 169–177
Copyright © 2009 by Information Age Publishing
All rights of reproduction in any form reserved.

Dewey's observation holds truer today than it did almost 100 years ago. When discussing the engaging effect that immersive technology can have on children, Gee (2003) said, "Wouldn't it be great if kids were willing to put so much time on task on such challenging material in school and enjoy it so much?" We agree. A recent study reported that nearly one third of all public high school students in the United States drop out before attaining their diploma. In urban schools the rate is even higher. A majority of those dropouts explained that they were adversely affected by the lack of relevance and engagement that their school curricula provided (Bridgeland, Dilulio, & Morison, 2006). Of those who do graduate from these public schools, many enter the workforce equipped with only basic standardized skill sets (Shaffer, 2006). These are the very skills that scores of American companies now outsource to countries like India and China, and to Central Europe—places where well trained workers can be employed much more cheaply than in the U.S. (Friedman, 2006). Some argue that traditional schooling is not preparing American children, especially in urban schools, to be "innovators at the highest technical levels that will pay off in a high-tech, global economy" (Shaffer, 2006, p. 3). McEwan (2000) states that "The discipline, academic knowledge, basic skills, ability to compete, and subject-matter competence that you think your children will acquire in school are vanishing faster than the pygmy owl and bighorn sheep ..." p. 53. While the severity of the problem is open for debate, the fact that schools are struggling to keep up with innovation in the digital age seems certain.

Jenkins (2003) observed a participatory culture that is growing outside of schools—one with lower barriers to artistic expression and civic engagement, support for creating and sharing, informal mentorship, and spaces where contributors feel that their input is valued. This emerging culture is in contention with the current organization of formal education in the United States.

A new divide along familiar lines is forming between privileged and disadvantaged students in public schools. As privileged digital "haves" take advantage of informal learning opportunities made possible by advances in information technology, the disadvantaged digital "have nots" are relying solely on formal educational institutions and are thus getting further behind in their ability to adapt to the emerging social culture of the internet. In addition to the new take on the digital divide, an older problem continues to plague education. Initial teaching experiences, especially in urban contexts, can be daunting and many beginning teachers—especially in low-income, urban schools—leave their position by their fifth year (National Commission on Teaching and America's Future, 2003). Perhaps our schools are in need of change that emulates what has been observed as the distributed, participatory, knowledge-based nature of our global human condition, and that allows for more input from both teachers and students (i.e., key stakeholders in a school system).

Human social and political interaction increasingly occurs using digital communication technologies. One sweeping advance in communication technologies is called Web 2.0 or the social web. It is comprised of applications such as, blogs, wikis, YouTube, MySpace, Second Life, and the like. Web 2.0 is basically a highly collaborative, participatory web of knowledge that allows for unprecedented levels of collective creation and meaning making. We see this increased collaboration as an epistemological change facilitated by a technological one. As this change affects the very root of how our society functions, it needs to be addressed in disciplines from philosophy to programming, from math to economics to fine arts, as well as modern languages, studies of literacy, and education. Concepts such as constructivism, social cognition, social justice/change and grass roots reform are not new to our discipline, but Web 2.0 is new, is rapidly changing, and is affecting how we think, operate, and educate. We at universities can philosophize and debate whether or not this is positive change, but we also need to research, learn about, and teach others how to deal with this phenomenon in a collaborative, participatory fashion that emulates how Web 2.0 works.

As Ellis (2006) notes, "Colleges (and public schools) have the opportunity to create a 21st-century paradigm that would educate students by allowing them to be active partners in the discovery and communication of new knowledge. (p. B20)" The authors would like to propose a conceptual model for just this kind of participatory, technology-enhanced program.

SIMSPACES—BACKGROUND

SimSpaces may be seen as an indirect descendent of the Instructional Software Design Project (ISDP) (Harel, 1990). The ISDP was a project based on the work of Seymour Papert that involved students in designing instructional software to teach fractions to younger students. The older students learned concepts of programming and mathematics by creating an instructional application. The fact that the younger students then used this application to gain knowledge of fractions was almost a secondary outcome. This educational process was based on Papert's (1991) notion of *constructionism*, the idea that learning is facilitated by the act of building or constructing a public artifact. Unlike the ISDP however, students in SimSpaces are designing a virtual learning environment for themselves, and then using it to further explore the content. In this way they further enhance the participatory learning culture of which they are a part.

SimSpaces are similar to the collaborative, user-created nature of Web 2.0 applications. The SimSpaces program is an inclusive, participatory learning-by-design process for teachers and students. Technically, SimSpaces would be developed using a virtual world engine. That is the engine would be utilized to create open source, 3D, immersive learning environments on closed servers. The specific intent of this process is to allow groups of teachers and students to collaboratively and actively design these environments, but also to allow them to later inhabit them for teaching and learning purposes. These environments would allow the participants to explore beliefs, theories, and approaches to teaching and learning without some of the administrative, logistical limitations and/or potential negative impact associated with experimenting in physical schools. "Learners take risks in a space where real-world consequences are lowered." (Gee, p. 67) In sum, implementation of the SimSpaces project would entail two distinct, yet integrally linked phases: 1) the collaborative, systematic design and development of the 3D immersive learning environments; and 2) the purposeful use of these simulated environments to explore teaching and learning.

SIMSPACES—A SCENARIO

The SimSpaces project is proposed to target students and teachers who are underserved and disadvantaged in the urban areas of the United States. The SimSpaces model begins in a less formal setting such as an afterschool environment or in summer intensive science and technology camps. For example, some of the design work would happen in the summer with implementation activities in the fall and spring. This way, the SimSpaces environment would be ready to support standards –based, curriculum-focused activities in science and/or technology during the regular school year. It therefore should complement the current school curriculum calendar but also allow for some innovative ways to explore and learn the material.

Phase I

The first phase of the project entails groups of teaching professionals, researchers, content experts, and high school students using the virtual world engine to collaboratively create virtual learning spaces. The process of knowledge construction and knowledge creation can hone both content knowledge and metacognitive ability in students (Chen & McGrath, 2003; Jonassen, Howland, Marra, & Crismond, 2008; Lehrer, 1993; Papert,

1980; Resnick, 1998). Logo (Papert, 1980) the programming language for children, and Lego/Logo (Resnick, 1998) the programmable construction blocks that are now *Lego Mindstorms*, are classic examples of this constructionist philosophy. "In recent years there has been a growing recognition of the educational value of design projects, in which students create external artifacts" (Resnick, 1998, p. 44). Resnick pointed out that manipulative materials play an important role in young children's learning, but often become replaced by more abstract formal methods later on. He argued that new (digital) manipulatives allow this method to also be applied to learning more complex concepts that are often presented to older children. Moreover, epistemic games, "games that are fundamentally about learning to think in innovative ways," can provide learning opportunities that are authentic, fulfilling and motivating (Shaffer, 2006, p. 9). Squire (2006) argued for framing game play as "*designed experiences* in which participants learn through a grammar of *doing* and *being*" (p. 19). Think of high school students' participation in SimSpaces as a game similar in its attractive and engaging qualities to world building games such as the Sims, Civilization III, or Roller Coaster Tycoon.

Groups of participants would first discuss issues such as curriculum, methodology, classroom layout, computer networking, and scheduling. The results of these decisions would then be used as plans to guide the development of the virtual learning space. The space could be any relevant learning context from a simulated classroom, to a laboratory, to a hospital building, to an ocean floor. Let's take the hospital as an example. Imagine a group of American high school students working together with their teachers, graduate students of education, researchers, and content experts from the U.S. Center for Disease Control to design a simulated hospital building in a fabricated town that has been decimated by a mysterious virus. Once the design plans have been drawn up, the SimSpaces design team(s) would work together with virtual world developers to learn how to create their virtual learning spaces using the virtual world engine mentioned earlier in this chapter. In this case, they would build 3D structures such as hospital buildings and rooms; they could create avatars of victims and health professionals; and together with CDC staff and high school teachers, they would create a story line driven by real world cases and high school science curriculum. When the "SimSpace" has been satisfactorily developed, the design team would work together to come up with ideas for implementation. An exemplary strategy for implementation of the "epidemic breakout" SimSpace might be a game in which participants compete to find the cause of the mysterious virus that has plagued the fictitious town they created in Phase I.

Phase II

This leads to the second phase of the project that is inhabiting and interacting within the collaboratively built SimSpaces (e.g., the "epidemic breakout" game). This could be when participants would assume the identity of avatars, populate the SimSpace, and role play the activity as both learners and facilitators. Each participant in the "breakout" SimSpace would be assigned a particular script or set of tasks to accomplish. Victims, for example might be given different symptoms to enact, while health and emergency preparedness professional characters might be given a mission to fulfill. Together with both content and curriculum experts, students and teachers could then play a health science-based learning game within the "epidemic breakout" SimSpace. That is, using their avatars, participants could try out innovative approaches to teaching and learning, in this case science, but also mathematics, engineering, and technology without the high impact and logistical ramifications of working in traditional, physical-world school settings. In a discussion of *identity and learning* Gee (2004) describes how learners need to associate themselves as the kind of person who can exist in a given domain to be able to effectively learn within it. He uses the science classroom as an example of how students take the virtual identity of a scientist by assuming certain sets of beliefs, vocabulary, interactions, etc. of real world scientists. While enacting the "breakout" simulation, for example, high school students would learn health science content by acting the part of a health science professional. This activity could be supported by the input of actual professionals (i.e., CDC employees). Thanks to the virtual world technology, the boundaries for how content could be presented and interacted with can extend far beyond the limitations of traditional school settings. It is important to note that activities generated by the SimSpaces project were initially designed to help traditionally marginalized metropolitan public school students experience interdisciplinary content like Science, Technology, and Media/Communications in more relevant, hands on, and realistic ways. A major goal has been to help change some of their stereotypical aversions to these disciplines.

Both phases of the SimSpaces project could also enhance opportunities for the professional development of public school teachers. Characteristics of virtual worlds (e.g., Second Life, There, Entropia Universe) and massive multiplayer online role playing games (e.g., World of Warcraft, The Sims Online) provide great potential for development of teachers. In role-playing video games, for example, "...players get practice in trying out new identities that challenge some of their assumptions about the world" (Gee, 2004, p. 117). The situated nature of practice teaching theoretically provides novices with the kind of authentic experience they need prior to entering the classroom as a certified teacher. It can be difficult to provide novices the opportunity to truly practice in a situated, realistic manner due to the technical and logistical constraints of operating physical world schools. Using simulated classrooms (or other learning environments) could provide novices the ability to try out unique and innovative approaches to teaching and learning in mathematics and the sciences. More specifically, in virtual learning environments, they can fail, critique one's actions together with peers and mentors, and accordingly re-create the situation using a new and improved approach in a way not possible when working with real children in a real school. There are some good examples of how to help novice teachers learn in this manner. Koehler and Mishra (2005) offer the concept of *Learning by Design*. In their study, teachers learned about technology by designing solutions to authentic educational technology design tasks in small collaborative groups. Koehler and Mishra (2005) argue that this activity allowed their participants to explore the ill-structured nature of authentic educational technology undertakings and develop "flexible ways of thinking about technology, design and learning" that go beyond the simple acquisition of educational technology skills traditionally taught in educational technology courses. "Because video games so nicely exemplify the nature of meaning as situated and embodied, they are also capable of capturing—and allowing players to practice—a process that is the hallmark of 'reflective practice' in areas like law, medicine, teaching, art, or any other areas where there are expert practitioners." (Gee, 2003, p. 90). Remember that these novice teachers would be designing and implementing alongside seasoned professionals, researchers, and real high school students. They would also be provided the opportunity to play the role of various related professionals within the SimSpaces and thus potentially gain valuable insider knowledge and dispositions. A larger number of K–12 students could be impacted by having teachers who have experienced SimSpaces—teachers who would more likely be versed in state of the art technologies and empowered by the opportunity to practice novel, often technology-infused approaches to teaching and learning.

THE FUTURE OF SIMSPACES

As the power of computers increases and the costs and physical size continue to fall we expect that we will see a greater blending of the real and the virtual. Distributed computing will advance apace with distributed work. The current rise in the amount of telecommuting will continue and even increase in the near term. Corporations will become less dependent on physical presence and more associated with virtual presence. We already see this happening today with some of the most recognizable company brands worldwide such as Google and Amazon. As work becomes more virtual so too must education. While there will be brick and mortar schools for the foreseeable future, a growing part of education will take place virtually. Students may be organized in virtual classes by interest and ability in the topic and not by the happenstance of geographical proximity. Faculty will draw subject resources from around the world and from the most current sources, not just from a print edition of a textbook that becomes outdated as soon as it is published. The question is whether education will take the lead in developing technologies and strategies that are compatible with the societal shifts already taking place, or whether our educational institutions will continue to fit an anachronistic square peg in a hole that is becoming rounder.

CONCLUSION

The authors should acknowledge that as this chapter is being written, virtual world engines may not be user friendly enough to be harnessed by teachers and students without the aid of a team of technologically savvy designers and developers. This should not be seen as an insurmountable obstacle, however. Newer technologies and their ease of use have tended to develop more rapidly than carefully planned programs for purposeful utilization (especially within the educational realm). This chapter should be read as both a springboard and a potential blueprint for SimSpaces and related endeavors that will undoubtedly be technologically feasible in the very near future. The authors argue that the participatory, malleable, and richly simulated nature of virtual worlds lend themselves to learning experiences that can be at once situated, inquiry based, collaborative, and transformative. An endeavor like SimSpaces has not been undertaken in the past likely because it was not possible without the proposed enabling technology.

REFERENCES

Chen, P., & McGrath, D. (2003). Knowledge construction and knowledge representation in high school students' design of hypermedia documents. *Journal of Multimedia and Hypermedia, 12*(1), 33–61.

Ellis, A. (2006). Creating a culture for innovation. *The Chronicle of Higher Education, 52*(32), B20.

Gee, J. P. (2003). *What video games have to teach us about learning and literacy.* New York: Palgrave Macmillan.

Harel, I. (1990). *Children designers.* Norwood, NJ: Ablex.

Jenkins, H. (2006). *Confronting the challenges of participatory culture: Media education for the 21st century.* Chicago: MacArthur Foundation.

Jonassen, D., Howland, J., Marra, C., & Crismond, D. (2008). *Meaningful learning with technology*. Upper Saddle River, NJ: Pearson.

Koehler, M. J., & Mishra, P. (2005). Teachers learning technology by design. *Journal of Computing in Teacher Education. 21*(3), 94–101.

Korthagen, F. A. J., Kessels, J. (1999). Linking theory and practice: Changing the pedagogy of teacher education. *Educational Researcher, 28*(4), 4–17.

Lehrer, R. (1993). Authors of knowledge: Patterns of hypermedia design. In S. P. Lajoie and S. J. Derry (Eds.), *Computers as cognitive tools* (pp. 197–227). Hillsdale, NJ: Erlbaum.

McEwan, E. (2000). *Angry parents, failing schools*. Wheaton, IL: Shaw Publishers.

Papert, S. (1980). *Mindstorms*. New York: Basic Books.

Papert, S. (1991). Situating constructionism. In I. Harel & S. Papert (Eds.), *Constructionism* (pp. 1–14). Hillsdale, NJ: Erlbaum.

Resnick, M. (1998). Technologies for lifelong kindergarten. *Educational Technology Research and Development, 46*(4), 43–55.

Shaffer, D. (2006). *How computer games help children learn*. New York: Palgrave Macmillan.

Squire, K. (2005). From content to context: Videogames as designed experience. *Educational Researcher 35*(8), 19–29.

CHAPTER 11

COURSE CO-CREATION VS. COURSE MANAGEMENT

Wikis as a Potential Alternative to Traditional Learning Management Systems

Michael L. W. Jones
Sheridan Institute of Technology and Advanced Learning

David Gelb
York University

ABSTRACT

Learning management systems (LMS) have been used extensively and effectively in educational settings for over a decade. By facilitating interaction within and outside of classrooms using an integrated set of online tools, LMSs have opened up the scope and reach of education in both online and traditional class settings.

However, it should be noted that the information architecture of traditional LMSs embody a power dynamic that leaves administrators and instructors

Wired for Learning: An Educator's Guide to Web 2.0, pages 179–194
Copyright © 2009 by Information Age Publishing
179

firmly in control over the design and maintenance of online educational environments. The architecture of control (Lockton, 2008) of traditional LMSs operates in distinct opposition to the ethos of Web 2.0 technologies, which enable and encourage robust user input and control. These hardwired power relations of the traditional LMS pose significant challenges in creating truly collaborative learning experiences, especially at a time when emerging Web 2.0 technologies enable a more democratic and user-generated educational experience.

This chapter suggests that the power differentials inherent in traditional LMSs can be radically redefined by adopting wiki technology as a complement to or even replacement of the traditional LMS. The chapter is based on observations and lessons learned from the authors' use of wikis as an alternative to their institutionally supported LMSs, and concludes with an analysis of potential future trends in co-creation as a metaphor for class and curriculum management.

INTRODUCTION

Learning management systems (LMS) are core technologies supporting computer-supported collaborative learning (CSCL). LMSs such as WebCT/Blackboard, ATutor, Angel and Moodle (among others) serve as a focal point for interaction among and between students and instructors by providing an integrated portal of information and a collection of tools for administrators and instructors to structure and manage the online educational environment.

The traditional LMS has played a central role in expanding the reach of online education and integrating online support tools into traditional face-to-face education. Given the ubiquity and reach of various social media Internet technologies today, it is often stunning to recall that fifteen years ago, the Internet was a cloistered environment largely restricted to the most technically inclined researchers in higher education.

The Internet user population remained highly specialized until 1994 and the release of graphic user interface based browsers to access an emergent Internet technology—the World Wide Web. This shift in technology allowed a great number of non-technical users to enter cyberspace—but not without considerable assistance. Early Internet service providers such as America Online and portals such as Yahoo! facilitated new users' acculturation to the online environment by simplifying a rapidly growing information space and targeting their attention to core elements of interest.

Early LMS suites emerged around the same time for much the same purpose—enabling millions of education users to leverage the power of Internet technologies through relatively easy to use environments while providing instructors the power to manage the learning environment effectively.

Over the last fifteen years, however, early Web technologies have evolved significantly. Somewhat loosely defined as social media or Web 2.0 technologies (O'Reilly, 2005), the current Web supports a more decentralized power dynamic in which users are not simply consumers of published content but also actively and easily co-create content. Social networking tools such as Facebook, content co-creation utilities such as Google Documents and photo/video sharing sites such as Flickr or YouTube have opened up many possibilities for radically decentralized and massive co-created user experiences. Through decentralizing and making accessible what McAfee (2006) termed SLATES (searching, linking, authorship, tagging, extensibility and signaling) Web 2.0 technologies have extraordinary potential to redefine online interaction in a variety of fields.

Unfortunately, designers of traditional LMSs have been slow to respond to the Web 2.0 phenomenon and continue to build systems based on metaphors of centralized control of information architecture and content. As such, they risk being overshadowed by emerging technologies that enable and encourage strong user input and control.

This chapter investigates the potential impact to the management and delivery of one Web 2.0 technology in particular—the wiki. A wiki is a collection of collaboratively created Web-based resources in which all registered members have the right to shape and contribute content. While wikis have successfully been used in specialized projects at various levels of education, this chapter argues that the real power of wikis is tapped when the technology is used as a learning management system. Wikis privilege decentralized collaborative authorship, freeing teachers and students alike from the limitations of centralized administration and information architecture design imposed by traditional LMSs. Examples from two wiki course co-creation efforts will help outline the benefits and challenges adopters of wikis as LMS may face in their own efforts, and the chapter concludes with a look at potential changes in LMS and wiki technology that may influence future adoption.

LEARNING MANAGEMENT SYSTEMS AS ARCHITECTURES OF CONTROL

While LMS technologies may have been essential in broadening the user base of online and hybrid education fifteen years ago, the emergence of popular, free, and easily used Web 2.0 alternatives risk overshadowing LMS use in educational environments.

We suggest here that the core problem at hand is the design of the traditional LMS. Traditional LMS design is constrained by what Lockton refers to as architectures of control:

> Architectures of control are features, structures or methods of operation designed into physical products, software, buildings, city layouts—or indeed any planned system with which a user interacts—which are intended to enforce, reinforce, or restrict certain modes of user behaviour. (Lockton, 2008)

It should be noted that architectures of control are not necessarily problematic. Indeed, as Norman (1990) rightly noted, affording optimal and constraining counterproductive actions is key to successful product design.

However, if the architecture of control of traditional learning management systems necessarily restricts access to and engagement with an educational environment, the limitations imposed may compromise the vitality and value of the environment. There are two major facets to how traditional learning management systems act as an potentially limiting architecture of control: 1) controlling general access to course content and interaction and 2) creating hard-wired individual roles and responsibilities within educational environments.

Controlling Access to Course Content and Interaction

An educational institution may feel it necessary to restrict access to course content to registered students only for a variety of reasons. An elementary school, for example, may have valid safety concerns in unleashing its students into the wider Internet population without appropriate supervision. Maintaining limited access to course content and interaction through a closed LMS may be very appropriate in such instances.

Other reasons for maintaining control speak to intellectual property concerns. In some institutions, content created by instructors becomes the property of the institution that employs them. In others, an instructor may retain copyright control—but may also wish to hold work close to the chest for his/her own reward (e.g., repurposing course notes into a book for sale, licensing software, etc.) In both instances, administrators and instructors alike may fear that open access to content compromises the potential value of that content.

It should be noted in response, however, that MIT's OpenCourseWare project (MIT, 2008) strongly suggests that open access to content can be adopted even by elite institutions with little overall negative consequence to an institution's brand or contribution to world knowledge development.

As Shapiro and Varian (1998) suggest, the value of information as an economic good may indeed increase as it is shared and decrease if hoarded. Lessig (2004) goes further by suggesting hoarding of intellectual property has put serious strains on the activities of cultural actors (educators and students included) in successfully engaging their work and creating a common cultural space. As such, it can be argued LMSs that are primarily leveraged to hide the intellectual property of educational institutions behind institutional firewalls may ironically limit the value of educational work by keeping the vitality of intellectual discussion and creation unnecessarily shielded from view and consumption in the creative common.

Structuring Individual Roles and Responsibilities

Traditional learning management systems also play a role in restricting access to information based on individual accounts and intended roles in an educational environment. As with controlling access to course content, this is often done for perfectly valid reasons. For example, access to personal information (e.g., individual student assessment and evaluation information or interpersonal email communication) is necessarily limited in LMSs to protect personal privacy.

Traditional LMS systems accomplish this goal not only by providing individual accounts but also arranging such accounts in an access hierarchy. It is here where the architecture of control of traditional LMSs may arbitrarily limit interaction and frustrate true computer supported collaborative learning.

As Bowker and Star (1999) note, while classification is an inherently human act, specific classification schemes may not only arbitrarily simplify individual entities but also serve to define relations among said entities. The classification of roles in a traditional LMS is no exception. In LMS design, individuals are assigned to various structural roles common in educational environments—for example, instructor, teaching assistant, or student. Other roles specific to the system may also exist—for example, system administration, educational administration, or course designer.

The limited nature of the student role is of specific concern here. The student role in traditional LMS design is more passive by design. Access is granted to course materials but the overall design of the course itself remains exclusively under administrator and instructor control. While instructors may choose to integrate some tools to encourage student collaboration and discussion, the responsibility for setting up these tools and integrating them into overall course design remains exclusively theirs. The same applies to the organization and aesthetics of the class space—only those at higher levels in the hierarchy have the power to create, organize, maintain and/or beautify class spaces.

This uneven power dynamic is not only problematic for creating a truly collaborative learning space. By giving instructors ultimate authority over the information architecture of a class space, they inherit ultimate responsibility for that space—a responsibility that may be daunting, especially for instructors not strongly familiar with the intricacies of LMS features. While some faculty may enjoy the challenge of mastering a new learning environment, it is arguable that the technical maintenance and design work required is tangential to what should be the core mission at hand—facilitating student learning.

THE CASE FOR WIKIS AS AN ALTERNATIVE
TO TRADITIONAL LMS

This chapter suggests that wikis may serve to address the above limitations of traditional LMS technologies. Social media platforms such as wikis can, if properly integrated into curriculum, create an intuitive collaborative learning environment drive by the actions of students and their peers.

The distributed nature of wiki co-creation provides multiple opportunities for students to share and learn with their colleagues. Not only can students create new content, they can denote contextual hyperlinks among content pieces and revise existing materials to extend current ideas. By sharing their work and engaging in iterative collaborative editing, students create and elaborate a semantic network of information and in doing so, create the very context of the class itself. Individual work is now part of the bigger whole and is amplified by its inherent visibility. Even when asked to post individual assignments, students soon experience the work of others, which can lead to a deeper reflection of their own contributions in this community. Collectively, all learners benefit as ideas are captured, published and ultimately consumed by wiki peers for further improvement.

While individual authorship is not initially obvious, it can be derived through edit logs to discern who did what and when—a necessary condition both to avoid the "free rider" phenomenon (Marwelland & Ames, 1979) that plagues collective resources and to correlate wiki activity with the common educational requirement of individual assessment. Individual edit history is also an important component of revision control; participants can analyze the co-creation process by peeling back the outer skin of a seemingly coherent page to reveal the temporal development of a document. In this way, the progression of ideas can be mapped in reference to time and contributor, transparently revealing the evolutionary process leading to the document's current state.

The co-creation process enabled by wikis embodies the work of Lev Vygotsky's notion of the Zone of Proximal Development (Vygotsky, 1978). The learner's "zone" is the gap between the development level of what an individual can accomplish independently and the level of accomplishment with the guidance of a teacher or more knowledgeable peer. Individual wiki contributions approximate what a learner currently knows (independent development level) and is further developed with input, advice, and editing assistance from academic peers.

Wikis also explicitly enable Vygotsy's concept of social constructivism, which suggests that learning is more successful when socially mediated as individuals are better able to solve problems together. When learning socially, a higher level of engagement and motivation can result in more creative and satisfying results (Vygotsky, 1978).

Educators have primarily leveraged wiki technologies by designing classroom activities suitable to co-creation. In such projects, students negotiate and build consensus through the process of constructing a shared artifact. Individual projects focused on co-creation of specific course deliverables are examples of student created wiki exercises and assignments. Co-authoring course texts, glossaries of key terms, annotated resource building and creation of instructional modules is common instances of these kinds of course wiki projects. Such a focused approach not only constrains the potential complexity of a wiki-based educational effort, it benefits from being conceptually similar to the governing ethos of the popular and arguably gold-standard Wikipedia, making the project intuitive to even lay users of the Internet.

To consider the value of wikis as an alternative to traditional learning management systems participants must think about the wiki as a holistic entity that reflects the current state of the classroom and acts as a central gathering point. When wikis are used as a core information architecture for a course, we begin to see the deep collaboration inherent in Lave and Wenger's notion of communities of practice (1991). Communities of practice refers to groups that are "are formed around shared commitments to have the knowledge and practice be applied, effective and produce results that forward the interests of the whole" (McMaster, 1998). Communities of practice have an emergent quality that surface from the bottom up as opposed to being directed and pre-conceived from a top level authority.

Communities of practice are often described as informal but require some maintenance and leadership to encourage growth. Wiki-based classes also need structure and purpose to foster a synergistic and community-oriented environment. While the instructor is normally charged with the role of community maintenance and leadership, the dynamics of this leadership in a wiki environment are markedly different. In traditional classroom settings, the learning dynamic is focused on the teacher as the gatekeeper and evaluator of knowledge structures. The social constructivist nature of wiki technology challenges the notion of teacher as knowledge authority by replacing the authoritative specialist role with a more egalitarian and democratic model of knowledge sharing. In other words, the instructor moves from being the sage on the stage to the guide on the side (King, 1993).

This can be challenging from an instructor's perspective—the pedagogy of student-centered constructivism is more complicated and less predictable than accepted and conventional teacher-centered methods (Burns & Humphreys, 2005). In a constructivist paradigm using wiki technology, students can follow their own research interests and connect with others to negotiate meanings and produce shared understandings. Less control over course content also means more challenges for teachers in regulating and evaluating student achievement (Lamb, 2004). The networked nature of individual authorship may also make empirical assessment a challenge for teachers in grade-focused education.

The benefits and challenges of adopting wikis as a learning management solution are complex and, to the unfamiliar, may seem daunting. It is our hope that our largely successful implementations of wiki-centered education may help contextualize the abstract phenomenon of collaborative co-creation through example.

LESSONS LEARNED FROM TWO CASE STUDIES OF WIKI-CENTERED LEARNING MANAGEMENT

The cases noted below were facilitated by the authors of this chapter and are available for public viewing at the URLs below.

Case Study 1: CCT300—Critical Analysis of Media— 3rd Year Undergraduate Communication, Culture, and Information Technology Course
(http://ccit300-f06.wikispaces.com)

In the fall of 2006, the CCT300 class focused on critical analysis of media form and structure with special attention to graphic novels as a medium. Major course deliverables included collaboratively building an inventory of media genres and creating a culture jamming/social influence campaign in small groups. Course activity was coordinated in the course wiki, which was edited over 9000 times by 116 students and the authors of this paper, with 97% of edits done by students.

Case Study 2: YSDN3006—Design and Information Architecture—3rd Year Undergraduate Design Course
(http://3006f07.wikispaces.com)

In the fall of 2007, the Design and Information Architecture class focused on Toronto's public spaces as a theme for the term project. The coursework was carried out over a 12-week semester following a design process involving research, analysis and synthesis phases. All course material was housed in a wiki to act as both a learning management system and as a presentation environment for the student coursework throughout the project timeline. This studio based course was taught into two separate sections with 29 students sharing a single wiki contributing 4800 edits, in which 92% done by students.

Wiki Technology Selected

In both cases, Wikispaces was chosen as the supporting wiki technology. A notable irony of Wikipedia's popularity is that the editing process of its supporting technology, MediaWiki, is complex to learn. Editing Wikipedia pages requires significant investment to learn MediaWiki's unique and powerful code structure. Given Wikipedia's global audience and reach, perhaps the high barrier of entry imposed by a steep learning curve is an effective architecture of control it itself, helping reduce potential noise by limiting editing to those willing to make the effort. In a wiki-centered educational environment, however, a steep learning curve could prove unnecessarily disenfranchising and increase student dissatisfaction with the wiki environment.

Thankfully, other wiki tools such as Wikispaces, PBWiki and Wetpaint have emerged to facilitate the average Internet user's participation in wiki environments. By leveraging familiar user interface elements and hiding the complexity of wiki coding to all but advanced users, these wiki technologies have enabled participation to a broader user base. As Wikispaces' strong user base in the K–12 market suggests (Davis, 2007), users need not be extraordinarily technically sophisticated to use the system and use it well.

Wikispaces' attention to the needs of education users was also a strong influencing factor in the decision to use this platform. For example, Wikispaces offers ad-supported "protected" spaces which were viewable by the general public but editable only by accepted users. Keeping editing power to class members only eliminates the potential chaos that may result in a fully public platform while still making the course itself open and transparent to interested onlookers. Similarly, in the case of the first case study class, instructors needed to get a full log of student edits for evaluation purposes. Wikispaces staff were not only happy to comply with the request, they eventually integrated publicly accessible edit logs organized by user ID in response to educator requests and feedback.

Both case studies led to interesting observations of how best to integrate wikis as an alternative learning management system, particularly with respect to a) facilitating effective learning environments using wiki technology, b) encouraging individual participation in collective spaces, and c) integrating the wiki LMS with other supporting technologies.

Facilitating an Effective Learning Environment

As noted earlier, the flattened hierarchy of wiki contribution and co-creation has the potential of transcending traditional student and instructor roles, which are unfortunately hard-wired in traditional learning management systems. Facilitating such a shift in practice is not necessarily a simple transition however. Both students and instructors have to refashion their roles and expectations to create a truly collaborative space.

For instructors, this primarily means ceding considerable control over course content, design and layout to students—for better or worse. Using wikis as an LMS explicitly affords course co-creation, with students playing more equal co-authorship roles. Now, the hierarchy is never perfectly flat—for example, in most instructional environments, students cannot unilaterally alter course syllabi or institutional regulations to meet their individual needs. In the above cases, formal courses documents were locked to prevent further editing from anyone but space owners (i.e., the instructors).

The rest of the course pages in both cases were freely edited by all members of the community. Instructors played a facilitative role, monitoring the development of the course wikis but generally engaging the community only when necessary. For example, in the course's frequently asked questions (FAQ) pages, students were encouraged to not only ask questions, but answer the questions of their peers. Instructors monitored the pages for accuracy and to ensure that all questions would indeed be answered. Instructor participation was minimal however - most student-generated answers were correct and that students often provided answers before instructors had a chance to respond.

For some instructors, this transference of authority may cause discomfort. Those more comfortable with traditional instructor-led education models may feel more secure possessing the ultimate authority traditional LMSs grant them, and will accept the burden of responsibility as a necessary condition of continuing to work in their comfort zone. It should be noted, however, that an online environment that is too tightly controlled is increasingly unlikely to be effective. Given the ubiquity, popularity and accessibility of Web 2.0 technologies, students who find that a traditional LMS does not meet their creative or communicative needs will simply seek out alternative tools and environments that will exist wholly outside instructor control or even awareness.

For students, the transition from traditionally passive content consumers to active content co-creators can be similarly difficult to facilitate. Unfortunately, too many educational environments still strongly reward superficial information retrieval vs. deep engagement with course content. In courses and programs where this approach to education is common, students may be strongly conditioned to be little more than traders of information in exchange for grades vs. active participants in the co-creation of knowledge.

This is frustrated further in highly competitive environments where sharing one's information can be perceived as ceding control over one's comparative grade. This was evident in the creation and sharing of study notes for course tests—while the class community as a whole appreciated their existence for obvious reasons, few really contributed to the effort. While those few were rewarded with participation points (see below for more discussion of this) the creators of the notes were somewhat frustrated by the free riders.

While some students in the case courses noted found this active role challenging at first, many came to appreciate and enjoy the freedom to create and share work of their own design, as is evidenced in the course feedback available on the wiki. Some, however, still felt frustrated by the open possibilities of co-creation, wanting to know what "the right answer" or "the right amount of participation" was. Reversing this conditioning can be tough—but increasingly it's necessary. High-level jobs and careers are increasingly conceptual and creative in nature, whereas jobs dependent on simple information mastery and retrieval are increasingly outsourced or automated (Pink, 2005). Higher education in particular should be explicitly encouraging creative and conceptual engagement with course material as a result, else we fail to prepare students for the world they will inherit.

Even if individual members of a wiki-based community largely accept their roles and responsibilities, there remains the potential for conflict in the collective space. For example, the first case course had 120 members, raising considerable potential for disagreement about what should be edited when. These disagreements can be both socially and technically rooted. Technically, the biggest issue was concurrent editing (e.g., many students trying to add their name to the roster of personal pages simultaneously). While some collaborative co-creation platforms attempt to manage concurrent editing by either locking down edit control to one user (e.g., PBWiki) or attempting to handle and integrate multiple sources of input simultaneously (e.g., Google Docs), Wikispaces unfortunately offers only limited awareness of potential simultaneous co-authors on a page and no means of constraining simultaneous edits. As contributors to the Wikispaces feature request page suggest (Wikispaces, 2008), it is a notable limitation of the platform, and as such one likely to be addressed in future releases.

Socially, it is entirely possible for a community of co-editors to have conceptual disagreements about the content and presentation of a given page. While this was surprisingly rare in both case courses, some conflict did occur. Interestingly, it was often over mundane issues such as the look and feel of the space (e.g., competing title banner designs for a page.) In such cases, students were encouraged to work out the disagreements amongst themselves and build a consensus decision. In another related course taught by the authors, one of the protagonists of a new design for the whole course site put his option to a class vote. On losing the vote, he abandoned his effort, but did so happy in the knowledge that he had the chance to make his option known and vetted.

Mitigating the potential conflict in this case was that individuals both the original and revised designs received credit for their efforts. The role of individual credit for collective work is examined further below.

Encouraging and Evaluating Individual Participation in Collective Spaces

While it would be nice to believe that students would participate in a course wiki out of intrinsic interest, such enthusiasm is hard to expect in any social medium, much less one structured by the extrinsic motivator of individual grades. As Li (2007) notes, fewer than one in five users can be expected to contribute in any substantive manner in the Web 2.0 sphere. The instructors thus felt it necessary to incorporate some metric to gauge the quality of an individual's wiki contributions. Rewarding participation in the classroom positively not only reinforces student accountability for their own actions, but also explicitly encourages participation from a broader spectrum of students that would otherwise contribute.

Value was placed on providing resources and input that could assist the class in furthering the course objectives, whether directly project related or more generally in their overall design education.

Asking and answering frequently asked questions, maintaining calendars of events, sharing inspirational examples and building technical documentation for related course software were some of the ways students supported each other's learning. Others chose to contribute by improving the overall organization and design of the space—for example, the course and assignment banners in the CCT300 wiki were the work on one especially creative student who took it upon himself to improve the look and feel of the space. Students also took it upon themselves to create and share content that was somewhat or wholly tangential to the course learning environment. While this was tolerated by course instructors, instructors took time to highlight what was quality work and to remind students that quality and relevance of edits—not sheer quantity—was the key to earning high wiki participation grades.

Instructors also encouraged participation by requiring all students to note their significant contributions in a personalized wiki page with accompanying hyperlinks to referring documents and assets.

In doing so, tracking and reporting participation performance was the primary responsibility of individual students. These self-reports were verified by accessing the wiki's edit logs. In these particular case studies, the administrators of Wikispaces provided the edit logs, thousands of individual page edits. The personal page would often become a point of personal pride and self-expression. The transparency of the Wikispaces platform offers participants exposure not readily visible by most standard LMS, thereby promoting a higher degree accountability and engagement with one's own learning success.

Integration with Institutionally Supported LMS and Other Web 2.0 Technologies

As the cases were primarily designed to replace the use of the institutionally supported traditional LMS, integration between the two systems was deliberately weak. Still, some cross-linkage had to be formed—for example, students familiar with the LMS from other classes had to be made aware of the existence of the wiki and be advised that the internal email system of the LMS would not be an effective means of communication with instructors. This was done through simply making the provided LMS space bare, hosting only a link to the wiki.

A major limitation noted in adopting the wiki as an alternative platform for learning management was posting individual grades. Students have become quite accustomed to instantaneous online access to their grades when an assignment is returned. Wikispaces as a platform, however, does not yet support secure and private distribution of individual grades, save for individual email communication. The gradebook utilities in most traditional LMS settings have normally been quite effective in compiling student grades while ensuring private access. This noted, one of the instructors' main complaints about the institutionally supported LMS in the above cases was its failure to successfully and reliably import grade spreadsheets from external sources, making the gradebook function rather cumbersome when it worked at all. In both cases here, the instructors reverted to personalized email or face-to-face communication out of necessity, but acknowledge that a functioning gradebook would be a considerable benefit in any LMS, wiki-based or not.

What was especially interesting to note, however, was the ease that other forms of social media could be integrated into the wiki environment. Indeed, such integration is explicitly encouraged and supported through "widgets" (small bits of source code that can be embedded into the wiki to extend and integrate functionality). In the second case study course, student research involved acquiring and annotating visual material. Many students posted annotated photos to the photo sharing site Flickr and fed the stream directly into the course wiki using a widget. These presentations were then embedded in a final research report for quick and easy reference by their peers and the instructor for evaluation purposes. As research reports were done in small groups, a portion of the grading scheme involved peer evaluation to ensure reasonable distribution of workload. This was facilitated by using SurveyGizmo, a third-party online survey tool, and integrated into the wiki via widgets.

From an instructional angle, the wiki and its available widgets extended the ability to effectively manage the course and underscored the value of open platforms in leveraging existing services to augment and support the learning experience for students. This ability to integrate specialized tools for particular tasks in regards to instructional administration, typifies the nature of using an open platform like wiki to conduct course management. Reliance on an exclusive piece of LMS limits the customization capabilities to the current version of the software and does not allow for easy extensions like third party widgets. The proprietary model of first generation LMS creates a closed situation where the technology dictates the course delivery rather than an open and adaptable LMS that allows for more flexibility in pedagogical designs.

CONCLUSION

The domain of Web 2.0 technology is still a rather fluid space. The inventory of Web 2.0 services at Go2Web20.net is nothing short of overwhelming—over 2000 services are listed, with new services being added regularly and others disappearing due to merger or lack of interest (go2web20.net, 2008).

Some speculate that this market bubble will eventually bust, as happened by the end of the .com bust in the late 1990s (Hirschcorn, 2007). While market rationalization is certainly plausible, the principles embodied by SLATES (McAfee, 2006) are powerful and empowering indeed, and as such are not likely to disappear outright. The most successful, socially valuable utilities are likely to survive and, like 1990s era survivors, remain as a core component of our Internet environment.

This likely causes no shortage of concern for closed, proprietary LMS providers, which are being challenged on two related fronts. On one side, Web 2.0 technologies such as wikis challenge the LMS model altogether by allowing students and instructors to stitch together a learning environment integrating a variety of free and accessible Web 2.0 services. On the other, open-source alternatives to proprietary LMS technologies (e.g., Moodle) have gained solid institutional and instructor support, largely due to its free license and dynamic developer and support community. In combination, these forces may severely threaten traditional LMS market position and the substantial revenues gained from institutional licenses.

How proprietary services adapt to these challenges remains an open question, but evidence suggests adaptation is occurring. Angel Learning's tagline for its LMS targets the Moodle challenge by declaring Angel's product to be "Simple. Powerful. Open" (Angel Learning, 2008), and not only does Blackboard's recent service pack integrate blogs and wiki technology within the LMS, it is marketed to institutional buyers as a value-added feature for young, social media savvy students (Blackboard, 2008).

Equally interesting to note will be how Web 2.0 services such as Wikispaces adapt to the needs of the educational market. The aforementioned Wikispaces feature request list is compiled by users, many of which come to the site from educational contexts. Wikispaces and other public wiki providers have been quick to respond to user demands to improve their services, and many of these service improvements have resulted in benefits for the educational user community. However, public wiki providers are, in the end, charged with meeting the generic needs of a generic audience. One strong argument for the continued development of learning management systems is the focus on tools and features central to the learning community. It is highly unlikely that a public wiki provider such as Wikispaces will, for example, integrate an online gradebook for its user base—for many users, such a tool would be rather pointless. The highly extensible nature of Web 2.0 technologies might be the more realistic evolutionary path for education-centered wikis to leverage—if education-centric tools and technologies could be integrated through widgets vs. integrated into the core of a service, the needs of educators and the priorities of public Web 2.0 service developers might be able to strike a workable balance.

Whatever the future holds, it is plausible to suggest that social media will impact the future of learning management system design. This chapter suggests that continued use and experimentation with wikis as learning management systems will continue to put pressure on the limitations of traditional LMS architectures of control to the benefit of students, instructors and educational administrators alike.

REFERENCES

Angel Learning (2008). *Homepage*. Retrieved June 1, 2008, from http://www.angel-learning.com.

BlackBoard. (2008). *Wiki FAQ.* Retrieved June 7, 2008, from http://www.black-board.com/products/Academic_Suite/wiki_faq.htm

Bokwer, G. C., & Star, S. L. (1999). *Sorting things out: Classification and its consequences.* Cambridge, MA: MIT Press.

Bruns, A., Humphreys, S. (2005). *Wikis in teaching and assessment: The m/cylopedia project.* WikiSym '05. Proceedings of the Wiki Symposium Conference, October 16–18, 2005. San Diego, CA: ACM.

Davis, M. R. (2007). Wiki wisdom: Lessons for educators. *Education week's digital directions, September 12, 2007.* Retrieved May 25, 2008, from http://www.edweek.org/dd/articles/2007/09/12/02wiki.h01.html

Hirschcorn, M. (2007). The web 2.0 bubble. *Atlantic Monthly,* April. Retrieved June 4, 2007, from http://www.theatlantic.com/doc/200704/social-networking

King, A. (1993). From sage on the stage to guide on the side. *College Teaching, 41*(1), 30–35.

Li, C. (2007). *Forrester's new social technographics report.* Retrieved May 22, 2008, from http://blogs.forrester.com/charleneli/2007/04/forresters_new_.html

Norman, D. A. (1990). *The design of everyday things.* New York: Doubleday.

Lamb, B. (2004). Open spaces: Wikis, ready or not. *EDUCAUSE Review, 39*(5), 36–48.

Lessig, L. (2004). *Free culture: How big media uses technology and the law to lock down culture and control creativity.* New York: Penguin Press.

Lockton, D. (2008). *What are architectures of control in design?* Retrieved May 29, 2008, from http://architectures.danlockton.co.uk/what-are-architectures-of-control-in-design/

Marwelland, G., Ames, R. E. (1979). Experiments on the provision of public goods: Resources, interest, group size and the free-rider problem. *American Journal of Sociology, 84*(6), 13–35.

McAfee, A. P. (2006). Enterprise 2.0: The dawn of emergent collaboration. *MIT Sloan Management Review, 47*(3), 21–28.

McMaster, M. (1998). *Communities of practice: An introduction.* Retrieved May 30, 2008, from http://www.co-i-l.com/coil/knowledge-garden/cop/mmintro.shtml

MeatBall Wiki. (2006). *Learning community.* Retrieved August 22, 2006, from http://www.usemod.com/cgi-bin/mb.pl?LearningCommunity

MIT OpenCourseWare (2008). *Homepage.* Retrieved May 27, 2008, from http://ocw.mit.edu/OcwWeb/web/home/home/index.htm

O'Reilly, T. (2005). *What is web 2.0?* Retrieved June 9, 2008, from http://www.oreilly.net.com/pub/a/oreilly/tim/news/2005/09/30/what-is-web-20.html

Pink, D. (2005). *A whole new mind: Moving from the information age to the conceptual age.* New York: Riverhead Books.

Shaprio, C., & Varian, H. R. (1998). *Information rules: A strategic guide to the networked economy.* Cambridge, MA: Harvard Business School Press.

Vygotsky, L. S. (1978). *Mind in society.* Cambridge, MA: MIT Press.

Wikispaces. (2008). *Feature requests.* Retrieved June 7, 2008, from http://www.wikispaces.com/feature+requests.

PART IV

LEARNING MANAGEMENT WITH WEB 2.0

CHAPTER 12

MEANINGFUL LEARNING WITH WIKIS

Making a Connection

Yufeng Qian
St. Thomas University

ABSTRACT

Recent years witnessed a rapid proliferation of the use of wikis in education due to its radical simplicity and versatility. As its emergence is a potential powerful tool for enabling new types of learning, it is necessary to base instructional uses of wikis on sound pedagogical framework in order for this innovation to live up to its promises and potentials. The purpose of this chapter, therefore, is to explore the pedagogical framework of wikis and how David Jonassen and his colleague's framework for meaningful learning can guide the design of wikis for instructional purposes. Major types of wikis use in education are also discussed with illustrative examples.

Wired for Learning: An Educator's Guide to Web 2.0, pages 197–213
Copyright © 2009 by Information Age Publishing
All rights of reproduction in any form reserved.

INTRODUCTION

The use of Wikis in education has rapidly proliferated in recent years. Along with other Web 2.0 technologies such as blogs, Really Simple Syndication (RSS) feeds, and folksonomy, wikis have been embraced by more and more schools and universities across the country, in an effort to increase information dissemination, improve collaboration, and meet the needs and preferences of the millennial generation of learners. Special conferences have been and continue to be organized to explore potential uses, current practice, and future directions of wikis in education. Campus Technology's 2008 summer conference of Next Gen.Edu, assembling the nation's leading experts and innovators in higher education, is such an effort toward exploring the new realm of teaching and learning in a Web 2.0 world.

Made famous by Wikipedia, wikis are Web publishing tools that allow public editing; that is, a wiki website is fully editable by its visitors from a Web browser who have access to it and/or are allowed to edit. Without knowledge of programming languages (such as HTML and JavaScript) or design skills of sophisticated Web development tools (such as Dreamweaver), wikis provide predefined templates where people can quickly set up and edit a Web page. Like other Web 2.0 technologies, wikis are a type of social and collaboration tool that enables people to do things together on the Internet—to articulate, communicate, share, collaborate, and learn from each other. Many have claimed that the wiki, along with other Web 2.0 tools, is an exciting technology innovation and has the potential to enable new types of learning that meets the needs of the 21st century (Owen, Grant, Sayers, & Facer, 2006; Richardson, 2006).

However, as Kulik (1994) cautioned, there have been many examples of unfulfilled promises of innovations in the history of educational technology. Many innovative technologies have taken on fad status and have failed to live up to their initial expectations and promises. Inspired by the novelty and educational possibilities of motion pictures, Thomas A. Edison in 1913 proclaimed that "(b)ooks will soon be obsolete in the schools. . . . It is possible to teach every branch of human knowledge with the motion picture. Our school systems will be completely changed in ten years" (cited in Saettler, 1968, p. 98). Despite the premature enthusiasm, enormous investment in educational film production, and massive media-comparison research efforts on the use of films in education (Allen, 1960; Carpenter & Greenhill, 1956; Hoban & van Ormer, 1951), the film has not reached its expected potential (Saettler, 2004) and its effectiveness in education is inconclusive and marginal, if any (Hoban, 1971; Wagner, 1978).

Maddux and Cummings (2004) have identified the lack of theoretical connections of innovations as the main contributor to their premature end. Without a foundation in learning theory, any technology-based instruction and learning may be driven predominantly by state-of-the-art technologies, thus, losing sight of the purpose of learning. Many researchers have therefore contended that effective and meaningful technology-based learning should be rooted in a sound theoretical basis, advocating linking constructivist views of learning to design practice (Bednar, Cunningham, Duffy, & Perry, 1991; Dabbagh, 2005; Jonassen, 1998).

Because the emergence of wiki is viewed as a potentially powerful tool for enabling new types of learning, we need to ensure that it does not turn into just another "fad" in educational technology. An exploration of its pedagogical foundations is needed before it becomes widespread. Therefore, the purpose of this chapter is to explore the current thinking on how people learn and how the technical affordances of wikis can support the learning.

DESIGN PRINCIPLES OF MEANINGFUL LEARNING

In the past few decades, constructivist learning theory has emerged as one of the greatest influences on education (Brooks & Brooks, 1993). In the constructivist view, knowledge is a consensus of beliefs, a consensus open to continual negation. Learning is therefore a knowledge construction process, a process that involves both active individual construction of meaning (Piaget, 1977) and an individual enculturation into a community (Vygotsky, 1986). In practice, the ultimate goal of instruction is to facilitate learners' meaningful learning of knowledge construction (Jonassen & Strobel, 2006).

What is "meaningful learning?" Definitions of this concept vary. Researchers have approached it from different perspectives and come up with definitions with differing focuses. As early as in the 1960s, David Ausbel's meaningful learning theory, as opposed to rote learning or memorization, emphasized relating new knowledge (concepts and proposition) to what students already know (prior knowledge) and proposed the notion of an advance organizer as a way to provide "mental scaffolding" to help learners acquire new knowledge. Based on Ausbel's theory, Novak and Gowin (1984) have developed "concept maps" as an instructional technique to promote meaningful learning, which also emphasizes the importance of prior knowledge. Wiske (1998) provided another perspective about meaningful learning with a focus on subject matter content, advocating that teaching of subject matter be central to the domain or discipline; accessible and interesting to students; exciting for the teacher's intellectual passions; and easily connected to other topics, whether inside or outside the discipline.

More recently, Jonassen (1994) examined the concept of meaningful learning from a constructivist perspective, asserting that meaningful learning is *active, constructive, intentional, authentic, and cooperative*. That is, meaningful learning is an *active* knowledge *construction* process that is driven by fulfilling a cognitive goal (*intentional*), usually through an *authentic* learning task, in a *collaborative* manner within a community. This community could be as small as a pair (such as the commonly used pair-work in class,) or as large as the whole community on a subject (such as the whole world online community working on the Wikipedia project). The term "meaningful learning" has coexisted with, and sometimes been used interchangeably with terms like "authentic learning," "situated learning," "engaged learning," "collaborative learning," or even "project-based learning" and "problem-based learning," given that these terms have derived from similar theoretical underpinnings—constructivist views of learning. Meaningful learning appears to be a more generic term that encompasses characteristics of current thinking on how people learn, such as "authentic," "collaborative," and "engaging." This chapter will adopt Jonassen's view on meaningful learning and use it as a pedagogical framework for learning design of wikis.

Jonassen, Howland, Marra, and Chrismond (2008) suggest five major roles technologies can play to support meaningful learning. First, technologies are *knowledge construction tools* with which learners can represent their thinking and produce knowledge bases in a multimedia format. Second, technologies are *information exploration tools* that learners use to locate, access, compare, and analyze information. Third, technologies provide *authentic learning contexts* that represent and simulate the real-world environment. Fourth, technologies are *social media* that facilitate communication and collaboration among knowledge-building communities. Fifth, technologies are *intellectual partners* of learners that support the learning processes of exploration, articulation, collaboration, and reflection.

Jonassen and his colleagues' framework for meaningful learning has been widely used in designing technology-enhanced teaching and learning, such as web-based instruction (Jonassen, 1999), video-enhanced learning (Karppinen, 2005), and virtual learning environments (Martinell, Sime, & O'Donoghue, 2006). Is wiki an ideal tool to support meaningful learning? The following section will explore how the unique features of wikis have correlated nicely with the attributes of meaningful learning.

HOW WIKIS CAN SUPPORT MEANINGFUL LEARNING

Created and released on the Internet in 1995 by Ward Cunningham, the earliest version of wiki was intended to be a group work tool for scientists at CERN (the European Organization for Nuclear Research), but has morphed into different forms and runs in different directions. From the early server-based wiki engines to the later hosted wikis, the number of wiki engines has grown exponentially since 2006 (Woods & Thoeny, 2007), with varied and expanding characteristics. But all wikis appear to share the following three fundamental characteristics that are highly suitable for facilitating meaningful learning.

First—Quickness and Simplicity

Wikis are technically quick and easy. Wiki, meaning "quick" in Hawaiian, allows for quick and easy creation of a website and change of the content on the site with no knowledge of HTML or skills of sophisticated web development tools. Different from the traditional way of web development that has relied on servers and FTP, requiring the burden of administration and sophisticated technical skills, current wiki engines provide hosted wikis (also known as wiki farms)—wiki engines that are installed and hosted on public servers, which allow anyone to create a website by simply signing up for an account. Hosted wikis usually provide design templates from which users can choose and later modify the look and feel of their wiki sites. The number of free hosted wikis has exploded since 2005, thus opening the floodgate to easy-and-quick web publishing (Woods & Thoeny, 2007).

While wikis' quickness and simplicity has originally referred to the set-up, running, and updating of a site and its pages, these features also hold true when multimedia components are concerned. Most hosted wikis allow users to upload and display multimedia elements on a page with a few clicks, including still images, YouTube videos, MP3 files, slideshow, and the like. The procedure is as simple as inserting an image into a word processing program (e.g., MS Word documents). Some wiki engines, such as Twiki. com, have further expanded the power of wikis by supporting widgets and plug-ins to increase the interactivity and usability of a wiki site. Widgets, such as *Slide.com*, spice up a wiki page with interactive photo slide shows and picture galleries. Plug-ins that have preinstalled in Twiki engine add more functions to a wiki page, including calendar, RSS feeds, threaded discussion, polling, searching, and so on. All these features enable users to create a full-fledged interactive Web site quickly and effortlessly.

The quickness and simplicity of wikis has significant implications in education. Throughout the history of instructional technology, the learning curve of an emerging technology has always been one of the major barriers to the wide adoption and further integration of that technology into teaching and learning environments (Cuban, 2001). Wikis' quickness and ease of use ease the way for knowledge construction, allowing learners to articulate and produce ideas and understanding represented in a multimedia format effortlessly. The flattened learning curve of wikis frees learners from grappling with mastering the tool; they can instead concentrate more on thinking, reasoning, and learning.

Second—Openness and Self-Regulation

Closely associated with quickness and simplicity, wikis level the playing field of Web publishing, allowing anyone to create and publish in the online world. The open access nature of wikis allows any participants to add, change, edit, or delete the content on a wiki page, enabling information access, sharing, and collective knowledge building in a truly democratic way. While recent wikis have added the access control feature that has split the current wiki world into two fields—fully open and gated, the wiki, along with other Web 2.0 tools, still remains the top open and democratic online tool that facilitates free publishing. Wikis' open and democratic nature opens the door to a wider and wilder world where learners have much more access to individuals' minds. Serving as an authentic learning context, the wiki exposes learners to a real-world environment—an environment where the good, the bad, the ugly; the true, the false, and the unknown coexist and intertwine, which requires higher levels of thinking and reasoning of learners.

In addition to the openness is the *revision control*, also known as *revision tracking*, another key feature of wiki that enables users to track the editing history of the page and to revert a page to a previous version or restore a damaged page. The page revision tracking is critical in guarding against vandalism (intentional or accidental) in an open access Web publishing world. It has also important value in learning because it is a great "mirroring tool" (Jermann & Dimitracopoulou, 2004) that prompts learners' awareness of self-regulation. Strictly linked to reflection, self-regulation is an important life-long learning skill and critical to tackling complex real-world learning tasks. Self-regulated learners monitor their behavior in terms of their goals and self-reflect on their increasing effectiveness (Zimmerman, 2002). In addition to promoting self-regulation and reflection, wiki's *revision control* could help teachers keep track of the learning process of a learner as well as the progress of the group work. Along with *revision control, revision diffs*, a feature that shows the differences between two page revisions, makes it easy for teachers to spot changes between different versions. Meaningful learning has emphasized the importance of the knowledge construction process in which learners actively explore, articulate, and reflect to build up their own understanding and knowledge. Wikis' revision tracking feature is a viable tool to "document" this learning, thinking and growing process.

Third—Collaboration

It is a widely held opinion that wikis are an ideal tool for supporting collaboration and harnessing the power of crowds. Wikis require true collaboration within a community that goes beyond "work alongside" each other. Since wikis operate on the principle of mutual trust and self-governing, people who contribute to a wiki site or page should share common interest and goal, which is the driving force for true collaboration. In a true collaborative environment, knowledge is collectively constructed and the final product is something that an individual could not be able to produce alone. Thus, shared authorship and ownership of the content of a wiki is becoming an essential attitude among the wiki community (Woods & Thoeny, 2007).

While openness has been the trademark and defining feature of wikis, recent wikis have added the *access/editing control* feature to protect wiki sites. Most hosted wikis have offered several choices for access and editing. Wikispaces, for example, provides three options to its users: public (pages can be viewed and edited by anyone), protected (pages can be viewed by anyone but can be edited only by invited members), and private (pages can be viewed and edited only by invited members). Meanwhile, most hosted wikis make inviting participants quite easy, requiring only the email address or the member's username. Invited users have the option to accept or decline the invitation; site moderators also have the option to delete the participants or change options of access and editing. This is a great feature to facilitate effective management and smooth and dynamic collaboration among a group of participants.

With the advance of the wiki technology, more features have been developed and added to support collaboration and group work. Some wiki engines, such as Confluence, come with built-in *blogging* and *threaded discussion* functionalities, allowing a group to write quickly and publish instantly their blog posts, news items, and discussion threads. As learners need prompt scaffolding and coaching during their knowledge construction process, wikis' blogging and threaded discussions can be used to provide continuing and on-time feedback and guidance to learners from teachers or more able peers. In addition, the *Mark for Review* plug-in provided by Confluence allows users to submit feedback about page content by using the "Review" tab on each wiki page, a list of which can help group leaders or moderators responsible for that site or page effectively collect and summarize feedback from the online community and make revision if necessary.

Obviously, wikis' unique features open up new possibilities for teaching and learning. Technologies have traditionally been used as a "teaching" tool to transmit knowledge to students, removing any active control of the learning process by the learners (Jonassen, Howland, Marra, & Crismond, 2008). The wiki, on the contrary, appears to be an ideal "mind tool" (Jonassen, 2000) that can be used to engage learners in authentic learning tasks that require active and collaborative thinking and learning.

MAJOR TYPES OF WIKI USE IN EDUCATION

The past few years have seen growing interest and increased use of wikis in education. More and more schools and colleges are turning to wikis for better collaboration and group projects (Deubel, 2008; Villano, 2008). This section will discuss the major types of wiki used for facilitating meaningful learning, with each type illustrated with examples identified in current literature.

E-Journaling

As early as in the 1960s, Progoff (1965), advocator of Intensive Journal Method, saw the value of personal journals in enhancing growth and learning. Since then, journaling as an instructional technique for promoting self-reflection has gained increasing attention in education, especially when it is enabled by the Web technology (Hiemstra, 2001; King & LaRocco, 2006; Phipps, 2005). E-journaling on the Web (such as blogs) has emerged as a new way for people to record, share, and reflect on their inner capacity. While many people are e-journaling using blog engines, wiki-based journaling appears to be more flexible in terms of interface and layout. E-journaling in blog way is arranged chronologically and enables commenting for each entry. Wiki interface, however, can be simple or sophisticated to meet the needs and skill levels of users who can design the "look and feel" of their journals their way. "A wiki can be a blog, but a blog does not have to be a wiki" (Mattison, 2003).

At Penn State University, "Epochewiki" (http://epochewiki.pbwiki.com/RhetoricAndComposition), a Rhetoric wiki project, uses PBWiki for students to blog about their experiences during the class and develop ideas for their writing projects. Journaling on wikis provides opportunities for personalized intellectual exchange between learners and the instructor and among a group of learners. It is also an ideal form for learners to document their growth or record their thinking path in a course or on a subject. Journal writing is a real-life task that many people have experienced and the personal nature inherent to diary-style writing involves learners emotionally. Online journaling takes this task to a new level by connecting the learner to a wider range of readers.

E-Portfolios

Portfolios have been widely recognized as a great tool for enabling authentic assessment of learning of both the final products and the learning process. The digitization of text, graphics, sound, and video has made creation, manipulation, and management of portfolios much easier than ever before. The wiki is an extremely simple tool to aid learners in collecting and organizing digital assets for a course or on a subject. The wiki-based portfolio could be an individual or collaborative endeavor and be shared among students in a class or made public for a wider audience. Publishing a learner's or a group of learners' learning to real audience would highly motivate learners, and enforce their sense of fulfillment and accomplishment.

An example of wiki-based e-portfolio is the "e-Folio 2008" project, created by students in Westwood Schools, Camilla, Georgia (http://westwood. wikispaces.com/eFolio+2008) (Figure 12.1). This wiki site is a collection of the school's ninth grade students' multimedia projects in a Computer Fundamentals class. Each student has a page listing his/her projects completed in this course, including MS Word, MS Excel, MS PowerPoint, movies, activist reports, and technology programs used this year. Westwood Schools' E-Folio site is a great example of showcase e-Portfolio that provides students opportunities to present accomplishments and share with not only the class but also the whole Web community.

Group Projects

Collaborative learning has been used as an instructional technique for some time and its effectiveness has been boosted by emerging computer technologies, especially Web technology (Johnson & Johnson, 2004). Be-

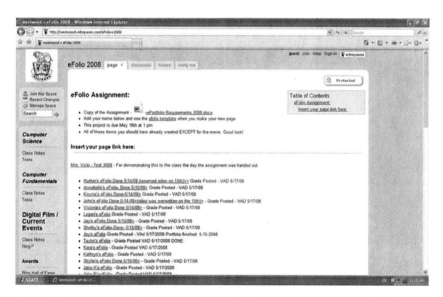

Figure 12.1 A screen of the "e-Folio 2008" at Westwood Schools, Camilla, Georgia. Reprinted with kind permission of Vicki A. Davis.

cause of its inherent simplicity and democratic nature, wiki is an ideal tool for facilitating and promoting student collaboration online. Students can use wiki to collaborate on a project, whether writing a term paper, preparing a presentation, collecting data or materials for an assigned topic, or collaboratively programming a computer game. Wiki-based collaborative projects engage learners in meaningful learning by providing them the opportunity to mimic how people work in the real world, and by promoting "pride of authorship, ownership, and friendship" among a group of learners. In addition to learning from each other, learners acquire interpersonal, negotiation, reasoning, and many other groupwork skills that are needed in real-life situation.

"The Flat Classroom Project" (http://flatclassroomproject.wikispaces. com/) (Figure 12.2), a global project for middle and senior high school students, jointed virtually two or more classes from the world and had students study and discuss real-world scenarios based on *The World is Flat* by Thomas Friedman. Using the wiki engine of wikispaces.com, students were grouped (e.g., one or two students from Bangladesh with one or two students from southern US) to work together on a specific topic. Wikis have enabled the collaboration in its truest sense—the collaboration being more than just "working alongside" each other, rather the joint development of meaning and understanding that each individual has shared, contributed to, reflected on, and finally agreed upon.

Figure 12.2 A screen of "The Flat Classroom Project 2007." Reprinted with kind permission of Vicki A. Davis and Julie Lindsay.

Wikipedia-Like Projects

What makes wiki famous is Wikipedia, a free online encyclopedia that allows anyone to edit and add. In addition to Wikipedia, Wikimedia Foundation has launched several other wiki-based projects, including Wikitionary (a free content dictionary and thesauri), Wikibooks (a collection of free e-book resources), Wikicommons (a collection of free video, images, music, spoken texts, and other free media). Such wiki-based projects run by Wikimedia have enormous implications for instruction. As with any field, there are key terms and definitions that form the basic "language" of a subject area. Wikipedia or Wikitionary is an ideal form for a class to collaboratively develop an online encyclopedia/dictionary on a subject matter that is under study. All members of a class can collaboratively work on the definitions and illustrations of key concepts/terms. Such projects require individual learners to research in a specific area of a term/concept and share findings with the class; the class as a whole would then come up with comprehensive information on the term/concept that an individual would otherwise not be able to accomplish.

Similarly, learners in the same field can collaborate to write a wiki-based book over a semester or across-semester on a subject matter. One such example is "Blended Learning in K–12" published on Wikibooks (http://en.wikibooks.org/wiki/Blended_Learning_in_K-12) (Figure 12.3). This wiki

Figure 12.3   A screen of a wiki book "Blended Learning in K–12." Source: Wiki-Books.

book examines the concept of "blended learning" and how it relates to the integration of technologies in the K–12 environment. The contributors are faculty and teacher-participants of the Curriculum, Technology, & Education Reform (CTER) Online—a master of education program offered at the College of Education, University of Illinois, Urbana-Champaign. [Insert Figure 3 about here.] Another example of wiki-books is Code and Other Laws of Cyberspace, written and put on wikis by Lawrence Lessig, a Law professor at Stanford University, at http://codebook.jot.com/WikiHome. First published in 1999 in print, the code in the book needs revision and updating to reflect the change in law, technology, and the context in which they reside. Lessig is using wiki to open the updating process to the whole online community, allowing any interested users to edit this book.

Course Web Sites

Course Web sites have been considered an effective communication and instructional tool for teachers and students. Designing and developing a class Web site is very time-consuming and technically demanding for educators. The simplicity and openness of wikis make Web publishing and updating a much easier task that allows all members of the class to collaborate in organizing and developing common course assets, such as developing the syllabus and topics of study, collecting learning materials, and compiling final products for showcase. Meanwhile, a class Web site can consist of an individual student's home page and how the class Web site looks and feels depends largely on every class member's contribution. Wiki-based class Web site involves every student who has essentially the same rights, abilities, and responsibilities.

A widely cited wiki course site is "The Romantic Audience Project" (http://ssad.bowdoin.edu:9780/snipsnap/eng242-s05/space/start), a British Literature class taught by Mark Phillipson at Bowdoin College, Maine (Kinzie, 2005; Read, 2005) (Figure 12.4). This site is a collaborative study of romanticism with contributions by all students enrolled in this course. The instructor, as the site moderator, issued weekly posting assignment that designated certain poems for everyone in the class to comment upon, and required responses to peer entries. Students were free to comment on each other's work and the source text. "An atmosphere of collectivity" was paramount during the collective course construction process (Phillipson & Hamilton, n.d.).

Another exemplar of wiki course site is Boston College's "Computers in Management" class taught by Jerald Kane (http://www.socialtext.net/cim/index.cgi), who has been using the wiki (SocialText.Inc) as the primary teaching tool (Figure 12.5). The wiki is the platform and repository where

Figure 12.4 A screen of "The Romantic Audience Project." Reprinted with kind permission of Dr. Mark Phillipson.

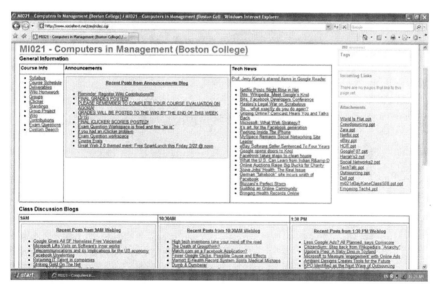

Figure 12.5 A screen of the course "Computers in Management" at Boston College. Reprinted with kind permission of Dr. Jerald Kane.

the course information and content (such as the text) is generated collectively (Havenstein, 2007). Students collaborated to build out the course by, for example, suggesting exam questions, additional articles and news clips from remote sites such as the *Wall Street Journal*, *New York Times*, and *Business Week*, and creating course content through individual and group projects, the content of which can be used for both the current and future classes. As a lead learner of his course and witnessing the power of the crowd, Professor Kane contended that wikis are ideal tools to create productive collaborative environments where the end product is better than what he could have done himself (Instructional Design & eTeaching Services, 2007).

Obviously, wikis are a viable tool to facilitate the active, authentic and collaborative knowledge construction process. The abundance of wiki's technical features can be used effectively and effortlessly to facilitate the meaningful learning/thinking process of exploration, articulation, collaboration, and reflection. Wikis can be used for a range of purposes: personal expression (e.g., e-journaling), database (e.g., e-portfolios), web publishing (e.g., wikibooks, wikipedias), knowledge management (course web sites), and group project management (group projects). Wikis appear to be a flexible web development tool that allows various forms of group work. E-journaling and e-portfolio are mainly for individual use of personal expression and database, and the authorship and ownership of the site and its content are owned by an individual, viewed and commented on by many. In contrast, the authorship and ownership of group projects, Wikipedia-like projects, and course web sites will be shared by all participants/collaborators. Such sites could be viewed by all members of the web community, but can be edited only by invited members, depending on the setting of the control access.

CHALLENGES AND FUTURE RESEARCH DIRECTIONS

While wikis' shared authorship and ownership has been regarded the trademark of this technology, it is this very feature that also poses questions for schools and universities where assessments are still largely based on individual efforts (Boulos, Maramba, & Wheeler, 2006). Careful planning of group work and clear assessment guidelines are needed to meet this challenge and address the assessment issue. Similarly, wikis' anonymity (unless identification is transparent) and openness may not prove itself to be an ideal tool for group work on controversial topics or issues. To avoid unexpected "warring wiki" and failed collaboration for a group project, teachers should be mindful of which wiki to choose as the collaboration tool.

As an emerging technology, the use of wikis in education is still a relatively new development and research on the use and evaluation of its effectiveness is in its infancy. While there exists an abundance of trade magazine style articles (see for example, Carpenter & Roberts, 2006; EduCause, 2005; Lamb, 2006) and testimonials/case studies (see for example, Augar, Raitman & Zhou, 2004; Bold, 2006) about the use of wikis discussing students' experience and insights, they are largely based on anecdotal observations that lack scientific rigor. There is an urgent need for rigorously designed research studies to establish a pedagogic evidence base about the wiki. Studies could analyze the benefits and limitations of wikis (as well as other Web 2.0 applications) used in various learning contexts and academic disciplines. Studies could also investigate whether and to what extent wikis are actually making a difference in the ways students collaborate.

CONCLUSION

Just like the wide space it offers, the opportunities and potential the wiki provides to education are wide open. This paper is an exploratory effort to identify the pedagogical foundations and theory-based design principles to maximize wikis' potential for supporting meaningful learning. The major types of wiki use in current education may serve as a startup for educators who plan to incorporate wikis into the classroom. With the advance of Web 2.0 technology, new educational applications may emerge as people become more familiar with this emerging tool. Careful planning of group work and rigorous research studies are needed in order to make optimal use of the wiki as a tool to facilitate meaningful learning.

REFERENCES

Allen, W. H. (1960). Audio-visual communication: Administration of AV programs. In C. Harris, & W. Harris (Ed.), *Encyclopedia of educational research* (pp. 115–136). New York: Macmillan.

Augar, N., Raitman, R., & Zhou, W. (2004). Teaching and learning online with wikis. In R. Atkinson, C. McBeath, D. Jonas-Dwyer & R. Phillips (Eds), *Beyond the comfort zone: Proceedings of the 21st ASCILITE Conference* (pp. 95–104). Perth, 5–8 December. Available at http://www.ascilite.org.au/conferences/perth04/procs/augar.html

Bednar, A. K., Cunningham, D., Duffy, T. M., & Perry, J. D. (1991). Theory into practice: How do we link? In T. Duffy, & D. Jonassen (Eds.), *Constructivism and the technology of instruction: A conversation* (pp. 17–34). Hillsdale, NJ: Erlbaum.

Bold, M. (2006). Use of wikis in graduate course work. *Journal of Interactive Learning Research, 17*(1), 5–14.

Boulos, M., Maramba, I., & Wheeler, S. (2006). *Wikis, blogs, and podcasts: A new generation of web-based tools for virtual collaborative clinical practice and education.* Retrieved April 6, 2008, from http://www.biomedcentral.com/1472-6920/6/41

Brooks, J. G., & Brooks, M. G. (1993). *In search of understanding: The case for constructivist classrooms.* Alexandria, VA: The Association for Supervision and Curriculum Development.

Carpenter, C. R., & Greenhill, L. P. (1956). *Instructional film research reports: Vol. 2* (Technical Report No. 269-7-61). Port Washington, NY: U.S. Navy Special Devices Center.

Cuban, L. (2001). *Oversold and underused: Computers in the classroom.* Cambridge: Harvard University Press.

Dabbagh, N. (2005). Pedagogical models for e-learning: A theory-based design framework. *International Journal of Technology in Teaching and Learning, 1*(1), 25–44.

Deubel, P. (2008). A taste of Web 2.0. Retrieved May 9, 2008, from http://www.thejournal.com/articles/22266

Educause. (2005). *7 things you should know about wikis.* Retrieved March 1, 2008, from http://net.educause.edu/ir/library/pdf/ELI7004.pdf

Hiemstra, R. (2001). Uses and benefits of journal writing. In L. A. English & M. A. Gillen (Eds.), *Promoting journal writing in adult education* (Vol. 90, pp. 19–26). San Francisco: Jossey-Bass.

Hoban, C. F. (1971). *Instructional films: State of the art.* Stanford, CA: Stanford University.

Hoban, C. F., & Van Ormer, E. B. (Eds). (1951). *Instructional film research (rapid mass learning) 1918–1950.* New York: Arno Press.

Jermann P., & Dimitracopoulou A. (2004). *Future research directions on interaction analysis indicators.* Retrieved March 8, 2008, from: http://telearn.noe-kaleidoscope.org

Johnson, D., & Johnson, R. (2004). Cooperation and the use of technology. In D.H. Jonassen (Ed.), *Handbook of research for educational communications and technology* (pp. 785–812). Mahwah, NJ: Erlbaum.

Jonassen, D. H. (1994). Thinking technology. *Educational Technology, 34*(4), 34–37.

Jonassen, D. H. (2000). Computers as mindtools for schools: Engaging critical thinking. Upper Saddle River, NJ: Merrill.

Jonassen, D. H. (1999). *Constructivist learning environments on the web: Engaging students in meaningful learning.* Retrieved January 6, 2008, from http://www3.moe.edu.sg/edumall/mpite/edtech/papers/d1.pdf

Jonassen, D. H., Howland, J., Marra, R. M., & Chrismond, D. (2008). *Meaningful learning with technology* (3rd ed.). Upper Saddle River, NJ: Pearson Education.

Jonassen, D. H., & Strobel, J. (2006) Modeling for meaningful learning, in D. Hung & M. S. Khine (Eds), *Engaged learning with emerging technologies* (pp. 1–27). Dordrecht, The Netherlands: Springer.

Karppinen, P. (2005). Meaningful learning with digital and online videos: Theoretical perspectives. *AACE Journal, 13*(3), 233–250.

King F. B., & LaRocco D. J. (2006). E-journaling: A strategy to support student reflection and understanding. *Current Issues in Education* [On-line], *9*(4). Available at http://cie.ed.asu.edu/volume9/number4/

Kinzie, S. (2005, March 11). Blogging clicks with colleges–Interactive Web pages changing class participation. *Washington Post.* Retrieved March 1, 2008, from http://www.washingtonpost.com/wp-dyn/articles/A25305-2005Mar10.html

Kulik, J. A. (1994). Meta-analytic studies of findings on computer-based instruction. In E. L. Baker & H. F. O'Neil (Eds.), *Technology assessment in education and training* (pp. 9–33). Hillsdale, NJ: Erlbaum.

Lamb, B. (2004). Wide open spaces: Wikis, ready or not. *EDUCAUSE Review, 39*(5), 36–48.

Maddux, C., & Cumings, R. (2004). Fad, fashion, and weak role of theory and research in information technology in education. *Journal of Technology and Teacher Education, 12*(4). 511–533.

Martinell, A., Sime, J., & O'Donoghue, M. (2006). *Design of a constructivist virtual learning environment composed by video summaries.* Retrieved May 1, 2008, from http://www.lancs.ac.uk/postgrad/ramirezm/papers/Edutec2006/EDUTEC2006_Ramirez.htm

Mattison, D. (2003). Quickiwiki, Swiki, Twiki, Zwiki and the Plone wars: Wiki as a PIM and collaborative content tool, [Electronic version]. *Searcher, 11*(4), 32–48.

Novak, J. D., & Gowin, D. B. (1984). *Learning how to learn.* New York: Cambridge University Press.

Owen, M., Grant, L., Sayers, S., & Facer, K. (2006). Social software and learning. Retrieved September 29, 2006, from http://www.futurelab.org.uk/research/opening_education/social_software_01.htm

Phipps, J. (2005). E-journaling: Achieve interactive education online. *Educause Quarterly, 28*(1).

Piaget, J. (1977). The Role of action in the development of thinking. In W. F. Overton & J. M. Gallagher (Eds.), *Advances in research and theory.* New York: Plenum Press.

Progoff, I. (1975). *At a journal workshop.* New York: Dialogue House Library.

Read, B. (2005, July 15). Romantic poetry meets 21st-century technology. *The Chronicle of Higher Education.* Retrieved March 30, 2008, from http://chronicle.com/free/v51/i45/45a03501.htm

Richardson, W. (2006). *Blogs, wikis, podcasts, and other powerful Web tools for classrooms.* Thousand Oaks, CA: Corwin Press.

Saettler, P. (1968). Instructional materials: Educational media and technology. *Review of Educational Research, 38*(2), 115–128.

Saettler, P. (2004). *The evolution of American educational technology.* Greenwich, CT: Information Age.

Wagner, R. W. (1978). Film research: The need for a new breed. *Educational Technology Research & Development, 26*(1), 65–78.

Wiske, M. S. (1998). What is teaching for understanding? In Wiske, M. S. (Ed.) *Teaching for understanding: Linking research with practice.* San Francisco: Jossey-Bass.

Woods, D., & Thoeny, P. (2007). *Wikis for dummies.* Hoboken, NJ: Wiley Publishing.

Villano, M. (2008, April 1). *Wikis, blogs & more, Oh My!* Campus Technology.

Vygotsky, L. S. (1986). The genetic roots of thought and speech. In A. Kozulin (Trans. & Ed.), *Thought and language.* Cambridge, MA: MIT Press.

Zimmerman, B. J. (2002). Becoming a self-regulated learner: An overview. Retrieved May 20, 2008, from http://findarticles.com/p/articles/mi_m0NQM/is_2_41/ai_90190493/print

CHAPTER 13

YOU'VE GOT TO SEE THIS

Looking Back On/Forward from On-Line Hypermediated Art Criticism and Collaborative Digital Technology

B. Stephen Carpenter, II
Texas A&M University

Pamela G. Taylor
Virginia Commonwealth University

INTRODUCTION

We previously explored ways in which Type II computer technology applications (Maddox and Johnson, 2006a) offer learners and educators ways to interpret works of art and visual culture that expand traditional linear conventions and encourage multi-linear possibilities (Carpenter and Taylor, 2006). Our previous work with computer hypertext applications *Tinderbox*™ and *Storyspace*™ suggests that collaborative, multi-linear interpretations of works of art and visual culture enable users to construct meanings that they would otherwise not encounter (Carpenter and Taylor, 2003; Taylor and Carpenter, 2005; Taylor and Carpenter, 2007; Taylor, 2000; Taylor; 2006; Taylor, 2007). While effective for expanding the discourse and levels of en-

Wired for Learning: An Educator's Guide to Web 2.0, pages 215–232
Copyright © 2009 by Information Age Publishing
All rights of reproduction in any form reserved.

gagement with interpretations of visual art and visual culture, such technologies do not allow for more global forms of collaborations that interactions on the World Wide Web provide. Maddox and Johnson (2006b) have since offered web-based examples of Type II technologies such as blogs, wikis, *WebCT,* webquests, and video conferencing. These and other web-based technologies lend themselves to the hypermediated criticism approaches we developed and used with Type II technologies in that users become more than mere readers of content. With blogs and wikis for example, users may also add content to what they read and thereby become active participants in the construction of web-based content. Similarly, *VoiceThread* allows users to upload presentations that combine images, video, text, and voice. Readers may add their own text and voice comments as well as visual elements that embrace and extend the hypermediated criticism approaches we used with Type II applications. In this chapter we consider how to take our previous engagements with hypermediated criticism and apply them to the interpretation of visual culture, using Web 2.0 technologies of *Voice-Thread*, blogs, image galleries, and *Second Life.* Our focus on visual culture emphasizes a shift from traditional interpretive practices in visual studies from the perspectives of producers to those of the consumers (Mirzoeff, 1999) who become participants in the process of meaning making. Further, as we focus our hypermediated criticism on examples of visual culture we underscore our theoretical perspective to empower the interpretive contributions of users and viewers with content from their own lived experiences. From our analysis of these Web 2.0 hypermediated criticism experiences we provide suggestions for pedagogical and curricular implications of engaging Web 2.0 in K–12 and other educational settings.

What would it take to get students to say to each other upon entering a classroom, "You've got to see this!"? Actually, this vision for engaged and meaningful art education was one we shared when we began our work on multilinear interactive hypertext in art education many years ago. We explored ways in which Type II computer technology applications (Maddox and Johnson, 2006a) offer learners and educators ways to interpret works of art and visual culture that expand traditional linear conventions and encourage multi-linear possibilities (Carpenter and Taylor, 2006). Our previous work with computer hypertext applications *Tinderbox*™ and *Storyspace*™ to interpret works of art and visual culture suggests that collaborative, multi-linear interpretations of works of art and visual culture enable users to construct meanings that they would otherwise not encounter on their own (Carpenter and Taylor, 2003; Taylor and Carpenter, 2005; Taylor and Carpenter, 2007; Taylor, 2000; Taylor; 2006; Taylor, 2007). Our initial projects were developed, designed, and implemented with the use of applications housed within our Macintosh computers (Taylor, 2000). The only way to share files—or thoughts, images, and videos—between and among different users was to construct a slightly complicated work-around that would link part of one user's file to part of another user's file. When attempting to make a connection among and between files created by different users, one had to eject the current 3.5" floppy disk on which the current file was saved and replace it with another disk when prompted by the computer. As memory on computers increased, our files grew in size, as did the files our students created. We migrated to larger ZIP disks, only to face the same limitations of size and interactivity among users. Our next step was to share files as e-mail attachments and to work collaboratively on the same document (Carpenter and Taylor, 2003). This approach solved, temporarily, the limitations imposed by size until the files became too large to send as attachments and we resorted to saving the file on a server. This solution was limited further in that only one person could make additions to the hypertext at any given time and this approach did not necessarily replicate the kinds of interactivity we imagined might be possible with computer technology in art education. For example, with the use of Google Docs we constructed initial drafts of this manuscript—we both wrote, edited, and moved around text simultaneously—as well as other written documents in an online, real time collaborative format. These kinds of real-time, simultaneous interactions refer to the collaborative engagements we had in mind in our previous work but were unable to realize given the limitations of the software applications. Simply, we were frustrated because we were hoping to do more than the software was designed to do while at the same time, it was our use and exploration of the software that motivated and propelled us to push its limits and seek ways to engage collaboratively.

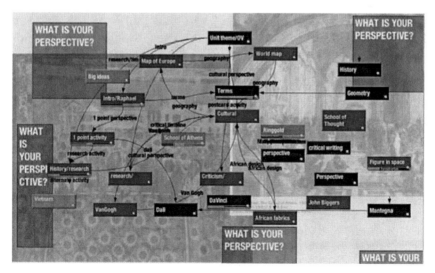

Figure 13.1   Screen shot of Tinderbox document map view.

We were not alone in our frustration. According to "Taking the 'A' out of Asynchronous," a recent *Campus Technology* article by Matt Villano (2008), more and more universities are both clamoring for and developing technologies that support more synchronous collaboration. From real time office hours for faculty to IT workers developing software programs together from remote locations, such asynchronous e-learning activities move our ideas of Web 2.0 capabilities to even more exciting possibilities than previously imagined. More frequently, conferences on computer technology and education are including presentations to and by entire teams of IT staff as forms of professional development for local schools, districts, and universities. Adobe's Acrobat Connect™ enables educators to set up on-demand virtual meeting rooms where people can come in and communicate in real time. Although the idea of getting immediate feedback on a project or idea, from a professor to a student, seems exciting and needed, the expectations associated with such possibilities can be problematic. This situation stems from traditional face-to-face interactions with teachers and students. Some participants in digital educational contexts expect them to always function like real world situations. As e-mail use and online classes become more prevalent, students appear more likely to ask questions in these digital communication environments than in face-to-face classes, so much so in fact, that some faculty members feel inundated with student e-mails at all hours of the day and night.

Other problematic issues include the "Big Brother syndrome," where we are no longer alone with our computers. When shopping, a pop-up message may appear asking if we need help finding a specific item or suggesting that we may want to purchase another item along with the one we are currently contemplating. These pop-ups are designed to encourage our consumerist behaviors. They remind us of scenes in the Tom Cruise movie *Minority Report*, in which citizens become potential consumers as they become victims of customized marketing campaigns as a result of the artificial intelligence embedded in the advertisements they pass by. We see the initial signs of such technology actually reaching our own experiences as we shop in grocery stores outfitted with flatscreen televisions that broadcast commercials for food and other items as we stroll past them up and down the aisles pushing our carts or imagine the possibilities of bypassing long checkout lines as our items are scanned and our cards charged as we walk out of the store.

With the increase in attention to online learning and interactive technologies we must not forget that access is not as universal as we might like. The early problems we both faced—like most educators who began to gravitate their instruction to on-line environments—with student access to computers and computer literacy still remain, but to different degrees. Further, the "digital divide" is still very much a real world issue that separates the "computer haves" from the "computer have-nots." The *New York Times* (Barboza, 2008) reports that for the first time there are more Internet users in China than in the United States. While sheer population numbers of each country should make this story a non-issue, what is relevant for educators and learners in this example is that with increasing numbers of on-line users comes increasing numbers of on-line consumers and producers of content for commercial, educational, informational, social, and other purposes. As this increase in users continues, educators will no doubt face additional issues with respect to learning styles, volume of learners, forms of digital interactivity, levels of computer literacy, and ways to create, share, receive, and reproduce visual and other content, and perhaps most importantly, provide access to those who do not have it.

YOU'VE GOT TO SEE THIS

Mary Panzer (2008) writes about MediaStorm (http://mediastorm.org), a contemporary Internet-based photojournalism company in which the producers "start with the photographs" rather than with the stories. In comparing this new photojournalism approach to the more traditional approach one might associate with *LIFE* magazine for example, Panzer (2008) observes, "Old *LIFE* stories began with an idea, and editors would assign photographers to produce pictures and a writer to produce text to fit that concept. MediaStorm producers start with photographs" (p. D-7).

> Among the many award-winners, a commission from Reuters called "Bearing Witness: Five Years of the Iraq War" (http://iraq.reuters.com) has won enormous praise from the news community. Another assignment, "Katrina: An Unnatural Disaster" (www.soros.org/resources/multimedia/katrina), for the Open Society Institute, has turned a good but predictable project on life in Louisiana after the hurricanes into vivid segments in which the subjects tell their own frank stories. The most talked-about posting, "One Man Brand" (http://mediastorm.org/workshops_0001.htm), is the product of a weeklong professional workshop and concerns a self-made New York tourist attraction, the Naked Cowboy who performs in Times Square. (Panzer, 2008, p. D-7)

Brian Storm, the president of the *MediaStorm* company, seeks the value of "making connections" to publicize the stories that *MediaStorm* produces.

> Another unique property of the Web has to do with making connections— frictionless transactions that Mr. Storm keeps looking for. After viewing a story, *MediaStorm* viewers can comment, download a transcript, buy a DVD, a book or a song. They can connect to related sites. They can send the story to their friends around the world. "You've got to see this," is probably the endorsement that he values most. (Panzer, 2008, p. D-7)

This new approach to photojournalism takes advantage of the very character of the contemporary "Web generation" who are just as likely to host a blog, buy and sell merchandise online, and inhabit a virtual world all during the course of a typical day. As is inherent with Web 2.0, the emphasis and success of MediaStorm—the recipient of several awards—lies in the connections and interconnections it fosters and relies on for the production, transmission, and publicity of its content. On the MediaStorm blog, Jessica Sturt (2008) makes the following connection,

> If you haven't seen it yet, head over to Interactive Narratives, and check out their newly relaunched site. Originally launched by Andrew DeVigal in 2003, Interactive Narratives is back and better than ever. On the new site, users can view, rate, and submit stories, chat in the forums, check out gear reviews and interviews with multimedia journalists—it's designed to be a "gathering place for multimedia journalists." With backing from the Online News Association, it will be exciting to see where this goes. (Retrieved online July 14, 2008 at http://mediastorm.org/blog/?p=448)

How might educators encourage such a "you've got to see this" atmosphere among learners using Web 2.0 applications and resources? While effective for expanding the discourse and levels of engagement with interpretations of visual art and visual culture, the technologies we used previously do not allow for more global forms of collaborations that interactions on the World Wide Web provide. Maddox and Johnson (2006b) have since offered web-based examples of Type II technologies such as blogs, wikis, WebCT, webquests, and video conferencing. These and other web-based technologies lend themselves to the hypermediated criticism approaches we developed initially and used with Type II technologies in which users become more than mere readers of content. With blogs and wikis for example, users may also add content to what they read and thereby become active participants in the construction of web-based content. Similarly, Voice-Thread™ allows users to upload presentations that combine images, video, text, and voice. Readers may add their own text and voice comments as well as visual elements that embrace and extend the hypermediated criticism approaches we used with Type II applications.

In this chapter we look forward from our work in interactive computer hypertext. By looking back to our previous work, we establish a vantage point from which we consider our current and future engagements with Web 2.0 technologies. This merging of past, present, and future perspectives exemplifies a proleptic pedagogical moment and stance as described by Slattery (2006) and allows us to see that what is to come is embedded within what is now.

In this chapter we consider how to take our previous engagements with hypermediated criticism and apply them to the interpretation of visual culture—visual constructs or devices for seeing that we experience in our daily lives such as television commercials, video conferencing web cams, or virtual worlds—using Web 2.0 technologies. Specifically, we consider our own uses, frustrations, and visions for using on-line image galleries, wikis and blogs, *Google Docs*™, *Voicethread*™, *Second Life*™, and Instant Messaging. Our focus on visual culture emphasizes a shift from traditional interpretive practices in visual studies and the perspectives and practices of producers to those of the consumers (Mirzoeff, 1999) of these cultural constructs and practices who become participants in the process of meaning making. Further, as we focus our hypermediated criticism on examples of visual culture we underscore our theoretical perspective to empower the interpretive contributions of users and viewers with content from their own lived experiences. From our analysis of these Web 2.0 hypermediated criticism experiences we conclude with suggestions for pedagogical and curricular implications of engaging Web 2.0 in K–12 and other educational settings.

Our intention for this chapter is to address nontraditional, alternative, and informal learning with Web 2.0 technologies and related pedagogical issues and instructional uses. We share actual examples from our own classes and collaborations as well as projections and speculations about what might, could, or should be possible in on-line educational settings. We recognize that there are many more collaborative technology tools available than we are familiar with or that we can conceivably mention in this chapter. We, therefore choose to share our explorations of on-line image galleries, wikis and blogs, *Google Docs*™, *Voicethread*™, *Second Life*™, and Instant Messaging as means to engage in imagining extensions of our early hypertag work (Carpenter and Taylor, 2003). Our musings in this chapter are built on empirical, real world case studies and exemplars of uses of Web 2.0 in university and K–12 instruction.

ON-LINE IMAGE GALLERIES

Sharing images between family members, friends, and other acquaintances seems to be a practice as old as photography itself. The translation of these practices from real world experiences to on-line interactions has been relatively easy. While many on-line image galleries are associated with social networks such as MySpace™ and Facebook™, some educators are using on-line image galleries like Picassa™, Flickr™, and Coppermine™ in conjunction with their courses as a forum for students to post work and comment on the contributions of their students. For example, *Seeing Culture* is a site that promotes the development of learning networks among students within the same course, other courses, and visitors who are no longer or were never enrolled in these courses. Author Carpenter, in collaboration with Texas A&M University colleague Lauren Cifuentes and graduate student Sanser Bulu, created *Seeing Culture*, an on-line image gallery based on Web 2.0 theory and technology. Both Carpenter and Cifuentes use *Seeing Culture* in their respective courses on visual culture, curriculum development, and educational technology. They designed *Seeing Culture* as a means to develop a growing but common resource of images and examples of visual culture for the purpose of sharing research and instructional possibilities. They have used *Seeing Culture* as a forum to "gather data to assist us to better understand how, when, and why responses to visuals evolve as learners socially negotiate meanings of images and concepts" (Cifuentes, Carpenter, and Bulu, 2008, unpublished manuscript). This ongoing collaboration is not limited by timetables set by semesters, courses, or instructors and thereby reflects the very elements of Web 2.0 and the interdisciplinary multilinear approaches we have encouraged in our previous work with hypertext in art education.

WIKIS AND BLOGS

As we began sharing our work in computer hypertext through conference presentations, we received feedback on several occasions about how similar our work sounded to a new and growing collaborative on-line environment known as wikis. While similar in the intention to enable multiple users to become both readers and authors, wikis in their early and current forms, do not enable viewers to "see" the connections in a visual map, web, or other format than the linear, text-based interface similar to written words on a page. Perhaps the best-known wiki is Wikipedia™ (http://www.wikipedia.com). Essentially a collaborative on-line encyclopedia, Wikipedia allows readers to become authors of the content of each page and entry. New entries are called stubs and can be expanded and edited by other users. The validity and credibility of entries on Wikipedia is always in question as any user can change content that can then be verified and edited by other users. Some educators construct their own wikis for courses whereby the students and instructors are the authors of the content.

In a similar way, blogs—a shortened and condensed term for web logs—are used by educators, journalists, families, and other users as both a public forum and chronicle of information. The use of blogs as a legitimate media source has been discussed and critiqued in popular and news media. The first incarnations of these so-called "alternative news sources" took the form of websites like *The Drudge Report*, but more recently corporate news agencies have started their own blogs. Independent blogs like *The Huffington Post* are considered among some of the more credible sources of breaking and probing news. An example of the possibilities of where such musing on interactive and Web 2.0 reporting and information sharing might lead can be seen in the video *EPIC 2014.*

> In the year 2014, *The New York Times* has gone offline.
> The fourth estate's fortunes have waned.
> What happened to the news?
> And what is EPIC?
> (Retrieved online July 26 at http://www.robinsloan.com/epic/)

These words are the only introduction the viewer receives before watching the video, a speculative, collaborative work that is the result of multiple revisions and mutations. Below these words on the opening page appears a white box with the following information:

> You're about to watch a future history of the media by Robin Sloan and Matt Thompson, with music by Aaron McLeran.
>
> Click here to watch EPIC 2014!
>
> Thanks to all the folks helping us share this with the world: Daniel, Ido, Arno, and Eduardo.
>
> Also, Robin Good did a transcript in
> English (ends a little too early, though),
> Coldwind did one in Spanish, Bobby
> in French, Eneko in Basque, Maciej in Polish,
> Fabio in Italian, Henry in Brazilian
> Portuquese, Li in Chinese, and Osman
> in Turkish. Cool, right?
>
> Questions? robinsloan at robinsloan dot com. (retrieved online July 26, 2008 at http://www.robinsloan.com/epic/)

EPIC 2014 exemplifies the proleptic nature of collaborative Web 2.0 content and interactions as it functions as a "future history." The video, in its current version and each of its previous versions that lead to this point, is part satire, part intertextual interpretation, part collaborative video wiki, and part prophetic cautionary tale. The current document has a recorded history that can be found through a simple Google search whereby users can see for themselves the growth, modifications, and variations of this collaborative document that has evolved through Web 2.0 technology.

Although we have not used wikis to enhance the content and delivery of our courses or scholarship, like so many other contemporary scholars and educators, we have used blogs for these purposes (Figure 13.2).

Blog features are built into online course distribution software such as WebCT™ and Blackboard™, however, educators seek and use other free blog services such as Blogger and WordPress as they promote more flex-

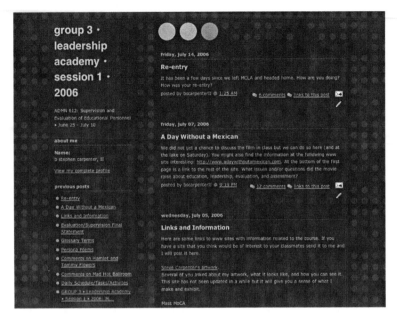

Figure ■ 13.2   Blog screenshot from a 2006 Summer Graduate course.

ibility in course design and management, while they also allow for contributions by not just the students enrolled in class but also by other readers should the instructor choose to open the documents for public consumption and production. In blogs, students can post comments and images in response to course assignments, as well as attach documents for larger distribution. Readers can follow threads of discussions or begin their own posts and encourage other responses. While services such as WebCT™ and Blackboard™ allow for threaded discussions, such technologies are typically dismantled after a semester has concluded, a practice that limits the extent to which students can continue the conversations, inquiries, and engagements with course content. The use of free blog and wiki services online encourages ongoing interactions among students, instructors, and other readers long after a semester brings traditional discourse about a course to a close.

GOOGLE DOCS

Single users with one keyboard and computer create most documents used in educational contexts. Even when working with a partner or with members of a group, only one user tends to write, edit, or modify the document at any given time. In this approach, collaborators tend to rename the same

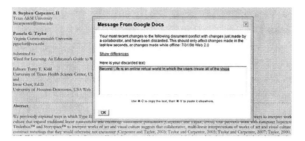

Figure 13.3 Message from Google Docs.

document to indicate the current version and as a means of archiving past versions. In this model, multiple users can work on different versions of the same document, but at a later time one user must use a "compare and merge documents" feature of their word processing application in order to construct a single manuscript. With the use of Google Docs™, the web-based authoring application, multiple collaborators can work on the same document simultaneously. In fact, we used Google Docs™ to write most of this manuscript and spent hours working individually and then later together in real time, adding, editing, deleting, correcting, and moving text. From our different authoring locations—Texas and Virginia—we could see the changes the other made periodically as we both saved our new additions every few minutes. This approach is not without its own complications. At one point we learned when we both attempted to modify the exact same section of the manuscript at the exact same time, the software rejected one of our contributions (Figure 13.3).

VOICETHREAD

Classroom 2.0 is a "social networking site for those interested in Web 2.0 and collaborative technologies in education" (http://www.classroom20. com/). Among various content featured on the site, users will find information about using VoiceThread in education. This site is an excellent source of information, support, and examples for using Web 2.0 for educational applications. With the inclusion of a built-in resources wiki and links to numerous technology and education user groups, it is itself the embodiment of Web 2.0 technology. For an informative description of Web 2.0 for education see "Web 2.0 and collaborative technologies" (http://web20in-education.wikispaces.com/Intro).

Among the most intriguing approaches to on-line collaborative environments is VoiceThread. Users construct stand-alone audio and video presentations to which other readers can add text and verbal commentary as well as other visual elements. An icon representing each contributor appears along the border of the viewing screen of the presentation. Each contributor's icon is highlighted as her or his segment of the presentation plays on the screen. Depending on the means by which contributors add content, either text or audio may accompany the images. Images may be stills or video and readers who become contributors can draw or make marks on the images that appear in the presentation. VoiceThread provides a means of asynchronous collaboration rather than the synchronous collaboration we used to write this manuscript on Google Docs while on-line at the same time. While similar to PowerPoint or Keynote whereby creators build a presentation through a series of still images, text, or videos, VoiceThread allows multiple authors and readers to contribute to the content of the presentation.

We have used VoiceThread in our courses as a low-tech and inexpensive means for students to produce digitally mediated presentations. For more high-tech means of producing digitally mediated presentations our students use PowerPoint or Keynote or applications for producing digital videos that can be saved and read as either QuickTime or Windows Media Player documents. These three formats require different levels of experience with creating digitally mediated presentations and therefore students with more experience and comfort with creating digitally mediated presentations can opt for more sophisticated formats. With the option to work alone or with a partner, our students are required to identify, investigate, analyze and construct a presentation using VoiceThread about a cultural institution—a person, place, event, or object—in the community. This project requires all visual documentation of the cultural institution under investigation take the form of a self-contained, digitally mediated presentation of about five-minutes in length with both visual and audio components. A basic format we have used with students for these types of projects includes a clear introduction, a description and analysis of the cultural institution, and suggestions of the educational significance of the cultural institution. Students may work with a partner on this project. We identify the most successful students as those who cite or reference at least five sources, three of which can be from course chapters or articles.

Once uploaded to VoiceThread, the students simply send the URL to the instructor where the presentations can be viewed and comments can be added (Figure 13.4). Further, during one class session, students made in-class presentations by logging in to their VoiceThread online and playing them from the site. Although no additional comments had been added to the presentations at that point, such additions would have become part of the in-class presentation. While students had access to department and university facilities and equipment to create and produce these digitally mediated projects, most chose to use their own computers and equipment.

Figure 13.4 VoiceThread Screenshot with student audio comments (left) and instructor audio comments (right).

Some students discovered that they could use their cell phones to function as microphones with which to record their audio voice-overs. Through a feature of VoiceThread, these students called a telephone number, recorded their audio files and then transferred the audio to their presentations online. These students saw no barrier in making such use of their cell phones in this way. For them, it was simply another means of taking advantage of multiple forms of digital technology for the purpose of communication and the construction of cultural productions.

SECOND LIFE

Second Life is the free user-created virtual world on the World Wide Web where the method of building or making is the method of living (Rosedale & Ondrejka, 2006). Avatars—graphic representations of people—populate this online, three-dimensionally rendered environment. In Second Life, the user as her or his avatar can teleport, fly, live in a house, go to clubs, take classes, make and view art, or just "hang out" in a virtual space on a computer screen (Figure 13.5). Second Life spans more than 42,000 acres in real-world scale. From press conferences and convention plenary sessions (Arrington, 2006; NYLC, 2006) to political speeches (Mistral, 2006), and live musical performances (Campbell, 2007), to film debuts (Meyers,

Figure 13.5 The authors' avatars (Carpenter and Taylor, left to right) meet in Second Life™.

2007), Second Life (SL) is a second home to millions of residents, who collaboratively create, purchase, and comment upon its content.

We venture in Second Life for a number of reasons including: building virtual environments, teaching, holding class discussions, making art, dancing, riding bikes, playing games, flying, exhibiting art, meeting, and researching. A common experience we have in Second Life especially when working with students is the somewhat perpetual obsession with avatar construction. We often hear, "You've go to see this" as our students share a new outfit, hairstyle, body type and/or gesture with their fellow avatars. In Second Life our students and we attend art exhibitions, cultural events, and lectures. We are members of several in-world groups and receive notices about events through SL note cards and e-mail. Author Carpenter is currently working on a virtual interpretation of a real world social justice project that requires knowledge of the scripting language that enables objects to move and perform other interactive tasks. Author Taylor continues the construction of the eLASTIC arts island. We both teach classes in Second Life that require students to take virtual field trips to other spaces and interact with guest lecturing avatars from other real world universities and institutions.

For the purposes of this chapter, we began looking to Second Life as a provocative collaborative tool. That is, Second Life has provoked questions for us that we have previously collaboratively addressed through Instant Messaging (see next section). The questions included: What lies beneath the skin of an avatar? Do avatars have souls? What are we made of in the virtual world? How do you "uncover" an avatar?

One aspect of these collaborative tools that we find most appealing in terms of our investigations of hypermediated criticism is their use as a format and context in which to theorize about them. We believe that some of the most provocative features of Web 2.0 collaborative tools are these kinds of questions that make us think in more critical and innovative ways than we would without the tools or each other. Second Life in particular, with its vast possibilities for unobstructed creative ability seems to burst with possibilities. On the down side, so many possibilities and the ability to achieve them requires multiple upgrades (both system and software), and Second Life is often slowed by its numerous users all over the world, and does not, as yet, work with any other software so copying and pasting, among other abilities, are not possible. In addition, creating and maintaining a "second life" is very time-consuming and we find that being very task oriented is mandatory, or else we lose track of real world time completely—a concern that many colleagues, educators, students, and parents who hear about this world have voiced to us.

INSTANT MESSAGING AND VIDEO CONFERENCING

There are a number of instant messenger clients that facilitate real time discussions through text, audio, and/or video including iChat, AOL Instant Messenger, and Skype. In addition, chat features of such social networking sites as Facebook and MySpace, as well as the instant message component of Gmail, and of course, cell phone texting, establish a varied and rich land-

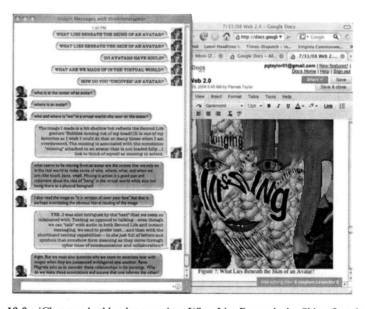

Figure 13.6 iChat sparked by the question: What Lies Beneath the Skin of an Avatar?

scape for text-based approaches to digital real-time communication. Instant Messaging is just that—real time communication between two or more people. (See Figure 13.6). Although some parents and teachers equate instant messaging shorthand such as NP (no problem), LOL (laugh out loud), and TTYL (talk to you later) with a scourge of language skills, Mark Peters (2008) reports that instant messaging (IM) actually represents:

> ...an expansive new linguistic renaissance." Sali Tagliamonte and Derek Denis at the University of Toronto, Canada, say teenagers risk the disapproval of their elders if they use slang, and the scorn of their friends if they sound too buttoned-up. But instant messaging allows them to deploy a "robust mix" of colloquial and formal language. In a paper to be published in the spring 2008 issue of American Speech, the researchers argue that far from ruining teenagers' ability to communicate, IM lets teenagers show off what they can do with language. (para. 1–2.)

We find that Instant Messaging is reliable and we often use it when some other form of communication fails or when we want to keep an image or document on our screen at the same time. Chatting and instant messaging with more than one person can get confusing, especially in a class situation where one instructor attempts to manage multiple conversations with, or questions from, students simultaneously. We see such confusion as an exciting challenge and we know that we can save an instant messaging session to refer back to or draw upon later.

CONCLUSION:
PEDAGOGICAL AND CURRICULAR IMPLICATIONS

Because definitions of curriculum include visual as well as text-based literacy, uses of Web 2.0 technologies fit well with current conceptions of visual culture in education. Users take advantage of Internet technologies to engage critically with visual culture in its three distinct but interrelated areas of inquiry: ontological (ideas, roles, implications, and effects of visual culture on our lives), substantial (objects, events, sites, and experiences), and pedagogical (curriculum and content that can be taught, interpreted, and learned) (Tavin, 2003; Carpenter, 2005). Increasingly, educators are using YouTube and other on-line content to supplement and to take the place of conventional course content. In fact, we use such content in the graduate courses we teach in curriculum development and visual culture. The combination of visual and audio content presented in and represented by online videos in these courses provides rich, common, real world examples for students to deconstruct and analyze critically.

But what is next? What else is available in the context of Web 2.0 technology that would encourage students and educators to insist, "You've got to see this"? Among many possibilities that we are now just beginning to explore includes the availability of RSS feeds. Short for "really simply syndication," RSS feeds now function as "you've got to see this" content sources as they keep us informed constantly of the latest updates and posts to our favorite blogs and web sites. We wonder how RSS feeds might help us extend our efforts to continuously expand the interactive and interconnected approaches to computer mediated art education and visual culture. We remain vigilant in our ongoing search for other "you've got to see this" possibilities on the horizon as we continue to develop our use of VoiceThread, blogs, image galleries, and Second Life and other Web 2.0 technologies in our research and teaching.

REFERENCES

Arrington, M. (2006). Dell to make announcement in Second Life. *TechCrunch*. Retrieved April 22, 2007, from http://www.techcrunch.com/2006/11/13/dell-to-make-announcement-in-second-life/

Barboza, D. (2008, July 26). China surpasses U.S. in number of internet users. *The New York Times*. Retrieved February 5, 2009, from http://www.nytimes.com/2008/07/26/business/worldbusiness/26internet.html

Campbell, V. (2007). *On the bleeding edge of performance: Second Life musicians*. Retrieved April 8, 2007, from http://campbell.vertesi.com/blog/on_the_bleeding_edge_of_performance_second_life_musicians.

Carpenter, B. S. (2005). The return of visual culture (Why not?). *Art Education* 58(6), 4–5.

Carpenter, B. S., & Taylor, P. G. (2003). Racing thoughts: Altering our ways of knowing and being through computer hypertext. *Studies in Art Education, 45*(1), 40–55.

Carpenter, B. S., & Taylor, P. G. (2006). Making meaningful connections: Interactive computer hypertext in art education. *Computers in the Schools... The Interdisciplinary Journal of Practice, Theory, and Applied Research, 23*(1/2), 149–161.

Cifuentes, L., Carpenter, B. S., & Bulu, S. (unpublished manuscript). An online collaborative environment for sharing visual culture.

Maddox, C. D., & Johnson, D. L. (Eds.). (2006a). *Computers in the Schools... The Interdisciplinary Journal of Practice, Theory, and Applied Research, 23*(1).

Maddox, C. D., & Johnson, D. L. (Eds.). (2006b). *Internet applications of type II uses of technology in education*. Binghamton, NY: Haworth Press.

Mirzoeff, N. (1999). *An introduction to visual culture*. New York: Routledge.

Meyers, M. (2007). Sundance holds screening in "Second Life" for first time. *C/NetNews.com*. Retrieved April 8, 2007, from http://news.com.com/Sundance+holds+screening+in+Second+Life+for+first+time/2100-1026_3-6153064.html

Mistral, P. (2006). Ex-governor Mark Warner reveals SL actions figures' identity. *The Second Life Herald.* Retrieved April 7, 2007, from http://www.secondlifeherald.com/slh/2006/08/exgovernor_mark.html.

NYLC (National Youth Leadership Council). (2006). The 18th annual national service-learning conference enters Second Life. NYLC. Retrieved April 22, 2007, from http://www.nylc.org/happening_newsarticle.cfm?oid=5497.

Panzer, M. (2008, July 8). Photojournalism for the web generation. *The Wall Street Journal.* p. D-7.

Peters, M. (2008, May 15). Instant messaging "a linguistic renaissance" for teens. *NewScientist.com* news service. Retrieved July 26, 2008, from http://technology.newscientist.com/article/mg19826566.600-instant-messaging-a-linguistic-renaissance-for-teens.html.

Rosedale, P., & Ondrejka, C. (2006). *Glimpse inside a metaverse: The virtual world of Second Life.* Retrieved December 15, 2006, from http://www.opendemocracy.net/arts/alterego_4620.jsp.

Slattery, P. (2006). *Curriculum development in the postmodern era.* New York: Routledge.

Sturt, J. (2008). Interactive narratives 2.0. *Media Storm blog.* Retrieved July 14, 2008, from http://mediastorm.org/blog/?p=448.

Tavin, K. (2003). Wrestling with angels, searching for ghosts: Toward a critical pedagogy of visual culture. *Studies in Art Education, 44*(3), 197–213.

Taylor, P. G. (2000). Madonna and hypertext: Liberatory learning in art education. *Studies in art education, 41*(4), 376–389.

Taylor, P. G. (2006). Critical thinking in and through interactive computer hypertext and art education. *Innovate, 2*(3).

Taylor, P. G. (2007). Press pause: Critically contextualizing music video in visual culture and art education. *Studies in Art Education, 48*(3), 230–246.

Taylor, P. G., & Carpenter, B. S. (2005). Computer hypertextual "uncovering" in art education. *Journal of Educational Multimedia and Hypermedia, 14*(1), 25–45.

Taylor, P. G., & Carpenter, B. S. (2007). Hypermediated art criticism. *The Journal of Aesthetic Education, 41*(3), 1–24.

Villano, M. (2008). Taking the 'A' out of asynchronous. *Campus Technology,* July, 38–43.

CHAPTER 14

WEB 2.0 AFFORDANCES FOR LITERACIES

Using Technology as Pedagogically Strong Scaffolds for Learning

Julie McLeod
University of North Texas

Sheri Vasinda
Texas A&M–Commerce

ABSTRACT

This chapter illustrates an approach to using technology in the K–12 classroom in which research-based literacy strategies are carefully and purposefully matched with Web 2.0 affordances. Using an established literacy strategy that is well known to the teacher and making a new application of that strategy with a technology adaptation provides a bridge for educational practice that combines the known with the new. By maintaining the integrity of the strategy and identifying and harnessing the affordances of the Web 2.0 tool, the combination can move educational practices forward to the technology-rich teaching and learning of the future. The process is described and illuminated with three elementary classroom examples.

Wired for Learning: An Educator's Guide to Web 2.0, pages 233–246
Copyright © 2009 by Information Age Publishing
All rights of reproduction in any form reserved.

INTRODUCTION

This chapter will attempt to map a path for educators that will leverage Web 2.0 affordances as scaffolds for strong, research based learning strategies. We believe the careful and purposeful match of literacy strategies with Web 2.0 affordances can strengthen the literacy strategies while supporting use of new technologies that are and will be standard tools for students of the 21st century. Using literacy strategies that may be familiar to teachers can motivate teachers to experiment with new technology tools that they may have otherwise not considered. The reciprocal effect is that the technology may motivate the student to be more engaged in a particular literacy strategy. While this chapter specifically describes three elementary classroom examples, the concepts can be adapted to all ages.

BACKGROUND

Web 2.0 offers many affordances for teaching and learning. The collaborative, user-created, ease of publication "style" of Web 2.0 (O'Reilly, 2005; Surowiecki, 2004; Tapscott & Williams, 2006) matches social constructivist learning theories (Lave & Wenger, 1991; Vygotsky, 1978, 1987). However, transitioning from traditional teaching methods to those well suited for Web 2.0 can seem an arduous task for educators. While most educators will agree that traditional teaching methods must be updated to utilize technology, there is little agreement as to what teaching and learning will actually look like in the future (Warlick, 2004).

Rogers (2003) studied the adoption or diffusion of innovations in general noting that adoption typically followed a curve with a small group of innovators first, followed by larger groups of early adopters, early majority and late majority and finally the last and typically smaller group of laggards. However, when a certain technology is particularly disruptive, for example the introduction of computers into education, Moore (1991) argues that a chasm develops between the early adopters and the early majority. Further, because of the rapid changes in technology that take place regularly, the educational technology chasm can appear particularly broad and deep. In this chapter, we will attempt to bridge that chasm by matching the best of literacy strategies with appropriate Web 2.0 technologies.

While Moore (1991) created a marketing roadmap for businesses that were trying to cross the chasm, the principles of business do not always translate directly into education. Figure 14.1 begins to integrate Moore's chasm with education depicting school sitting comfortably and safely where it has always sat, for the most part teaching the way it has always taught but aside a chasm. Most know well some iteration of the story of time travelers

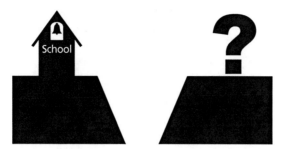

Figure 14.1 Chasm between school and the unknown.

from a hundred years ago who were baffled by a modern operating room, but felt at home in the classroom (Papert, 1983). Even today when almost all classrooms in the developed world have computers and Internet access, the access to the computers is still low, with an average of six students per computer (OECD, 2006). Further complicating the situation, across the chasm lays the unknown. We do not have a picture of the classroom of the future not to mention the path we should take to get there.

Prensky (2005) discussed a progression or a path for technology adoption in education specifically. The main progression begins with "doing old things in old ways," moves next to "doing old things in new ways," and ends with "doing new things in new ways" (Prensky, 2005). In reflecting back to Figure 14.1, Prensky's progression could be superimposed upon the figure and is included in Figure 14.2. Doing old things in old ways refers to the current state of school, safely on the left side of the figure. On the right side of the figure is doing new things in new ways, clearly an unknown place at this point. In the middle, the bridge represents doing old things in new ways. We contend that this bridge represents the focus of this chapter, matching research-based strategies (old things) with new Web 2.0 technologies (new ways).

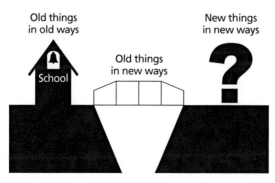

Figure 14.2 Progression of technology adoption.

Figure 14.3 What we actually see.

The problem with this figure is that in the real world we cannot see the entire picture. Generally speaking, what we see looks more like Figure 14.3. We know with certainty only where we have been. We cannot even see the fullness of the bridge. If we decide to step out onto the bridge, we cannot always see even far enough forward for the next step. We do not know where the bridge will end nor when we have "arrived" at the place that we have called the unknown. All we know with certainty is that we will never arrive at the place of doing new things in new ways if we never step onto the bridge. The bridge is not the future of school, but it is the best way we have found to thoughtfully move closer to the unknown.

A crucial element to stepping onto the bridge is a commitment to praxis (Freire, 1997). Acting reflectively, or exercising praxis, informs educators on the bridge. With each action, or each step, there is real work that is done. This real work is followed by reflection so that the next step can be illuminated. While taking steps toward the unknown can be risky, using praxis creates calculated risks that can be more easily managed. In other words, when we use proven, research based strategies as the old things and carefully match those strategies with appropriate Web 2.0 tools, we can make calculated steps across the bridge that lead to powerful teaching and learning, bringing us all closer to the future.

It is important that we start with a common understanding of literacies, the research-based strategies used to teach those literacies and the affordances of Web 2.0.

Definition of Literacies

The definition of literacy continues to evolve beyond the traditional concept of the ability to simply read and write. As we consider developing fluent, or literate, understandings in a variety of contents and contexts, such as computer literacy, math literacy, science literacy, and critical literacy, to name a few, our definition of literacy involves a broader range of meaning. Scribner (1984) suggests that literacy be viewed in terms of integrating three metaphors: 1) as adaptation to societal expectations; 2) power to achieve personal aspirations and make social change; and 3) as a state of grace, or becoming a well read, or "cultured" person.

Using Scribner's metaphors and Web 2.0 opportunities, a literate person of the twenty first century would include becoming fluent, or adapting to new expectations of platforms and texts available. As text moves beyond only two dimensional reading of hard copies, across and down, it now also includes three dimensional reading of electronic texts that are read across, down and deeper (Warlick, 2007). Internet based reading includes hyperlinked texts in which you can click "deeper" into the text to find the definition of a term or access a related article. Scribner's metaphor of power might also be thought of as the ability to contribute to a knowledge and thought base available through the Internet, a key component of Web 2.0. Thus, as a contributor to the knowledge base, or even entertainment or social networking base, a sense of power in terms of influence can be achieved, as is the admiration of a thought provoking blogger or self-publishing one's own work; achieving Scribner's state of grace.

Definition of Literacy Strategies

According to the Literacy Dictionary (Harris & Hodges, 1995) a strategy is a "... systematic plan, consciously adapted and monitored, to improve one's performance in learning." Literacy strategies may include a teaching move determined by examining the needs of a particular student or the flexible thinking of learners as they grapple with a difficult math problem or monitoring their reading comprehension. For example, when readers comes to an unknown word, they may read past the word to use context as a strategy for solving the word, sound out the word using phonics as a strategy or use the structure of the word, such as roots and affixes using etymology as a strategy.

Description of Web 2.0 Affordances

Affordances can be described as the properties that determine how something can be used (Norman, 1988). Affordances are those essential elements that define something, in this case a Web 2.0 tool. For example, an affordance of podcasting is the use of audio and ease of broadcast and syndication. An affordance of a blog is not only ease of publication, but also the engagement of readers through the comment functionality. These affordances, when capitalized upon, can add a powerful dimension to carefully planned learning activities.

The careful match of strategy to Web 2.0 affordance deserves some discussion before we offer some examples. Generally speaking, when we talk of careful matches, we strive to maintain the integrity of the strategy while also creating something that was not there without the technology. In other words, for these first steps across the bridge, we believe it is important to maintain the elements of the strategy that have proven effective through the research. When we speak of the integrity of the strategy, we are really speaking of these essential elements. Then, we look for Web 2.0 affordances to purposefully match those essential elements so that the combination creates positive changes in the learning environment that were not possible without the technology. This concept of careful and purposeful matches can best be illuminated with specific examples.

CLASSROOM EXAMPLES OF PURPOSEFULLY MATCHING STRATEGIES WITH WEB 2.0 AFFORDANCES

These stories are a few of the examples of the purposeful matching of strategies to Web 2.0 affordances. Within these elementary classroom stories, read beyond the story to identify how the strategy was matched with the affordance as well as the student excitement and engagement.

Language Experience Approach with Wikis and Blogs

Language Experience Approach is a strategy in which children's oral compositions are transcribed and then used as reading material (LEA). The trademark of this reading approach is a child dictating their own meaningful stories to the teacher who writes them down verbatim in its most pure form. Children are encouraged to read and re-read their stories to build fluency and word recognition. The deeper pedagogy of this approach is that children are active agents in their own learning (Allen, 1968; Stauffer, 1970). We have used the LEA in two different situations, once with a wiki and once with a blog (Vasinda, McLeod & Morrison, 2007).

Wiki Example: The Story of Story
We were designing technology integration projects with two inquiry-based multiage classes in a North Texas suburb public school. Part of the social studies curriculum included a study of the local community and "the lives of heroic men and women who made important choices, overcame ob-

stacles, sacrificed for the betterment of others, and embarked on journeys that resulted in new ideas, new inventions, and new communities" (TEA, n.d.). Working from a student's question of, "Why was our school named after Alvis C. Story?" the two classes set about to find answers. In this community, schools are named for important community figures, so researching a school namesake would clearly lead to important knowledge about the history of the community. However, this would be primary source research since no other texts were available on Alvis Story. Interviewing would be a major source of data collection and, while Alvis Story was no longer living, his son Chester agreed to come to the school for the interview.

Interviewing is a skill that many spend years learning and perfecting. Thus, students were given a mini lesson on interviewing based partly on the book Radio: An Illustrated Guide (Abel & Glass, 1999). Days before the first interview with Chester Story arrived, the students busily formulated their questions ranging the "Why was our school named after your dad?" to questions related to hobbies, sports and favorite foods. There was a quiver of excitement as the day of the interview arrived. As Chester Story enthusiastically answered questions and told stories, the children took notes and the teachers moderated and videotaped. Later, Chester was joined by his sister June for another interview so students could learn more about Alvis Story. The children were now rich with experiences of the Depression era time period, the history of the community and the life of our school namesake.

Meanwhile, students also were learning about the means with which the "Story of Alvis Story" could be published. Wikimapia.org, which is a satellite map based wiki whose tagline is "Let's describe the whole world," seemed to be a good match because the maps gave the students a sense of connection to the medium and provided them with another visual perspective of their community while the wiki allowed students to authentically publish their work, creating powerful reading and writing experiences.

When introducing wikis to the students, one student immediately worried that people might enter wrong or misleading information. We used the Giles (2005) study to discuss with the students that researchers had noted no statistically significant difference in the number of errors in Wikipedia and Encyclopedia Britannica. Further, when errors or major changes in knowledge are recognized, these can be fixed immediately on Wikipedia. To further clarify, we used an example of something many of the children in the classes were both knowledgeable and passionate about, Pokemon.

"If you were reading an entry in a wiki about Pokemon and you read some wrong information about Charmander . . ."

There was an audible gasp as several children said, "Not, Charmander!"

"You wouldn't like that, would you? Well, you could go into the wiki and correct the information right away, so that it would be correct. Because you care so much about Charmander and you know so much about Charmander, you would want to make it right."

While exploring wikimapia with the classes, we had our navigating student click on one of our local schools, Rountree Elementary. As commonly happens, the school was labeled as a compound word, Roundtree.

Sheri said, "Wait, I noticed something about Rountree's label. It's spelled wrong. I worked at Rountree once and I care a lot about that school. Lots of people think it is spelled like a "round tree," but it's not. I want to go in and correct the spelling of Rountree. I'm guessing the person who labeled Rountree really cares about the school or else he or she wouldn't even take the time to label it, but they didn't realize the spelling is not like a compound word. This person cared enough to label the school. I care enough that I want to make sure it's spelled right, too."

A student was navigating at the computer that was being projected and Julie walked the student through the process of correcting the error while the other students watched it immediately change. We had a serendipitous learning moment in which we were able to authentically illustrate the care, knowledge and passion of the "expert" user's knowledge and the way wikis can be organically grown and immediately corrected.

Working together, the children composed an entry about Alvis Story's life and watched it emerge on the wikimapia site projected on the wall as Sheri transcribed their words on the computer. Students brainstormed strong lead statements and then selected the best one. They determined the important information to include. They also discussed the structure of the entry and then together vocalized the story. The children tried out different ways to communicate Mr. Story's life. They arranged, rearranged and reread their work many times until the final entry satisfied the group. In all, the writing and editing experience took about 45 minutes. When complete, a small group stayed in from recess with Julie to post it on the World Wide Web via wikimapia. Extending the rereading, many students accessed the story from home and students and parents were able to publicly comment on the story. Honoring and capitalizing on children's experiences is part of what makes LEA such a powerful strategy. The collaborative and public nature of the wiki extends its potential through the potential of a larger audience pool. (To view the wikimapia entry, navigate to http://www.wikimapia.org/#lat=33.097725&lon=-96 .658573&z=14&l=0&m=a&v=2&show=/1759693/)

Blogging at the ASA

Central Dallas Ministries' After-School Academy (ASA) is a Kindergarten through fifth grade after school program located in a public housing development in a remote area of the city. During the summers, Sheri often assists the director, Janet Morrison, with staff development and collaborates on curriculum and when ASA had more access to technology, Julie became another resource. After reading articles about teaching first and second graders how to blog (Intel, n.d.; Jackson, 2005), Janet began thinking about more meaningful and interactive ways to engage the students in technology that would help develop their reading and writing skills during their summer program as well as provide insight as to what the children were learning. Since many of the students had just finishing kindergarten, first or second grades, their literacy (and typing) skills were still emerging.

To scaffold the children's experiences, students were allowed the choice of dictating their daily experiences and reflections for a staff member to type in or they could draw the day's events in their journals, which would then be scanned in and posted on the blog. To further develop their reading skills, Sheri suggested that the children reread their blog post after each composition and reread them as they shared them with family members. Though the children sometimes struggled, hesitated, or stumbled over some of their simpler words when reading them back, with little help they were able to decipher the entire entry they had dictated. For example, students used and easily recognized words such as "gluteus maximus," which became part of their language bank from the frequent references during the exercise and fitness classes of the summer's health and nutrition theme. Using their dictated text as authentic and organic reading material changed the work from strictly blogging to a new format of language experience.

At the end of each of their posts, children were asked to create "labels" (or "tags," depending on the blog site one uses). Labels allow the blog author to create searchable key words, an important component of Web 2.0. In essence, the labels become the main idea of the post. Though nearly all of the children in the After-School Academy had tested low in main idea and comprehension skills, when asked to label their post, the children had little difficulty identifying their labels. Technology gave the students an authentic reason to identify the main idea of their post and the LEA strategies allowed students to be successful in this endeavor, perhaps for the first time in their emerging reading lives. (To view the ASA blog, navigate to http://ourasafamily.blogspot.com)

Readers Theater with Podcasting

The work we did pairing LEA with blogs and wikis increased our awareness of the power of using technology to strengthen a literacy strategy. We began to look for more opportunities for a purposeful marriage of literacy strategies and technology. As podcasting became more and more available, we saw it as a medium to pair with a reading intervention strategy that had already demonstrated effectiveness in both reading fluency and reading comprehension: Readers Theater (Griffin & Rasinski, 2004; Martinez, Roser & Strecker, 1999). Readers Theater requires no props or costumes. It is much like old time radio shows where voices are used to convey the meaning and set the pace. In fact, in the absence of props, costumes and sets, the reader is compelled to use only voice and expressive reading to enable the audience to envision the text. The reader must think critically about how a character would respond in the particular situation of a story to read it in such a manner to convey meaning, thus strengthening reading comprehension. Even without podcasting, the performance aspect motivates students and gives an authentic purpose to engage in repeated reading of the text. Because the reader's voice is the tool for this strategy, podcasting is a technology match perfectly suited to showcase voice and Readers Theater. By utilizing the Internet, podcasting affords a wider audience, including parents, grandparents and other family and friends who may not be able to come to the school during school hours. This wider audience raises the level of importance to the performance (See Vasinda & McLeod, 2008).

Three second-grade classes and two third grade classes participated in a ten-week integration of Readers Theater as part of the practice component of their reading instruction. Three of the five classrooms were on Title One campuses in which approximately sixty percent of students enrolled receive free or reduced lunch. The teachers committed to allocating ten to fifteen minutes per day for students to practice reading a short script. The students received a new script of the teacher's choice each Monday, they practiced each day and recorded their performances digitally on Fridays. The files were uploaded to a district Readers Theater site for students and their families to access. Students also listened to their podcasts during the following week evaluating their progress. Student reading comprehension levels were pre-tested before beginning Readers Theater and post tested at the end of the project using informal reading inventories. After ten weeks students made an average grade level gain of 1.15 years in reading comprehension. This corroborates similar comprehension gains from earlier Readers Theater studies (Griffin & Rasinski, 2004; Martinez, Roser & Strecker, 1999).

The difference the podcasting seemed to make was in the permanency of the voice recording and the potential for a wide and unknown audience. Student focus group interviews provided insight into the engagement of the students' listening and re-listening to their performances many times developing a more critical ear for their own reading and motivation to do a better job the next time, as well as an enchantment of listening to their own voice, as Harrison answered when asked what he liked about the Readers Theater Project, "What I like about readers theater, because when you would hear it on the computer you would hear your voice. And if you say something kind of funny, you would laugh about yourself and the next thing I liked: it was fun."

A surprising discovery was the way in which students described "watching" their Readers Theater or "showing" it to their families. Students seemed to make visual connections with their voice recorded stories, which is exactly the intention of radio or other audio mediums (Abel & Glass, 1999) and the charge of Readers Theater to use voice to help the audience envision the text. However, never before have students communicated this type of discovery through Readers Theater. We believe the permanency of the podcasting medium brought about this visual realization for the students. Certainly, with much research supporting the importance of using visual images to reading comprehension (Gambrell & Koskinen, 2002; Sadoski & Paivio, 1994), this finding is crucial.

Problem Solving Strategies and Screencasting

For mathematics learning, one of the fundamental approaches is to offer students experiences with various problem-solving strategies (NCTM, 2004). These strategies can then be used by the students to approach various problems of differing content and challenge. In Texas, the number of strategies the students must know and use increase over the years. Specifically for sixth graders in Texas, the problem solving strategies include drawing a picture, looking for a pattern, systematic guessing and checking, acting it out, making a table, working a simpler problem and working backwards (TEA, n.d.). These strategies, which stem from fundamental mathematical problem solving processes such as proving, reversing, specializing, generalizing and extending (Contreras, 2007) are likely very similar to the strategies used across the United States. Of course, it is important that students become familiar with the problem solving strategies. It is equally important that they gain experience using each strategy and understand how and when to apply different strategies. Thus, you have all likely heard the mathematics teachers' favorite mantra, "Show your work!"

When students show their work, they are becoming consciously aware of the problem solving strategy they are using and they are learning to communicate mathematically. Importantly, they are making their thinking visible. Yet, thinking is a process and processes are not captured as well on a static medium such as paper. Technology can be utilized to capture processes more fully. For example, if a student is studying the process of the life cycle of plants, he/she might look in a book and see three pictures, one of a seedling, one of a medium sized plant and one of a large, full grown plant. These three pictures capture moments in time of the process, but they do not capture the entire process nor do they expose the students to the complexities, intricacies and nuances that can be a part of many natural processes. A time-compressed video or animation of a growing plant that can be manipulated by the student is a far superior method to demonstrate the process. Similarly, the thinking and problem solving processes can be better documented if we can capture not just students' written documentation, but also the evolution of those writings and the thinking that is occurring while writing. Thus, in this match, students create screencasts of their problem solving while working a problem.

Screencasts are digital video and audio recordings of a computer screen. Students have a problem they are solving and they use a microphone to record themselves narrating their thinking and sometimes using a drawing tablet as an input device. These screencasts can then be viewed like a video on a computer. When problem-solving strategies are matched with screencasting, the resulting product is called a mathcast. (To view mathcasts, navigate to http://math247.pbwiki.com/). A further benefit of this strategy is that when appropriately placed online, these mathcasts can begin a conversation about the problem at hand. For example, when mathcasts are posted online using a blog, it opens the opportunity for comments and feedback. Also, sites such as CrowdAbout (http://crowdabout.us/) and VoiceThread (http://voicethread.com/) can be used to target feedback to a specific part of the mathcast. These sites can be used to help teachers offer specific feedback to students at the point in the mathcast where students might have stumbled, for example. They also afford a wider audience.

CONCLUSION

Currently we are preparing students for an unknown future. Success in the twenty first century will depend on continuous learning, unlearning and relearning as new technologies continue to develop. To move toward this unknown territory, teachers must develop an adaptive capacity (Bennis, 2003) in which opportunities are identified and capitalized upon. The future of Web 2.0 tools in education is strong, particularly when its use can be tied to research-based strategies. The public and collaborative nature of this new read/write web brings an authentic platform to anyone's work and is especially powerful for children. While the specific future of technologies such as Web 2.0 is unknown, the trend toward enabling users and honoring the content those users generate will not likely curb. Honoring and enabling learners ties this technology-rich learning environment with social constructivists, offering a glimpse into the unknown of "doing new things in new ways."

As we have stepped out onto the bridge of "doing old things in new ways," we believe that we have found a path to the unknown that embraces and enlarges a strong educational research base of literacy strategies. Our first work on the bridge was a serendipitous discovery. We wanted to use the

Web 2.0 tools and collaborated on a project to use a wiki. It was because of our reflective stance, or our praxis, that we realized that we had taken an established literacy approach, LEA and brought it to a new more public venue with both a wiki and a blog. We were determined to repeat the success and joined podcasting with Readers Theater, as always maintaining the integrity of the literacy strategy with a careful technology match. With that success, we have become convinced of the power of this approach. We have planned many new purposeful matches such as problem solving and screencasting, math vocabulary and podcasting and more. We also have the opportunity to model the responsibility Web 2.0 collaborators and authors have in accuracy and integrity. In our desire for the place of doing new things in new ways, educators must not lose sight of the work of past scholars. In fact, this work can be used to guide our steps. The bridge of doing old things in new ways may be long, but it is a worthy journey to help move the profession toward the future.

REFERENCES

Abel, J., & Glass, I. (1999). *Radio: An illustrated guide.* Chicago, IL: WBEZ.

Allen, R. V. (1968). How a language experience program works. In E. C. Vilscek (Ed.), *A decade of innovations: Approaches to beginning reading.* Newark, DE: International Reading Association.

Bennis, W. (2003). *On becoming a leader.* New York: Basic Books.

Contreras, J. (2007). Unraveling the mystery of the origin of mathematical problems: Using a problem-posing framework with prospective mathematics teachers. *Mathematics Educator, 17*(2), 15–23.

Freire, P. (1997). *Pedagogy of the oppressed: New revised 20th-anniversary edition.* New York: Continuum.

Gambrell, L. B., & Koskinen, P. S. (2002). Imagery: A strategy for enhancing comprehension. In C. C. Block & M. Pressley (Eds.), *Comprehension instruction: Research-based best practices* (pp. 305–318). New York: Guilford.

Giles, J. (2005). Internet encyclopedias go head to head. *Nature, 439,* 900–901.

Griffith, L. & Rasinski, T. (2004) A focus on fluency: How one teacher incorporated fluency with her reading curriculum. *The Reading Teacher, 58*(2), 126–137.

Harris, T. L. & Hodges R. E. (1995). *The literacy dictionary: The vocabulary of reading and writing.* Newark, DE: International Reading Association.

Intel. (n.d.). A space of your own. *Intel Education: An Innovation Odyssey.* Retrieved August 19, 2007, from http://www97.intel.com/odyssey/Story.aspx?StoryID=302

Jackson, L. (2005). Blogging? It's elementary my dear Watson! *Education World.* Retrieved August 9, 2007, from http://www.educationworld.com/a_tech/tech/tech217.shtml

Lave, J., & Wenger, E. (1991). *Situated learning: Legitimate peripheral participation.* New York: Cambridge University Press.

Martinez, M., Roser, N., & Strecker, S.(1998/1999). I never thought I'd be a star: Reader's theater a ticket to fluency. *The Reading Teacher, 52*, 326–334.

Moore, G. (2002). *Crossing the chasm.* New York: HarperCollins.

National Council of Teachers of Mathematics. (2004). *Standards for school mathematics: Problem solving.* Retrieved May 12, 2008, from http://standards.nctm.org/document/chapter3/prob.htm

Norman, D. (1988). *The design of everyday things.* New York: Basic Books.

O'Reilly, T. (2005). *What is web 2.0?* Retrieved September 23, 2006, from http://www.oreillynet.com/pub/a/oreilly/tim/news/2005/09/30/what-is-web-20.html?page=1

Organisation for Economic Co-operation and Development. (2006). *Are students ready for a technology rich world?* Paris: Author.

Papert, S. (1983). *The children's machine: Rethinking school in the age of the computer.* New York: Basic Books.

Prensky, M. (2005). Adopt and adapt: Shaping tech for the classroom. *Edutopia.* Retrieved May 1, 2008, from http://www.edutopia.org/adopt-and-adapt

Rasinski, T. (2003). *The fluent reader: Oral strategies for building word recognition, fluency, and comprehension.* New York: Scholastic Professional Books.

Richardson, W. (2006). *Blogs, wikis, podcasts and other powerful web tools for the classroom.* Thousand Oaks, CA: Corwin Press.

Rogers, E. (2003). *Diffusion of innovations* (5th ed.). New York: Free Press.

Scribner, S. (1984). Literacy in three metaphors. *American Journal of Education, 91*(1), 6.

Surowiecki, J. (2004). *The wisdom of crowds: Why the many are smarter than the few and how collective wisdom shapes business, economics, societies and nations.* New York: Doubleday.

Sadoski, M., & Pavivio, A. (1994). A dual coding view of imagery and verbal processing in reading comprehension. In R. B. Ruddell, M. R. Ruddell, & H. Singer (Eds.), *Theoretical models and processes of reading* (4th ed., pp. 582–601). Newark, DE: International Reading Association.

Stauffer, R. G. (1970). *The language-experience approach to the teaching of reading.* New York: Harper & Row.

Tapscott, D., & Williams, A. (2006). *Wikinomics: How mass collaboration changes everything.* New York: Penguin Group.

Texas Education Agency. (n.d.). *Texas essential knowledge and skills.* Retrieved August 12, 2007, from http://www.tea.state.tx.us/teks/index.html

Vasinda, S., & McLeod, J. (2008). *Extending reader's theater: Podcasting to push performance reading to new levels of engagement and student success.* Paper presented at the International Reading Association Annual Conference. Atlanta, GA.

Vasinda, S., McLeod, J., & Morrison, J. (2007). 1 + 1 = 3: Combining language experience approach with web 2.0 tools. *LEA SIG (of the International Reading Association) newsletter. 38*(1), 6–10.

Vygotsky, L. (1978). *Mind in society.* Cambridge, MA: Harvard University Press.

Vygotsky, L. (1987). *Thought and language.* Cambridge, MA: The MIT Press.

Warlick, D. (2004). *Redefining literacy for the 21st century.* Worthington, OH: Linworth.

CHAPTER 15

SEMESTER WITHOUT END

Keeping the Class Connection Open via RSS

Ray Schroeder
University of Illinois at Springfield

ABSTRACT

Whether we called it semester, quarter, intersession, session, term, or module—instructional units have been just that, quantifiable measures in terms of time, content, and location. Classes had a beginning, duration, and end. When the term of that instructional unit was met, there was a cessation of teaching and learning. Instructor and students went their own way to continue their lives and careers. Now, instructors are using RSS syndicated Web 2.0 tools such as blogs, podcasts, and wikis to disseminate class materials to students. With RSS, there is the potential to keep the class connection open beyond the end of the term. Increasingly, as instructors use RSS-enabled tools in class, students continue to subscribe long after they have graduated.

Wired for Learning: An Educator's Guide to Web 2.0, pages 247–252
Copyright © 2009 by Information Age Publishing
247

INTRODUCTION

Over the ages, whether we called it semester, quarter, intersession, session, term, or module—instructional units have been just that, quantifiable units, measured in terms of time, content, and location. Classes had a beginning, duration, and end. Most commonly, they were offered in one location—a particular room in which the students would gather to glean wisdom from the teacher. When the term of that instructional unit was met, there was a cessation of teaching and learning. Instructor and students went their own way to continue their lives and careers. Certainly, a select few students would keep in touch with their instructor or their class peers, but that was the clear exception, not the rule. In even more rare cases an instructor would maintain a newsletter or a listserv to push out occasional information to former students.

With the emergence of RSS syndicated Web 2.0 technologies, we have the means to continue to engage students after the end of the instructional term. The very nature of these technologies is to facilitate two-way communication in text, audio, and video; to interact, to engage over time and distance. Increasingly, as we integrate these technologies into our classes, we open the door to engage our students along with our former students. We are no longer bound by the classroom, by the term, by the university. With the emerging virtual world environments, we seemingly are no longer bound by the definitions and persona of this world!

The liberating aspects of Web 2.0 enable users to continue to teach, interact, and gain input from students who have completed the course alongside (virtually) those who are currently enrolled. This creates the potential for a rich learning community spanning the student, the graduate and the professional. It provides continuing education for those who completed the initial course; it provides the insight and perspective of graduates and professionals to those who are first encountering the course material. And, it expands the learning experience beyond the artificial boundaries of the institution.

It is the objective of this chapter to describe how this new phenomenon is unfolding in higher education and to explore the implications and possible future ramifications of this in the context of our current educational institutions.

BACKGROUND

At its core, RSS is an xml document that allows users to receive content delivered to a computer or mobile device as soon as it is published online. (What is RSS?, 2008) RSS was originally developed in 1999 by Netscape as a way of creating portals to popular online news sites. Though Netscape eventually dropped it when the company decided it was too complex, others picked up the technology. (Pilgrim, 2002) The Berkman Center for Internet & Society holds ownership of the current RSS 2.0 specification, granting permissions through the Creative Commons Attribution/Share Alike license for the specification to be customized, excerpted and republished. (History of RSS, 2007)

An alternative standard to RSS was developed in order to address some shortcomings in the RSS standards was developed in 2003 and subsequently adopted by Google as its primary feed standard. (Atom (Standard), 2008). Yet, RSS remains the generic term by which such instant feeds of content updates are known.

A BLOG EXAMPLE

In the 1980s and 1990s I taught a graduate seminar in New Technologies in the Electronic Media. The seminar focused on new and emerging technologies—with an emphasis on learning technologies and their impact and influence on the delivery of education. As is common in such seminars, students were required to critique articles and monographs, presenting their comments to the class at large. Given the emergent nature of the subject, relevant articles would be published even during the course of the semester. To efficiently push those articles out to students so I could help direct their choices toward the most relevant and valuable articles to critique, a listserv was set up. The listserv provided regular summaries with links to complete versions of articles I thought were good choices for reviews. As students completed the seminar and launched or continued their careers, a number continued their subscription to the list. This provided them with a relatively steady stream of reports of recent research in the field. It was one-way; students did not have permission to post to the list.

In 2001, the list was converted to a blog entitled "Techno-News." The web site is http://people.uis.edu/rschr1/blogger.html. With RSS dissemination, updates were pushed out to subscriber computers via aggregators. Comments were enabled so that students, and others, could respond to the postings. Additional blogs were added; "Online Learning Update" (http://people.uis.edu/rschr1/onlinelearning/blogger.html) and "Educational Technology" (http://people.uis.edu/rschr1/et/blogger.html) to address the two most popular areas of the seminar. The blogs are now available to students in the class that eventually grew out of the original seminar–Internet and American Life (the title and readings for the class taken with permission from the Pew Charitable Trust Project of the same name)—a class that I currently teach entirely online. Students enrolled in the class monitor the blog postings via aggregators or links included in the Blackboard class site. Former students continue to aggregate the blog and continue to post comments to the blog that are then read by students in the class and enhance the online discussions. Course materials are shared via the blog with former students (and others) beyond the end of the semester, thereby keeping the two-way connection open with those who have taken the class.

Through the blogs, the original class continues as it has in one form or another for the past 25 years—addressing the impact of new and emerging technologies with an emphasis on learning technologies. Daily summaries and links to the latest news and research articles in the field of New Technologies in the Electronic Media are shared. As of this writing in mid 2008, among the three blogs there are more than 3,000 RSS subscribers. These blogs are syndicated online at dozens of sites ranging from universities to professional associations (including the Sloan Consortium) to textbook publishers. Clearly the reach of these materials—originally intended merely as classroom materials—has expanded far beyond the dozen students who took the seminar most semesters. Among those thousands of RSS subscribers and regular web visitors to the blogs are those students who have taken that original seminar or my more recent Internet and American Life class. For those former students, the class continues week after week, month after month, year after year. Their comments to the blogs enlighten the students (and others world-wide) who read the blogs. This makes for an exciting cycle of continuing study and contribution to a class that does not end.

APPLICABILITY IN RANGE OF CLASSES

Application of RSS-enabled syndication of class materials is not discipline-specific. The ability of podcasts, wikis, blogs and many of the other Web 2.0 technologies to handle a wide range of materials from text to image to scientific notation, makes them equally useful in nearly all courses that cover topics where there are updates, new research, on-going debates and discussions. The use of technologies to disseminate these perspectives to persons beyond those on the current class roster is true to the "gravitational core" of Web 2.0 and engages the collective intelligence of students, former students, and potentially others. The opportunity also exists to share such communications among related classes at the same, or different, institutions and even across disciplines. Expanding the learning community in this way enhances the learning experience, enables contacts and promotes collaborations.

If one makes the feeds open to all as I do with the blog feeds for my classes, the probability exists, of course, that students or graduates who never were part of the original class community may become part of the interactive cycle of publication and comment/revision. This portion of the class becomes open learning. The opportunity exists for informal learning. The reach and impact of the class materials is multiplied many times through the reach of the Internet.

FUTURE TREND: AN AVATAR VISION

Virtual world environments such as Second Life are opening the potential for even richer collaborations within the extended learning community. Such environments now support RSS standards so that all who have an interest may be informed when new materials are added, or virtual events are scheduled. Alerted by the RSS feed, the potential exists for students at various institutions to interact with former students via avatars in virtual worlds at scheduled events. "In world" sessions in the future may provide yet another robust opportunity for exchanges. The rich multi-media environment in Second Life provides opportunities for chats, instant messages, shared objects and more. Extended learning communities may thrive in such an environment.

Imagine the possibilities! Students who have graduated and moved into careers in a profession associated with the field would be encouraged to "drop-in" to join students who are just beginning to learn the discipline. One-on-one interactions, or one-to-group interactions, are entirely possible. Virtual guest speakers could pop up with regularity—both scheduled and unscheduled—at virtual locations where the class takes place. The graduates could browse student projects in the virtual classroom, meet, and interact with the new students in the class. Dialogs between and among the graduates who have become professionals in the field could enlighten the students. The students could test new ideas and perceptions out on those who have completed their course of study and are now applying what they have learned in real life. Certainly this vision would include the possibility for graduates of one program to "drop in" to join students from another university. Whole groups of students, and former students, could gather at one or another university site to view student projects or participate in live discussions.

CONCLUSION

The use of Web 2.0 RSS-enabled technologies for dissemination of class materials opens many doors. Widespread adoption could be transformative in higher education. It opens the doors of higher learning much like the MIT OpenCourseWare initiative (MIT, 2008). The difference is that the RSS syndicated materials are instantly and continuously updated and expanded, as well as commented upon by former students at the public at large. The potential exists for higher education to expand its key role in continuing professional education—informing and updating the perspectives and knowledge base of professionals. This would be done automatically via RSS.

The reach and impact of using RSS to broadly disseminate class materials remains to be seen. But, the potential is enormous. Students could become lifelong participants in classes; professors could continue to mentor and enlighten students throughout their careers. Education would no longer be truncated by the academic term. It would be infused into the lives and careers of active professionals.

Perhaps the most exciting aspect of this movement is that it requires no central base of organization, no major investment, no major technological capacity. Individual faculty members, by adopting the new Web 2.0 technologies are joining and leading the movement, in many cases without prior intent. In seeking to develop collaborations venues for classes, they are opening the doors of their classrooms to the world, including their past students. The joy that was reserved for that very occasional return visit of a successful graduate to the professor's office is multiplied a hundredfold by the on-going communication and collaboration between the faculty member and the graduate.

REFERENCES

Atom (standard). (2008, May 2). Wikipedia. Retrieved May 11, 2008, from http://en.wikipedia.org/wiki/Atom_%28standard%29.

History of RSS. (2007). RSS Specifications. Retrieved May 11, 2008, from http://www.rss-specifications.com/history-rss.htm

MIT OpenCourseWare. (2008). MIT OpenCourseWare. Retrieved May 31, 2008, from http://ocw.mit.edu/OcwWeb/web/home/home/index.htm

Pilgrim, M. (2002, December 18). *XML.com: What is RSS?* XML.com. Retrieved May 11, 2008, from http://www.xml.com/pub/a/2002/12/18/dive-into-xml.html

What is RSS?. (2008, May 1). .Net Development Information and Resources. Retrieved May 11, 2008, from http://searchwindevelopment.techtarget.com/sDefinition/0,,sid8_gci813358,00.html

PART V

WEB 2.0: CASE STUDIES AND IDEAS FOR EDUCATORS

CHAPTER 16

PLANNING FOR 21ST CENTURY TECHNOLOGIES

Jeff Utecht
International School of Bangkok, Thailand

ABSTRACT

With the onset of Web 2.0 tools in the 21st century, schools have had to re-think the use of technology within the learning environment. School stake-holders from teachers to parents to students are asking schools to allow them seamless access to information via the Internet. Schools are increasingly har-nessing the power of the web to make anytime anywhere information sharing a reality. This chapter focuses on creating a web-based school portal that puts student learning at the center of a comprehensive technology plan. From communication between school wide systems to supporting and implement-ing a technology plan within a school, this chapter looks to connect the power of Web 2.0 tools in creating a comprehensive information system for all users within a school community.

Wired for Learning: An Educator's Guide to Web 2.0, pages 255–275
Copyright © 2009 by Information Age Publishing
255

INTRODUCTION

With the uncontrollable use of social networks and media sites by both teachers and students, schools must revisit their technology plans and re-think technology's role within the wider school system. From lunch cards to student databases that hold everything from addresses to nurse reports, technology is a part of our school system. With a computer on almost every teacher's desk and overhead projectors slowly being replaced by LCD projectors, the technology revolution in schools is taking on a new face. Over the past decade, schools have purchased and implemented technology hardware at an amazing pace. Taking advantage of government and private grants, schools have found ways to wire themselves to the growing body of knowledge that is the Internet. They have adopted e-mail systems and internal communications to make the workflow of a school easier and more efficient. With the onset of Web 2.0 tools and the abundance of new learning tools the web now holds, it is time to rethink how schools are designed. This plan looks at just that. It offers a new infrastructure for schools. One that focuses on student learning and creates a system of support around students so that schools can build a learning landscape that allows them to prosper in a new digital society (Figure 16.1).

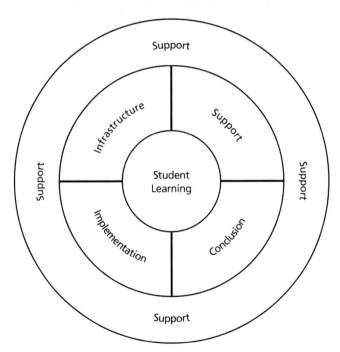

Figure 16.1 Building an educational portal focused on student learning.

Student Learning

In order to create a technology plan that supports student learning, schools must understand how students learn in this new digital landscape. The new Bloom's Taxonomy (Smythe & Halonen, 2008) and George Siemens' Connectivism Theory (Siemens, 2004) both outline these new changes in student learning. These two documents, along with endless resources from the blogosphere and Educational technology articles, can help any technology plan in defining why changes need to be made. A good technology plan should include a pedagogical theory of how the plan, and in the end the tools, are going to impact students. A school's goal is to teach students for their future and a technology plan should include a pedagogical reasoning for how these tools and new teaching and learning methods will meet that need. Without a solid pedagogical section of the plan, it cannot and should not move forward. It is in this section that a school must have buy in from all involved stakeholders (School Board, Superintendent, Parents, and Teachers). Karl Fisch's *Did You Know* video (Fisch, 2006) is one that can cause a significant ripple of interest in a School Board or parent presentation. Without everyone understanding how technology changes the way educators teach and students learn, the plan will unlikely reach its full potential.

Course Management System

Every school should have a Course Management System (CMS). Whether it is Moodle (moodle.org) or Blackboard (blackboard.com) or something else depends on the preference of the school. What is important is that this system starts to replace the school networks of the past. No longer should files only be accessible at school. By implementing a web based CMS, one can easily move all classroom documents into a web platform where a computer's operating system does not matter. This also allows anytime anywhere access to documents and learning materials. The list below highlights some of the functions a CMS should allow a school to do:

- Be able to have both private and public sections
- Be able to scale to the size of the school
- Be able to allow for different assignment types (forums, chats, assignments, journals, etc)
- Be able to create weekly/monthly/yearly backups (daily if preferred)
- Be fast and reliable
- Be easy to navigate
- Be as cost efficient as possible

In the end, the CMS should take the place of file systems in the school and at the same time add the functionality to allow for students to interact and courses to have an online component if chosen. At the very least, it should be used as a way to store and share files within a class, club, or community. The CMS begins to create a new web based information backbone for the school.

School Portal

A school portal should be the homepage for the school. Some schools might opt to use the public side of their CMS to be their school portal while others opt for a separate system. Either way, with the CMS being web based, linking the two can easily be accomplished allowing for complete information integration.

The school portal should be a public access site (although it too can have a private side) where the larger school community comes for information. Someone at the school—not central administrators—must manage the site. Only by having the site managed locally, can the site truly reflect the happenings of the school. The use of pictures, articles, podcasts and videos can all be used as evidence of student learning on the site. Drupal (drupal.org), an open-source content management system is one program that can be used for a school portal. It allows individual teachers to have a blog section where they can post events in their classroom. If a school wishes, blog posts can be promoted to the front page, making it rather easy to create a dynamic site where the content is constantly changing and up-to-date. For a good example of a school portal have a look at Lewis Elementary School's site in Portland, Oregon (lewiselementary.org). This site is a Drupal install that is managed locally by the principal, Tim Lauer (timlauer.org). Tim has local control over the look and feel of the site. This is in keeping with most job descriptions for a principal. A primary responsibility of the principal is to communicate regularly with parents and the community. Principals or assistant principals should be the gatekeepers to the school portal. Does this mean new communication skills for principals? Absolutely!

Teacher Websites

The newsletter was the communication vehicle of the 20th century. In the 21st century, schools need to move their communication to a more relevant form. Throughout the late '90s and into the early 21st century, teachers were pushed to create web pages. Schools and educators spent endless hours in training sessions learning to use FrontPage, Dreamweaver, or a host of other web page creation tools. Some teachers took to making web pages while others never grasped the concept of a well-constructed web page. Add to that the fact that someone also needed to understand File Transfer Protocol (FTP) or some other web file hosting system and one can easily see how creating a web page quickly became overwhelming.

However, the tools are now ready. Web 2.0 has simplified the process to the point that it is time to mandate a web page for each teacher. Now writing a blog post is easier and faster than writing and formatting a newsletter.

If a school adopts a school portal that has both a public and private side to it (as Drupal allows) then setting teachers up with a login and a simple preformatted page is quick and easy. All a teacher needs to do is know how to type and upload pictures (if they so choose).

Another option is to have a separate install for teachers to house their sites. Wordpress MU (mu.wordpress.org) is an easy to use program for this. Although technically a blogging piece of software, it can easily be customized on a teacher-by-teacher site to run the way that teacher feels most comfortable. Shanghai American School is one school that utilizes Wordpress MU in this format (teachers.saschina.org). In the end, it is a simple piece of software that a school can implement for use as a teacher website.

Student Network

During the 2006 K12online pre-conference (k12onlineconference.org), David Warlick discussed the idea that schools "cut off their tentacles" in reference to students and their learning (Warlick, 2006). It is time that schools understand the need for a school supported student network that allows students to create personal learning communities around subjects and activities.

Elgg (www.elgg.org) is a social networking install that is showing a lot of promise. It gives the freedom that students are accustomed to in creating groups, and having "friends." The social network however, can be controlled by the school and installed as part of the school's overall learning network. It comes with built in file uploading capability and a built in RSS reader. Students can start creating their learning networks that reach outside the students in their grade level or school, and into the larger school community. As a school, you can decide to keep this social network private to only your school, or make it public and allow people from outside to view, comment, and learn from your students.

Wordpress MU (mu.wordpress.org) is an installation that gives each student their own blog where they can customize their online learning portal. They can upload and share documents and reflect on schoolwork. It does not have all the social networking functions of Elgg. However, it is a well-supported blogging program that students pick up easily.

In the end, it does not matter what software platform a school chooses. What does matter is that a school does not cut the tentacles off of students. Instead, a school needs to create learning systems that allow those tentacles to reach where educators want. Educators can push and pull tentacles in the direction wanted, but if students' tentacles are cut off, they do grow back. These tentacles will then grow back underground where they are unseen and schools have no idea where those tentacles are reaching to, who they are connecting to, and what they are being exposed to. Only by allowing the tentacles to grow within the school, can educational institutions train students how to use the network for good, how to learn from the network and how to make the network work for them.

Program Integration

There are a number of different programs that can be used to create a learning system for today's school. By no means is this list complete, these are programs that schools have tried or are in the process of implementing in development of a school wide learning network that focuses on student learning. A school does not need to install all of these programs, but instead look at the different programs and decide for itself which ones best meet the school's needs. Three programs from the list below can give a school everything it needs to create a complete learning and communication network. Combined in different ways, these programs can offer a customized learning platform for schools. The list is not a comparison of programs but rather a look at the functionality that each can provide for a school system.

Different School setups that could be successful:

Option 1
Drupal: School portal and teacher websites
Moodle: Student blogs and Course Management System
Wordpress MU: School portal, student network, teacher webpages

Option 2
Blackboard: Course Management System
Drupal: School portal and teacher websites
Elgg: Student Social-Network

These are just two of the setups that could be combined to create an educational portal. Of course, these are not all the combinations. These tools can be combined in a multitude of ways. A school must take the time to research, experiment and design a system that best meets its needs.

School Information Systems

Technology reaches into every aspect of schools today. The Student Information Systems that run our schools hold more critical data than any other single program. As 21st century school wide systems are being designed, schools must think about how all this information is connected, how and who needs access to what information and how it can be made available to stakeholders in as few clicks as possible.

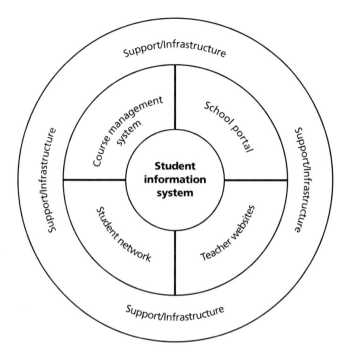

Figure 16.2   Building a student information system.

In examining Figure 16.2, one can see that not much has changed from the educational portal plan (Figure 16.1) that focuses on student learning to the infrastructure plan for the school. The significant change is replacing Student Learning with Student Information System (SIS) as the central focus. As previously discussed, the way a school manages the educational side of its technology should revolve around Student Learning. From a school wide systems approach, the central focus should be the Student Information System. This core piece of software will determine much of what a school can and cannot do as it creates a school wide system.

There are a number of Student Information or Student Management Systems available to schools. SASI, Admin+, and PowerSchool being just three in what is a long and complicated list.

This one fundamental piece of software can either make or break how the system as a whole works. Choosing the Student Management System that is right for the school is a key part in starting to build a school portal. What follows are functions that a Student Management System should allow a school to do.

Open Access

The Student Information System must have an open database that allows a school to incorporate other programs into it to allow for a seamless system. A program built in a database like mySQL would allow easy integration into the educational programs talked about in the School Portal section. By having an open database (a database that allows other programs to link to it and pull information from it) a Student Information System allows schools to customize their school portal using the tools they want. Most database programs today are proprietary and have a closed database, or a database created by them that does not integrate well with other programs. This trend appears to be shifting and moving toward the creation of more open database systems. By using open systems, schools have the control they need to create a system that is easy, secure, and if possible gives ubiquitous access. These systems must be accessible and customizable.

Ubiquitous Access

In today's anywhere, anytime, learning environment stakeholders want access to the information where they are and not where the information is. In other words, someone should be able to access anything and everything wanted from an Internet connected computer. Student Information Systems of the future must be web based, they must allow teachers, parents and students access when they need it. Having a closed system that runs on closed applications is a dying breed. Parents should be able to access information when they want it, students should be able to check grades from the lunchroom, and teachers should be able to complete report cards on a Saturday on their couch with their favorite coffee mug.

By making SIS web based, schools no longer need to worry about which platform their school is running (Windows, Linux, or Mac) or what the issues would be if they decide to upgrade or switch platforms. The web browser is the single best cross platform piece of software. Teachers (for the most part) already know how to use it, and students and parents would need little training as well.

All-in-One Solutions

The Student Information System of the 21st century needs to be all encompassing. No longer should schools have to synchronize information between programs. For example, teachers have a grading program that they have to synchronize with the SIS system. The SIS system then has to be synchronized to the web program that displays the information. That is excessive synchronizing of information and if the syncing of these programs does not happen on its own we are wasting human resources on these functions.

The SIS should have all of this within one system that is scalable to the needs of the school. A teacher should be able to enter grades into a web based reporting program. Those grades (if the school so chooses) should be accessible by parents and/or students without any other steps having to take place. A teacher should be able to take attendance and (if a school so chooses) have that information available to all parents via the web in real time. By setting up permissions, a school should be able to allow different stakeholders access to different parts of the system.

The SIS needs to be an all-in-one student information portal where all stakeholders can access the student information they need. It should offer a one-login solution to everything one could possibly want to know about a child, a student, and a student body.

Integrated System

By having a SIS that is web-based, it is easier for schools to create an integrated system of student information and educational access. What follows are scenarios of how users should be able to interact with data in a school portal that is web-based.

Student: Eva has a 15 minute break between classes. Just enough time to check and see if Ms. Galloway has posted the grades from Eva's essay that she handed in on Monday. Eva fires up her laptop and browses to her school's portal. There she sees that tonight's varsity baseball game has been canceled. . . . go figure after the three days of rain they have had recently. She logs into the system and navigates to her courses where she finds that Ms. Galloway has posted her essay grade. A 'B' not bad for a late night cram session. She moves her cursor over the grade and a bubble pops up with a comment from Ms. Galloway: "Good work! I think you should add this essay to your portfolio."

Eva decides that she will add the piece to her portfolio collection; knowing that she can later go back and either not include it as a final portfolio piece or write a reflection about it and turn it into one of her 3 pieces needed for English class. Eva quickly navigates to her portfolio, opens up her web folder and drags the essay from her desktop directly into her web folder through her browser. After the file uploads, a box pops us asking Eva to tag the essay with key words so that it can be found later.

With 5 minutes left Eva checks her school e-mail quickly . . . nothing worth reading. She logs out and heads to class.

Parent: Mr. Johnson is counting down the hours until 4 when he will be leaving work early to go watch his son pitch in the baseball game after school. It is his son's first as a starting pitcher. Mr. Johnson is concerned the game will be canceled due to the heavy rain this week so he heads to the school's website where he sees a message posted by the Athletic Director that the game has indeed been canceled. He is disappointed but at least it saved him a trip to the ballpark. While on the school's site, Mr. Johnson decides to login and check his children's grades. After logging in, he clicks on Paul's name and is instantly taken to a page that shows that Paul was present in all his classes today. He clicks on Algebra to see how Paul is doing. He knows Paul has been struggling with some of the concepts and wants to see how his grades are progressing. He quickly scans the grades and finds that Paul is pulling a B⁻. Not too bad! In the upper right hand corner, he clicks on a link that says "Student Blog" and is taken to another part of the website where he sees a list of reflections and other writings from Paul. He clicks on the category Algebra and starts reading, getting a feel for how Paul is feeling about Algebra and where he is struggling. He is a typical teenage boy who does not talk a lot about school at home. Mr. Johnson finds it refreshing that he gets a glimpse into his son's thoughts through his school blog.

While logged in, Mr. Johnson checks on his 9th grade daughter Eva. He notices she got a B on an essay that was turned in earlier this week, which he finds strange because he does not remember her telling him she had an essay assignment due. He makes a note to talk to her when he gets home.

Before signing off, he can't help but head over to the sports section and once again watch the highlights from last week's game where Paul hits a double in the gap. All baseball games are streamed live through the school's web site and archived. A video class at school also takes each game and creates a highlight reel. At the end of the year, the media class sells a DVD of all the highlights from sporting events throughout the school year. Mr. Johnson buys one every year and finds it a great way to document his children's athletic life through high school.

Teacher: It is early in the morning as Ms. Power gets to her classroom. She takes her laptop out of her bag and presses the power button. As she walks over to hang up her jacket, she flips the LCD projector on for the day. She remembers last year when the school installed it that she was nervous. She knew this meant that soon the school would be taking away her overhead projector and she was not very comfortable with that at the time. However, today she smiles as this year she did not even ask for an overhead projector in her room, in fact she had not used one the second part of last year and asked that they take it out of her room over the summer.

As she sits down at her computer, she starts her browser and navigates to the school's portal. There she is greeted with a message from the principal about happenings this week. She clicks on the calendar on the left and a new window pops up with a weekly view of after school activities and assemblies happening this week. She also notices a new podcast created by the 5th graders has been posted. She clicks on the link that reads "episode #10" and is taken to another part of the web site where she clicks play and listens to two students talking about what's happening in 5th grade this week. As the podcast plays in the background, she signs into the portal for the day. As she logs in, the portal changes to reflect information for teachers. Under the heading "Reminders" there is a note from the principal that reminds her that there will be a Fire Drill at 1:30 today. On the left under the heading "Resources Needed," she notices that someone has posted in the resource forum looking for cardboard tubes for a project. In the middle of the page is a posting called "A Week Ahead" that the principal posts every Monday that gives a rundown of everything happening this week.

Ms. Power clicks on her link that says blog and begins to write today's outline in a blog post. When she finishes, she chooses who she wants to see the blog post: Students, Parents, Teachers, Public, there is also a button that says 'Promote to Front Page'. Every day a different teacher writes something for the front page of the school's portal explaining what is happening in an individual class. By taking turns, the teachers only have to post something about once a month.

For today's outline, she just clicks Parents and Students. The blog post is instantly saved and she checks the LCD to make sure it is displaying properly on the whiteboard. She next clicks on the SIS link which takes her to the Student Information System. She loves this new system where she only logs in once and can access all she needs for the day. Once there she clicks on attendance and finishes preparing for her students to arrive.

These are just a few examples of how a 21st century school portal should work for all stakeholders. Information that is important to them, information they can access where they want when they want just a click away. We need to create school portals like Amazon.com creates online stores: one log in to a vast amount of knowledge and resources. Everything one could possibly need in a single integrated system.

At this time, finding this all in one system already intact is a challenge. Currently, schools must create this system by putting programs together that function as a whole. As a school creates its educational portal, these are some other ideas to consider:

Media Area

If schools are going to block sites like YouTube.com and OurMedia.org then they need to give students and staff another way to post video and audio files. Schools should have their own media area for the community to use. Imagine the power of a school having its own YouTube-type site.

Built-in RSS Reader

If it were just there, just sitting in front of teachers and students would they use it? Would teachers use it with students if it did not mean another username and password for both students and teachers?

Site-Wide Tags

The system should use site-wide tags that allows users to find information on any tagged artifact from any part of the site. For example, if parents click on the tag "Football" they could see articles written by both staff and students, they might find videos and podcasts from players, and maybe even a story from a 4th grader about playing football.

In the end, it is about access to information. The easier a school can make the information available to those that need and want it the better a 21st century system will be received by all.

Support

Support Structure

A school can have the best educational portal and the best infrastructure, but if it does not have the support in place to both help teachers use/ understand technology and support infrastructural needs, then the money spent on hardware will be lost.

Throughout the late '90s and into the 21st century, schools spent a great deal of money on computer hardware and technology systems and infrastructure. Now that these systems are in place, a school must think and rethink the support needed to not only keep these systems up-to-date but also how they affect teaching and learning in the classroom.

Below is a two-pronged approach to technology support in schools (see Figure 16.3).

ITs (Informational Technologists): These people know networks; their job is to make sure day in and day out that the network is healthy. They fo-

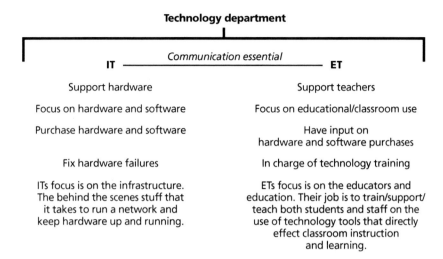

Figure 16.3 The two sides of an educational technology department.

cus on keeping viruses out, keeping computers running, and making sure that the overall school network is in place, up-to-date, and working.

ETs (Educational Technologists): These people know education. They will likely have had classroom experience and have been put into positions as ETs because of their use of technology in the classroom. Although they may be familiar with networks and the hardware of the school, their focus is on the tools, the learning, and the training to embed technology into day-to-day classroom use.

Schools begin by hiring IT positions. People that can make sure the network and computers are running. But many times these ITs are pushed into the positions of ETs where they may not have classroom experience, may not be familiar with new learning tools, new approaches, or new methods in teaching and learning in a networked classroom. ETs, on the other hand, are hired to help teachers and students utilize the technology skills and approach the district has adopted.

A key component that was left out of the original support structure was the media/literacy specialists. These people are key in the support structure of the school's technology plan. Figure 16.4 has been reworked to now include this new position.

The Literacy/Media specialist is not a new position but instead an evolution of the librarian post that today focuses not only on written text, but also on other information sources. The Literacy/Media specialist needs to be a specialist in the area of 21st century Literacy skills and should teach those skills in the context of the media/library center. The Literacy/Media specialist must understand that tags, categories, and Boolean searches are

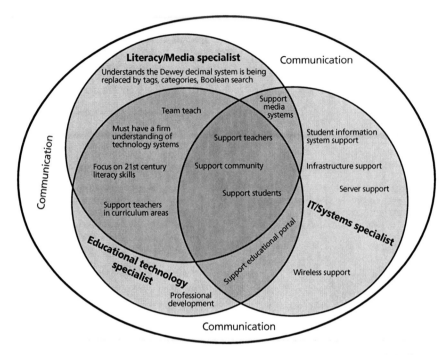

Figure 16.4 The convergence of roles between the IT, ET, and Literacy/Media specialist.

augmenting the Dewey Decimal system. That is not to say that the Dewey Decimal system is going away, just that students today engage with information that is digital more than in print. They do Google searches before they check out a book. Arguing whether or not this is right or wrong is beside the point as it just is the way students gather information today.

Support Team

The technology support team is made up of Literacy/Media Specialist, Educational Technologists, and Information Technologists. It is the collective power of this team to work together to support the overall use of technology in the school. This support includes professional development for staff, teaching research skills to students, and making sure that the network systems are running smoothly. The communication between all team members is critical and if possible, their offices should be within close proximity to each other. This helps to facilitate communication among all team members. Grade levels or departments are grouped together in schools so that teachers can support each other and work together. The same accommodation should be made for the technology support team.

Support Personal

Informational Technologist: There should be enough IT positions to support the schools needs. There is a wide disparity among schools in the ratios of IT positions to students. Some schools have anywhere from 2500 students per IT position to 100 students per IT position. If a school has implemented a 1:1 laptop program, then more IT positions will be needed in order to support the infrastructure needs of such a system. Each school should have an IT support person on campus. That IT support needs to be decentralized and each school should have a dedicated IT person starting at 300 students. In general, 300 students is a guide for many specialist positions within schools and the same guide should be used when looking at technology.

Educational Technologist: These positions are new dedicated positions that many schools do not have or are just now realizing that they need if they want to move forward with technology use in the classroom. A ratio for this position of 300:1 (Student: ET) also is recommended. This would then allow for the ET to support both the students and teachers in an embedded technology model.

Literacy/Media Specialist: Every school should have a Literacy/Media Specialist. Searching on the American Librarian Association (http://www.ala.org) website to try and find what it recommends as a student to librarian ratio did not return any conclusive results. Regardless of this, each school should have at least one Literacy/Media Specialist.

Therefore, a school of 300 students should have a support structure that looks like this.

> IT: one position
> ET: one position
> L/M Specialist: one position

For a large high school of 2500 students or so the support structure would be:

> IT: eight positions
> ET: eight positions
> L/M: one or more positions

Of course, this is a perfect scenario. Can schools afford that many positions? Probably not, but in a perfect world teachers would not need this support if they were coming out of teacher training programs that focused on educating teachers how to utilize 21st century skills. Until this happens, these positions are critical to a school as it continues to move forward in its use of technology as a tool in the classroom.

IMPLEMENTATION

In regards to implementation, all the technology in the world and the best support structure are nothing if a school does not take the time to implement the technology in a way that supports the structure of the entire plan. The process of implementing a technology plan can have lasting consequences on the buy in from stakeholders. Implement the plan correctly, and a school can bring the stakeholders and the system along at the same time. Implemented incorrectly, a school can end up alienating stakeholders or never fulfilling its technology plan's goals.

Most schools do not have the financial freedom to implement a complete technology plan in the span of one year. Therefore, schools are forced to implement new technologies, new plans, over several years. In the end it has to do with money. A school needs money to implement the technology plan. From switches and wires, to teacher training and support, it all costs money. Because schools are forced into multi-year plans, it is easy to get stuck in a routine of working on or focusing on one part of the plan without ever moving on. Infrastructure is usually where this happens. Many schools decide they are going to focus on upgrading their infrastructure over a period of time. By the time they are done upgrading, it is time to replace the 3 to 5 year old equipment to meet new standards. In these cases, schools continually work on their infrastructure and never truly implement the technology into the school or classroom.

There are two things a school can do when creating a technology plan and implementing that technology plan. First, a school must identify what it wants end users to be able to do on a year-to-year basis. From there, a school can work backwards and create an infrastructure based on what it wants teachers and students to do that year. A school should be wary of overbuilding its infrastructure and instead focus on creating a foundation to meet its users' needs. Secondly, a school should evaluate its technology and implementation plan on a yearly basis. A school might create a three or 5-year technology plan, but technology is changing and advancing so rapidly, that accurately predicting the future of technology and education is impossible.

Start with the End in Mind

Doug Johnson provides a nice visual of the different layers of technology needs in school. Figure 16.5 shows that it is the technology infrastructure that is the foundation on which to build. A school cannot add hardware and software that its infrastructure cannot support.

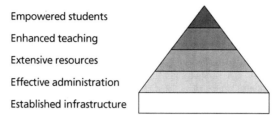

Figure 16.5   Doug Johnson's Hierarchy of Educational Technology Needs. (Johnson, 2007).

The use of a triangle depicts that the infrastructure must be wider than the student and teacher use at the top of the triangle. Although a solid foundation is necessary, the base should be in-line with the use. In other words, there is no need to have a base that is state-of-the-art if users are only word processing. Build an infrastructure to support only what is needed. So in reworking the diagram, it would look something like Figure 16.6.

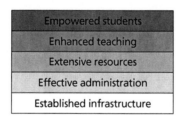

Figure 16.6   Educational technology needs reworked.

In this way the infrastructure, resources, support, and outcomes are all in-line and supported by each other. A school does not need to add more than necessary, instead it should build the system just large enough to support what is needed. Once this is understood, a school can then look at what it wants students and teachers to do with technology and work backwards to create a system that can support those outcomes.

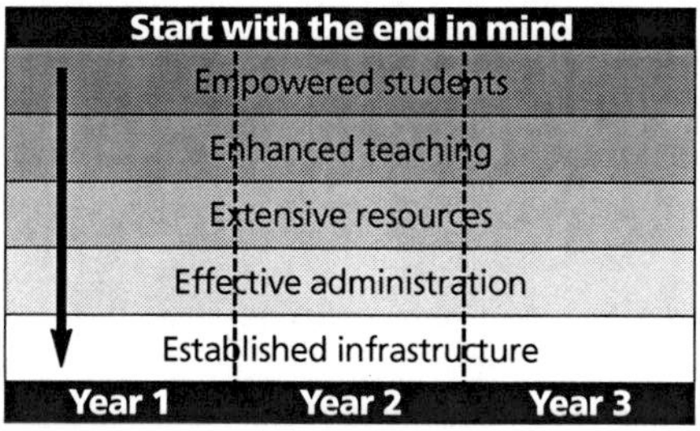

Figure 16.7   Implementing a plan horizontally rather then vertically ensures all stake holders needs are met.

Even though the layers of support must be horizontal, the implementation of the whole system must be vertical. By implementing in a vertical format, each year sees added value to the end user. This allows stakeholders to buy into a system and "see" results on a yearly base.

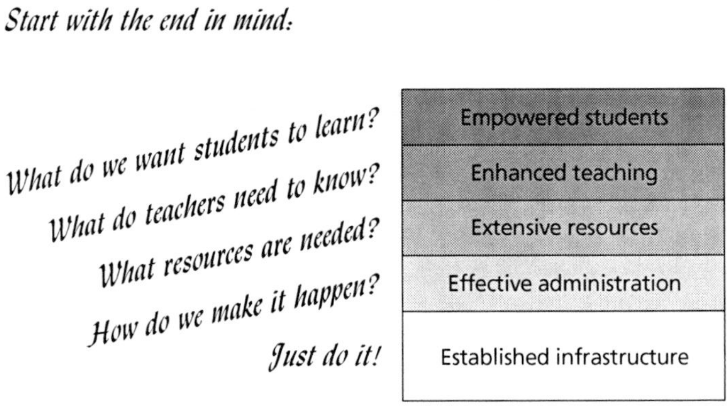

Start with the end in mind:

Figure 16.8 From students to infrastructure make sure everyone's needs are met.

When a school only focuses on infrastructure, in many cases the end user does not 'see' results. A new server means nothing to a teacher. However, being able to work with new content or enter grades online does. By implementing the plan in a vertical way, a school ensures that the users see results yearly. The users are able to see the impact the money and hard work is having on the education system as a whole.

In word form, it might look like this:

> **Students will learn:** to upload multimedia projects to the web and embed them into their e-folios
> **Teachers will:** be able to support students in the creating of multimedia projects and learn how to embed projects into e-folios
> **Resources needed:** Time to train teachers, Time to train students
> **Infrastructure:** Internet connection, server to house files, a way for students to upload videos and embed them on e-folios

Starting with knowing what a school wants students to do, it can work backwards to ensure there is an infrastructure in place to make these outcomes happen.

Too often, schools think horizontally when implementing technology. Trying to anticipate everything that an infrastructure may need to support is unrealistic. Technology evolves too fast to try and guess what may be needed in the future. Instead, a school must start with what it wants students to be able to do with technology today, create an infrastructure that can support that, and continue to revise and improve that infrastructure as schools head into tomorrow.

By looking at technology implementation through a vertical lens, schools also can decide how much they can afford to do any given year. Each school's budgetary demands are different. Some schools might take smaller chunks of their plan based on the financial resources they have available. No matter what a school's financial resources are, by implementing in a vertical format, a school ensures that the students are impacted in some way. This provides the end users with tangible results and not just servers and wires in a locked closet.

Each school must decide how to best implement its plan, but by taking a vertical approach a school can focus on affecting education and student learning. Again, keeping the focus on student learning from the design through the implementation stage is a key factor in successfully bringing all stakeholders on board with a 21st century technology plan.

CONCLUSION

In the 21st century, schools need to support locally but think globally. Schools must have a local infrastructure that supports learning but that also allows students and teachers to learn and interact globally. Technology plans of the 21st century need to focus on student learning and continue to ask the questions "What do students need to learn and what skills do they need to accomplish that learning objective?"

If schools embrace the changes of the 21st century: the new skills, learning theories, and literacy, then creating a system that supports learning in this new digital age should be a top priority.

A 21st century technology plan looks to bring people and resources together. It is a system that allows all school stakeholders to log on through a single user interface and access the information they need when they need it. It should allow stakeholders to communicate more efficiently. This creates a network of users and allows them to connect to each other, forming relationships that are natural to students today.

Schools must embrace the changes that the digital age has brought. Schools need to understand that by not creating a digital landscape for their learners, they are alienating them and missing opportunities to engage them in the learning process.

No technology plan is easy to implement. Technology is a moving target. A multi-year technology plan is really a year-to-year technology plan with a guide to the direction the school wants to go. This is why it is critical to meet the needs of the school today with an eye on tomorrow. A technology plan must be fluid and adaptable. In this digital age, one skill that everyone must have is to be able to learn, unlearn and relearn information as it changes. The same is true with a technology plan. Build it, evaluate it, and revise it on a yearly basis. Good schools in the 21st century will always have a three-year technology plan because they are constantly changing their end goals based on new emerging technologies. For example, the programs that have been mentioned in this chapter are ones that *currently* would allow schools to build an educational portal. They are merely examples of programs that are available to schools *today* for little or no cost that can create a digital landscape ripe for learning, interacting, connecting, and conversing. However, with the rapid changes in this digital age, these programs may not exist tomorrow.

The first step is to understand that when students are at the center of a technology plan, that teaching and learning must change. With an infrastructure and support model in place, and an implementation process that brings the school along in a vertical fashion so that all pieces of the plan are adequately supported, schools can change. Teaching and learning can and will change.

This is a time of rapid change. The world continues to flatten and become more connected. Students today already live and learn in this globally connected world. Education has a responsibility to prepare students for their connected future. In order for that to happen, students must be engaged in their learning spaces. A 21st century technology plan puts in place a system that allows teachers to teach successfully and allows students to engage in the learning process. Only then can education continue to move forward with society into a globally connected digital future.

REFERENCES

Content Management System. (2008). Content Management System. In *Wikipedia* [Online]. Retrieved March 12, 2008, from http://en.wikipedia.org/wiki/Content_management_system

Fisch, K. (2006, August). *Did you know.* The Fischbowl. Retrieved March 12, 2008, from http://thefischbowl.blogspot.com/2006/08/did-you-know.html

Johnson, D. (2007, July 5). *Maslow and motherboards: Technology planning.* Doug Johnson's Blue Skunk Blog. Retrieved April 23, 2008, from http://www.doug-johnson.com/dougwri/maslow-and-motherboards-technology-planning.html

Siemens, G. (2005, December 4). *Connectivism: A learning theory for the digital age.* elearning space. Retrieved March 12, 2008, from http://www.elearnspace.org/Articles/connectivism.htm

Smythe, K., & Halonen, J. (2008). *Using the New Bloom's Taxonomy to design meaningful learning assessments.* APA Online. Retrieved March 12, 2008, from http://www.apa.org/ed/new_blooms.html

Warlick, D. (2006, Oct 16). *Derailing educatoin: Taking sidetrips for learning.* K12 Online Conference 2006. Retrieved April 23, 2008, from http://k12online conference.org/?p=26.

CHAPTER 17

IS THERE A PLACE
IN SECOND LIFE®
FOR K–12 EDUCATION?

Amanda Jost
Houston Independent School District

Irene Chen
University of Houston Downtown

ABSTRACT

This chapter documents a dialogue between an Educational Technologist for a large urban school district and a faculty member of teacher education. The Educational Technologist has taught for 19 years, 18 of them in Pre-Kindergarten through 6th Grade computer labs. She is interested in exploring new virtual reality technologies and how they can be useful for increasing student achievement.

A Dialogue between Amanda Jost, (Educational Technologist, Curriculum, Instruction, and Assessment Department, Houston Independent School District) and Dr. Irene L. Chen (Department of Urban Education, University of Houston Downtown).

Wired for Learning: An Educator's Guide to Web 2.0, pages 277–290
277

Amanda Jost is an Educational Technologist for a large urban school district in Houston, Texas. She has taught for 19 years, 18 of them in Pre-Kindergarten through 6th grade computer labs. She is interested in exploring new technologies and how they can be useful for increasing student achievement. She wants to find ways for teachers to connect and share ideas that will help students to be more successful.

Dr. Irene L. Chen is an Associate Professor in Urban Education Department at UHD. Dr. Chen has helped train teachers in Houston Independent School District and other districts. She has diverse professional experiences. Previously, she was an instructional technology specialist, a computer programmer/analyst, and department learning technology coordinator. Her research interests are: instructional design, technology and culture, assessment and evaluation educational technology, and multicultural education.

Dr. Chen: *I understand in your role as an Educational Technologist you have been looking into Second Life. What's it all about?*

Jost: Second Life is an online 3D virtual world. People interact with each other by creating virtual selves called avatars. The avatars can walk around, talk, and even fly, all at the direction of a real person at a computer. In Second Life there are buildings, trees, chairs, tables, etc. so it looks and feels a lot like a real world. When you are in Second Life directing your avatar you really feel like you are there. At first it can feel very strange because people create their avatars to look like anything they want, so you might find yourself talking to a wolf person or a snake person. Many avatars do look like people but may or may not look anything like the people do in real life. In Second Life you can be younger, thinner, and have more hair than you have in real life!

Some rules in Second Life are the same as in real life, like if you step off a cliff you will fall. Some rules are different, like if you end up under water after stepping off the cliff you will not drown. In fact, when you get out of the water you won't be wet. One big difference is that in Second Life you have new methods of transportation. You can fly, which is a great way to look around a new place and you can teleport to other locations, which is a way to jump from one place to another in just a few seconds. Second Life has day and night as in real life, but you can choose to make it look like day whenever you want to by clicking on World—Force Sun. It will only change your view, not the view of everyone else who is there. In real life we live in time zones and Second Life has a time zone, too. All of Second Life is in a time zone called SLT (Second Life Time), which is the same as real life San Francisco, California. The time zone is needed as a reference for people scheduling events.

Dr. Chen: *Who started Second Life?*

Jost: Second Life was created by Linden Lab® which is located in San Francisco (hence, the Second Life time zone). Linden Lab was founded in 1999 to create a virtual world and Second Life has been open to the public since 2003. Linden Lab has over 200 employees in the US, Europe, and Asia. Second Life now has members in the millions.

Dr. Chen: *So is Second Life a game?*

Jost: Second Life is not a game and was not created to be a game. Members of Second Life are called "residents." There is no specific goal and no winners or losers. There is not a beginning and end like there is in a game. People create their avatars and interact as they wish. They build structures and objects, hold events, and invite others to participate. So the people who go there create the Second Life environment. There is as much diversity in Second Life as you find in real life. People have built schools, night clubs, shops, and art galleries and have formed groups for creating music, discussing theology, forming campaign strategies, viewing art, and many other activities. Some people choose to play games while in Second Life just as some people choose to play games in real life but Second Life should not be confused with a Massive Multiplayer Online Role Playing Game (MMORP). The attribute that Second Life shares with a game is that it can be a lot of fun.

Dr. Chen: *If I want to join Second Life, how do I get started? If I go to the Internet and search for "second life" will I be able to click on a Web site and be in Second Life?*

Jost: No, you will be on the Internet on a website about Second Life. That is where you begin. Go to http://secondlife.com, click "Join," and fill out the form (Figure 17.1).

Figure 17.1 Second Life.

Be careful when choosing a name for your avatar because you cannot change it after you set up your account. You can delete your account and set up a new one, but you can't change the name on an existing account. Type in any first name you like and choose a last name from a list on the website. If you don't like any of the last names offered, you can navigate away from the Second Life website and go back. The names offered will be different.

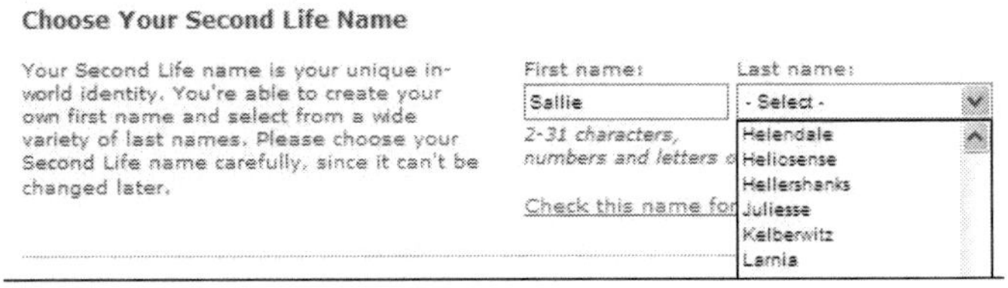

Choose Your Second Life Name

Your Second Life name is your unique in-world identity. You're able to create your own first name and select from a wide variety of last names. Please choose your Second Life name carefully, since it can't be changed later.

First name:
Sallie
2-31 characters,
numbers and letters
Check this name for

Last name:
- Select -
Helendale
Heliosense
Hellershanks
Juliesse
Kelberwitz
Lamia

Figure 17.2   Second Life name selection.

Select an avatar from a set of 6 female and 6 male choices. Continue to fill out the information required. Here is a sample of the avatars offered. A free account is fine.

Figure 17.3   Avatar selection.

You will be directed to go to your e-mail and open the message from Second Life that will activate your account. When you open the e-mail message you will find a link to activate your account. You will be told to download and install the Second Life client program. A link for the download is in the message. Check the system requirements. Currently a cable or DSL Internet connection is required, along with at least 512 MB of RAM and 800 MHz processing speed. There are a variety of graphics cards listed. For Windows, XP or higher is required and for Mac, OS 10.3.9 or better is required. If you don't have the minimum system requirements, you may not be able to run Second Life.

After you have downloaded and installed the program, you are ready to go. Open the program from the shortcut on your desktop. Logon with your password and agree to the Terms of Service.

Figure 17.4   Terms of service.

The first place you arrive will be Orientation Island. Here, you will learn to do a few basic things. You will learn to move, communicate, search, and change your appearance. After you finish the tutorials you will be given the opportunity to teleport to Help Island, where you can take more tutorials or you can go ahead and explore Second Life. Orientation Island and Help Island are just for "newbies" (newcomers to Second Life), so after you leave you cannot return. However, there are mirror locations called Orientation Island Public and Help Island Public. You can visit these whenever you want to go through the tutorials again. Here I am at the entrance of the Search Tutorial on Orientation Island.

Figure 17.5   Inside Second Life.

Dr. Chen: *That's sounds very interesting. How can I find out more?*

Jost: Besides the tutorials in Second Life, you can find many tutorials about Second Life on the Internet. You can find them in various forms, from written instructions to videos. One video I found very useful as an introduction to Second Life was Episode 66 of AsktheTechies.com. Another helpful item was the Unofficial Complete Fool's Guide to Second Life. You can find both of these resources on the Internet.

If you get physically stuck anywhere, as I have (one time I took at trip on an airplane, then couldn't figure out how to get off the plane; another time I fell into a crevice and couldn't get out) you can always click Search, find a new location, and click to teleport to it. This will instantly get you out of your problem and into a new place. I have also found that people I encounter are generally helpful if I ask for instructions.

There are lots of blogs about Second Life, so that is another good way to find out more. Search the Internet and you will find many resources. You can join some listservs that will send you e-mail messages automatically if you want to stay connected. I belong to the Second Life Educator's Listserv also known as SLED (go to https://lists.secondlife. com/cgi-bin/mailman/listinfo/educators and fill out the subscription), the ISTE Second Life Listserv (go to www.iste. org/secondlife/ and fill out the subscription at the bottom), the Official Linden Blog (go to http://blog.secondlife. com/ and click Subscribe by e-mail at the top left), and the Second Life Research Listserv (http://list.academ-x.com/ listinfo.cgi/slrl-academ-x.com).

Dr. Chen: *I've heard that you can spend real money in Second Life. How does that work? Is it expensive?*

Jost: As a matter of fact, in Second Life you can only spend Linden dollars, which is the virtual currency of Second Life. You can obtain Linden dollars by having a paid account or by purchasing them in Second Life. If you choose to have a paid account, you will pay a monthly amount of real money and receive Linden dollars for it. You can also gain Linden dollars by winning contests held in Second Life and by building something in Second Life that people want to buy. There are locations in Second Life where people will pay you for simply being there so that they can build up their traffic statistics, the records that show how many people are spending time on their land. You can also earn Linden dollars by having a job in Second Life.

I think it is important to know, however, that you do not need to buy anything in Second Life. You can sign up for a free account and not feel like you need anything else. If you do have Linden dollars you can purchase clothing, objects, land, hair, different looking skin, vehicles, and many other things. I have to admit I would like some better hair!

Dr. Chen: *It sounds like it could be fun. But why would any K–12 educator want to know about Second Life?*

Jost: First, our students are growing up in a digital world that includes 3D interactive environments. Children as young as five are participating in virtual worlds like Webkinz, Nicktropolis (by Nickelodeon), Club Penguin, and Virtual Magic Kingdom (by Disney). These include elements such as games, social interaction, and virtual shopping. We certainly need to know about this type of world so that we can understand our students, be able to connect with them, and engage them in educational activities.

Second, students can learn in Second Life. You can set up classes for your students in Second Life where they can work on collaborative projects. Under your direction your students can work on projects with each other or they can participate in activities with students in other countries. In addition to classes, there are simulations for your students to experience such as those created by the National Oceanic and atmospheric Administration (NOAA) and the Earth System Research Laboratory (ESRL) involving hurricanes, tsunamis, and glaciers. There are other simulations created by the National Aeronautics and Space Administration (NASA) involving space travel. There are rules and limitations involving minors, so there are some things you will need to learn if you want to use Second Life with your students.

Third, there are many professional development opportunities for educators in Second Life. There are educational groups to join, meetings to attend, and educators to meet from all over the world. There are universities who have created learning spaces in Second Life. Some notable examples are Harvard, Princeton, Penn State, Columbia University, NYU, and a variety of universities around the world, such as ones in Scotland, Australia, England, Canada, France, Denmark, Finland, and more. There are research projects involving education going on in Second Life right now that may interest you.

If you are interested in the schools involved in Second Life, it will help you to know that they cannot always be found by doing a search in Second Life. On more than one occasion I have needed to use a search engine on the Internet to find them. For example, search for "Columbia

University Second Life" on the Internet and you will get instructions on how to find it in Second Life. Also, the public cannot visit some school locations because they are restricted to their own students.

Dr. Chen: *OK, so let's say I am a K–12 teacher. Why would I want to use Second Life with my students? What's possible and what are the issues?*

Jost: My focus is on K–12 education, so we are dealing with students that are minors. Let's talk first about students who are 13 through 17 years old. These students cannot join Second Life because it is only for adults. You must be 18 years old to join Second Life. However, teens from 13 through 17 can join a virtual world created by Linden Lab that is just for them called Teen Second Life. This is their own virtual world where they can interact with other teens and not be bothered by inappropriate adult content. So if your students are 13 through 17 years of age, they can join Teen Second Life and not Second Life. Here's the problem. You, as an adult educator can only join Second Life but not Teen Second Life. So how do you hold a class? I have discovered two ways.

You can buy your own private island in Teen Second Life. You will need to submit to a background check and you will be confined to your island. You cannot freely roam around Teen Second Life. Students can come to your island if and when they choose, and they will automatically be notified that there is an adult present. To me, these are minor concerns because if you are their teacher and your students come to your class in real life, they will come to your class in Second Life. The major issue is the cost. Currently, an island costs $700 real US dollars if you qualify as an educator and there are monthly maintenance fees of $147.50, which is also an educator discount. Educators are allowed to buy smaller spaces for as little as $175 with a monthly fee of $37.50. In spite of the costs, a private island or space may be a good solution for you, especially if you work for a district or organization that supports the use of virtual worlds in education, meaning that they will pay for it.

Another way to teach students in Second Life is to join Skoolaborate.com. This is a "by invitation only" project. You will need to submit to a background check and you will need to agree to what they call a minimum commitment. This includes attending a meeting in Second Life for 1 hour every two weeks, developing and documenting at least one Second

Life activity every six months, using these services for at least one year with at least six students, actively pursuing a collaborative project with a school from another country, and more. The time commitment is high. This looks like an exciting possibility because you would be connecting your students with students from other countries and would be working with teachers who are highly motivated to make the activity a success.

Dr. Chen: *What about the younger kids, especially those who are under 13?*

Jost: There is no virtual world created by Linden Lab for children under 13. I have asked educators that I have met in Second Life about how they use Second Life with younger students. Some teachers feel comfortable using a projector in their classrooms to let their students experience educational simulations in Second Life.

Others have told me they create short videos in Second Life (called "machinima") and show them to students. Developing the skills needed to create these movies takes time, more time than most teachers have. Also, after creating the movies, your campus or school district may have a movie approval process that would need to be endured before the movie could be shown. Therefore, I think only a small minority of teachers would want to do this. However, in the future, there may be banks of these movies available for educators to download from Creative Commons. There are already machinima to be found in Creative Commons, but I don't see any for educators to use with young students yet.

Maybe sometime in the future there will be a Second Life virtual world for teachers and their younger students. At this time, if you teach students under 13 years old, the best opportunities are not in engaging students in Second Life but in using Second Life for your own professional learning. Connect with other educators, share knowledge and resources, and attend workshops, because Second Life is a rich, ever-changing world from which you can benefit. As you interact with other educators, some valuable ways to use Second Life with younger students may be discovered.

Dr. Chen: *What other issues and concerns do educators have to watch out for in Second Life?*

Jost: One issue involves the technical performance of Second Life. You may experience something called "lag" which is noticeable when you are communicating with someone. There can be a bit of a delay while you wait for them to respond. It is also noticeable when you are moving in Second Life. As you approach an area the objects (including buildings and other structures) may take some time to appear. Also, Second Life itself will sometimes go down or portions of it will go down. The people at Linden Lab work quickly to resolve the issues. It is really quite a technical feat in my opinion, since their programmers are not in charge of what's being created in Second Life—the residents are. In spite of these issues, I have not experienced any real problems. However, if I had a group of students depending on Second Life for an assignment, I would be more concerned over these things.

Another issue is the time it takes to learn to use Second Life. It does take a while to get comfortable moving around, finding locations, and communicating. If you want to work with students, they will need time to develop their skills as well. So be prepared to spend some learning time and bring your sense of humor with you. I was at a meeting recently and was trying to move to another seat so that I could see better. Instead, my chair moved with me and I started riding my chair around the room accidentally. When I figured out how to stop and get off I was standing right next to the presenter. I'm pretty sure this was distracting but everyone was really nice about it.

Another issue is that people don't always behave as they should. Just as in real life, people in Second Life don't follow the rules all of the time. If someone seriously interferes in other people's enjoyment of Second Life (for example, by assaulting them in a weapon-free area) this can be reported as abuse. The Lindens investigate all reports of abuse and will give warnings and/or banish those who harass or abuse others in Second Life. Just to let you know, if someone does attack you, you can't really be harmed. The worst that can happen is that you get sent back to your home location and feel annoyed.

Dr. Chen: *If it is difficult to learn to use Second Life and costly to find space, why would you want to bother? I mean, why not just do your good old teaching and learning in real life? Is there any advantage to teaching in Second Life?*

Jost: Second Life is uniquely suited to some types of learning and can, in some cases, be an improvement over real life teaching and learning. For example, it is an ideal place for students to work on foreign language skills, as they can interact with native speakers to improve their reading, writing, speaking, and listening skills. Also, Second Life can be used to engage and motivate students to learn programming (called "scripting" in Second Life). One teacher reports that students spend longer on their projects and endure through their programming difficulties because of the sense of ownership they feel in Second Life. After they build something, they don't want to give up on making it move.

Second Life is also well suited for cultivating global consciousness and cultural connectedness, which can lead to solutions for big problems. It is being used effectively by Global Kids, a program out of New York City, to foster an awareness of global issues, develop leadership skills, and to empower students to make a positive difference on a global level. On Global Kids Island in Teen Second Life, high school students host forums to increase understanding among young people all over the world about issues such as racism, child sex trafficking, international justice, the Holocaust, and genocide in Darfur. They have raised money through fundraisers in Second Life to help solve some of these international problems. Global Kids has attracted students that were at risk for dropping out and is turning them into tomorrow's leaders. That's inspiring!

Second Life is a perfect place to reach all kinds of learners, too. Gifted students, at risk students, students learning English as a second language, and students with many different learning preferences learn skills and knowledge in Second Life that will help them improve their achievement in real life.

An exciting aspect of Second Life is the interaction between students. They are teaching each other rather than sitting and listening to a teacher (or too often, not listening). Teachers who have worked with students in Second Life report increased excitement and engagement of students, an increased willingness to continue to work on difficult projects, and much better attendance. Students don't want to miss their Second Life classes.

Dr. Chen: *Tell me more about the professional development opportunities of the Second Life in the area of educational technology.*

Jost: My favorite place to go in Second Life is ISTE Island. It was created by ISTE (the International Society for Technology in Education) to be used by educators for meetings and events. ISTE holds educator meetings every Tuesday and Thursday evening. Even when there is not a meeting-taking place, there is almost always a docent at ISTE Headquarters. A docent is a person who is there to answer your questions about ISTE events in Second Life or any general questions you might have. As a new person I have found this to be very helpful. In addition, ISTE allows educators to use some of their space for meetings. To find out more, go to ISTE Island Headquarters in Second Life, look at their calendar of events, and talk to the docent. There is a sign next to the calendar to tell you how to reserve space for a meeting. Of course, you will need to join Second Life before you can visit ISTE Island.

I also like to go to Discovery Educators Network on EdTech Island. They have workshops in Second Life for educators, with topics ranging from "Uses of Graphic Organizers in the Classroom" to "Playing QuickTime Movies in Second Life for Professional Development." Real life teachers get together in Second Life to share resources and tips involving education in both real life and in Second Life.

I also like Lighthouse Learning Island. It was created by four school districts in Massachusetts to be a professional learning community of educators. It's worth exploring because you will find resources of information about Second Life and education there. For example, if you walk into the Nauset Public Schools building and look for the Resources and Info area, you will be able to "touch" many laptops that will give you links to websites about the use of Second Life in education.

The ELVEN Institute is a great place in Second Life, too. This organization was created specifically to help PreK–12 educators use virtual environments for teaching and learning. They hold workshops for educators to help them learn basic Second Life skills and to help them find ways to use Second Life to promote student achievement.

These are just a few of the opportunities in Second Life. Groups I can recommend joining are K–12 Educators, Real Life Education in Second Life, EdTech Community, ISTE, and Discovery Educator Network. Locations I suggest that you explore are SciIsland, Second Louvre Museum, Ball State University Campus, and Info Island. I encourage you to join Second Life and look for groups, locations, and events. I also suggest that you do an Internet search for educational groups and events in Second Life. Sometimes it is easier for me to find what I am looking for in Second Life if I find out about it on the Internet first.

Dr. Chen: *I am aware that there is not a good selection of educational applications of simulations and animations in K–12 software market. What can teachers do to take advantage of the online 3D virtual world environment of Second Life to fill the gap?*

Jost: Teachers who feel comfortable using Second Life as a presentation platform can use the simulations in Second Life to teach in a whole class setting. The whole class setting allows the teacher to be in full control, which is important when using a new technology that allows interaction with the public. If and when Second Life becomes more mainstream (like the Internet), some controls or filters may be developed to prevent inappropriate interactions. At that time, teachers may be able to allow students to use Second Life each at individual computers. For now, teachers should check on their district and campus regulations involving the use of Second Life with students and should be in control. Teachers who enjoy exploring and learning to use new technologies can master the needed skills.

Teachers with districts who are willing to spend some money exploring new technologies can become involved in creating their district's Second Life environment. Within that environment, teachers can build their own simulated experiences to use with students. They can also attract other educators to contribute simulations. The skills required to create simulated experiences will take some time to develop and will not interest all teachers.

Dr. Chen: *Do you plan to implement the Second Life in workshops or teacher training activities? What is HISD's response to Second Life? Is it likely to be encouraged or banned? Are there any firewall concerns or regulations regarding allowing Second Life on campuses?*

Jost: At this time, my plan is to investigate Second Life from home with other educators in small virtual groups to learn more about what is possible and what is useful. I will continue to attend educational meetings in Second Life that other people have set up. I may organize some virtual meetings of my own. These will be held after hours from people's home computers. Houston Independent School District (HISD) does not currently allow the use of Second Life on its network. In order to be approved for use on the HISD network, programs must be fully tested and be shown not to interfere with the network. They must also have the backing of research to show their educational value.

Dr. Chen: *Do you foresee a warm welcome from teachers for Second Life? Or will they take it as just another new technology toy?*

Jost: What I expect is a variety of responses to Second Life. Yes, some teachers will definitely see Second Life as a toy. I myself was afraid of Second Life because of reports I heard in the news. I thought it was a recreational game that had nothing to do with education. When Second Life was mentioned as an educational tool in my master's level educational technology class I thought I should take time to explore it. As other educators hear about educational uses for Second Life, I believe they will create accounts and look for ways to use it, too. Based on my experience, however, it will be the teachers who love exploring new technologies that will look into Second Life. I think many teachers will feel it takes too much of their time to learn how to use it. My hope is that the teachers who do explore Second Life will pave the way for others to follow. They could do this by writing instructions for others to learn how to use it, by creating new educational uses for Second Life, and by spreading the word through blogs and presentations.

Dr. Chen: *This has been an interesting conversation. Do you have any final thoughts?*

Jost: Second Life is intriguing and engaging. There is potential for a positive impact on student achievement in the hands of creative educators who are willing to let students take more control of their own learning, which is what we need if we want to develop lifelong learners. I expect that Second Life or another virtual world will become increasingly worthwhile to educators as they learn to use it and create unique learning environments for their students.

At one time the Internet was thought to be too dangerous, difficult, or costly for student use and yet it is now the resource of choice for many students and teachers. It is used in PK through grade 12 on a daily basis in many schools. When teachers have had a chance to explore the possibilities of Second Life, I expect that virtual teaching, learning, and professional development will grow into an exciting and valuable resource. I look forward to seeing the innovations of teachers as they discover ways to engage and instruct students from many cultures and of various abilities and learning styles.

CHAPTER 18

USES FOR WEB 2.0 TOOLS IN INSTRUCTIONAL SETTINGS

Dominique Turnbow, MLIS
University of California, San Diego

Andrea Lynch, MLIS
University of California, Los Angeles

ABSTRACT

Many instructors are using Web 2.0 tools in in-person and online settings. While many of these tools are accessible and easy to use, one must be careful that the technologies being used are improving learning for students. This chapter will focus on current Web 2.0 tools and how to effectively use them in instruction. The purpose of the chapter is to provide practical strategies for using Web 2.0 tools in instruction and beyond the classroom. After reading the chapter, readers will be able to: list reasons for incorporating Web 2.0 tools into instruction and outreach; identify ways to incorporate the tools into class curriculum to reach a variety of learners; and identify ways to incorporate the tools into activities in order to reach users where they are and with the tools they are using.

Wired for Learning: An Educator's Guide to Web 2.0, pages 291–300
Copyright © 2009 by Information Age Publishing
All rights of reproduction in any form reserved.

INTRODUCTION

Throughout the years education has undergone many changes. Educators strive to keep up with new pedagogical practices, changing student behavior and technologies. The World Wide Web has greatly increased the speed at which technology has changed the way students learn and provided new opportunities for incorporating active learning into instruction. Many instructors are using Web 2.0 tools for in-person and online settings. While many of these tools are accessible and easy to use, one must be careful that the technologies being used are improving learning for students. Educators now find themselves in an environment where, more than ever, technologies can be harnessed to provide new learning environments to meet students' diverse learning styles.

This chapter assumes a basic understanding of Web 2.0, but will provide a brief definition of it. The authors will discuss why educators should consider using Web 2.0 tools as a part of their instructional pedagogy and provide examples of tools that work well in traditional and non-traditional instructional situations. Some tips for best practices when using these types of tools in instruction will also be provided. After reading the chapter, one will be able to:

- list reasons for incorporating Web 2.0 tools into instruction
- identify how different tools appeal to a variety of learning styles, and
- identify ways to incorporate the tools into activities beyond the classroom in order to reach users where they are and with the tools they are using.

BACKGROUND: A BRIEF DEFINITION OF WEB 2.0

The best way to define Web 2.0 is in relation to Web 1.0, which is characterized by static HTML pages. Content for Web 1.0 pages was created and updated by a single person—the one who had access to the Web site. In a Web 1.0 world, form (e.g., the way text looked and functioned) and content were inseparable. What a creator *wanted to say* (content) could not exist independently of *how one said it* (form). The basic difference between Web 1.0 and Web 2.0 is that Web 2.0 separates form from content. Table 18.1 provides a detailed comparison of Web 1.0 and 2.0.

For example, one could put content on a Web page and then create an RSS feed that delivers it to blog or wiki where people can read the content, even comment on or change it, as well as receive it in their preferred way. Suddenly, content that once existed on a static Web page is now in a form that encourages collaboration among and participation from people. Key features of Web 2.0 tools are that they are participatory and collaborative.

TABLE 18.1   Characteristics of Web 1.0 and Web 2.0

Web 1.0	Web 2.0
Publishing	Participation
Content management, presentation	Content reappropriation (e.g., mashups)
Individual, large-scale Web sites	Blogs, wikis
Directories	Tagging
Users observe; "listen to" Web sites	Users add value, co-create
Subscription services	Low-cost or free services
They, the media (control held by few)	We, the media (we create the media)
Macro-content	Micro-content
Authority is key	Collective decision-making
Versions and major releases	Continuous micro-enhancement
Creator defines content, design	User defines content, design (e.g., Web desktop)
Taxonomy	Folksonomy
Value indifferent to amount of usage	Value increases the more it is used
Business model	Blogosphere
In author we trust	In users we trust
Harnessing of authority's intelligence	Harnessing of collective intelligence
Best-sellers	The "Long Tail"
Control	Cooperation
Example: *Encyclopedia Britannica*	Example: *Wikipedia*

Source: "Mashing up the Once and Future CMS," by Malcolm Brown, March/April 2007, *EDUCAUSE Review, 42*(2), p. 8. Reprinted with permission of the author.

Experts have different ways of defining Web 2.0. The term became popular after Tim O'Reilly defined it in 2005.

> Web 2.0 is the network as platform, *spanning all connected devices* [emphasis added]; Web 2.0 applications are those that make the most of the intrinsic advantages of that platform: delivering software as a continually-updated service that *gets better the more people use it, consuming and remixing data from multiple sources, including individual users, while providing their own data and services in a form that allows remixing by others, creating network effects through an "architecture of participation,"* [emphasis added] and going beyond the page metaphor of Web 1.0 to deliver rich user experiences. (para. 1)

MAIN FOCUS: WHY USE WEB 2.0 TOOLS IN INSTRUCTION?

There are many reasons to consider using Web 2.0 tools in instruction. The authors' have a constructivist philosophy. Constructivists argue that an educator is not the "sage on the stage," instead s/he is the "guide on the side."

Learning happens when individuals are able to create their own meaning. A constructivist curriculum fosters students' prior knowledge and experiences by using them as a starting point to create new understandings and meanings about the content. Constructivism requires that "instructors tailor their teaching strategies to student responses and encourage students to analyze, interpret, and predict information. Teachers also rely heavily on open-ended questions and promote extensive dialogue among students" (On Purpose Associates, para. 8).

Web 2.0 technology enables constructivist learning and teaching to happen in new ways. The dialog, for example, does not have to be confined to in-person class time. It can happen online synchronously or asynchronously using instant messaging, blogs, collaborative Web-based software, etc. In addition, constructivist theory focuses on the process of learning, not just the outcomes or competencies achieved by the learners. If one takes a close look at Table 18.1 created by Brown, one will probably agree with him when he writes, "If one studies this table long enough, a gestalt emerges: the Web 1.0 looks uncannily like the teaching paradigm, whereas the Web 2.0 resembles the learning paradigm" (2007, p. 9). Web 2.0 tools allow the learner to demonstrate their learning in new, relevant ways. Through online discussions and contributions, students' learning processes and understanding of material is illuminated. Instructors can use these tools to guide student learning, provide feedback quickly, and review confusing or difficult concepts. For example instead of waiting for an in-person quiz, test, or essay, students can be asked to blog a response to a prompt. Not only will the instructor be able to view and comment on a student's response, but so will other students in the class. Furthermore, if anonymity is important, there are aspects of these tools to remove personal information from open discussions.

In addition to supporting constructivist learning, Web 2.0 tools also support many learning styles and provide more opportunities for active learning in and outside of the classroom. This is not to say that before the World Wide Web different learning styles could not be accommodated. It is that Web 2.0 tools provide new opportunities new for all learning styles to be accommodated. Kolb (1999) offers a model where learners fall into one of four categories: diverging, assimilating, converging and accommodating. People in each of these categories have different, preferred learning styles. The bullets below (Chapman, Kolb Learning Styles Descriptions and Definitions, para. 2) provide a brief description based on Kolb's Learning Styles Inventory (1999). Alan Chapman's Web site (2008) provides more details about the Kolb Inventory and how it can be used to address learning styles.

- **Diverging.** People in this category like to "feel" and "watch" in order to view situations from many points of view. They prefer to learn through activities that generate ideas, like brainstorming.

- **Assimilating.** People in this category like to "watch" and "think" to put information into a logical form. They prefer to focus on theory rather than the practical and learn through lectures, reading, and the opportunity to explore analytical models.
- **Converging.** People in this category like to "do" and "think" to find practical applications for ideas. They prefer to learn through experimentation by simulations and practical applications.
- **Accommodating.** People in this category like to "do" and "feel". They prefer to learn through hands-on activities and thrive in environments that require group work.

Web 2.0 tools provide instructors with technologies that facilitate learning in the ways that work best for students.

Types of Web 2.0 Tools

Table 18.2 describes the advantages and disadvantages of different Web 2.0 tools and suggests how the tools appeal to each learning style.

Tips for Best Practices

There are many examples of best practices for how to incorporate Web 2.0 tools in instruction. Taking time to see what others have done can give instructors ideas about how to use these tools in a curriculum. This section of the chapter will help you examine how instructors can use Web 2.0 tools to enhance your current activities, assignments, and exercises

Instructors have developed a repertoire of tools to assess student learning. These tools currently "work" for what one needs them to do, so why add Web 2.0 Tools? Web 2.0 technology can enhance what one is already doing. Consider the following example. An instructor likes to engage students in a discussion of plagiarism and usually asks them a series of questions starting with a definition of plagiarism. Incorporating a Web 2.0 tool into this discussion, like a blog, the instructor could get everyone to participate. There are always some students who don't like to raise their hands, others who don't like to speak in front of others, and additional students who are uneasy with the definition that came to mind and don't want to share it verbally. If the instructor were to post the plagiarism definition question to a blog and then ask the students to answer the question using the comments feature, they would be able to do so anonymously and therefore, feel comfortable and confident to participate in that virtual discussion.

TABLE 18.2 Web 2.0 Tools and Kolb's Learning Styles

Technology	Learning Styles Addressed	Advantages	Disadvantages
Blogs *Think of these as online individual or group journals.*	• **Diverging**—learners can read different points of view • **Assimilating**—learners can observe the thoughts of others and reflect on them • **Accommodating**—learners can contribute to the group conversation	Blogs are good for narrating experiences or sharing information. • Chronological order allows one to see the interchange of ideas about a topic • Easy for anyone to post or comment on entries • Comments can be anonymous • Many blogs allow one to easily add its feed to a reader • Blogs allow keywords to be assigned to entries as an additional way to organize them	Not as good for people who are not prolific or those that want succinct information. • Needs to be maintained on a regular basis • Entries can only be displayed in the order they were created; they cannot be customized unless you add keywords to each entry
RSS Feeds *Think of these as another way to keep up with news, research, and what bloggers are writing.*	• **Diverging**—learners can read different points of view • **Assimilating**—learners can observe the thoughts of others and reflect on them • **Converging**—learners provide examples of practical applications of concepts • **Accommodating**—learners follow the group conversation	Good for tracking new blog items without visiting the blog directly. Provides an easy way to keep track of news and alert items in one place	Not as good for people who don't want to read blogs regularly. Feed posts can "pile up" and become overwhelming if not read on a regular basis and can contribute to "information overload."
Wikis *Think of these as collaborative web sites.*	• **Accommodating**—learners can contribute to the group conversation • **Diverging**—learners can read different points of view	Good for creating a continually modifiable easy access web page. • Display of information can be customized • Anyone can contribute to the	Not as good for people that want to maintain control of the content being posted on the wiki. • There is more of a learning curve to initially design a wiki

Tool	Learning Styles	Uses	Considerations
	• **Assimilating**—can observe the thoughts of others and reflect on them	wiki—it doesn't rely on a single person to maintain content • Encourages collaboration among peers and workgroups	• Many wikis require a password to edit (although increasingly wiki software services allow you to create a level of access where anyone can edit without a password)
Social Tagging *Think of these as online tools (e.g., del.icio.us, Technorati, etc.) to organize and keep track of frequently visited or important web sites or other web-based items.*	• **Assimilating**—facilitates the need of the learner to put ideas into a logical form. • **Accommodating**—fosters collaboration through creating "tags" that describe information in diverse ways	Good for keeping track of web sites so you can easily find them again (e.g., pulling together a list of sites for a class or about a specific topic). Accessible from anywhere (with a browser and Internet access) One can see how resources are grouped by keyword "clouds" Anyone can organize the web sites by assigning it a "tag" that describes the content	Not as good for people who prefer standardization and logical distinctions and groupings. Anyone can organize the web sites by assigning it a "tag" that describes the content—which means that tags lack standardization and may not group together in a way that makes sense to everyone
Social Networks *Think of these tools (e.g., Facebook, MySpace) as your virtual place, space, and/or persona*	• **Diverging**—learners can interact with others with similar and different points of view.	Good for communicating and building a relationship with friends, family, students, and colleagues. • Another way to communicate with people • Shows your "human side" to students • Very easy to post and share notes about anything you want	Not as good for people who don't want to be bothered with continually updating their profile. • Can be time consuming to initially set up a profile • Can provide a distraction since it is very easy to get caught up in updating your profile and poking around looking for other people
Open/Share Documents or Notes *Think of this tool (Google Docs) as a free, Web-based, easy way to create documents and spreadsheets with others*	• **Diverging**—can facilitate idea generation among learners • **Accommodating**—encourages and provides an opportunity for group work synchronously or asynchronously	Good for collective development of documents among students and colleagues. • A free way to create documents with people • Very easy to edit, format, share, and publish documents with people	Not as good for people who like all the fancy bells and whistles of word processing applications. Also the revision control is a bit clunky.

Instructional Methods and Benefits of Web 2.0 Tools

There are many instances where Web 2.0 tools can add an extra benefit to your active learning techniques. Table 18.3 ties some popular instructional assignments, exercises and/or activities and maps them to Web 2.0 tools and describes the benefits. This will give one an opportunity to look at what one does in instruction that might lend itself to using a Web 2.0 tool to do the same thing with, hopefully, added benefits with minimal concerns and disadvantages.

CONCLUSION

The authors' goals for this chapter were that one would be able to:

- list reasons for incorporating Web 2.0 tools into instruction
- identify how different tools appeal to a variety of learning styles, and
- identify ways to incorporate the tools into activities beyond the classroom in order to reach users where they are and with the tools they are using.

In this chapter, we have provided a brief introduction of Web 2.0 with a comparison to Web 1.0 in order to create a foundation for discussing incorporation of these tools into one's instruction. A table of Web 2.0 tools mapped to Kolb's learning styles provides insight to help one make a decision about tools for instructional purposes. Another table was included to help identify which Web 2.0 tools work with specific instructional activities to enhance and improve student learning (Table 18.2).

But one may be asking, "In the future, what other tools will be developed to incorporate into my teaching and improve student learning?" What the authors hope is that one will find some practical strategies for approaching incorporating future tools, whatever they may look like and in whatever shape they may be, into their instructional toolbox. In the end it is about improving student learning and achieving the objectives that an instructor develops for a session or course. New technology does not replace the deliberate and thoughtful way instructors create curriculum and assignments with students in mind; technology enhances what an instructor is already doing. Once a student-centered curriculum has been developed, Web 2.0 tools can provide new methods for teaching and address a variety of learning styles.

TABLE 18.3 Benefits of Web 2.0 in Instructional Design

Assignment/Exercise/Activity	Web 2.0 Tool(s)	Benefit(s) of Web 2.0 Tools
Short writing assignments	Blog	Blogs facilitate writing, peer-review of the assignment by other students as well as the public (Brown and Adler, p. 25)
Long writing assignments	Open/Shared documents	Blogs facilitate writing, peer-review of the assignment by other students as well as the public (Brown and Adler, p. 25)
Open-ended questions and/or needs assessment	Blog	Blogs compile answers and feedback and can be anonymous. Also, because they are accessible beyond the classroom walls and outside of the discussion that prompted the questions and/or assessment, students can continue to add feedback over time.
Journal or log	Blog	Because blog entries are chronological, it creates the look and feel of written journal or log entries. Using this tool also facilitates comments by the instructor and/or fellow students.
Group paper assignment	Wiki or Open/Shared documents or notes	Wikis are good for creating a single source that is written by the class or sub group. It can be accessible by the group, however you define it. Also, since wikis offer revisions to be tracked, one can go back and see which students did what sections and/or pieces of the assignment.
In-class exercise	Blog	Blogs compile answers and feedback and comments can be anonymous.
Formative or summative assessment and/or class evaluation	Blog	Blogs compile answers and feedback and can be anonymous. Also, because they are accessible beyond the classroom walls and outside of the discussion that prompted the questions and/or assessment, students can continue to add feedback over time.
Contact and/or office hours	Social networking site or blogs	Being part of the systems where students are, like social networking sites (i.e., facebook) is another way to conduct office hours and answer questions. Using this tool also allows one to post questions publicly or keep them private. Making the interactions personal and letting the students see an instructor's personal side, depending on how much they reveal in their profile, may make them more willing to contact you with their questions and concerns. Alternatively, instructors can use a blog which gives them some of the features of a social networking site, but less of the extra bells and whistles.
Reference List/Bibliography	Social tagging or Open/Shared notes	Use social tagging sites (e.g., del.icio.us) and shared notes (e.g., Google Notebook) to encourage students to keep track of Web sites they are using for research projects and papers. These tools can help students organize resources into groups and keep track of information they will need for citations.

ACKNOWLEDGEMENTS

The authors would like to acknowledge Nancy Stimson, Outreach Services Librarian at the University of California, San Diego, Biomedical Library. The "Web 2.0 Tools and Kolb's Learning Styles" (Table 18.2) table was based on a similar one co-developed by Stimson and Turnbow.

REFERENCES

Brown, J. S. (2008). Minds on fire: Open education, the long tail, and learning 2.0. *EDUCAUSE Review*, 43(1), 16–32. Retrieved September 5, 2008, from http://connect.educause.edu/Library/EDUCAUSE+Review/MindsonFireOpenEducationt/45823?time=1221146132.

Brown, M. (2007, March/April). Mashing up the once and future CMS. *EDUCAUSE Review*, 42(2), 8–9. Retrieved September 5, 2008, from http://connect.educause.edu/Library/EDUCAUSE+Review/MashinguptheOnceandFuture/40696?time=1220636150.

Chapman, A. (2008). *Kolb learning styles*. Retrieved September 5, 2008, from http://www.businessballs.com/kolblearningstyles.htm.

Kolb, D. A. (1999). *The Kolb learning styles inventory* (version 3). Boston, MA: Hay Resources Direct.

Learning Theories Knowledgebase (2008, September). Constructivism at LearningTheories.com. Retrieved September 11th, 2008, from http://www.learning-theories.com/constructivism.html.

On Purpose Associates. (2001). *About learning: Constructivism*. Retrieved September 5, 2008, from http://www.funderstanding.com/constructivism.cfm.

On Purpose Associates. (2001). *About learning: Learning styles*. Retrieved September 5, 2008, from http://www.funderstanding.com/learning_styles.cfm.

O'Reilly, T. (2005, October 1). *Web 2.0: Compact definition?* Entry posted to O'Reilly Radar, Retrieved September 5, 2008, from http://radar.oreilly.com/2005/10/web-20-compact-definition.html.

CHAPTER 19

DESIGNING PROFESSIONAL DEVELOPMENT TO SUPPORT TEACHERS' TPACK AND INTEGRATION OF WEB 2.0 TECHNOLOGIES

Drew Polly
University of North Carolina–Charlotte

Clif Mims
University of Memphis

ABSTRACT

The emergence of Web 2.0 technologies has transformed the way that people collect, organize and generate knowledge. Still, like most digital technologies, Web 2.0 tools are not being used to their full potential in classrooms. Using the framework of technological pedagogical and content knowledge (TPACK), we describe an empirically-based model of learner-centered professional development that shows promise to impact student learning by supporting the effective integration of Web 2.0 technologies in PK–12 classrooms.

Wired for Learning: An Educator's Guide to Web 2.0, pages 301–316
Copyright © 2009 by Information Age Publishing
301

INTRODUCTION

The myriad of Web 2.0 technologies that are currently being developed and distributed are impossible to keep up with (Hedberg & Brudvik, 2008). Educational technology resources, such as magazines, blogs and repositories of Web 2.0 tools are updating their lists of tools daily in order to keep up with the technological developments and advancements. These technologies allow teachers and students with Internet access to locate, organize and generate knowledge in robust ways, and hold the potential to greatly change traditional modes of teaching and learning (e.g., Alexander, 2008; O'Reilly, 2005; Hedberg & Brudvick, 2008; International Society for Technology in Education [ISTE], 2007).

In depth overviews of some of these Web 2.0 tools are provided in other chapters in this book. However, this chapter focuses on ways to support teachers' integration of Web 2.0 tools in their teaching. The first section provides an overview of effective technology integration and technological pedagogical content knowledge (TPACK). TPACK represents the knowledge that teachers need to effectively integrate technologies, including Web 2.0 tools, into their teaching (Koehler & Mishra, 2005). In the next section, I provide a theoretical framework of learner-centered professional development (LCPD), based upon the American Psychological Association's Learner-Centered Principles (APA Work Force, 1997) and other empirically based recommendations for teacher learning. Next, LCPD is described in the context of hypothetical classroom vignettes, which include details about professional development and the classroom integration of Web 2.0 tools. Lastly, implications for both research and practice are shared.

TECHNOLOGY INTEGRATION AND TPCK

Technology Integration and Learning

Earle (2002) suggested that in education, integration brings together all the elements of teaching and learning, including technology. Hence, *technology integration* represents an intersection between teachers, learners, pedagogies, content and technologies. If technology is appropriately integrated it can substantially impact both teaching and learning (Brown, Collins, & Cocking, 1999; Schacter, 1999).

National surveys continue to indicate that technology access In PK–12 classrooms continues to reach all-time highs (Milken Family Foundation, 1999, 2002; United States Department of Education [USDE], 2007). State departments of education, school districts and schools are spending large portions of their budgets on hardware, software and infrastructures related to technology and Internet access.

While access is at an all-time high, copious research studies have shown that simply using technology does not always yield positive student learning outcomes (Loveless & Pellegrino, 2007; Ringstaff, 2002; Pea et al., 2002). Only technology-rich activities that support higher-order thinking skills have been shown to consistently impact student learning (Brown, Collins, & Cocking, 1999; Lawless & Pellegrino, 2007; Schacter, 2002). Hence, technology-rich instruction is most effective if technology is integrated into the curriculum while also developing students' higher-order thinking skills. In order for effective technology integration to occur, teachers need adequate support in learning how to use these technologies.

Supporting Teacher Learning: Technological Pedagogical Content Knowledge

Just as Earle (2002) stated that technology integration was the intersection of technology with multiple aspects of teaching and learning, educational technologists (Harris, Mishra, & Koehler, 2007; Mishra & Koehler, 2006; Neiss, 2005; Thompson, 2005) have posited that in order to effectively integrate technology teachers must have technological pedagogical content knowledge (TPACK). TPACK is an intersection of knowledge about technological tools, pedagogies and content (see Figure 19.1). Within the TPACK framework, Koehler, Mishra and Yahya (2007, p. 743) describe technology, pedagogy and content as:

> *Technology* (T) broadly encompasses standard technologies such as books and chalk and blackboard, as well as more advanced technologies such as the Internet and digital video, and the different modalities they provide for representing information.
> *Pedagogy* (P) includes the process and practice or methods of teaching and learning, including the purpose(s), values, techniques or methods used to teach, and strategies for evaluating student learning.
> *Content* (C) is the subject matter that is to be learned/taught. The content to be covered in high-school social studies or algebra is very different from the content to be covered in a graduate course on computer science or art history.

Without knowledge in all three areas, efforts to integrate technology typically become ineffective in a variety of ways. First, without a focus on content, technology-rich lessons become tool-based, where technology is used but the focus is not on student learning. Activities are used because

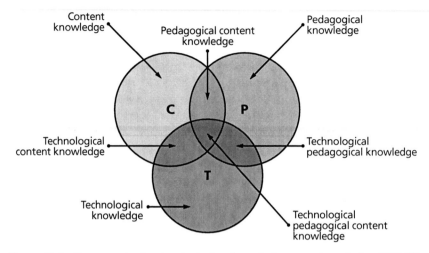

Figure 19.1 Framework of technological pedagogical content knowledge (TPACK). From Koehler & MIshra (2005).

teachers like the technologies. Second, without the emphasis on proper pedagogies, teachers take student-centered tasks and make them teacher-directed (Cognition & Technology Group at Vanderbilt, 1997). Teachers must be afforded the opportunities to extend their knowledge of technologies, pedagogies and content, if they are expected to integrate Web 2.0 tools into their classroom.

THEORETICAL FRAMEWORK: LEARNER-CENTERED
PROFESSIONAL DEVELOPMENT (LCPD)

Overview of LCPD

Professional development has been advanced through research studies (Fullan, 1995; Garet et al., 2001; Kennedy, 1999; Penuel, Fishman, Yamaguchi, & Gallagher, 2008; Wilson & Berne, 1999), syntheses of research (Loucks-Horsley, Love, Stiles, Mundry, & Hewson, 2003; Loveless & Pellegrino, 2007), theory development (Putnam & Borko, 2000; Borko, 2005), practitioner guidelines (NPEAT, 2000a) and national standards (National Staff Development Council [NSDC], 2001; NPEAT, 2000b; Sparks & Hirsch, 2000). Despite the wealth of published work, there is little agreement among professional development researchers or practitioners regarding the criteria for effective professional development (Guskey, 2003; Loveless & Pellegrino, 2007).

In search of empirically-based recommendations for professional development, our recommendations for learner-centered professional development (LCPD) are grounded in the *APA Learner-Centered Principles* (herein, referred to as *Principles*), a set of 14 recommendations for instruction that are based on research in the fields of education and educational psychology (Alexander & Murphy, 1997). Table 19.1 shows these 14 Principles. From these 14 recommendations and other research on teacher learning, I have identified six components of learner-centered professional development. They include: 1) a focus on student learning, 2) teacher ownership, 3) ongoing activities that are sustained over time, 4) opportunities to collaborate with fellow teachers and professional development personnel, 5) emphasis on knowledge of content and pedagogy and related tools such as technology and 6) experiences that promote teacher reflection. Table 19.2 shows the components of LCPD along with a description of the related Principles and empirically based knowledge about teacher learning.

TABLE 19.1   APA's Learner-Centered Principles

APA Principles	Description and Research
1. The learning of complex subject matter is most effective when it is an intentional process of constructing meaning from information and experience.	Learners form knowledge from their prior knowledge and experiences (Cognition and Technology Group at Vanderbilt, 1990; Alexander, Jetton, Kulikowich, & Woehler, 1994).
2. The successful learner, over time and with support and instructional guidance, can create meaningful, coherent representations of knowledge.	The learning process must be ongoing and supported by others (Lave, 1991; Brown & Palinscar, 1989). Learning must be extended over time (McCombs, 1988).
3. The successful learner can link new information with existing knowledge in meaningful ways.	Prior knowledge influences attention (Anderson, Pichert, Shirey, 1983), perception (Gibson, 1966) and knowledge value (Alexander, Jetton, Kulikowich, & Woehler, 1994; Shaw & Dennison, 1994).
4. The successful learner can create and use a repertoire of thinking and reasoning strategies to achieve complex learning goals.	Both general cognitive and metacognitive and metacognitive strategies are essential for learning (Alexander & Judy, 1988).
5. Higher order strategies for selecting and monitoring mental operations facilitate creative and critical thinking.	Learners are able to reflect on their own thinking, oversee their work and assess their own performance (Ernis, 1989, Nickerson, 1989).
6. Learning is influenced by environmental factors, including culture, technology, and instructional practices.	Learning is a social process that is influenced by the classroom environment (Lave, 1991; Resnick et al., 1991; Pea, 1989, Greeno & Moore, 1993).

(continued)

TABLE 19.1   APA's Learner-Centered Principles (continued)

APA Principles	Description and Research
7. What and how much is learned is influenced by the learner's motivation. Motivation to learn, in turn, is influenced by the individual's emotional states, beliefs, interests and goals, and habits of thinking.	Learners who believe that they are in charge of their own learning (Deci & Ryan, 1991) and have goals of understanding rather than performing (Dweck, 1986) are more apt to achieve in schools.
8. The learner's creativity, higher order thinking, and natural curiosity all contribute to motivation to learn. Intrinsic motivation is stimulated by tasks of optimal novelty and difficulty, relevant to personal interests, and providing for personal choice and control.	Learners are more effective when they have personal interest and intrinsic motivation (Ames & Ames, 1985, 1989; Dweck & Leggett, 1988; Gottfried, 1990).
9. Acquisition of complex knowledge and skills requires extended learner effort and guided practice. Without learners' motivation to learn, the willingness to exert this effort is unlikely without coercion.	Learners' motivation influences learning (Jetton & Alexander, 1997; Deci & Ryan, 1991). Learning requires extensive effort from the learner and guidance from teachers (Brown & Palincsar, 1989).
10. As individuals develop, there are different opportunities and constraints for learning. Learning is most effective when differential development within and across physical, intellectual, emotional, and social domains is taken into account.	Learners develop at different rates and their development levels must be accounted for in the classroom (Case, 1993; Scarr, 1992).
11. Learning is influenced by social interactions, interpersonal relations, and communication with others.	Classroom interactions influence learning (Berieter & Scardamlia, 1989; Brown & Palicsar, 1989; Collins, Brown, & Newman, 1989; Lave, 1991).
12. Learners have different strategies, approaches, and capabilities for learning that are a function of prior experience and heredity.	Prior knowledge and experience serve as a scaffold for future learning (Alexander et al., 1991; Schraw & Dennison, 1994).
13. Learning is most effective when differences in learners' linguistic, cultural, and social backgrounds are taken into account.	Teachers must base instruction off of the various backgrounds of their learners (Case, 1993, Piaget, 1952; Erickson, 1963).
14. Setting appropriately high and challenging standards and assessing the learner as well as learning progress— including diagnostic, process, and outcome assessment—are integral parts of the learning process.	Learners able to assess their own performance (Ernis, 1989, Nickerson, 1989); should be given information about their performance to modify or adjust behavior (Alexander & Judy, 1988).

Source: Alexander & Murphy, 1997

TABLE 19.2 Characteristics of Learner-Centered Professional Development (LCPD)

Characteristic	Literature on Teacher Learning and Professional Development	APA Learner-centered Principles (APA Work Group, 1997)
Student-focused	Professional development should focus on analyzing the gap between (a) goals and standards for student learning and actual student performance and (b) prepare teachers to bridge that gap (Hawley & Valli, 1999).	The learning of complex subject matter is most effective when learners construct meaning from information and experience (Principle 1). The successful learner, over time and with support, can create meaningful, coherent representations of knowledge (Principle 2).
Teacher-owned	Professional development should involve teachers in selecting the content of professional development programs and, if possible, give teachers choices about learning activities (Hawley & Valli, 2000; NPEAT, 2000a).	Individual's learning is influenced by their motivation (Principle 9). An individual's motivation is influenced by their beliefs and interests (Principle 7), the learner's creativity and curiosity (Principle 8), and their background and experiences (Principles 10, 12 and 13)
Collaborative	Professional development should allow teachers to collaboratively work together (NPEAT, 2000a; Sparks & Hirsch, 2000) and develop the problem solving skills needed to teach effectively (Putnam & Borko, 2000).	Social interactions, interpersonal relations, and communication with others all provide opportunities for learning (Principle 11).
Ongoing	Professional development should be connected to a comprehensive change process focused on improving student learning (Hawley & Valli, 1999).	The successful learner, over time and with support and instructional guidance, can create meaningful, coherent representations of knowledge (Principle 2).
Content and pedagogically based	Student learning can be influenced by increasing teachers' content knowledge (Ball, Lubienski, & Mewborn, 2001), pedagogical content knowledge (Marzano, Pickering & Pollock, 2001) and by examining how students learn (Fennema, Carpenter, Franke, Levi, Jacobs, & Empson, 1996).	The learning of complex subject matter is most effective when it is an intentional process of constructing meaning from information and experience (Principle 1). The successful learner, over time and with support and instructional guidance, can create meaningful, coherent representations of knowledge (Principle 2). Individual's learning is influenced by their motivation (Principle 9).
Reflective	Professional development should allow teachers to reflect on evidence of their teaching; (a) student work samples and (b) artifacts from their own teaching (Hawley & Valli, 1999; NPEAT, 2000a).	The learning of complex subject matter is most effective when it is an intentional process of constructing meaning from information and experience (Principle 1). Assessment is an integral part of the learning process (Principle 14).

These components of LCPD are empirically based recommendations for all contexts of professional development. In this section, we provide a general overview of the components. Vignettes that connect LCPD in the context of Web 2.0 tools follow this section.

Components of LCPD

Student Learning

The goal of all professional development programs is to positively impact student learning outcomes (Hawley & Valli, 1999; Loucks-Horsley, Love, Stiles, Mundry, & Hewson, 2003). Numerous Principles cite the potential for learning to occur when learners are able to construct new knowledge that is grounded in prior experiences. In the case of Web 2.0 tools, these tools must be introduced in the context of how they can address various curriculum needs and positively impact students' learning of content. Using an instructional design approach, teachers should identify content that students have trouble learning and look to design technology-rich instruction to enhance the teaching of that problematic content. For example, Toondoo (http://www.toondoo.com), a Web 2.0 tool that allows students to create cartoons, should be introduced to teachers as a way to support students' creation of a project related to content (e.g., language arts, social studies, etc.) rather than simply a technological tool. Teachers need explicit guidance about how to align Web 2.0 tools to the content that they teach.

Teacher-Owned

Professional development programs that have provided teachers with choices about the content and activities have been linked to high rates of adopted practices in teachers' classrooms (Desimone, Porter, Garet, Yoon, & Birman, 2002; Garet, Porter, Desimone, Birman, & Yoon, 2001; Hawley & Valli, 1999). Various Principles discuss the significance of motivation during the learning process. Learners more readily create knowledge when they participate in tasks that are interesting, challenging and relevant to their lives (Principles 7, 8, and 9). Further, since learners are at different developmental levels, LCPD should be adaptable to meet teachers' individual needs (Principles 12 and 13). Effective professional development related to Web 2.0 technologies should provide teachers with overviews of tools, but give them ample time to explore and actively examine technologies that they are interested in using in their classroom. For example, provide teachers with a repository of Web 2.0 tools (e.g., http://www.go2web20.net/), and provide guidance as they search for tools that align with content that they teach.

Ongoing

Research on most professional development projects does not see substantial change in teachers' practices or student learning until teachers have had ample time to learn new pedagogies and knowledge and also apply them in their classroom (Banilower, Boyd, Pasley, & Weiss, 2006; Orrill, 1999; Richardson, 1990). In their large scale analysis of the Local Systemic Change Professional Development Initiative Banilower et al. (2006) found that teachers' practice did not change until they had over 30 hours of professional development. This is supported by the second Principle, which states that learning is not effective unless it is supported over time. Effective professional development for Web 2.0 tools includes ongoing learning experiences for teachers to use the tools, plan how to integrate them, and refine their lessons after their students have used them.

Collaborative

In recent years, professional development projects have involved teachers learning in group settings where teachers learn together, co-plan, teach and collaborate to examine student work and discuss their teaching. These approaches have been linked to improvements in teachers' instruction (e.g., Hollins, McIntyre, DeBose, Hollins, & Towner, 2004; Strahan, 2003; Vescio, Ross, & Adams, 2006) and slight gains in student learning (Strahan, 2003; Supovitz & Christman, 2003; Vescio, Ross, & Adams, 2006). The eighth Principle cites learning as a social process, while the sixth Principle discusses the influence that the learning context has on the learner. Teachers need to be given ample opportunities to discuss with their colleagues and the professional development staff how Web 2.0 technologies could be used to impact student learning in their classroom. Further, research cites the benefit of having a teacher-leader or professional developer guide the process of planning technology-rich lessons (Glazer & Hannafin, 2006).

Focused on Pedagogy and Content

Professional development needs to be comprehensive; when teachers learn about Web 2.0 tools, they must also learn about appropriate pedagogies and related content. According to the Principles teachers' construction of these different types of knowledge must be linked to prior knowledge and experiences (Principle 1), supported over time (Principle 2), and based on teachers' interests (Principles 6, 7, 8 and 9). Previous projects, such as the Learning Environments with Technology in Urban Schools (LeTUS) at the University of Michigan, provided middle school science teachers with learning opportunities to learn about science content, inquiry-based approaches to teaching, and technologies that supported teaching content in an inquiry-based approach (Penuel et al., 2008; Fishman, Marx,

Best, & Tal, 2003). Similar approaches are needed to support the effective use of Web 2.0 technologies.

Reflective

Learning is an ongoing process that is most effective when learners are given feedback on their performance (Principle 14) and they are able to apply their metacognitive skills to self-assess their progress (Principle 4). Professional development projects are now using video-based technologies and artifacts of student work to support teachers' learning. Teachers meet after a lesson to collaboratively examine a lesson and/or artifacts of learning (Borko, Michalec, Timmons, & Siddle, 1997; Fallon & Watts, 2001; Shepherd & Hannafin, under review; Sherin & van Es, 2005). LCPD to support Web 2.0 integration would extend this idea. Students could use Web 2.0 technologies to produce artifacts of learning, such as a wiki or Google Documents. Teachers could examine both students' products and their lesson in order to determine if students' work met the goals of the lesson, and how they could modify future lessons in order to make a greater impact on student learning.

Summary of LCPD. The components of LCPD highlighted in this section apply to all forms of professional development. In this next section, we provide vignettes of LCPD in the context of supporting teachers' integration of Web 2.0 tools.

VIGNETTES OF PROFESSIONAL DEVELOPMENT AND WEB 2.0 TOOLS

Based on the components of LCPD, below we describe some hypothetical classroom vignettes of how professional development can support teachers' integration of Web 2.0 technologies.

Social Bookmarks

Overview

Social bookmarks, such as Diigo (http://www.diigo.com) and Delicious (http://www.delicious.com) create a web-based compilation of websites that are labeled by tags. Users can search by tags to find bookmarks that they and others have identified. Teachers and students and can use this information to create a searchable list of resources about content that they are teaching or learning. This information can be used to supplement other instructional resources, and for students to create products to demonstrate their understanding of content.

Professional Development for Social Bookmarks

A second grade teacher, Mrs. Valdez, learned about WebQuests in a workshop she attended at her local university. After the teacher's students completed a WebQuest about snakes, she shared the WebQuest and her students' work with other second grade teachers (focused on student learning and collaborative, Principle 8). While Mrs. Valdez was happy with the Web-Quest, she was discouraged that students lacked a way to efficiently archive websites so that other students could also use that resource. Mrs. Valdez had been reading about social bookmarks, and decided to use them when students completed their next WebQuest (teacher-owned, Principles 7, 8 and 9). She created a class account for all of her students to use. Anytime her students found a website they stored the website within the bookmarking tool. Since the bookmarks were online, others (e.g., teachers, parents, students from home computers) who had an Internet connection could access them.

In order to support the other teachers in her building, Mrs. Valdez helped the other teachers learn how to use social bookmarks in a computer lab during their planning period (focused on content and pedagogy and collaborative, Principle 8). Mrs. Valdez provided in-class support for teachers who expressed anxiety using bookmarks with their class; a teacher assistant covered her class, while she assisted her colleagues in their classrooms. In addition to in-class support (ongoing, Principle 1), after students completed WebQuests, teachers used a planning period to examine student work, and the social bookmarks that students had created (reflective, Principle 4). In addition, teachers shared their work with teachers in other grades, which led to further use of social bookmarks (collaborative).

Aggregators

Overview

Aggregators like Google Reader (http://reader.google.com) or Feedburner (http://www.feedburner.com) collect information from Really Simply Syndicated (RSS) feeds and organizes it for readers. RSS feeds can include news websites (e.g., CNN, The New York Times), blogs from experts in the field, and audio or video-based podcasts. Both teachers and students can use aggregators to gather content and resources related to topics that they are teaching or learning. By gathering information from multiple sources, learners are exposed to varying perspectives and must use their higher-order thinking skills to evaluate the material that they view.

Professional Development for Aggregators

A high school Advanced Placement United States government class spends the year studying the federal government. Prior to the year, the high school Social Studies department analyzed scores from the Advanced Placement test and found that their students struggled to synthesize, analyze and evaluate information that they read (focused on student learning). Teachers decided that they would like to address this learning gap by integrating more current event information from news websites (teacher ownership). The department chair arranges for the school district's technology coordinator to come work with the U.S. Government teachers.

During a few meetings prior to the school year, the technology coordinator models how to teach students how to collect information with aggregators. Further, during the meetings teachers undertake the role of high school students, as they use an aggregator to organize news reports and blogs about the upcoming election (focused on content and pedagogy). Further, after evaluating and synthesizing this information in small groups (collaborative, Principle 8), the teachers choose how they represent their knowledge. Some teachers used a word processor to create a newspaper, presentation software to prepare a speech, a video recorder to record a podcast of a mock news report or a dramatization about the election. With guidance from the technology coordinator, teachers were able to determine their final product and evidence that they had learned the main concepts about the election process. Teachers were charged with using these pedagogies with their own students (teacher-owned, Principles 6, 7, 8 and 9).

The classroom teachers begin this project in their classroom at the beginning of the school year. For those technology-savvy teachers, the technology coordinator supported their work by answering questions via e-mail. For the teachers who required more support, either the technology coordinator or a technology-savvy teacher assists them by providing one-on-one mentoring or in-class support (collaborative and ongoing, Principles 2 and 8). After teachers started this project, they met with each other during planning times to share how the project was going. Also, at the conclusion of the project teachers met with the technology coordinator to examine students' projects and make preparation for other technology-rich lessons for later in the year.

Collaborative Document Sharing

Overview

Applications like Google Documents (http://docs.google.com) and Wikis (http://www.wikispaces.com, http://www.wetpaint.com) provide opportunities for people to collaborate with others on various documents.

Google Documents allow people to share word processing documents, spreadsheets and presentations. Wikis, meanwhile, allow teachers to share the publishing a web-based document. Students can create documents and share them with others that they are collaborating with, with teachers in order to get feedback on their work, or with parents who are interested in reading their children's work.

Professional Document for Collaborative Document Sharing

Elmer Elementary School is interested in establishing a partnership with a local university to improve their writing scores (focused on student learning). The school's technology teacher, Mr. Morse, surveys every teacher in the building and finds that the faculty has an interest in using the Internet to work on collaborative writing projects (teacher-owned, Principles 6, 7, 8 and 9). Mr. Morse and an educational technology professor arrange for students to collaborate with preservice teachers in writing a wiki about children's books that both groups will read. Mr. Morse spent an hour-long planning period with each grade level of teachers. During the hour, teachers learned about the basic editing tools by working on a wiki with other teachers (collaborative, Principle 8). Mr. Morse modeled how to teach basic wiki skills to students with a combination of demonstration and guided independent work time (focused on content and pedagogy). Meanwhile, preservice teachers at the university were also learning how to edit a wiki.

Each preservice teacher partnered with a class. The preservice teachers visited their partner class to meet the students. Classes of students chose a book to read, and the preservice teachers also read those books. Students and preservice teachers posted comments about the book on the wiki. Comments included discussions of characters, the plot, and predictions about the book. After the book was completed, the students and the preservice teacher used the wiki to publish an advertisement about their book, convincing others to read it. The wiki was shared with the school community (e.g., other students, teachers, administrators and parents).

During the scope of the project, teachers had access to Mr. Morse's assistance during planning periods to assist in various ways (ongoing, Principle 2). As the project concluded, the teachers, students and preservice teachers provided input about the experience and insight about how to improve the collaboration in the future (reflective, Principles 4 and 14).

IMPLICATIONS

Professional development to support technology integration is challenging (Harris, 2008a, 2008b, 2008c; Loveless & Pellegrino, 2007). The various components of learner-centered professional development (LCPD) show promise to substantially support teachers' integration of Web 2.0 technologies, such as social bookmarks, aggregators and collaborative sharing tools. However, the use of LCPD to support Web 2.0 integration raises numerous issues for both research and practice. They are described below.

Examining How to Best Develop TPACK

Advocates of technological pedagogical content knowledge (TPACK) contend that teachers must deepen their understanding of all three components of TPACK in order to effectively integrate technologies, such as Web 2.0 tools, in their classroom (Mishra & Koehler, 2006; Thompson, 2007). The TPACK model seen earlier in Figure 1 accounts for the overlaps between the three components; hence, LCPD cannot focus solely on the Web 2.0 tools, the instructional practices or the content of teachers' classroom. Due to TPACK's comprehensive nature, LCPD must be comprehensive as well.

In order to identify how specific professional development activities influence TPACK, researchers must identify specific LCPD experiences and collect data on these as well as the impact of these activities on teachers' knowledge of the various TPACK components (Loveless & Pellegrino, 2007; Penuel et al., 2008). Data sources should vary and include evidence of participants' learning (e.g., performance-based tasks, lesson plans, classroom observations, student work samples) and participants' self-report (e.g., interviews and surveys).

Examining Impact Beyond Workshops

Historically, professional development research does not follow teachers back to their classroom (Guskey, 2002; Loucks-Horsley et al., 2003). As indicated earlier, teachers must receive ongoing support during both their planning periods and their instructional time. If professional development is going to be ongoing and continuous, research must also be.

For example, if teachers learn how to use collaborative document sharing tools in workshops, and receive support during the school year, researchers must continue to collect evidence about the follow-up nature of professional development, support during implementation, and participants' reaction to the various professional learning experiences. Data sources should include evidence cited above (e.g., lesson plans, student work samples, classroom observations, interviews, surveys), and specifically will be used to identify the extent and impact of follow-up professional development.

Change in Beliefs versus Change in Practice

Professional development research has not been able to clearly identify whether teachers' beliefs or instructional practices change first (e.g., Song, Hill, & Hannafin, 2007; Ertmer, 2003; Loucks-Horsley et al., 2003). Since Web 2.0 tools are fairly new and not widespread among K–12 teachers and students, LCPD must address teachers' beliefs by giving them ample time to explore and learn the tool, and providing educators with concrete examples about how these teachers could integrate Web 2.0 technologies.

Research must be comprehensive enough to collect data on participants' beliefs towards technology, teaching and teaching with technology. Studies should examine teachers' beliefs and instructional practices from the beginning of professional development until the completion of the project. Specifically, the interaction between teachers' beliefs and instructional practices needs further attention.

CONCLUSIONS

When used in conjunction with activities that develop higher-order thinking skills, technologies, including Web 2.0 tools, show promise to improve student learning outcomes. In order to effectively integrate Web 2.0 tools, teachers must experience rich professional development experiences to deepen their knowledge of technology, pedagogy and content, and the intersections of each. LCPD and its six components have the potential to support the integration of Web 2.0 tools. However, further research is needed regarding how to best support teachers' use of these technologies.

REFERENCES

Alexander, B. (2008). Web 2.0 and emergent multiliteracies. *Theory into Practice, 47*(2), 150–160.

Borko, H. (2004). Professional development and teacher learning: Mapping the terrain. *Educational Researcher, 33*(8), 3–15.

Bransford, J. D., Brown, A., & Cocking, R. (Eds.). (2000). *How people learn: Mind, brain, experience and school, expanded edition.* Washington, DC: National Academy Press.

Cognition and Technology Group at Vanderbilt. (1997). *The jasper project: Lessons in curriculum, instruction, assessment, and professional development.* Mahwah, NJ: Erlbaum.

Earle, R. S. (2002). The integration of instructional technology into public education: Promises and challenges. *Educational Technology, 42*(1), 5–13.

Ertmer, P. A. (2005). Teacher pedagogical beliefs: The final frontier in our quest for technology integration? *Educational Technology Research and Development, 53*(4), 25–39.

Glazer, E. M., & Hannafin, M. J. (2006). The collaborative apprenticeship model: Situated professional development within school settings. *Teaching and Teacher Education, 22*(2), 179–193.

Guskey, T.R. (2000). *Evaluating professional development.* Thousand Oaks, CA: Corwin Press.

Harris, J., Mishra, P., & Koehler, M. J., (2007, April). *Teachers' technological pedagogical content knowledge: Curriculum-based technology integration reframed.* Paper presented at the 2007 Annual Meeting of the American Educational Research Association, Chicago, IL.

Hedberg, J. G., & Brudvik, O. C. (2008). Supporting dialogic literacy through mashing and modding of places and spaces. *Theory into Practice, 47*(2), 138–149.

International Society for Technology in Education (2007). *National Educational Technology Standards for Students, Second Edition (NETS-S).* Eugene, OR: Author. Retrieved September 17, 2007, from: http://cnets.iste.org/inhouse/nets/cnets/students/pdf/NETS_for_Students_2007.pdf

Koehler, M. J., Mishra, P., & Yahya, K. (2007). Tracing the development of teacher knowledge in a design seminar: Integrating content, pedagogy, & technology. *Computers & Education, 49*(3), 740–762.

Loucks-Horsley, S., Love, N., Stiles, K. E., Mundry, S., & Hewson, P. W. (2003). *Designing professional development for teachers of science and mathematics* (2nd ed.). Thousand Oaks, CA: Corwin Press.

Mishra, P., & Koehler, M. J. (2006). Technological pedagogical content knowledge: A new framework for teacher knowledge. *Teachers College Record. 108*(6), 1017–1054.

Niess, M. L. (2005). Preparing teachers to teach science and mathematics with technology: Developing a technology pedagogical content knowledge. *Teaching and Teacher Education, 21*, 509–523

O'Reilly, T. (2005). *What is web 2.0?* Retrieved March 24, 2008, from http://www.oreillynet.com/pub/a/oreilly/tim/news/2005/09/30/what-is-Web-20.html

Putnam, R., & Borko, H. (2000). What do new views of knowledge and thinking have to say about research on teaching? *Educational Researcher, 29*(1), 4–15.

Song, L, Hannafin, M. J., & Hill, J. (2007). Reconciling beliefs and practices in teaching and learning. *Educational Technology Research and Development, 55*(1), 27–50.

Thompson, A. (2005). Technological pedagogical content knowledge: Framing teacher knowledge about technology. *Journal of Computing in Teacher Education, 22*(2), 46–48.

CHAPTER 20

TECHNICALLY SPEAKING

Supporting 1.0 Teachers in a 2.0 World

Jeanne C. Samuel
Tulane University

Jarrod L. Sanson
Northwestern State University

Janice M. Hinson
Louisiana State University

ABSTRACT

The purpose of this chapter is to help educators assemble their Web 2.0 tool-kits to enable the creation of Web 2.0 learning objects. Our primary objective is to discuss infrastructure, interfaces, hardware, and software to fill in information gaps. Too often, teachers return from Web 2.0 seminars to discover during classroom implementation that they do not have enough information or technical expertise to make the applications work. They may also need help supporting students as they retrieve content at school via high bandwidth or remotely from home via dial-up access, or creating feeds that render correctly in different feed readers and media players. This chapter, in essence, is "look-

Wired for Learning: An Educator's Guide to Web 2.0, pages 317–332
Copyright © 2009 by Information Age Publishing
317

ing behind the curtain" to understand what must be in place in order to take advantage of Web 2.0 tools.

Initially, Web use was "read only." This type of Web use is now being referred to as Web 1.0. Although there are many definitions of Web 1.0, Daniel Miessler (2007, July 11) writes that Web 1.0 is "a system of interlinked, hypertext documents accessed via the Internet. With a Web browser, a user views Web pages that may contain text, images, and other multimedia and navigates between them using hyperlinks."

Web 2.0, also referred to as the Read/Write Web, is a perceived change that describes the use of interactive tools, such as blogs and wikis that facilitate collaboration and sharing (Miessler, 2007, July 11). The differences between the two versions of the Web, and the possibilities now available through Web 2.0, are radically changing instructional delivery. As a result, teachers and students are experiencing an entirely new way to teach and learn. Soloman and Schrumm (2007, p. 23) developed a differences comparison between Web 1.0 and Web 2.0 (see Table 20.1).

Currently, many school districts are providing professional development to help teachers integrate Web 2.0 tools into instruction. Too often, technical issues are not addressed adequately at these workshops, if at all. Consequently, when teachers return from Web 2.0 seminars, they find that they do not have enough technical expertise to make the applications work. Our goal is to provide technical information to help teachers understand what must be in place in order to take advantage of Web 2.0 tools. We have two objectives. First, we want to increase educators' knowledge of the techie side of digital communication so that they can diagnose problems and contribute to technical conversations. Second, we want to help educators understand the things that need to be in place so they can create Web 2.0 learning objects to keep information flowing.

TABLE 20.1   Comparison of Web 1.0 and Web 2.0

Web 1.0	Web 2.0
Application based	Web based
Isolated	Collaborative
Offline	Online
Licensed or purchased	Free
Single creator	Multiple collaborators
Proprietary code	Open source
Copyrighted content	Shared content

Throughout this chapter, we describe the efforts of two fictional 5th grade teachers, Ms. Rodriguez and Mr. Richard, as they integrated Web 2.0 tools into their teaching practices. Additionally, we outline the hardware and software required to make these tools work. The discussion focuses on podcasting and video casting; blogs, wikis and RSS feeds; and reusable content and Web-based resources. The chapter ends with a detailed description of how to create, edit, and post podcasts. All resources mentioned in each section appear at the end of the section so that readers can refer to these resources quickly. All links were retrieved on August 11, 2008 from their respective sites.

POD- AND VIDEOCASTING

Ms. Rodriguez's 5th grade students in Louisiana are studying birds that are indigenous to their state. In addition to recognizing the birds by sight, Ms. Rodriguez would like for her students to identify the birds by their calls as well. To do this, she decides to create a podcast of different birdcalls so students can listen to the recordings repeatedly at their convenience.

Audio

There are three basic things that Ms. Rodriguez needs to create, post, and retrieve podcasts: recording equipment, a server (a place to post the recorded bird calls), and student media players (retrieval devices such as computers, iPods, Smartphones, and other mobile and portable media devices) to listen to the recorded bird calls. The cost of recording equipment ranges in price. An inexpensive way to create a podcast is to use a computer's built-in microphone and Audacity freeware. An affordable option is purchasing an individual or classroom retail package such as the Tool Factory Podcasting bundle. The expensive option is using enterprise solutions such as an Echo 360 or Apple OSX Server with Podcast Producer. These options differ in ease of use rather than good, better, best quality. Enterprise (turnkey) solutions tend to be one-button solutions.

Audacity and Garageband are two popular programs for creating audio content. Mixcraft is an affordable PC-platform recording studio similar to Garageband. If needed, audio files may be converted to MP3 format using freeware or shareware applications such as Switch Audio File Format Converter. If Ms. Rodriguez decides to host her own podcasts or additional course materials, she will need access to at least one computer to function as a server. This server at minimum will require a lot of storage space and high bandwidth network card(s) if it is used to serve audio and video files.

- Audacity/Lame (http://audacity.sourceforge.net/download/windows)
- Garageband (http://www.apple.com)
- Mixcraft (http://www.acoustica.com/mixcraft/index.htm)
- Switch Audio File Format Converter (http://www.nch.com.au/switch/)

Video

Joey is a student in Ms. Rodriguez's class, and his father works for the Louisiana Department of Wildlife and Fisheries. During a recent camping trip, Joey and his father filmed an eagle as it swooped down into a lake and caught a fish. Ms. Rodriguez wants to post this video on her class Web site.

Many people are turning to Apple's iMovie and Microsoft's Movie Maker to create, edit, and produce video content. These programs are often bundled with the software that comes with the computer when it is purchased. Another program, Adobe's Visual Communicator 3, also allows users to create video presentations that can be shared via the Internet. Visual Communicator is best to use when preparing professional-quality videos using up to three cameras. The program includes a teleprompter feature and a background feature using a green screen. The output will have to be converted to a podcast format. Camtasia and the Jing Project are robust packages available from TechSmith. Tegrity is another program to consider, especially when trying to manage a variety of different forms of presentations. Tegrity software records podcasts, vodcasts, and lecture presentations. It has a word search feature that enables students to locate the portion of a recorded lecture that has a specific word on the slide. Tegrity can also be used to capture presentations live. Conference XP is a Microsoft Research project, which in partnership with academia, continually develops effective classroom technology.

Mini-DV camcorders and high definition camcorders, if your application accepts it, are fine for recording video. Before purchasing a video recorder, it is helpful to know your application specifications. For example, some applications support Firewire (IEEE 1394) but not USB video input. The PV-GS320 3CCD Panasonic DV camera includes both FireWire and USB connectivity. The microphone, however, is a built-in zoom microphone. The sound quality is good, but restricted to the person in video frame. A camcorder that accepts an external microphone enables users to record more than one speaker at a time.

- Camtasia http://www.techsmith.com/
- Conference XP (http://research.microsoft.com/conferencexp/)

- Jing Project http://www.jingproject.com/
- Tegrity (http://www.tegrity.com/)
- Visual Communicator (http://www.adobe.com/products/visual-communicator/)

Blogs, Wikis, and RSS

For Ms. Rodriguez's birding unit, she locates a statewide birders' blog where kids discuss and post the location, number, and types of birds they see in their communities. Ms. Rodriguez is excited about the possibilities because this blog provides up-to-date information that is not available in any other format. She and her students plan to map the information by parishes (counties). They will use their data to graph the birds by type to determine which birds are spotted most frequently. Ms. Rodriguez decides also to start her own blog that contains resources for her class and for other teachers. This is the fundamental nature of Web 2.0. It is the creation of communities of similar interest.

Blogs. Blogs are Web 2.0 applications that enable students, teachers—the world—to participate in the read-write, social web. There are currently many applications available to help individuals create content, convert and compress media files, tag content (metadata/ information about the content), publish content, and advertise or subscribe to content (RSS). Podcasts and video casts are examples of content that can be easily downloaded from the web using web-based utilities and web browser add-ins. Blogs are similar to electronic discussion boards, but are not as restrictive. Blogs are becoming more accepted in K–12 because they expand educational opportunities for students. Blogs tend to be personal and reflective, while wikis are designed for group use (edited by many).

Wikis. A wiki is a dedicated web space that allows users to post and edit content collaboratively. Blogs archive posts in chronological order and content remains searchable. Wikis keep a history of changes but viewers only see the current version of edited content. There are many ways for teachers to use wikis in classrooms. For example, while riding home on the bus, Marla, one of Ms. Rodriquez's students, sees a Red-Winged Blackbird flying along the levee. She's never seen one before and asks Ms. Rodriguez if Red-Winged Blackbirds are common to Louisiana. Ms. Rodriguez decides that she wants to have her students use wikis to do reports on native birds. She asks a friend who teaches at a school in her district if his students would like to participate in the wiki. Mr. Richard agrees, and they assign their students to cross-school groups. To make it fun and interesting and to practice working and writing together, the first project is about famous birds. Some students research fictional birds such as Tweetie, Woodstock, and Big Bird, while others research famous sports birds such as the Philadelphia Eagles, the Baltimore Ravens, and the Pittsburgh Penguins. For the second project, the children research and write collaborative research reports about native birds while continuing to reference the birders' blog for data.

Some Web 2.0 tools, such as blogs and wikis are web-based and can be hosted in-house using applications such as Community Server and Word-Press (wordpress.org), or off-site using applications such as Blogger, pbwikie, WordPress (wordpress.com), Odeo, and OurMedia. Wikis can be created using in-house, open source wiki products such as TWiki or blogger applications such as B2evolution. Pbwiki also has an education wiki. Wikis are also being included as part of Learning Management Systems (LMS) such as Blackboard, Moodle, and Manhattan Virtual Classroom.

There are many reasons for choosing to host your own web content, using open source, turnkey, or 3rd party hosting sites. To decide which solution is best, you should compare desired features with needs, hardware specifications, and funding. Ms. Rodriguez and Mr. Richard decided to use PBWiki since it is free and membership secure. Also, PBWiki can be accessed both on and off-site from their respective schools.

RSS. While helping students gather information and resources for their wiki reports, Ms. Rodriguez notices that several organizations, such as Friends of the Earth, offer RSS feeds to provide news updates about environmental issues affecting wildlife. To increase her students' interest in the environment, she subscribes to several RSS feeds personally, and adds a blogroll to the class blog. A blogroll is a blog feature that lets you list your favorite blogs in the sidebar of your blog.

RSS stands for Really Simple Syndication and is a language used for content delivery. Content providers can advertise their content via RSS feeds and users can subscribe to the feeds to receive content. A feed is similar to a channel that only delivers the content as described by a provider. Many organizations, such as newspapers like the Washington Post, use RSS to send out daily news features or "breaking news" stories to keep their audiences updated. In other words, new content sent out by an organization to which you are subscribed will automatically load in your feed reader, feed-savvy browser, or download to your portable media device. The XML (Extensible Markup Language) or RSS document is called a feed. Feeds are referred to as RSS feeds, XML feeds, syndicated content, channels, or web feeds. Some feeds, in the case of newspapers, may only contain a headline and a link to the full story. Other feeds may contain full text web site content. In the past, to receive feeds, users had to install a News Reader. Today, most web browsers can maintain subscriptions and display feed data. Ms. Rodriguez uses FireFox since she uses many of the helpful add-on applets. Mr. Richard prefers Internet Explorer 7 since it displays visual cues to media types and includes searchable metadata information in the sidebar. Recommendations for stand-alone feed readers can be found on the website RSS Specifications.

A teacher may want to create her own RSS feeds, and there are several applications that help create RSS feeds and file tags. These include Feed-ForAll, Feedburner, and Feed Writer. If you plan to embed your RSS feeds within an LMS such as Blackboard, you may need to use a product such as Feed2JS (Feed to JavaScript), which summarizes content from other sites within your web site or course page. Basically, what Feed2JS does is keep your summary feed information up-to-date inside Blackboard as the subscription RSS feed items change. You can use a free-hosted Feed2JS site or install this software on your server. PHP scripts are also available to serve XML data from within HTML documents.

- B2evolution (http://www.b2evolution.net)
- Blackboard (http://www.blackboard.com)
- Blogger (www.blogger.com/start)
- Community Server (http://communityserver.com/?gclid=CLPw0s-r0ZMCFQrP GgodWRWhig)
- Feedburner (http://www.feedburner.com/fb/a/home)
- FeedForAll (http://www.feedforall.com)
- Feed to JavaScript (http://feed2js.org/)
- Feed Writer (http://www.mirabyte.com/en/products/feedwriter.html)
- Manhattan Virtual Classroom (http://manhattan.sourceforge.net)
- Moodle (http://www.moodle.org)
- Odeo (http://www.odeo.com)
- OurMedia (http://www.ourmedia.org)
- Pbwiki (http://pbwiki.com)
- RSS Specifications (http://www.rss-specifications.com/browser-based-rss.htm)
- TWiki (http://www.twiki.org)
- WordPress (http://www.wordpress.org)
- WordPress (http://www.wordpress.com)

Reuseable Content

Often, teachers search the Web for supplemental instructional materials to enhance lessons, and there are many, many content-related sites on the web. Multimedia Educational Resource for Learning and Online Teaching (MERLOT), for example, is a great site for lessons and general content for college faculty. It is a searchable collection of online resources that have been reviewed by members of the site and college faculty for overall quality. The content is divided into various educational categories, but is searchable if you need specific lessons. The web site also provides the ability to find colleagues in your field. Content-related sites specifically for K–12 include Kathy Schrock's Guide for Educators and the International Society for Technology in Education (ISTE) web site, which contains lesson plans as well as technology standards for students, teachers, and administrators.

TeacherTube is another great resource for teachers. TeacherTube was created to help teachers share relevant instructional videos with others. The web site itself works in the same way that YouTube works. When searching for content, you type in the content and a search engine matches the search topic. Uploading a video involves creating a title for the content, a detailed description, choosing the appropriate topics that apply to the content, and uploading the file. You can make your video private or public. There is no limit to file size, but TeacherTube does limit the video file types they accept. They accept video files in the WMV, AVI, MOV, MPG, MP4 and FLV file formats. Because Mr. Richard is using a Mac, he uses the free Flip4Mac WMV player. The file formats accepted by TeacherTube are .doc, .ppt, .pdf, .rtf, .txt, .csv, .xls, .mp3, .wav, .kmz, .swf, .zip and .gsp file formats.

TeacherTube provides a downloader option (http://www.download-toolz.com/files/ teachertube_d_setup.exe) since they acknowledge that students may be unable to view videos using dial-up access. The video will be downloaded as a Flash file, which makes the download much faster. You can watch the FLV-format video using FLV player, (http://www.download.com/FLV-Player/3000-2139_4-10467081.html) if you do not have the ability to view the file. If you need to convert the file to another format for playing on your computer, try out one of the easy to use online converters such as Vixy or Zamar. Other video-based web sites are SchoolTube and My Learning Tube. SchoolTube (http://www.schooltube.com) is a safe, free media sharing web site for students and educators and is nationally endorsed by premier education associations.

- Flip4Mac WMV player
  (http://www.flip4mac.com/wmv.htm)
- International Society for Technology in Education web site
  (http://www.iste.org)
- Kathy Schrock's Guide for Educators
  (http://school.discoveryeducation.com/ schrockguide/)
- MERLOT
  (http://www.merlot.org)
- TeacherTube
  (http://www.teachertube.com)

CREATING A PODCAST

The best way to understand the intricacies of podcasting is to walk through an example of how to create one. We will again refer to our fictional teacher, Ms. Rodriquez, who wanted to make a podcast of birdcalls for her students. This information is provided so that educators can use podcasting to create richer instructional materials.

Before Ms. Rodriquez begins recording information for a podcast, she should determine the type of file she should create based upon how the podcast will be listened to by her students. In her case, her recording equipment stores files as Windows Media Audio (WMA). WMA files may be played back as recorded in various client programs such as Windows Media Player, Apple computers with the Flip4Mac QuickTime plug-in, and some MP3 players. The distinction between a WMA audio file and a podcast is that a podcast may be subscribed to via a RSS feed and automatically downloaded to personal devices as new content becomes available. WMA files, on the other hand, need to be manually downloaded or synchronized with personal devices. Consequently, WMA files are not compatible with RSS feeds. Currently, MP3 and MP4 (AAC) are most commonly used file formats. M4V files are gaining popularity since they play well in iTunes. Many of her students still have dial-up connections at home. This makes listening to audio files online difficult. Ms. Rodriguez converts her WMA files to MP3. When she posts the files on the server, she saves her media page as a basic web-page for her students to manually download the files. She also creates an XML page saved with the RSS file extension. She creates a download button with the URL to the RSS media page and places the button on her basic web page. In Mr. Richard's class, almost all the students own iPods and he has enough loaner iPods to enable all students to use them. Mr. Richard's students can subscribe to the media page created by Ms. Rodriguez by using the button. Anytime new content is added to the site, the media will automatically download to his students' iPods when they synchronize the players. Consequently, Mr. Richard does not have to tell students when new content is available as long as they synchronize regularly. Ms. Rodriguez's class will have to manually download each new file as it becomes available. She will need to notify them when new content is available so they do not have to keep checking for content.

Recording

Before beginning, it is also important to consider how the actual recording will be made. One easy way to record audio content only lectures is to use digital voice recorders such as Olympus Digital Voice Recorders and lapel microphone such as the Olympus ME 15. These recorders store audio recordings as individual WMA (Windows Media Audio) audio files. Users can create different folders to organize files. Recorded files may be streamed or played in various portable audio players and computer-based media players such as Windows Media Player. Files can be uploaded to a computer or server by removing the battery compartment to expose the USB jack. Audio files can also be recorded directly to a file using computer applications such as Apple's GarageBand and Audacity (http://audacity. sourceforge.net) an open source, cross-platform sound editor. Lame MP3 Encoder is required to encode MP3 exported formats from Audacity.

- Apple's GarageBand
  (http://www.apple.com/ilife/tutorials/#garageband-podcast-51)
- Audacity
  (http://audacity.sourceforge.net)
- Lame MP3 Encoder
  (http://www.free-codecs.com/download/Lame_Encoder.htm)

File Format Conversion

If you are new to podcasting, the easiest way to create a podcast is to use a portable audio recorder/MP3 player. Audiocasts (podcasts) are in a MP3 file format. An MP3 file contains information about the artist, album, genre, etc. This info is stored in what is called ID3 tags. Although Audacity, an open source sound editor, is great for recording audio and converting audio, it will not convert WMA files directly to MP3. To be able to use WMA files as podcasts, each WMA file must be converted to the MP3 (MPEG-1 Audio Layer 3–Moving Picture Experts Group) file format.

There are freeware and commercial products available on the Internet for converting audio files. For example, NCH Swift Sound has both commercial and free versions of Switch Audio File Format Converter. Many technologists, such as those at Tulane University, prefer Koyote Soft's Free MP3WMA Converter because it's easy to use. The MP3WMA Converter is also easy to use. You just drop the file(s) into the frames, select the output format, select the conversion settings (parameters), and press convert. (See Figure 20.1.) Note that you are able to convert batches of files instead of just one file at a time.

You may also want to convert a WMA file to WAV to embed in a Power-Point presentation or to edit in Audacity. Audacity and Free MP3 WMA Converter permit adding some metadata to the file. Windows Media Player and iTunes use these tags to organize your MP3s. Another great free utility for tagging files is Softpointer's AudioShell. AudioShell is a Microsoft Windows Explorer shell extension plug-in which allows you to view and edit

Figure 20.1   File format conversion.

Figure 20.2   Tags—metadata.

music tags directly in Windows Explorer. You need only to right-click on the file icon to see the menu options. Figure 20.2 is an example data entry of file metadata. Metadata displays on browser pages or appears as scrolling data on playback devices.

File Conversion Rates

There is a trade-off between file size (storage space) and audio quality. Users can make a file smaller by adjusting its sample rate and bit rate. Music-only files require higher sample and bit rates, because files with higher bit rates have better sound quality. However, they also have larger file sizes. Voice recordings do not require high fidelity. As a result, voice-only podcasts use small sample and bit rates. Users can decrease files size by reducing the voice-only podcast from stereo to mono. For example, an audio file encoded with a stereo bit rate of 96kbps equals 48kbps for a mono file. The minimum recommended bit rate for talk-only podcasts is 32k bits; however, 48k bits is the most commonly used rate. For music podcasts, the recommended minimum rate is 96k bits, but the bit rate of 128k bits is the most common. A one-hour podcast encoded at 64kbps is about 28MB (voice only)

- Audio File Format Converter
  (http://www.nch.com.au/switch/)
- Koyote Soft's Free MP3WMA Converter
  (http://www.koyotesoft.com/appli/Setup_FreeConverter.exe)
- SoftPointer's AudioShell
  (http://www.softpointer.com/AudioShell.htm)

Advertising (RSS)

A confusing aspect of web content syndication is whether to use an XML file extension or a RSS one. As stated earlier, RSS is a type or dialect of XML. If you have a reader or web browser that interprets RSS and XML, the content will display properly in the browser when you go to the URL. But, if you see code, this means that your browser or reader cannot properly interpret the page. File extensions denote the program to use to open the file. The tip to remember is, if you use the RSS extension (the part that follows the dot in a file name on Windows OS systems), you can subscribe to the feed automatically when you click on the icon. [RSS Example] Or you can right-click on the icon, copy the shortcut, and paste it into your browser or preferred feed reader. If you use the XML file extension, you still can save the feed as a favorite and an RSS-savvy web browser will present the information properly. Otherwise, you have to copy and paste a URL for the feed into a browser or feed reader address textbox or subscription textbox. When creating feeds, you also need to define the MIME type. MIME stands for Multipurpose Internet Mail Extensions. Although originally used to define email content beyond a type of text document, MIME now refers to other web-based, non-email content. The FeedForAll website has a comprehensive MIME type list.

RSS feeds are easily created (often automatically) by software when you use hosting sites such as Blogger, or feed creation software such as stand-alone FeedForAll, or the web-based FeedBurner. If you wish to advertise your RSS feed(s) to many sources and not just people you know, you might try a pinging service such as Feed Ping or ping-o-matic. This will advertise your feed updates to other servers. If Ms. Rodriguez, for example, wants to advertise her content on iTunes, she would ping the Apple Server to update the Apple site about her content changes. The Apple site provides the information needed to create an account, post, and update content in iTunes.

If you do not have a host website which automatically creates RSS feeds for you, you will need to create your own feeds. A great place to learn about how to create an RSS feed is to refer to the RSS 2.0 Specification site. You also might want to buy a feed creation tool such as FeedForAll or try an on-line copy & paste feed generator such as Link Assure's Free RSS Feed Writer. In addition to the RSS 2.0 Specification website, Photoblogs.Org has a useful template to get you started. An RSS template for iTunes is also available from Apple. You can use this template even if you do not advertise your podcast on the iTunes site. Some of their code is not RSS specification-compliant, however. Expression Engine also provides a copy & paste iTunes RSS template (http://expressionengine.com/wiki/iTunes_Podcast_Template/).

- Apple site, http://www.apple.com/itunes/store/podcaststechspecs. html
- Blogger, https://www.blogger.com/start
- Expression Engine http://expressionengine.com/wiki/iTunes_Podcast _Template/
- FeedBurner, http://www.feedburner.com/fb/a/home
- FeedForAll (http://www.feedforall.com/mime-types.htm)
- Feed Ping, http://www.feedping.com/
- Link Assure's Free RSS Feed Writer, http://www.linkassure.com/ rss-writer.php
- Ourmedia, http://www.ourmedia.org/
- ping-o-matic, http://pingomatic.com/.
- RSS 2.0 Specification http://cyber.law.harvard.edu/rss/rss. html#hrelementsOfLtitemgt.

Throughout this chapter, we have described ways for educators to create Web 2.0 learning objects and integrate them into their teaching practices. We addressed the hardware and software needed to create and post these objects. However, as the Web continues to evolve, what future trends might educators expect?

FUTURE TRENDS

Moving from the static, read-only web to the social, read-write web (Web 2.0), can be problematic for education institutions. The information highway delivers a surplus of data with a shortage of scholarship. Additionally, many people agree that the Web is as much a time-waster as it is convenient. According to Tim O'Reilly (2005), Web 2.0 is a shift from directory-based taxonomy (where) to social network folksonomy-based information (who). Our students need to retrieve accurate information in a timely fashion. One solution is to develop software applications that can perform tasks humans now perform. Berners-Lee, Hendler, and Lassila (2001) call this solution the Semantic Web. Many refer to the Semantic Web as the Web 3.0 or version 3. We do not agree. Retired Stanford professor Bebo White sees the Semantic Web as one evolution of the Web, while the social web is another path (2006). Samuel, Daniel, Hinson, and Sanson (2008) agree with Dr. White but suggest expanding the model. We define the solution to information retrieval in closed systems, such as educational institutions, as the Contextually Partitioned Web (CPW). This web guides the student experience via consensually defined metadata (Figure 20.3).

Web 2.0 resources are identified using tags. Tags are information such as title, author, date, and comments. Many websites employ tag clouds. For example, the Indianapolis Museum of Art uses cloud tags to describe their art collection objects. Tag clouds are groups of tags generally ranked alphabetically and differing in font size and position. People scan these lists to find resources. The larger the font, the more popular the website or frequently the topic appears in the site. Tag clouds are visual indicators of popularity, frequency, and truthiness (things we wish were true) not of substantiation (fact). They are the product of folksonomy or individual classification rather than standardized or consensual categorization. Tags are therefore prone to classification and spelling variance. The CPW model employs a collabulary defined by subject matter experts and digital archivists. Word Spy defines a collabulary as a collaborative vocabulary to ensure content "relevance and consistency" (McFedries, 2007). In other words, we suggest

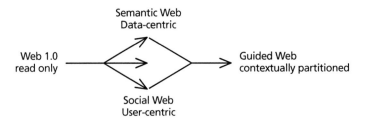

Figure 20.3 The contextually partitioned Web (Samuel et al., 2008).

that Library Science should become an integral part of any new web-based solution for a data archive and retrieval system. Careful planning and tag standardization should be employed along with database back ends, wikis, blogs, and cloud-based solutions. The effect of this model is that information retrieval time will decrease while usefulness of retrieved resources will increase.

CONCLUSION

Several years ago, Web 2.0 applications in education were primarily limited to blogs and wikis. Only the technically fearless were willing or able to take the time to figure out how to incorporate original podcasts in the classroom. Until recently, guidebooks about Web 2.0 technology were limited to definitions and creation information. What was missing was the essential information about how to post and advertise your content. Although this chapter is not a step-by-step guide, the intent is to provide you with the essential information and auxiliary links to help you create, post, and advertise Web 2.0 content and fully participate in the read/write (social) Web. Additionally, we hoped to ignite a dialog about how to best prepare students to use the web as a resource for authentic research and scholarship. Shouldn't our focus as educators be to drive the next Web wave from teaching students where to surf to creating shark-free oceans of information?

REFERENCES

Berners-Lee, T., Hendler, J., & Lassila, O. (2008). The semantic web. *Scientific American Magazine*. Retrieved August 1, 2007, from http://www.sciam.com/article.cfm?id=the-semantic-web.

Halvey, M., & Keane, M. (2007). *An assessment of tag presentation techniques*. Paper presented at the 16th International World Wide Web Conference (WWW2007), Banff, Alberta, Canada. Retrieved from http://www2007.org/htmlposters/poster988/.

Home Theater Glossary. (n.d.). *WMA*. Retrieved August 11, 2008, from http://www.hometheatermag.com/glossary/

Indianapolis Museum of Art. (2008). *IMA tags*. Retrieved August 8, 2008, from http://www.imamuseum.org/connect/tags

McFedries, P. (2007, January 17). Collabulary. *Word Spy*. Retrieved August 8, 2008, from http://www.wordspy.com/words/collabulary.asp

Merriam-Webster's Words of the Year. (2006). Truithiness. In *Merriam-Webster Online* [Online]. Retrieved August 8, 2008, from http://www.merriam-webster.com/info/06words.htm

Miessler, D. (2007, July 11). *The difference between Web 1.0, 2.0, and 3.0*. Retrieved May 1, 2008, from http://dmiessler.com/blog/the-difference-between-web-10-20-and-30

O'Reilly, T. (2005, September 30). *What is web 2.0?* Retrieved August 8, 2008, from http://www.oreillynet.com/pub/a/oreilly/tim/news/2005/09/30/what-is-web-20.html

PHP (2008). *History of PHP and related projects.* Retrieved August 11, 2008, from http://www.php.net/manual/en/history.php

Samuel, J., Daniel, A., Hinson, J., & Sanson, J. (2008, April). *The contextually partitioned web: What you need when you need it.* Paper presented at the Tulane University School of Medicine Education Day, New Orleans, LA.

Soloman, G., & Schrumm, L. (2007). *Web 2.0: New tools for new schools.* Eugene, OR: International Society for Technology in Education.

TechTarget. (2008). *XML.* Retrieved August 11, 2008, from http://searchsoa.techtarget.com/sDefinition/0,,sid26_gci213404,00.html

Webopedia.com. (2008). *MIME.* Retrieved August 11, 2008, from http://www.webopedia.com/TERM/M/MIME.html

Webopedia.com. (2008). *MP3.* Retrieved August 11, 2008, from http://www.webopedia.com/TERM/M/MP3.html

Webopedia.com. (2008). *RSS.* Retrieved August 11, 2008, from http://webopedia.com/TERM/R/RSS.html

Webreference.com. (2003). *Introduction to RSS.* Retrieved August 11, 2008, from http://www.webreference.com/authoring/languages/xml/rss/intro/

Webreference.com. (2003). *PHP.* Retrieved August 11, 2008, from http://www.webreference.com/programming/php/

White, B (2006, April). *The implications of web 2.0 on web information systems.* Paper presented at WEBIST 2006, Setubal, Portugal. Retrieved March 1, 2008 from http://www.webist.org/2006/Documents/Bebo_webist_keynote.pdf

CHAPTER 21

ACCESSIBILITY ISSUES FOR WEB 2.0

Becky Sue Parton
Southeastern Louisiana University

Robert Hancock
Southeastern Louisiana University

ABSTRACT

Multiple studies (Siegal, Parton, & Hancock, R; Zaparyniuk & Montgomerie, 2005; Witt & McDermott; 2004) reveal a pattern of accessibility problems for educational and popular websites. Especially alarming is the fact that fewer sites are accessible today than were accessible in 1997 due to the increased presence of multimedia elements on web pages (Hackett, Parmanto, & Zeng, 2005). Historically, "As web designers have increased their use of complex web design components, they have also added barriers to accessibility for persons with disabilities" (Hackett, Parmanto, & Zeng, 2005, p. 290). Given Web 2.0's heavy reliance on collaborative applications and the tendency to have content built by teachers and students, web accessibility training is paramount. This chapter will provide a rationale for addressing accessibility compliance, review historical failures of the web design community to address these standards, and provide solutions for what we can do as a community to improve Web 2.0 accessibility.

Wired for Learning: An Educator's Guide to Web 2.0, pages 333–342
Copyright © 2009 by Information Age Publishing
All rights of reproduction in any form reserved.

333

INTRODUCTION

Since 1996, the Americans with Disabilities Act (ADA) has required website accessibility for persons with disabilities. In a suit between the National Federation of the Blind (NFB) and AOL over the service's incompatibility with screen readers, the Department of Justice ruled that Web sites are public accommodations and must therefore offer access to the disabled (Heim, 2000). Yet, it is much harder to find a handicapped friendly site than a handicapped friendly building. Physical structures have been the primary emphasis of the ADA. According to Chong (2003, p. 1), "We in the National Federation of the Blind believe that although we don't have many problems accessing buildings, the world is moving in the direction that everything one does revolves around electronic services and the Internet. If the blind can't use that information, we will not be able to compete. We will be relegated to the backwaters of the electronic information highway." Unfortunately this issue is even worse on sites where the authors, such as K–12 teachers and students, normally have not had the opportunity or training to design for persons who are disabled. Joseph Lazzaro, director of the adaptive technology program at the Massachusetts Commission for the Blind and author of Adapting PCs for Disabilities (Lazzaro, 1995) stated, "If you're cut off from information, you're not going to go to school, you're not going to get a job. You're going to be left out of a lot that society has to offer." Indeed web options can be very limited for those who have trouble handling a mouse, seeing a web site, or hearing video. While there are options that can assist users in overcoming these issues, the site source must be designed with those options in mind. If our nation's educational institutions and corporations don't address the accessibility issue, they risk 20% (Loiacono and McCoy, 2004) of their potential students and customers. Web 2.0 applications make joining a community easier for traditional users; however, if the developer is not mindful of accessibility concerns in the initial design, a great many people may be left without access. A simple question to illustrate the point may be, "Is your wiki accessible to the blind as it is currently designed?" The answer given by the vast majority of amateur designers is probably no. A look at the first blind accessible wiki located at http://blind.wikia.com, highlights the obstacles that face developers. Significantly more groups are using Web 2.0 to get people involved, but we as a society have long neglected web accessibility. If we do not grow accessibility at the same rate we grow interactivity we risk excluding the folks who arguably could benefit the most from the type of interaction Web 2.0 has to offer. Thus, the timing is critical to address web accessibility problems in both the traditional format and in the Web 2.0 format.

The objectives of this chapter are:

- Familiarize the reader with the rationale for addressing Web Content Accessibility Guidelines (WCAG) and the lack of compliance in the literature.
- Delineate research conducted by the authors on web accessibility for sites created by K–12 school district in anticipation of heavy Web 2.0 development from this developer pool.
- Outline relevant issues, terms, and guidelines for educators who are creating accessible content on Web 2.0.
- Highlight a case study based upon a pilot project with high school Deaf students that reflects on the use of wikis to build dynamic, hybrid fieldtrip experiences
- Discuss future trends in accessibility for Web 2.0.

BACKGROUND

In 1999, the World Wide Web Consortium (W3C) established the Web Content Accessibility Guidelines (WCAG) to promote accessibility of web content to people with disabilities (WCAG, 1999). The guidelines were intended (1999) for use by all Web content developers (page authors and site designers) and for developers of authoring tools. W3C is an international consortium where member organizations (including Microsoft, Apple, IBM, and others), a full-time staff, and the public work together to develop international web standards. W3C operations are jointly administered by the MIT Computer Science and Artificial Intelligence Laboratory (CSAIL) in the USA, the European Research Consortium for Informatics and Mathematics (ERCIM) headquartered in France and Keio University in Japan (W3C, 2007). These guidelines, while developed initially before Web 2.0, obviously contain Web 2.0 content within their scope of authority. They were intended to be of positive impact to all users regardless of site interaction (e.g., client side or server side transaction) or user agent employed (e.g., desktop browser, voice browser, mobile phone, automobile-based personal computer, etc.) or environment (e.g., noisy surroundings, under- or over-illuminated rooms, in a hands-free environment, etc.).

A Brief Overview of WCAG 1.0 Guidelines

Multi-file formats of the full WCAG 1.0 Guidelines can be found at the W3C WCAG Site, http://www.w3.org/TR/WCAG10/. To simplify, there are three levels of WCAG 1.0 compliance. They are A (the lowest), AA (the middle) and AAA (the maximum). Compliance is judged based upon checkpoints that may or may not need to be satisfied based upon their priority. An example of a checkpoint follows:

> 1.1 Provide a text equivalent for every non-text element (e.g., via "alt", "long-desc", or in element content). *This includes:* images, graphical representations of text (including symbols), image map regions, animations (e.g., animated GIFs), applets and programmatic objects, ascii art, frames, scripts, images used as list bullets, spacers, graphical buttons, sounds (played with or without user interaction), stand-alone audio files, audio tracks of video, and video.

For the majority of Web sites, Priority 1 is considered a basic requirement [and] Priority 2 and 3, respectively 'should' and 'may' be satisfied (Williams and Rattray, 2003). Sites are evaluated as A, AA, or AAA, based upon satisfaction of checkpoints as follows:

Level A—Priority One

A Webmaster who wishes to have a WCAG compliant site must attain at least level A. This is also known as Priority One. Every Priority One checkpoint must be completed in order to claim Level A compliance status.

Level AA—Priority Two

A Webmaster who wishes to have a WCAG compliant site should satisfy all the Priority Two checkpoints. This will mean that more barriers to accessibility will be removed for users with disabilities. Once a Webmaster has satisfied all the Priority One and Priority Two checkpoints then the site can claim to be Level AA compliant.

Level AAA—Priority Three

A Webmaster who wishes to have a WCAG compliant site may satisfy all the Priority Three checkpoints. This will mean that more barriers to accessibility will be removed for users with disabilities. Once a Webmaster has satisfied all the Priority One, Priority Two and Priority Three checkpoints then the site can claim to be Level AAA compliant.

From WCAG 1.0 to 2.0 Guidelines

The W3C is in the process of redrafting the WCAG 1.0 guidelines to become WCAG 2.0 guidelines, (W3C, 2007b), yet there has been little historical compliance in complying with the standards as outlined in WCAG 1.0. The development process has been a long one. The W3C began work on the guidelines in 2001 and is just now in the process of finalizing those guidelines.

The Historical Failure of WCAG 1.0 Guidelines

Historically, the web-design community has not done a great job in meeting WCAG guidelines. In the year after the WCAG guidelines were initially drafted, Sullivan & Matson (2000) examined fifty of the web's most popular sites, as determined by web traffic statistics. This examination found that 41 of these 50 sites were deemed inaccessible through a combination of automated and manual testing. Two years later, Jackson-Sanborn et al. (2002) examined six categories of sites, finding that most (66.1%) failed accessibility testing for WCAG Priority 1. The majority of errors found would have no visible effect on the site's design if corrected, and other errors that would impact the design could be coded differently thus keeping the same site appearance. Subsequently, Lazar (2003) sampled the home pages of the fifty largest organizations in the Maryland area as reported by the Baltimore Business Journal. Only one out of the fifty was determined to be fully accessible according to the Priority Level 1 of the WCAG. Researchers have also noted, "...universities in some non-English-speaking countries have significantly less accessible web pages" (Kane, Shulman, Shockley, & Ladner, 2007,p. 154). Essentially, the attention to accessibility is dismal regardless of the type or origin of the website in question, although the extent to which that is true does vary.

In many studies, it was the home pages that were analyzed using a popular accessibility evaluation tool, Bobby, now called WebXACT, which was first developed by the Center for Applied Special Technology to check documents for conformance to W3C recommendations based on all three priority errors (Zaparyniuk & Montgomerie, 2005). Although a large number of research studies employ the use of an automated software program, others prefer manual checking. Often, a combination approach is advocated since automatic tools can be unreliable to a certain extent as reported by Witt & McDermott (2004). For example, an instance that would lead to this occurrence might be when graphics do have a corresponding 'alt' tag as required, however upon analysis of the tag it becomes clear that the content is meaningless text such as the word 'graphic'. In this situation, the automatic evaluation tool will assume compliance, whereas a manual check will flag the problem.

CURRENT RESEARCH

In a recent study conducted by the authors, an analysis of compliance to WCAG 1.0 standards in a variety of educational institutions (i.e., universities, public schools, schools for the Deaf and/or Blind) was undertaken.

Web sites were evaluated using EvalAccess 2.0 from the Laboratory of Human Computer Access for Special Needs.

A sample of university ($n = 50$) web sites was randomly selected from the results of an Internet search on top universities in the United States. The first link returned provided a list of schools that contained 124 entries. Fifty random numbers were generated with the aid of computer software from 1 to 124. The corresponding entries from the search results were selected for evaluation. A similar process was undertaken for K–12 districts ($n = 50$); an Internet search on K–12 districts in the United States resulted in thousands of 'hits' with the first fifty being accepted for this study.

The findings indicated overwhelmingly that little or no attention to WCAG 1.0 compliance has occurred nationally at the K–12 or university level. A finding with potentially farther reaching implications, however, was the gap between universities and K–12 districts. In contrast to the 70% of universities that met the Level A conformance (see Figure 21.2), only 34% of districts met that same minimal level (see Figure 21.1). An independent samples t-test was performed to evaluate the null hypothesis. When analyzing priority one errors, universities and K–12 districts showed dramatic differences in mean error rate (2.14 versus 14.76) for priority one errors that was statistically significant ($p < .05$). This issue is perhaps even more critical for Web 2.0 given its heavy reliance on collaborative applications and its tendency to have content built by teachers and students themselves.

Guidelines

Often in design and accessibility, there is more than one "right" way to do things—it is often a judgment call in determining what will result in the "best" or "most accessible" product. The guidelines are an excellent foundation upon which to build accessible Web content, but unless the developers understand the reasons behind the guidelines, they might apply the guidelines incorrectly or ineffectively. For example, the guidelines call for the use of the alt text to describe images. It is most important however, that the developer just not describe the image, but give the user a feeling of the image's purpose on the page. It is perhaps best to use the guidelines as a starting point for what must be done to make the site accessible. When one considers the amount of work accessibility can be, it becomes a very daunting task. However, there are many steps that a Web 2.0 developer can take to make his/her sight more accessible to people with disabilities. Begin by separating out your site's Web 2.0 content pieces into individual elements, and then determine how each element can be made more accessible. Then put yourself in the place of a person who is disabled and ask yourself what you could do to make each piece of content and the site itself more accessible for him/her. Make your site as accessible as your constraints allow in order to meet the needs of your particular audience. Although the WCAG guidelines are a good guide, there is no true consensus as to a specific methodology to employ. It is the author's intent to give you some good examples of things you can do to make life easier for users with disabilities.

Example One: Podcasting for the Deaf and Hard-of-Hearing

Traditional audio podcasts, are one of the most commonly used Web 2.0 tools, yet they are most often a total loss for a deaf or hard-of-hearing individual. This situation does not have to be the case as there are two approaches that can be of dramatic assistance to deaf and hard-of-hearing individuals in joining the podcasting phenomenon.

The first of these approaches is perhaps most useful for persons who are hard-of-hearing. It involves the use of a video podcast. While the simplest approach would be a PowerPoint presentation of the covered content in a video podcast format, a far more elegant solution would be the captioning of relevant video content (such as is done on most television programs), using software such as Media Access Generator (MAGpie), developed by the CPB/WGBH National Center for Accessible Media (NCAM). This software tool is designed to make it easy for multimedia content developers to add captions to their audio and video content. MAGpie allows the captioning of web audio and video content for use in QuickTime, which can then be easily set up for video podcast.

The second of these approaches would perhaps be more elegant for deaf individuals. Often for deaf individuals it is more comfortable to have an ASL interpreter than to read text, so for these folks it might be best to just begin with ASL interpreted video, ideally with captioning, and then convert this video to QuickTime to be set up for video podcast.

Example Two: Blogs and RSS Feeds for the Blind

Blogs and RSS feeds are a great resource for the visually impaired and blind individuals among us. However, there are many things a developer can do to make RSS and blogged content more accessible for the blind. Perhaps the most important of these is to avoid building automated pictorial verification—those abstract renderings of random characters that ask users to retype the word they see on the screen into developed aggregators or hosting sites. Also known as a captcha or the "vision test," these are meant to keep spam programs out of the system, but unfortunately they also keep out people with vision loss. Captchas are extremely difficult for people with low vision to decipher and screen readers cannot read them because they are unlabeled graphics. Another key issue in formatting hosts and content is to enable the user to skip the navigation segment of the relevant page or anything else that is going to give a long list of non relevant content to the screen reader (i.e., a drop-down menu with all 50 states in alphabetical order even though you can predict that most users will need to select 'Texas'. Finally, the developer should test the final product with a piece of software such as IBM's ADesigner to view the page as a visually impaired or blind person might.

There is much more that can be given by way of example, but space precludes us from going into greater detail here. Rather, we recommend that the developer take some advice from the WCAG guidelines. By focusing more on principles rather than techniques, version 2.0 of the guidelines is more flexible, and encourages developers to think through the process conceptually. The four main guiding principles of accessibility in WCAG 2.0 are:

- Perceivable
- Operable
- Understandable
- Robust

If developers focus on these key principles and uses the guidelines as a starting point, they will be well on their way to achieving a useful level of accessibility.

Mini Case Study

Web 2.0 tools are being successfully used by students who fall under the authority of the Americans with Disabilities act. Recently, a group of eight high school students from the Jean Massieu Academy for the Deaf took a fieldtrip to Tiger Creek Wildlife Refuge in Texas. While on-site, the students took videos, photos, and notes about their experiences. A wiki shell was created for the students who were then free to add information and reflections about the trip to the site. For example, one student posted a photo of paw marks in the sand and discussed the difference between cat and dog prints. This tool allowed the students to interactively share about a common experience not only with each other but also with other Deaf students who did not participate in the fieldtrip. It is interesting to note that little attention was overtly paid to the accessibility features of the wiki; however, the students automatically knew that videos would need captions.

In this case, the students used American Sign Language to communicate in the videos; so English captions were added for hearing visitors.

FUTURE TRENDS

Unfortunately, past evidence and current trends indicate that accessibility will continue to be a growing problem until we focus more energy upon addressing it. Finding information on accessibility for Web 2.0 tools is extremely difficult and studies on accessibility and 2.0 tools are few and far between. Both developers and researchers must reverse this trend toward inaction quickly.

CONCLUSIONS

"An accessible information technology (IT) solution is one that is usable by all people, regardless of ability or disability" (Brunet, et al., 2005). The techniques and guidelines of web accessibility were not invented to make life hard for web developers. They were invented to make life easier for people with disabilities and bring them into the web community. Web 2.0 likewise intends to make the web a communal resource by making it easier to access and publish information. Like everyone else, people with disabilities want and need to access the community offered on the web. Nothing could be more perfect in terms of making the world more accessible to people with disabilities.

Web 2.0 should not be a barrier to people with disabilities; it should be a solution to helping them overcome the barriers that for them are a natural part of everyday life. For Web 2.0 to reach its full potential for people with disabilities, developers must design with accessibility in mind, or risk creating yet another barrier in the lives of people whom just want equal access and participation.

REFERENCES

Brunet, P., Feigenbaum, B., Harris, K., Laws, C., Schwerdtfeger, R., & Weiss, L. (2005). Accessibility requirements for systems design to accommodate users with vision impairments. *IBM Systems Journal, 44*(3), 445–466.

Chong, C. (2003). America Online: Is it accessible now? *The Braille Monitor.* May 2003. Retrieved April 15, 2005, from http://204.245.133.32/bm/bm03/bm0305/bm030509.htm.

Hackett, S., Parmanto, B., & Zeng, X. (2005). A longitudinal evaluation of accessibility: Higher education web sites. *Internet Research, 15*(3), 281–295.

Heim, J. (2000, September). Locking out the disabled. *PC World.* 181.

Jackson-Sanborn, E., Odess-Harnish, K., & Warren, N. (2002). Web site accessibility: A study of six genres. *Library Hi-Tech. 20*(3), 308.

Kane, S., Shulman, J., Shockley, T., & Ladner, R. (2007, May). *A web accessibility report card for top international university web sites.* Paper presented at the 2007 International Cross-disciplinary Conference on Web Accessibility (W4A), Banff Canada.

Lazar, J. (2003). Web accessibility in the mid-atlantic United States: A study of 50 home pages. *Universal Access in the Information Society, 2*(4), 331–341.

Lazzaro, J. (1996). *Adapting PCs for disabilities.* Reading, MA: Addison Wesley.

Loiacono, E., & McCoy, S. (2004). Web site accessibility: An online sector analysis. *Information Technology & People, 17*(1), 87.

Siegal, W., Parton, B., & Hancock, R. (under review). An examination of web content accessibility guidelines compliance: Are universities and school districts making world wide web learning resources available to the disabled? *Journal of Information Technology Education.*

Sullivan, T., & Matson, R. (2000). *Barriers to use: Usability and content accessibility on the web's most popular sites.* Paper presented at ACM Conference on Universal Usability, Arlington, VA.

W3C. (2007). *Organizational information.* Retrieved January 19, 2007, from: http://www.w3.org.

Web Content Accessibility Guidelines 1.0 (WCAG). (1999). Retrieved January 19, 2007, from http://www.w3.org/TR/WCAG10.

Williams, R., & Rattray, R. (2003). An assessment of web accessibility of UK accountancy firms. *Managerial Auditing Journal.* Retrieved from ABI/INFORM May 17, 2007.

Witt, N., & McDermott, A. (2004). Web site accessibility: What logo will we use today? *British Journal of Educational Technology, 35*(1), 45–56.

Zaparyniuk, N., & Montgomerie, C. (2005). The status of web accessibility of Canadian universities and colleges: A charter of rights and freedoms issue1. *International Journal on E-learning, 4*(2), 253–269.

CHAPTER 22

WEB 2.0 IN TEACHER EDUCATION

Characteristics, Implications, and Limitations

Michael M. Grant
Clif Mims
The University of Memphis

ABSTRACT

Like the variety of Web 2.0 applications, theories of learning and instructional models are also primarily content independent. So it is left up to the teacher educator to match learner characteristics, content, pedagogy and technologies. This chapter will concentrate on the use of Web 2.0 technologies in contemporary constructivist and cognitivist learning environments. We will present the characteristics of Web 2.0 tools to support teaching and learning, including low threshold applications, a variety of tools and models, as well as access to tools and knowledge. Finally, we will identify the limitations and challenges that exist with using these tools, such as immature applications, longevity of applications, number of applications, unconsolidated services and security and ethics.

Wired for Learning: An Educator's Guide to Web 2.0, pages 343–360
Copyright © 2009 by Information Age Publishing
343

WEB 2.0 IN TEACHER EDUCATION:
CHARACTERISTICS, IMPLICATIONS, AND LIMITATIONS

We have arrived at the time in teacher education, both preservice and in-service education, where a large portion of the learners is deemed digital natives. In their personal, professional and academic lives, these individuals are plugged in. Differentiation is central to both Web 2.0 and education. In Web 2.0, small, niche applications address individual productivity needs. In education, differentiated learning calls for instruction that is tailored around the individual. Teacher education needs to accommodate for these trends.

Many Web 2.0 applications are content independent or can be repurposed to diverse instructional needs. Like the variety in these applications, theories of learning and instructional models are primarily content independent. However, with the excitement or apprehension surrounding new technologies, it is easy and tempting to remain focused solely on the technology. This would be a disservice to learners. So it is left up to the teacher to match learner characteristics, content, pedagogy and technology. Therefore, teacher educators and teachers must be cognizant of both the technology affordances and learning theory compatibilities.

This chapter will concentrate on the use of Web 2.0 technologies in contemporary constructivist and cognitivist learning environments. In particular, we will first examine the tenets and applications of constructivism and cognitivism. Then we will present the characteristics of Web 2.0 tools to support teaching and learning in these environments. Finally, we will identify the limitations and challenges that exist with using these tools. To consolidate and respect page constraints, a list of all the applications we have embedded throughout the chapter are aggregated into the "Resources" section at the end.

CONSTRUCTIVIST AND COGNITIVIST LEARNING

One's ideas about knowledge and the process of learning influence instructional practice. Educators that believe learners actively construct knowledge while making sense of the world will likely design instruction emphasizing the development of meaning and understanding. Educators, believing that learners passively receive information, will likely develop instruction that emphasizes knowledge transmission.

Constructivist Learning

Constructivism is based on the premise that learning is an active process and learners construct knowledge and understanding of the world by reflecting on their experiences. Learning becomes active when students are able to connect new knowledge with their prior understanding (Piaget, 1954, 1974; Mims, 2003). Piaget suggested that learners construct new knowledge from their experiences through the processes of assimilation and accommodation (Piaget, 1967). Assimilation occurs when learners are able to incorporate new experiences into their existing mental framework without having to change it. However, some experiences contradict a learner's mental model. Accommodation occurs when the learner reconstructs his/her mental framework allowing for integration of the new experience.

Constructivist learning is epitomized by key interactions with others and the environment (Driscoll, 2005) and meeting the needs of the learner at their instructional level. Constructivism is often associated with independent learning, self-regulation, and student-centered learning. Problem solving, hands-on activities and real-world scenarios provide new experiences and encourage learners to use active techniques as they assimilate or accommodate new knowledge.

Many researchers have considered technology's role in education and demonstrated that it can enhance instruction, facilitate learning and serve as a medium allowing students to more fully express themselves, often in creative ways (Grant & Branch, 2005; Papert, 1980; Schank, Berman & Macpherson, 1999). Web 2.0 technologies integrate well with constructivist learning as many of the tools are social and encourage interaction with others. The wide assortment of technologies (images, audio, video, text) allow for multiple representations of understanding, foster creativity and help teachers provide individualized instruction and tailored learning opportunities for students.

Cognitive Learning

Cognitivism, modeled by information processing theory, is organized by three serial apportionments: a sensory register, working memory and long-term memory (Driscoll, 2005). The sensory register allows stimuli to be perceived and attended, both of which have limited capacities, passing received stimuli to working memory. Similarly, working memory is a processing center for active learning, but it also has a limited capacity. This capacity can be extended through memory strategies, such as mnemonics, rehearsal and chunking of information. Finally, new learning can be processed from working memory into long-term memory, theorized as permanent unlimited storage. In long-term memory, new learning can be adapted and shaped with previous learning in the form of organizational structures called schemata (Ausubel, 1980).

Cognitive load theory highlights the specific limitations of working memory. Three types of cognitive load (i.e., intrinsic, germane and extraneous) have been associated with learning (Clark, Nguyen & Sweller, 2006). In particular, intrinsic and germane cognitive load are associated with the learning content and the learner, while extraneous cognitive load is often associated with poor instructional development, complex learning environments and poor usability. These types of cognitive load are significant given the capacity limitations of working memory. Since they are additive, the cognitive load types compete for space in working memory (Clark & Mayer, 2003). Particularly relevant to technology-enhanced learning, too much extraneous cognitive load associated with difficult software applications and poorly designed interfaces deleteriously affects learning.

Cognitive learning emphasizes strategies to meaningfully encode and decode knowledge to and from long-term memory (Driscoll, 2005). Several cognitive instructional models and strategies complement Web 2.0 applications. Schema construction and advance organizers consider the structure of a learner's knowledge (Ausubel, 1980). New knowledge can be added into long-term memory schemata by accretion, tuning and restructuring (Driscoll). Similarly, advance organizers offer an organizational strategy for learners to begin processing and encoding knowledge (Mayer, 1979). So using technology applications that support construction of schemata in long-term memory have the potential to relate new knowledge with prior knowledge in a multisensory way.

Reigeluth (1999) suggests that the sequence of learning is important for relating or distinguishing among traits in the learning content. Similarly, the sequencing strategy (i.e., topical or spiral) is also dependent on the learning content. The instructional sequences result "in the formation of stable cognitive schemata to which more complex understanding are more easily added" (p. 433). However, building effective instruction is not simple. Nevertheless, some Web 2.0 applications enable combining multiple sources of information, such as text, video, photographs, quickly. So, it may be easier for a teacher to produce a more effective instructional sequence with one of these applications.

WEB 2.0 TO SUPPORT TEACHING AND LEARNING

Web 2.0 is typically defined by the characteristics, or design patterns, set forth by O'Reilly (2005), including the long tail and perpetual beta. There are, however, several attributes of Web 2.0 that support constructivist and cognitivist teaching and learning. These are (a) low threshold applications, (b) variety of tools and models and (c) low cost and networked community. Each is described below.

Low Threshold Applications

Low threshold refers to how easily a tool—specifically, a technology-based tool—is to adopt and how easy it is to learn. Gilbert (2002) and his colleagues at the Teaching, Learning and Technology Group affirm that low threshold applications are (a) easy to learn by both teachers and students, (b) not intimidating to require re-examination of epistemologies and teaching practices, (c) simple enough to require little technical training for use and (d) almost ubiquitous (para. 4). From a teacher's perspective, these are attractive.

In contrast, Sade (2005) emphasizes student use of low threshold applications. Those technologies that afford a variety of technical skill levels among students should be the ones integrated into curricula by teachers. These technologies, Sade suggests, allow for the construction and sharing of learning artifacts. So students are able to represent their learning in a contemporary method most indicative of their experiences.

In both sets of characteristics, low threshold applications suggest a shallow learning curve and dedicating few cognitive resources to the tools. The entry point for teachers and students to learn the tools is quick. Both Gilbert (2002) and Sade (2005) suggest tools should be selected based on high usability characteristics (cf., Nielsen, 2000). This certainly reduces extraneous cognitive load.

The characteristics of low threshold applications to support teaching and learning are rooted in both cognitivism and constructivisim. Appropriate for both learning theories, low threshold applications allow the teacher and student to focus on the content and not the tool. For example, based in Oliver's (2007) work, in one of our preservice teacher education courses, we have students create self-paced instructional units with Trailfire (see Figure 22.1), a social bookmarking service that generates linear sequential sets of bookmarks, or trails, around a selected topic. A student can follow a trail a teacher has created with annotations or critical thinking questions displayed on each Web site. Through a Web browser plug-in, teachers can simply add new bookmarks to a trail by tagging the trail with the same title. The focus of the assignment is then on locating the best sources of content and adding annotated comments to the trail for students to consider. Similarly, we have had students create self-paced instructional units with WebSlides powered by Diigo.

In an online teacher education course, we have provided minimal instruction for Web 2.0 tools. As such, the return on investment as a teacher and a student is high. As teachers, we have had to provide little upfront instruction about how to use the tools and little subsequent support. As students, they are able to move forward with building a learning artifact without having an introductory type of assignment to learn the tool. As

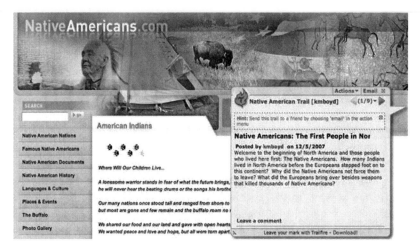

Figure 22.1 A self-paced instructional unit using Trailfire.

suggested by Gilbert (2002), very little training and follow-up support is required with low threshold applications. For example, Weebly is a Web site authoring tool with a drag-and-drop interface; no HTML programming is required (although it is possible). When using this with preservice and in-service teachers, it has been unnecessary to teach how to use Weebly. Likewise, Rieber (personal communication, 2008) described similar results with Google Pages/Sites in a preservice teacher education course.

Particular to constructivism and critical to Sade's (2005) recommendation, low threshold applications allow for the creation of multiple representations of knowledge and a variety of learning artifacts. These tenets are most strongly rooted in constructionism (Harel & Papert, 1991; Kafai & Resnick, 1996) and project-based learning (Grant, 2002; Moursund, 1998). Constructionism as a learning theory and project-based learning as an instructional model afford learners the opportunity to represent their learning in personally meaningful methods. Low threshold applications like Trailfire, Weebly and Google Pages/Sites very often provide an avenue for accomplishing this.

Variety of Tools and Models

Mental models can be considered as functional schemata. Driscoll (2005) suggests that mental models "guide and govern performance" (p. 130) during learning or problem solving. When using a Web site or software application, we have preconceived notions about how to accomplish a task within the system. User interfaces, the communication point between the designer and user, however, are what a designer considers to be the best tool, and users to a large extent are expected to adapt to the interface (Brusilovsky, 2001; Inan & Grant, 2008). In contrast, van Dam (2000) asserts that the aim of interface design should be to complement human abilities, including cognition.

But in the past teachers and students have primarily used the productivity tools typical of all-in-one office suites (e.g., Becker, 2001). As such the opportunities to select a tool that matches an individual's mental model has been limited. Instead, the choices have been primarily constrained to those with ubiquity. This requires that teachers and students adopt or adapt to these models of accomplishing tasks. Hallmarks of these large packages include unnecessary features and just-in-case features (e.g., Pogue, 2007).

In comparison, Web 2.0 applications are small, niche tools. At 37 Signals, which is widely recognized for developing tools such as Basecamp, Ta-da List and the application platform Ruby on Rails, Dimon and colleagues (37 Signals, 2006) have advocated for reduced features. They have also recommended focusing on the interface and core content or function first. As such they are adamantly creating smaller applications. So across the Internet, a number of compact applications have been constructed often with different mental models of how to accomplish a task. For example at the time of this writing, 13 concept-mapping applications were listed at the directory Go2Web20.net. Likewise, Fleck, Jumpknowledge and Diigo allow textual annotations on bookmarked pages. Of the three, Fleck is the most graphical; Jumpknowledge is strictly text-based (see Figure 22.2). Diigo and Fleck include social networking, while Jumpknowledge simply shares via email or hyperlinks. DrawHere, however, allows drawings and diagrams to be saved to a Web page as an annotation, and then shared. So, not only is it possible to parallel a mental model, it may also be possible to address preferences (i.e., visual, textual, audile, etc.) for learning.

The implications for teaching and learning to choose from a variety of small Web 2.0 applications are considerable. Instead of an all-in-one suite, teachers and students can selectively adopt tools that are most intuitive, and expressly appropriate to secondary students, preservice and in-service teachers, it may be inessential to select a single tool for use with an assignment. This is intimately related to the cognitive load of low threshold applications. Because a teacher or student can select a cognitively compatible tool, fewer cognitive resources are dedicated to learning how to use the tool, increasing the efficiency of learning. The choice of tools also dovetails

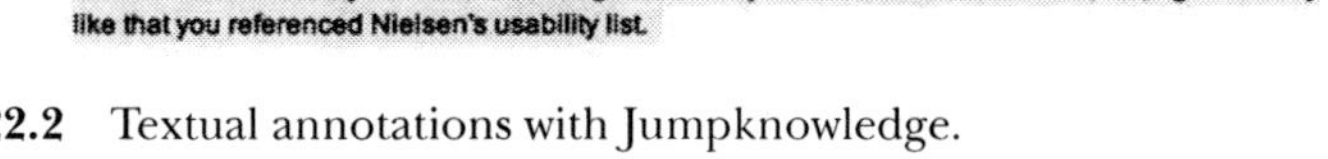

2. Can typical users utilize the system for its intended purposes? **1** I really like the questions here in 1 and 2. Good job. I think these align well with your critical success factors, too, right? I really like that you referenced Nielsen's usability list.

Figure 22.2   Textual annotations with Jumpknowledge.

with Sade's (2005) constructivist criteria for selecting tools to integrate into a curriculum. Learners can represent their learning in a variety of ways and through an array of applications.

Access to Tools and Knowledge

Not only are there myriad Web 2.0 tools from which users can choose, these technologies are available at little or no expense making them widely accessible. Chris Anderson (2008) describes an emerging business model called *freeconomics*, where with the rapidly decreasing costs of digital technology, it is best to give them away for free. This helps build awareness of a tool and a user base. In addition, there has been a commitment to providing knowledge and expertise openly. For example, Wikipedia relies of the expertise of individuals to create the content. Similarly, Curriki is committed to providing high-quality curricula for K–12 teachers and students. At the time of this writing, they are paying for individuals to develop units and course. The state of California is also exploring the creation of an online textbook for World History using Wikibooks. The opportunities result in teachers and students having greater access to tools and knowledge.

With the limitations related to access and expense greatly diminished, learners are able to try multiple tools, while there is little time lost. Since the applications are Web-based, there typically are not downloads only a registration process. Additionally for the teacher, it is easier and more accessible to use a variety of resources, such as embedding external media (e.g., YouTube, TeacherTube) or extending learning opportunities (e.g., external blog conversations). For example, in our online teacher education classes, we have embedded relevant videos, podcasts and slideshows into the learning materials. Moreover, Mims has incorporated blog discussions inside his course but within his own professional blog. These opportunities align well with constructivist learning.

Personal learning communities (PLCs) have also emerged as a result of the social aspects of many of the Web 2.0 tools. Learning is no longer confined to the physical classroom space or appointed meeting times. Access to experts and others interested in a topic of study is available through the social components of tools like Diigo, TeacherTube, Twitter, and blogs and wikis. This gives learners greater control over their learning, indicative of constructivist principles.

The community of expertise extends beyond the curricular content as well. There are typically active online support and development communities associated with Web 2.0 tools. This can be beneficial to teachers and learners as assistance is available when users encounter difficulties. In addition, developers consider user feedback in updating the technology.

With members of his PLC, Mims participated in a recent vigorous discussion about features inside Diigo that spawned responses and quick changes from the developers. Consequentially, an alternative educational version of Diigo will be released to districts and schools. Similarly, Grant's email feedback to Jumptags, a social bookmarking service, resulted in developer responses. This mutually beneficial relationship leads to more user-friendly versions of and experiences with the tool.

LIMITATIONS AND IMPLICATIONS

The sections above have articulated the strengths of Web 2.0 applications. We have advocated for their uses given the examples we provided from our own work. Unfortunately, the promise of Web 2.0 is not without challenges. In particular, we will discuss five categories of limitations to using Web 2.0 applications and their implications for teaching and learning. These are (a) immature applications, (b) longevity of applications, (c) numbers of applications (d) unconsolidated services and (e) security and ethics. None of these are distinct or isolated to one theory of learning. Instead, we present the following sections for teachers to consider as they progress through their instructional design processes. Moreover, it is left to the individual teacher educator and teacher to determine her position on the continuum of technology integration professional development stages (see e.g., Goddard, 2002) in order to gauge the personal impact of each of these limitations.

Immature Applications

One of the characteristics, or design patterns, O'Reilly (2005) aligned to Web 2.0 is termed *perpetual beta*. Rollett, Lux, Strohmaier, Dösinger and Tochterman (2007) describe Web 2.0 applications as "constantly evolving, never really leaving the beta state" (p. 91). While on the surface this may appear to be a strength, this can also be depicted as deploying immature, or premature, applications to users.

Because of this immaturity, the Web 2.0 applications have a tendency from our experiences to be susceptible to unexpected downtimes and software anomalies. For example, Zookoda, a blog post to email tool, was forced to suspend service after discovering it was being exploited by spammers (Murphy, 2007). Also, a number of applications we have used have had software inconsistencies, including unexpected errors, lost data and slow response times. Even popular Twitter has experienced recent fluctuations in stability (Twitter, 2008).

There is a well-known yet covert software axiom to deploy a product and let the users tell you what you are missing. Hence, the advice: Wait for version point one or service pack one. 37 Signals (2006) suggests the user feedback that is consistently received every day represents the features to implement. Above, we explained how Web 2.0 developers were sensitive to their communities of users. They, in fact, rely on the users to determine many features. For many Web 2.0 applications, there seems to be an imbalance between listening and responding to a community of users versus literally banking on a community of users. The challenging element to this is the often lack of features that do exist.

For teachers and students, the downtimes, software glitches and lack of features can lead to frustrations. When teachers plan lessons with these tools, there is an expectation for stability and reliability. The assumption that Web 2.0 tools are always available has been transferred from desktop applications. However, it may in fact be a faulty premise.

Longevity of Applications

As described earlier, many of the Web 2.0 applications did not exist two years ago and most tools within four years (Waters & Nuttall, 2008). With this chronology, it is simply impossible to determine which companies and tools will survive. As such, teachers and teacher educators should be reticent to recommend tools that do not at least have some reputation, whether through our networked communities or through reviewing sites, such as Buzzshout, Cnet Reviews or AppAppeal. LaMonica (2006) is suspicious of a "dot-com-like bubble" materializing (Boom or bubble? section, para. 1). In a similar fashion, Waters and Nuttall (2008) report a belief that many Web 2.0 companies will perish.

Certainly, the concern for teachers and students is investing significant development time in a product that may not persist. One method to combat this is to leverage Web 2.0 applications' widespread compatibility features. In many cases, the application will allow you to export your data into a variety of formats or download complete archives of files (see Figure 22.3). These can often be reused or imported into another similar service. Still, this is not a solution but a workaround. The skills to successfully transfer data across system may be more than we should expect teachers and students to do. In addition to the small niche applications, should we consider the transient potential of these applications as a defining characteristic and regard our data to be just as fluid?

Furthermore, some Web 2.0 applications are still struggling to determine an appropriate business model (Waters & Nuttall, 2008). Popular Twitter is one that has yet to create a revenue stream. Other tools that offered free

Figure 22.3   Exporting data in a variety of formats from Zoho Creator.

services in some instances have created limits or applied fees to their services. For instance, two of our favorite applications to use with teachers and teacher educators, Zoho Creator and Weebly, added business or professional plans, placing limits on their free accounts. Naturally, the appeal to teachers and students is the widespread low to no cost of these applications. Freeconomics and freemiums (Anderson, 2008) are new business models to attract customers. The fallacy is that teachers or students may be dependent on a service that then moves to a business model, making the tool unfeasible.

Number of Applications

Unlike the Web browser and search engine wars, which time has distilled to a few, there are currently a massive number of Web 2.0 applications to review and from which to select. At Go2Web20.net, a respected directory of applications begun in 2006, the number of listed applications at the time of this writing was 2,490. Similarly, the Center for Learning and Performance Technologies lists the number of tools for creating, delivering and managing technology-supported learning at over 2,400. While we discussed earlier the advantages of niche applications, this explosion has created a thick register of possibilities for teacher educators and teachers. While a few tools have moved to the forefront, such as Wordpress, Blogger, Wikipedia, delicious, Flickr and most recently Twitter, the litany of over 2000 possible tools remains daunting. Time has yet to create de facto tools.

The implications of this many applications for teaching and learning are similar to the challenge of locating meaningful sites on the Web. Social bookmarking services, like delicious and review sites like those mentioned above can help distill the possibilities, similar to Nettrekker's premise for Web sites. TeachersFirst Edge is one site that is attempting to provide this type of service.

Unconsolidated Services

Another challenge to using Web 2.0 applications is their dispersement across the Internet and different developers. In other words, tools and services are unconsolidated, where a blog may be hosted at Edublogs, a wiki created at WetPaint and presentations created at SlideRocket. The strength to all-in-one suites is their centrality and consistency across applications: Functions in one tool work identically or similarly in another. While Web 2.0 tools gain credibility for high usability and shallow learning curves, there is still a cognitive investment for teachers and students to learn each tool, which contributes to extraneous cognitive load.

Some companies have attempted to combat this limitation by creating or aggregating an all-in-one online suite. For example, Zoho offers approximately 20 different tools, including the standard office suite of a word processor, spreadsheets and digital presentations but also a wiki, a digital notebook and project management. Likewise, Google has launched Google Apps with an office suite and a Web site authoring tool among others.

By choosing an all-in-one suite, teacher educators and teachers lose the flexibilities described above for niche applications. However, sending teachers and students to different sites may be overwhelming or disorienting, particular to novices. Saving files in network spaces instead of personal hard drives will undoubtedly make some teacher educators and teachers nervous or skeptical. Moreover, it can simply be confusing to determine the correct URL for published work. For example, it is not uncommon for preservice teachers in our own classes to submit a URL to a password-protected space instead of the public address. Finally, each tool requires a separate user name and password, so keeping up with many logins is annoying at the least. OpenID, however, "a single sign-on mechanism for the Web," ("Major Tech Companies," 2008, para. 3) has the potential to reduce this challenge in the near future.

Security and Ethic

Security for student information and security of intellectual property persists as an issue on the Web. Encouraging students to use blogs and other

Web 2.0 tools requires significant investments in preparing students for protecting their privacy. Richardson (2006) recommends,

1. teachers follow state and district guidelines for publishing student information and photos on school Web sites;
2. teachers ask for parental permission to engage in publishing online;
3. teachers should be prepared to discuss what should and should not be published online; and
4. teachers determine protocols for publishing, such as using first names only, using pseudonyms or using anonymity (pp. 11–12).

These guidelines are important during information seeking and publishing but also for social software and networking sites where much of the content available is personal and public (Anderson, Grant & Speck, 2007).

Additionally, we must continue to teach children to respect copyrights and intellectual property of others. Students will illegally download text, images, music, videos and software, because they perceive it to be freely available and in the public domain (Rader, 2002). With the use of many Web 2.0 tools, it is easy to combine media from various sources with little regard to copyright. Plagiarism is synonymous with copyright infringement (Johnson & Groneman, 2003). In particular, Baron and Crooks (2005) warn against "cut and paste plagiarism."

Finally, we must continue to remind students of information and media literacies skills. Identifying sources of information, as well as the quality of information sources, remains important. Some Web 2.0 tools—blogs and wikis in particular—are susceptible to questions of quality. Wikipedia (2008a) in fact lists updated possible copyright problems within Wikipedia's pages. Wikipedia (2008b) also maintains a page to help students to conduct research with Wikipedia. Interestingly, a recent study (Giles, 2005; "Nature's response," n.d.) found relatively similar levels of quality between Wikipedia and Encyclopedia Brittanica. To help students maintain ethics and quality, Warlick (2004) recommends four guidelines for teachers and students to follow when publishing and working online:

1. Teachers and students should be honest, fair and courageous in gathering, interpreting and expressing information for the benefit of others.
2. Ethical teachers and students treat information sources, subjects, colleagues and information consumers as human beings deserving of respect.
3. Teachers and students are accountable to their readers, listeners and viewers and to each other.
4. Information, in the Information Age, is property. Information is the fabric that defines much of what we do from day to day, and this rich and potent fabric is fragile. (pp. 92–93)

CONCLUSION

Web 2.0 is not a panacea nor is it the end. In fact, many developers and technophiles are anxiously awaiting Web 3.0. Twine is one of the first applications that seem to begin to take advantage of the notion of the semantic Web. While the tools may change, the need for teacher educators and teachers to have a firm understanding of learning principles to guide the use of the tools has not. Aldrich (2005) reminds us,

> There are strongly mixed reactions about the new technology. Some end users like it (and some love it), but professionals who built a lifetime of skills around the old technology are very suspicious, often undermining it. Even the advocates admit the technology often has to be cajoled into working.... Invariably, people just did not realize how hard it was to pull it off. What seemed easy and obvious is in fact quite daunting. (pp. xxxvi–xxxvii)

Not every teacher educator and not every teacher will be attracted by Web 2.0 or Web 3.0. The technologies themselves may be easier and more accessible. But combining complex learning environments, learner characteristics, content, pedagogy and technology together creates a less distinct path to success. Skilled teacher educators and teachers are still key to meaningful student learning. Prensky's (2001) digital natives are using a variety of tools for entertainment, information learning and communication. Teaching and learning must respect the changes in learners and innovations. Changes in the current roles of teachers and students may be required in order to take full advantage of Web 2.0 applications and active learning.

WEB 2.0 RESOURCES

- AppAppeal (http://www.appappeal.com)
- Basecamp (http://www.basecamphq.com)
- Blogger (https://www.blogger.com/start)
- Buzzshout (http://www.buzzshout.com)
- Center for Learning and Performance Technologies Directory (http://c4lpt.co.uk/Directory)
- Cnet Reviews (http://reviews.cnet.com)
- Delicious (http://del.icio.us)
- Diigo (http://www.diigo.com)
- Draw Here (http://drawhere.com)
- Edublogs (http://edublogs.org)
- Fleck (http://fleck.com)
- Flickr (http://flickr.com)

- Go2Web20.net (http://go2web20.net)
- Google Apps (http://www.google.com/apps/business/index.html)
- Google Sites (http://sites.google.com)
- Jumpknowledge (http://info.jkn.com)
- Nettrekker (http://www.nettrekker.com)
- Ruby on Rails (http://www.rubyonrails.org)
- SlideRocket (http://www.sliderocket.com)
- Ta-da List (http://www.tadalist.com)
- TeachersFirst Edge (http://www.teachersfirst.com/content/edge.cfm)
- TeacherTube (http://www.teachertube.com)
- Trailfire (http://trailfire.com)
- Twine (http://www.twine.com)
- Twitter (http://twitter.com)
- WebSlides (http://slides.diigo.com)
- Weebly (http://weebly.com)
- Wetpaint (http://www.wetpaint.com)
- Wikipedia (http://wikipedia.org)
- Wordpress (http://wordpress.com)
- YouTube (http://youtube.com)
- Zoho (http://zoho.com)
- Zoho Creator (http://creator.zoho.com/home.do)
- Zookoda (http://zookoda.com)

REFERENCES

37 Signals. (2006). *Getting real: The smarter, faster, easier way to build a successful web application*. Chicago, IL: 37 Signals.

Aldrich, C. (2005). *Learning by doing*. San Francisco, CA: Pfeiffer.

Anderson, C. (2008, March). Why $0.00 is the future of business. *Wired, 16*(3), 140–149, 194.

Anderson, R. S., Grant, M. M. & Speck, B. W. (2008). *Technology to teach literacy: A resource for K–8 teachers*. Upper Saddle River, NJ: Merrill Prentice Hall.

Ausubel, D. P. (1980). Schemata, cognitive structure, and advance organizers: A reply to Anderson, Spiro, and Anderson. *American Educational Research Journal, 17*(3), 400–404.

Baron, J., & Crooks, S. M. (2005). Academic integrity in web based distance education. *TechTrends, 49*(2), 40–45.

Becker, H. J. (2001, April). *How are teachers using computers in instruction?* Paper presented at the annual meeting of the American Educational Research Association, Seattle, WA.

Brusilovsky, P. (2001). Adaptive hypermedia. *User Modeling and User-Adapted Interaction, 11*(1/2), 87–110.

Clark, R. C. & Mayer, R. E. (2003). *E-learning and the science of instruction*. San Francisco, CA: Pfeiffer.

Clark, R. C., Nguyen, F., & Sweller, J. (2006). *Efficiency in learning: Evidence-based guidelines to manage cognitive load.* San Francisco, CA: Pfeiffer.

Driscoll, M. P. (2005). *The psychology of learning for instruction* (3rd ed.). Boston: Pearson Education.

Gilbert, S. W. (2002, February 12). The beauty of low threshold applications. *Syllabus.* Retrieved June 13, 2008, from http://campustechnology.com/articles/38981/

Giles, J. (2005). Internet encyclopedias go head to head. *Nature, 438*(7070), 900–901.

Goddard, M. (2002). What do we do with these computers? Reflections on technology in the classroom. *Journal of Research on Technology in Education, 35*(1), 19–26.

Grant, M. M. (2002). Getting a grip on project-based learning: Theory, cases and recommendations. *Meridian: A Middle School Computer Technologies Journal, 5*(1). Retrieved June 13, 2008 from http://www.ncsu.edu/meridian/win2002/514/index.html

Grant, M. M., & Branch, R. M. (2005). Project-based learning in a middle school: Tracing abilities through the artifacts of learning. *Journal of Research on Technology in Education, 38*(1), 65–98.

Harel, I., & Papert, S. (Eds.). (1991). *Constructionism.* Norwood, NJ: Ablex.

Inan, F. A. & Grant, M. M. (2008). Individualized web-based instruction: Strategies and guidelines for instructional designers. In T. Kidd & H. Song (Eds.) *Handbook of research on instructional systems & technology* (pp. 581–594). Hershey, PA: Idea Group Publishing.

Johnson, K., & Groneman, N. (2003). Legal and illegal use of the internet: Implications for educators. *Journal of Education for Business, 78*(3), 147–152.

Kafai, Y., & Resnick, M. (Eds.). (1996). *Constructionsim in practice: Designing, thinking and learning in a digital world.* Mahwah, NJ: Erlbaum.

LaMonica, M. (2006, March 14). Google deal highlights Web 2.0 boom. *Cnet.com.au.* Retrieved June 16, 2008, from http://www.cnet.com.au/software/internet/0,239029524,240061041,00.htm

Major tech companies join OpenID board; the addition of Google, IB, Microsoft, Verisign, and Yahoo is expected to help build support for a single Web sign-on service. (2008, February 7). *Information Week.* Retrieved June 16, 2008 from General Onefile Gale database.

Mayer, R. E. (1979). Can advance organizers influence meaningful learning? *Review of Educational Research, 49*, 371–383.

Mims, C. (2003). Authentic learning: A practical introduction and guide for implementation. *Meridian: A Middle School Computer Technologies Journal. 6*(1). Retrieved June 16, 2008 from http://www.ncsu.edu/meridian/win2003/authentic_learning/

Moursund, D. (1998). Project-based learning in an information-technology environment. *Learning and Leading with Technology, 25*(8), 4.

Murphy, T. (2007, December 21). Broadcasts have been suspended. *Zookoda*. Retrieved June 16, 2008, from http://zooblog.zookoda.com/index.cfm/2007/12/21/Broadcasts-Have-Been-Suspended.

Nature's Response to Encyclopaedia Brittanica. (n.d.). *Nature*. Retrieved June 16, 2008, from http://www.nature.com/nature/britannica/index.html

Nielsen, J. (2000). *Designing web usability: The practice of simplicity*. Indianapolis, IN: New Riders Publishing.

Oliver, K. (2007). Leveraging web 2.0 in the redesign of a graduate-level technology integration course. *TechTrends, 51*(5), 55–61.

O'Reilly, T. (2005). *What is web 2.0?* Retrieved June 13, 2008, from http://oreilly.com/pub/a/oreilly/tim/news/2005/09/30/what-is-web-20.html

Papert, S. (1980). *Mindstorms*. New York: Basic Books.

Piaget, J. (1954). *The construction of reality in the child*. New York: Basic Books.

Piaget, J. (1967). *Biology and knowledge*. Chicago, IL: University of Chicago Press.

Piaget, J. (1974). *To understand is to invent: The future of education*. New York: Grossman.

Pogue, D. (2007, January 18). Purging bloat to fashion sleek software. *The New York Times*, p. C1.

Prensky, M. (2001). *Digital game-based learning*. New York: McGraw Hill.

Rader, M. H. (2002). Strategies for teaching internet ethics. *The Delta Pi Epsilon Journal, 44*(2), 73–79.

Reigeluth, C. M. (1999). The elaboration theory: Guidance for scope and sequence decisions. In C. M. Reigeluth (Ed.), *Instructional design theories and models: A new paradigm of instructional theory*, (Vol. II, pp. 425–453). Mahwah, NJ: Erlbaum.

Richardson, W. (2006). *Blogs, wikis, podcasts, and other powerful Web tools for classrooms*. Thousand Oaks, CA: Corwin Press.

Rollette, H., Lux, M., Strohmaier, M., Dösing, G., & Tochterman, K. (2007). The web 2.0 way of learning with technologies. *The International Journal of Learning Technology, 3*(1), 87–107.

Sade, G. (2005, May). *Weblogs as open constructive learning environments*. Paper presented at annual meeting of Blogtalk Downunder, Sydney, Australia. Retrieved June 13, 2008 from http://incsub.org/blogtalk/images/bog_talk_gsade_v71.doc

Schank, R. C., Berman, T. R., & Macpherson, K. A. (1999). Learning by doing. In C. M. Reigeluth (Ed.), *Instructional design theories and models: A new paradigm of instructional theory*, (Vol. II, pp. 161–181). Mahwah, NJ: Erlbaum.

Twitter. (2008). *Lost a database*. Retrieved June 16, 2008, from http://status.twitter.com/post/37338586/lost-a-database

van Dam, A. (2000). Beyong WIMP. *IEEE Computer Graphics and Applications, 20*(1), 50–51.

Warlick, D. (2004). *Redefining literacy for the 21st century*. Worthington, OH: Linworth.

Waters, R., & Nuttall, C. (2008, May 26). Web 2.0 fails to produce cash. *Financial Times.com*. Retrieved June 16, 2008, from http://us.ft.com/ftgateway/superpage.ft?news_id=fto052620081432231624

Wikipedia Foundation Inc. (2008a, June 15). *Wikipedia:Copyright problems.* Retrieved June 16, 2008, from http://en.wikipedia.org/wiki/Wikipedia:Copyright_problems

Wikipedia Foundation Inc. (2008b, June 10). *Wikipedia:Researching with Wikipedia.* Retrieved June 16, 2008, from http://en.wikipedia.org/wiki/Wikipedia:Researching_with_Wikipedia

GLOSSARY OF TERMS

AET Zone: A three-dimensional virtual, immersive world used by graduate programs in education at Appalachian State University.

Affordance: Affordances are properties that influence how something can be used. Affordances are those essential elements that define something, in this case a Web 2.0 tool.

AJAX: Acronym for Asynchronous JavaScript and XML. A combination of several programming tools to build interactive applications. Allows the content of a web page to be updated or changed without the entire page being reloaded.

Arguing to Learn: Online students collaboratively discuss or "argue" about course material. This kind of learning activity can lead to deeper learning as it provides opportunities for students to explain and prepare a justification or defense of their ideas and exposes them to other viewpoints either similar to, or different from, their own.

Atom: a recent version of RSS technology that is used by Google-owned Blogger among other Web 2.0 services. Many aggregators accept both RSS and Atom feeds.

Blended learning: The organic integration of thoughtfully selected and complementary face-to-face and online approaches and technologies.

Blog: A site maintained by an individual, organization or group or people, which contains recurrent entries of commentary, viewpoints, descriptions of events, or multimedia material, such as images, pictures or videos. The entries are typically displayed in reverse chronological order with the most recent post being the current focus.

Wired for Learning: An Educator's Guide to Web 2.0, pages 361–367
Copyright © 2009 by Information Age Publishing
361

Blogosphere: A collective term encompassing all blogs and their interconnections. It is the perception that blogs exist together as a connected community (or as a collection of connected communities) or as a social network.

Cognitive presence: The extent to which learners are able to construct and confirm meaning through sustained reflection and discourse in a critical community of inquiry.

Collaborative learning: The sharing of personal meaning and the validation of understanding through discourse and debate

Community of inquiry: A framework that directs attention to the process of constructing and confirming deep understanding through the intersection of cognitive, social and teaching presence.

Community of Practice (CoP): Refers to groups of individuals who share a common interest through working and learning together in order to further their shared purpose. In education, those who engage in collective practices to build knowledge in a particular domain (e.g. microbiology) can be thought of as a community of practice. The Community of Practice concept was formed by Jean Lave and Etienne Wenger and has since evolved and been adopted to scenarios like organizational development and knowledge management.

Digital disconnect: The discrepancy between the high informal use of narrative in a range of Web2.0 technologies by young people and the lower level within institutional systems, such as VLEs (Virtual Learning Environments).

Digital storytelling: A process in which digital technology is used to combine a number of media into a coherent narrative

Elgg: An open source social platform based around choice, flexibility and openness: a system that firmly places individuals at the centre of their activities. Users have the freedom to incorporate all their favorite tools within one environment and showcase their content with as many or as few people as they choose, all within a social networking site that you control.

Flickr: A photo sharing website and web services suite, and an online community platform, which is generally considered an example of a Web 2.0 application. In addition to being a popular Web site for users to share personal photographs, the service is widely used by bloggers as a photo repository. Its popularity has been fueled by its innovative online community tools that allow photos to be tagged and browsed by folksonomic means.

Folksonomy: Short for folk (or folks) and taxonomy. A user generated taxonomy used to categorize and retrieve Web pages, photographs, Web links and other web content using open-ended labels called tags.

FURL: A free social bookmarking website that allows members to store searchable copies of webpages and share them with others. Every member receives 5 gigabyte of storage space.

Information architecture (IA): The practice of mapping and organizing information to make usable and accessible. In the context of the Internet, IA often implies the design of non-linear information structures that are approached through a software interface. Findability of desired content is implemented through an effective and intuitive navigation system, playing an important role in the efficient access to needed information.

Instructional Design: The systematic process of analyzing students' needs and learning goals, designing and developing instructional materials.

Interactivity: Communication in distance education between faculty and students and among students themselves (Sherry, 1996). Interactivity can be via telephone, one-way and two-way audio and video, two-way streamed (real-time transmission) video with or without graphics interactivity, two-way computer hook-ups, or via response terminals (United States Distance Learning Association, 1996).

Intersubjective: Social relations can refer to a multitude of social interactions, regulated by social norms, between two or more people, with each having a social position and performing a social role.

Knowledge Community: A community of students collaborating to create collective knowledge for a particular domain.

Learning Management System (LMS): Software used for the facilitation of teaching and learning with functionality that may include: scheduling, posting assignments and notes, emails and announcements, grading and assessment tools. As a web-based system, the LMS can be the exclusive learning environment or serve to augment the physical classroom (blended course delivery). Some notable commercial examples of LMS are WebCT/Blackboard, Desire2Learn, ATutor, and Angel.

Maintaining Awareness: When online communities are in flux, the members of the community want to keep track of new events and developments within their online collaboration. Maintaining sufficient awareness helps users coordinate, share content, and plan future work.

Mashup: Merging content from different sources, client- and server-side.

Mass communications: The extensive dissemination of communications media and relates to newspaper, magazine publishing, radio, television, film, and electronic media, such as the Internet and has increasingly focused on the convergence of publishing, broadcasting and digital communication.

MP3: MP3 is a standard digital audio format used to encode music for playback in digital devices

MySpace: A social networking website offering an interactive, user-submitted network of friends, personal profiles, blogs, groups, photos, music, and videos.

Net Generation students: The present generation of undergraduate students who have grown up in a world dominated by technology and surrounded by multimedia.

Online collaboration/collaborative learning: Students learning online by interacting with one another, building knowledge and acquiring skill. Both the process of collaboration and the product of collaborative work can be of tremendous educational value. Web 2.0 technology can be exploited as a means to achieve online collaborative learning.

Online learning: Electronic (e)learning, and some forms of distance education that include the use of the Internet. Online learning can include a number of communication tools and technologies to help convey course content and encourage interactivities among students and the facilitator (instructor).

Perpetual beta: A design principle of Web 2.0 applications describing the constantly evolving nature of the tools, often making changes at the request of users.

Podcasting: A multimedia file distributed over the Internet using syndication feeds, for playback on mobile devices and personal computers. Though podcasters' web sites may also offer direct download or streaming of their content, a podcast is distinguished from other digital audio formats by its ability to be downloaded automatically using software capable of reading feed format.

Presence Pedagogy: A framework for teaching and learning utilizing virtual immersive worlds and Web 2.0 technologies, characterized by design and activities which facilitate consistent engagement between students and faculty, enabling the creation of communities of practice.

Reflective learning: An educational process in which the learner makes sense of an experience to inform future actions.

Rich Internet Application (RIA): Web applications that have the features and functionality of traditional desktop applications.

RSS Feed: An RSS feed is an XML file that provides content or summaries of content, including links to the full versions of the content and other metadata, that a user can subscribe to using an RSS aggregator.

RSS: Short for "Really Simple Syndication." This is a technique to easily distribute content such as news headlines; websites update notices, and sometimes movies and applications to a wide audience. An RSS document can be referred to as a "feed," "web feed," or "channel." The feed will contain either a summary of content being distributed from an associated web site or the full text of the article.

Semantic Web: The future evolution of the World Wide Web. The Semantic Web will allow people to more easily find, share, and combine information.

Semiotics: The study of patterned human communication behavior, including auditory/vocabulary, facial expressions, body talk, touch (proxemics), signs, and symbols.

SimSpaces: A protocol for a two-phased approach to developing and implementing virtual learning spaces influenced by a constructionist perspective of learning.

Situated Learning: Learning in which knowledge is constructed in a community of practice, situated in a specific context.

Social Bookmarking: A technique that users use to organize, categorize, search, share and manage bookmarks of web pages they are interested in on the Internet using metadata. Users save links to web pages and can either make the links public or keep them private and share with a specified user group.

Social Constructivism: A philosophy that holds that knowledge is created culturally, socially and within communities.

Social Networking: A website which is an online resource for building virtual social network communities of individuals with common interests or who are interested in exploring the interests and activities of others.

Social presence: The ability of participants to identify with the community (e.g., course of study), communicate purposefully in a trusting environment, and develop inter-personal relationships by way of projecting their individual personalities

Social Software: Web based applications which people use to communicate, collaborate and share resources online. Through links, comments, tags and aggregation, users can build interconnections and networks of knowledge.

Teaching presence: The design, facilitation and direction of cognitive and social processes for the purpose of realizing personally meaningful and educationally worthwhile learning outcomes.

Tool mediation: Tools of activities, represented in signs and symbols, acted as agents for, and subsequently provided definition for, culture, and served as intervening links to consciousness. Mediation of these tools, which Vygotsky called "tool mediation" (1985), was the structural and genetic central feature of mental functioning which, in turn, became a necessary liaison to consciousness.

Virtual learning space: An immersive or non-immersive distributed artificial environment that is intended to provide contexts for learning.

Virtual World Engine: Virtual world engines allow users to produce exclusive, customized, virtual environments on closed servers.

Virtual world: A virtual world is a computer-based simulated environment intended for its users to inhabit and interact via avatars. This habitation usually is represented in the form of two or three-dimensional graphical representations of humanoids (or other graphical or text-based avatars).

Web 2.0 Instructional Design: A model designed utilizing the socio-constructivist philosophies and it can be adapted to different settings where Web 2.0 tools are used to improve learning and performance.

Web 2.0 technologies: A variety of new technologies, such as blogs, wikis, and media sharing sites and social network sites that provide user-centered opportunities to create and share content.

Web 2.0: A trend in World Wide Web technology, a second generation of web-based communities and hosted services such as social-networking sites, wikis, blogs, and other new technology approaches, which aim to facilitate creativity, collaboration, and sharing among users. The term became notable after the first O'Reilly Media Web 2.0 conference in 2004. While Web 2.0 suggests a new version of the World Wide Web, it does not refer to any technical updates, but rather to changes in the ways software developers and end-users use webs.

Web Syndication: A form of syndication in which a section of a website is made available for other sites to use. Two examples include RSS and Atom feeds.

Widgets: Small software components that are usually embedded into a larger system (like a web browser) for increased functionality. Commonly, widgets consist of a graphical user interface for user customization of the widget's capabilities and allow for third party services to be embedded into the larger system. An example of this is iGoogle, which uses widgets (called "gadgets") for user's to display content from a wide array of sources like news, calendars, weather, email and other web services.

Wiki: Short for "wiki wiki" which means "rapidly" in the Hawaiian language is a website that allows users with access to collaboratively create, edit, link, and categorize the content of a website in real time covering a variety of reference material. Wikis have evolved from being purely a reference site into collaborative tools to run community websites, corporate intranets, knowledge management systems and educational sites.

Wordpress MU: A blogging program that allows you to run hundreds, even thousands of blogs within a single install (http://mu.wordpress.org).

YouTube: A popular free video sharing web site which lets users upload, view, and share video clips, the service utilizes Adobe Flash technology to display video. The wide variety of site content includes movie and TV clips and music videos, as well as amateur content such as videoblogging.

ABOUT THE EDITORS

Terry T. Kidd, PhD received his graduate education training from the Texas A&M University. Kidd has presented at international conferences on designing technology rich learning environments, technology diffusion and innovation, and issues dealing with faculty and staff development. His research interests include technology innovation and diffusion within an educational and community context to support teaching, learning, and development and the interaction of technology with individual and institutional factors in (re)structuring community computing solutions that lead to the (re)production of social inequality. Kidd is an experienced university educators, consultant, and scholar. He is the author of the *Handbook of Research on Instructional Systems Technology* and the co-author of *Social Information Technology: Connecting Society and Cultural Issues.*

Irene L. Chen, EdD received her Doctor of Education in Instructional Technology. She is an Associate Professor in the Department of Urban Education at the University of Houston Downtown. Dr. Chen has a diverse professional background. She previously served as an instructional technology specialist, learning technology coordinator, and computer programmer/analyst. She has taught numerous graduate and undergraduate courses in instructional technology as well as curriculum and instruction. She has delivered numerous K–12 in-service training and professional development activities in the areas of faculty and staff development. She is the co-author of *Social Information Technology: Connecting Society and Cultural Issues* and the author of *Technology Application Competencies for K–12 Teachers.*

Printed in the United States
218095BV00002B/23/P